Universalism without Uniformity

Universalism without Uniformity

Explorations in Mind and Culture

EDITED BY JULIA L. CASSANITI
AND USHA MENON

The University of Chicago Press
Chicago and London

The University of Chicago Press, Chicago 60637
The University of Chicago Press, Ltd., London
© 2017 by The University of Chicago
Published 2017
Printed in the United States of America

26 25 24 23 22 21 20 19 18 17   1 2 3 4 5

ISBN-13: 978-0-226-50154-3 (cloth)
ISBN-13: 978-0-226-50168-0 (paper)
ISBN-13: 978-0-226-50171-0 (e-book)
DOI: 10.7208/chicago/9780226501710.001.0001

Library of Congress Cataloging-in-Publication Data

Names: Cassaniti, Julia, editor. | Menon, Usha, editor.
Title: Universalism without uniformity : explorations in mind and culture /
    edited by Julia Cassaniti and Usha Menon.
Description: Chicago : The University of Chicago Press, 2017. | Includes index.
Identifiers: LCCN 2017010445 | ISBN 9780226501543 (cloth : alk. paper) |
    ISBN 9780226501680 (pbk. : alk. paper) | ISBN 9780226501710 (e-book)
Subjects: LCSH: Culture—Psychological aspects—Cross-cultural studies. |
    Culture and globalization—Cross-cultural studies. | Cultural pluralism—
    Cross-cultural studies. | Social psychology—Cross-cultural studies. |
    Multiculturalism—Cross-cultural studies.
Classification: LCC GN357.U65 2017 | DDC 306—dc23 LC record available at
    https://lccn.loc.gov/2017010445

♾ This paper meets the requirements of ANSI/NISO Z39.48-1992
(Permanence of Paper).

CONTENTS

ACKNOWLEDGMENTS

The present volume is the result of a conference event that brought together some of the most significant and established figures in the field of psychological anthropology and cultural psychology and some emerging junior scholars to honor the life and work of Richard A. Shweder. The discussions were thoughtful and wide-ranging, focusing on how to think cogently and substantively about psychological diversity within the world's single human race. At that event, which took place over two days on December 5 and 6 at the 2014 AAA meetings in Washington, DC, many of the issues that can be found in this book were raised by scholars dedicated to promoting cultural psychology as advocated for the past thirty years or more by Richard Shweder. For a variety of reasons, not all who participated in these events are represented in the book. Thus, Tanya Luhrmann, Stanton Wortham, and Hazel Markus, for instance, who made highly personal and fascinating presentations on the significance and timeliness of cultural psychology, have not contributed chapters while others—Robert LeVine, Roy D'Andrade, Alan Fiske, and Charles Nuckolls—who happened not to be present at the AAA events, have.

Over the course of the two days, Shweder's students, his students' students, and his colleagues discussed the challenges and promises of this growing field. Although the strengths and weaknesses of the disciplinary traditions of different participants sometimes took central stage, all were adamant that cultural psychological approaches in its many guises were crucial for a deeper and more valid understanding of human motivation and behavior. All participants also agreed on the fundamental importance of the central premise of cultural psychology—that culture and psyche make each other up such that neither can be thought of as prior to nor independent of the other. Subtle differences in emphasis, however, tended to emerge—differences that can be discerned in the chapters of this book as well—when participants discussed how the study of culture can best be integrated with the study of the mind: Is culture to be seen as a variable among others (such as "the reason for this person's psychological holistic orientation is because she is part of an Asian culture that promotes this, through the cultivation of local ideas like *uchi* [close circles of attachment] or because of historical patterns of farming practices, etc.")? Or, as a process that is embedded in and inseparable from psychological experience (such as "the reason for this person's concept of self is connected to these larger patterns but especially to her unique life narrative, which looks like this in this case and experienced through these close group dynamics")?

It is not surprising, perhaps, that these differences in approach often lined up along each participant's disciplinary tradition: those more closely aligned with the field of psychology (among them Alan Fiske, Jon Haidt, and Paul Rozin) tended to view culture as a variable in psychological analyses, and those more closely aligned with the field of anthropology (such as Jacob Hickman, Pinky Hota, Tom Weisner, and Byron Good) were more comfortable with the notion that cognitive processes are malleable, shaping and being shaped by the cultural contexts into which humans are born and raised and live. But, by the end of the conference, there was a shared sense that we, as psychologists and anthropologists, are now more able to address the kinds of questions that cultural psychology poses and offer thoughts about the past, present, and future state of the field to help this emerging enterprise move forward. The thoughts that resulted from these conversations in large part make up the substance of this book. Sadly, during the book's preparation, our colleague Roy D'Andrade passed away. We mourn his passing and celebrate the many great ideas he inspired.

We dedicate this book to Richard Shweder and the field of cultural psychology that he has so passionately helped to rejuvenate and promote. Through his dedication to research and teaching, Richard Shweder has challenged and encouraged several generations of emerging scholars to help knit together the difficult complexities at the edges of mind and culture.

Universalism without Uniformity

USHA MENON

Drexel University
Department of Anthropology

JULIA L. CASSANITI

Washington State University
Department of Anthropology

As the world population grows and our planet appears smaller each year, and as clashes over ideologies within and across cultural groups become more easily shared through new technologies and modes of travel, today is an exciting time to be alive. Arguments over claims of idealized human sameness are pitted against arguments for a recognition and celebration of deep difference. Far from the fall of the Soviet Union marking the "end of history," as the political philosopher Francis Fukuyama (1989) once claimed, our century has spawned an unanticipated, and sometimes unsettling, global diversity in cultural practices, religious ideologies, and socio-political movements. Together with assertions of primordial identities and the resurgence of premodern ontological ideologies, the world can no longer be neatly divided into the West and the non-West, or the developed and the developing—such neat dichotomies have become much too hybrid for such a distinction to reflect the lived variation in global experience. Within this need for an appreciation of diversity is a complementary need for an understanding of how we are in some sense all the same. As humans we all share basic qualities, but claims about what they look like are often problematic. Declarations of sameness raise questions about who is doing the declaring, and about how the declarer's proclamations are too often biased toward the perspective of their own privileged group, with the result that the imposition of a more powerful group's view of what that sameness looks like is taken as natural. Not attending to difference exacerbates these kinds of inequalities that too often disproportionately fall along lines of nation, class, gender, and other marks of identification that celebrate some people and marginalize others.

Universalism without Uniformity offers a new way to approach these issues. In each of the essays in this collection authors examine the mind as working in and through the cultural constructions around us, rather than apart from it, as so many disciplinary traditions suggest. The essays draw from multiple perspectives in the social sciences, especially those of anthropology and psychology, but also of political science and sociology; within this multiplicity, however, is a shared attention to the human mind as coconstitutive in and of culture. Their approaches to diversity and similarity as fundamentally part of our culturally embedded makeup is what Richard Shweder (2003) has called "universalism without the uniformity," a central feature of the growing field of cultural psychology. In the following essays, the authors of *Universalism without Uniformity* address important questions about the state of the world and our places in it through a cultural psychological engagement with their own and others' research.

The scholars that founded the field of cultural psychology were each in their own ways united in recognizing the importance of mental and social processes not as apart from each other (as the traditional disciplines of psychology, anthropology, and sociology have tended to do), but in their mutual construction together. The approach has grown from the work of a heterogeneous collection of scholars roughly two to three decades ago. It has never been singular in its theoretical or methodological approach; some of its founding figures (including Jerome Bruner 1990; Michael Cole 1998; Jaan Valsiner 2014a, 2014b; and James Wertsch 1991) drew their theoretical lineages from the Russian cultural-historical school of Lev Vygotsky and an attention to language, while others (including Hazel Markus and Shinobu Kitayama 1991, 1997; Richard Nisbett et al. 2001; Nisbett 2004; Richard Shweder 1991, 2003) drew from the psychological sciences and emerged from a cross-cultural perspective that includes the work of John and Beatrice Whiting and their attention to the diversity of behavioral practice. Other advocates of the movement for cultural psychology come at it from yet different angles. Although diverse, within these different traditions has been a standing commitment to paying attention to the role of historically formed strategies of communication in how we think and act, both as explanations for human differences and as part of the analysis and interpretation that scholars engage in, and with, as they process their data. What this commitment to both similarity and diversity means, as the cultural psychologist Richard Nisbett and his coauthors have stated, is that

> cognitive content is learned and indefinitely malleable and the assumption that cognitive processes are universally the same and biologically fixed may both be quite wrong. . . . [I]t is not possible to make a sharp distinction between cognitive process and cognitive content. Content in the form of metaphysical beliefs about the nature of the world determines tacit epistemology. Tacit epistemology in turn dictates the cognitive procedures that people use for solving particular problems. (2001, 306)

Though diverse in approaches, together the essays in this collection address what this malleable potential of human cognition looks like in practice, as it examines how "psyche and culture . . . make each other up" (Shweder 1991, 73). The essays in the collection each offers a different perspective in how we might want to go about exploring this makeup, drawing out critiques and advocating for new possibilities to help engage with the strengths and weaknesses of their own disciplinary traditions and forge a new era of cultural psychology. Making use of the authors' own ongoing empirical research projects, they show just how neither psyche nor culture is thought of as prior to, or independent of, the other. Although differing in the extent to which culture or mind is used as a starting point for analysis, and in the degree to which social context or mental processing is seen as the goal of this analysis, there are two premises that are central to each of the essays here: First, as humans we are motivated to search for meanings in everything around us; and second, the cultural worlds we live in are intentional worlds that exist because of our involvement in them. Thus, they maintain that we exist as human beings—with agency, identity, subjectivity, and a sense of self—because (not in spite of) the fact that we interpret and make sense of the events and experiences of our lives. And we do so in terms of the meanings and resources we seize from our worlds—the very worlds that we create and uphold through our thoughts and actions.

Through this attention to coconstruction *Universalism without Uniformity* endeavors to move past common disciplinary perspectives that have, historically, separated anthropological attention to culture from psychology's interest in mental processes (Bruner 1999). On the one hand, many psychologists, despite the existence of fields of investigation such as social psychology and cross-cultural psychology, tend to see culture as so much "noise" that obscures from view the functioning of the psyche (Fish 2000), even as they seemingly acknowledge the importance of social and cultural factors. But, as Clifford Geertz famously observed, a human being without culture would, in effect, be an "unworkable monstrosity," a meaningless and inhuman creature (1973, 49). Many anthropologists, on the other hand, laboring under the load of an excessive empiricism, are uncomfortable discussing subjective experiences that cannot be directly observed and studied. Preferring to deal with cultural constructs, anthropologists adopt either one of two strategies: (1) treat the mind as an unexamined (or even unexaminable) black box, or (2) invoke a "'common-sense psychology' of human motivation and learning" (Bock 1999: 2). Both strategies are problematic: The first results in removing cultural constructs from subjectively lived experience, thereby rendering them alien, and the second universalizes the anthropologist's own unexamined, often ethnocentric, ideas of how the psyche supposedly functions. In sharp contrast, this book, through adopting a cultural psychological approach that focuses squarely on the interrelationship of culture and mind, questions and tries to undermine these old, entrenched disciplinary foundations and divisions and argues for a new approach to study the differences that underlie apparent similarities and the similarities that get ignored because of the anthropological preference for recognizing difference and the psychological tendency for ignoring cultural influences. This is, of course, the promise and the challenge of cultural psychology. Quite apart from these disciplinary pulls and influences, all the contributors to this volume also are conscious of the fact that their subjectivity inevitably colors the gathering, analysis, and interpretation of data and try to be as self-aware as possible in their work.

What Is Universalism without Uniformity in the Study of Mind in Culture?

From a cultural psychological perspective, what is universal are the abstract potentialities of the human mind—the ability to think and act, to feel and desire, to possess norms and values, to have purpose and goals, and to envision the social and natural worlds. Rather than existing *a priori* in some precultural space, these very basic human traits are emergent, realizing their full potential only within the context of the symbolic and behavioral traditions of a community. There are two points that need to be made here to clarify the perspective we take in this book—one about the concept of culture that is being invoked, and the other about the significance of context in cultural psychological investigations. First, the concept of culture used here gives emphasis to doctrines and beliefs—that is, the symbolic component—equal to the emphasis it gives to the inherited practices of a community—the behavioral component. From this perspective, then, human beings become fully human only as members of their cultural communities, absorbing as they mature the symbolic inheritance and the behavioral practices of these communities. And as a result, to a greater or lesser degree, they come to exemplify in their everyday lives, in their actions and their thinking, the mentality (or mentalities) that characterizes their community (Shweder et al. 2006). And second, within cultural psychology, the idea of context is thought to be integral to higher-order psychological processes and activities: *what* one thinks about shapes *how* one thinks, a case of content influencing process (see Markus, Kitayama, and Heiman 1996). Cultural psychologists in this way tend to assume that there are hardly any "deep" or "hard-wired" mental structures, except perhaps "certain very early emerging inborn cognitive biases and heuristics" (Miller, pers. comm.), and perhaps not even those, that are immune to the surrounding sociocultural context or that function apart from it. Context in this sense is less about external noise and more a central mechanism of the creation of mental life.

The human mind is so protean and complex that it includes hidden and unexamined parts that only an encounter with an "other" will activate and bring into consciousness. This has been termed "the principle of original multiplicity" (Shweder 1996, 41). It is, of course, this multiplicity that is the source of our shared humanity, one that allows us to communicate across cultural and linguistic boundaries, and to understand the mental life of another culturally distinct human being. Because of the significance that cultural psychology grants symbolic and behavioral traditions in shaping the mentalities that prevail in various cultural communities, it is not surprising that the discipline tends to disavow the principle of human psychic unity, asserting instead that ethnic divergences in self-organization, in mental processes, and in moral and emotional functioning run deep. It does not deny outright the possibility of empirical universals in psychological functioning, but neither does it necessarily privilege such universals as verities about the life of the psyche (Shweder and Sullivan 1993). To the extent that cultural psychology does subscribe to psychic universalism, it is in the "original multiplicity" mentioned above that it is thought to be found.

In no culture and in no single human life, however, is this multiplicity homogeneous, but nor is it fully heterogeneous either. Sometimes inconsistent structures, tendencies, capacities, and abilities are never fully expressed or experienced. Instead, the particular contextual historical experience of a cultural community shapes its mentality (or mentalities), giving it character and substance by developing and deepening some structures and tendencies, allowing some capacities and abilities to grow and flourish while letting others atrophy and wither away (see Werker 1989 for interesting similarities between what is being described here and the ability of very young infants to distinguish sound shifts in nonnative languages). In assuming this process of selection from a vast array of cultural possibilities and the subsequent deepening and development of what has been selected, cultural psychologists harken back to Ruth Benedict's idea of culture, that each human culture represents "some part of the wide arc of human potentialities" (Mead 1974, 43).

Such a theoretical stance, as advocated in this book, echoes the Geertzian notion that there is no such thing as a generic or basic human being: "To be human here is thus not to be Everyman; it is to be a particular kind of man, and of course men differ" (Geertz 1973, 53). Each of us is, therefore, a particular kind of human being—Javanese or Moroccan or French, and also multiple at once. This is precisely the meaning of the phrase "psyche and culture make each other up"—culture completes us, shapes us into who are. At the same time, as Sapir's work reminds us (Irvine 1994) we are not *tabulae rasae*: each of us is born into this world with innate traits, talents, and abilities that interact in all kinds of subtle and not-so-subtle ways with one's sociocultural environment, with the cultural codes one is exposed to from (and perhaps even before) birth to produce the human beings we finally become. The intricate interconnections that exist between innate psychological traits and extant cultural codes, and how these interconnections are instantiated in behavior, is the subject matter of cultural psychology.

The approaches taken in this book share a general methodological commitment, one that emphasizes the importance of long- or short-term fieldwork to gather comprehensive data about the ways of life in various cultural communities. They also are united in their theoretical engagement with what has been called "custom complexes," sets of customary practices "and the beliefs, values, sanctions, rules, motives, and satisfactions associated with them" (Whiting and Child 1953, 27). These general methodological approaches, along with shared theoretical commitments to psychological pluralism, unite the essays in *Universalism without Uniformity* in the scholarly vision of understanding the interrelationship of culture and mind.

Within this shared vision, however, there are significant differences in the approaches advocated for how to best go about uncovering what such a project can look like in practice. We have termed the heterogeneous approaches taken up by the authors of this book under the umbrella term cultural psychology, but there are many significant differences in the approach taken by these scholars even as they each identify themselves and their work through it. Different disciplinary traditions are especially significant—not necessarily because one tradition is "better" than another at uncovering all the relationships of mind and culture, but because different traditions are oriented to particular perspectives on what kinds of methods to use and what kinds of findings are considered convincing for a given situation in a particular intellectual community.

To avoid reinforcing the disciplinary walls that often impede research into culture and psychology, we have not structured the essays in this collection according to the home disciplines of their authors, but we address some of the influences of academic tradition that inform this book here. We do this both to introduce some of the methodological and theoretical influences taken up in the following essays and to offer some thoughts on what we see as some of the strengths and weaknesses of them as they relate to the shared perspectives in this book. After all, as scholars we are also part of particular intellectual cultures, and escaping them is not an easy task, nor even one to necessarily aspire to. The authors in this collection engage with each of their own disciplinary problems and perspectives even as they seek to move past them, as they interrogate the often entrenched assumptions that go into their particular lineages of thought and show how cultural psychological approaches can help. They advocate for a particular take on a particular issue of intellectual interest to them, but as part of a larger shared emphasis on psychological pluralism in culture they also take the broader theoretical perspective that there may in fact be multiple good and effective approaches available to the project of understanding the mind in culture. The various disciplinary traditions they draw from are part of this project.

Cross-Cultural Psychology

Psychology, in its many guises, has tended to "assert that psychological processes are shared, pan-human qualities of all peoples, everywhere" (Berry 2014, 226). This assumption shapes and influences the research methodology and analysis of data of each subfield of psychological research, although in slightly different ways. Even a cursory familiarity with research and practice within general psychology is enough to reveal its aspiration to be regarded as a science in the tradition of the natural sciences: It seeks to formulate laws about the human mind and its operations that would hold true across all human populations, irrespective of cultural context. From the perspective of the mind as a central processing mechanism, culture is seen as problematic, because it interferes with, and muddies the process of observing, the human mind and its functioning. Therefore, general psychology seeks to minimize, if not entirely eliminate, culture's effects on the human mind. Thus, research within general psychology (though perhaps not all) often requires isolating human subjects—predominantly educated Westerners, very often college undergraduates—and having them perform tests and tasks in laboratories, thought to be preeminently context-free environments. The cultural psychologist Jaan Valsiner (2014b) has contended that general psychology's quest to formulate laws about the functioning of the human mind is the result of it being what he terms a "new and liminal science," liminal because it is located at "the intersection of natural and human sciences" (6). This location makes it subject to "powerful social ideologies" (fn1) about what it means to be a science, ideologies that compel it to gather and analyze "objective data" in order to postulate laws about psychological functioning, ignoring almost entirely the culturally patterned subjectivity that is so central to, and that so critically defines, human experience. By doing so, it abandons the study of higher-order psychological processes that involve intentionality, purposefulness, and resilience in accommodating to an ever-changing world, focusing, instead, on examining such supposedly stable and universal phenomena as personality traits, various kinds of "intelligence," attachment types, learning styles, and coping strategies (Valsiner 2014a).

Under the burden of being a science devoted to the creation of universal and stable knowledge, general psychology also has adopted experimentation, the research methodology of the natural sciences, as its own. And the results are sometimes a little strange: as Jerome Bruner (1999) describes it, general psychology postulates theories of memory based on undergraduates sitting in psychology laboratories—spaces that, to an anthropologist at least, appear to be saturated with cultural meanings—memorizing nonsense syllables "presented to them while seated alone in front of a memory drum that clicks out target syllables at, say, one each three seconds. The 'culture free' claim is, of course, that this is memory-without-meaning" (xiv). From a cultural psychological perspective, such research rarely yields a deeper understanding of human mental processes because to be human is to be cultural, and excising culture from the research agenda appears to undermine the very purpose of the research.

Cross-cultural psychology emerged when the field started to recognize that the West and Western understandings are part of a culturally diverse world. As a subfield of general psychology, cross-cultural psychology seeks to understand how the traditional foci of psychological research—especially those of emotion, selfhood, and mental health—may vary across cultural domains. Sharing general psychology's belief in the psychic unity of humankind, and employing the same research methodology of psychological tests and tasks to derive data, cross-cultural psychology has had to make sense of the indisputable fact that many of the findings that result from laboratory research with educated Western populations do not travel well across cultural, ethnic, and linguistic boundaries. In trying to resolve this problem, cross-cultural psychologists have tended to resort to one of two explanations: either that the non-Western populations they work with have not yet achieved their full psychological potential for a variety of reasons (lack of literacy, absence of formal schooling, emphasis on rote learning, to name a few) or that their non-Western subjects are unfamiliar with the testing environment, and it is this disabling unfamiliarity that prevents the central processing mechanism that is their minds from revealing itself through performing appropriately on the psychometric tests presented to them (see Cole 1971). It is not just that non-Western subjects are unfamiliar with testing and testing environments, however, but that the tests themselves are inherently culture-specific, tailored to the cultural, economic, and political conditions of modern Western societies. As Michael Cole, one of the leading thinkers in contemporary cultural psychology, found when he participated in the effort in the early 1960s to export "new mathematics" to the Kpelle of Liberia, Kpelle children are perfectly capable of categorizing, learning, memorizing, and reasoning in their own world, but they perform poorly on tests and experiments designed in modern Western societies to study changes in these faculties as children mature and develop—these tests and experiments were just too culture-specific, assuming conditions and situations that did not exist among the Kpelle. This creates a compelling problem for the field of cross-cultural psychology.

Then there is the emic–etic issue. As John Whiting has pointed out, psychological categories formulated in the West are frequently unable to describe the thinking and reasoning of people in another culture (1978, 390). Thus, when Shweder and Much attempted to implement Lawrence Kohlberg's famous Heinz dilemma in Bhubaneswar, Odisha, India, they found that the conflict set up in the interview protocol—the conflict between the right to life and the right to private property—hardly resonated with the interviewee. Instead, the interviewee discussed "the irrationality of committing a sin" and never once mentioned the idea of "rights." As Shweder remarked, the interviewee "provided an impressively cogent argument about the irrationality of committing a sin. This led us to realize that Western psychologists had imported into their moral development research a rather restricted conception of the moral domain, which was focused almost exclusively on issues of harm, rights, and justice. It led us to start thinking about other subdomains of the moral" (Shweder 1999, 69; cf. Miller 1997). Apart from these problems, Carl Ratner (2008), a rather trenchant critic of cross-cultural psychology, contends that cross-cultural psychologists are not interested in the concrete details of particular cultures; instead, they are interested in universal dimensions that can be abstracted from particular cultural contexts, and that, therefore, are thought to lend themselves to cross-cultural comparisons. He points to Hofstede's operational definition of individualism versus collectivism as an excellent example of such a research strategy. He contends that Hofstede believes that these concepts are "so simple, homogeneous, invariant and obvious that entire countries could be categorized as individualistic or collectivistic on the basis of three superficial statements about work—e.g., 'Have a job that leaves you sufficient time for your personal or family life'" (2008, 33). Cross-cultural psychologists find such conceptual frameworks attractive because they believe that it gives them a handle on the messiness that often characterizes fine-grained cultural data, that it allows them to make valid cross-cultural comparisons, ignoring the multiplicity of factors that distinguish one collectivistic culture from another or one individualistic culture from another. In this context, it is noteworthy that, according to Ratner, Triandis has identified as many as sixty factors that can separate collectivistic cultures from each other.

And finally, in their attempts to reduce culture into a set of easy-to-handle traits, cross-cultural psychologists tend to privilege biology over culture. Biology is, thus, thought to set the parameters for the psyche to operate and culture merely moderates these operations. Matsumoto's work on emotions and culture exemplifies this approach. He claims that emotional experiences are basic and universal because they are caused by "pan-human biological mechanisms" (Ratner and Hui 2003, 69) and the only role that culture plays is to regulate and manage the ways in which people express their emotions (2001). In this instance, culture is extrinsic to the psyche rather than constitutive of it.

Psychological Anthropology

Like general psychology and cross-cultural psychology, anthropology (and psychological anthropology in particular) also has at times assumed the psychic unity of humankind. Anthropology emerged as a field in an era of aspirations toward similarity. Thus, the psychological anthropologist Melford Spiro is not an outlier when he claims that "the human mind works (or has the capacity to work) the same everywhere" (1984, 327) nor when he states that human emotions are universal because of "the transcultural characteristics of the generic human mind" (1984, 342). Unlike general psychology and cross-cultural psychology, however, psychological anthropology derives its data in a fundamentally different way. Anthropologists study the quotidian details of ordinary people's lives and experiences that, among other things, include family life practices, religious beliefs, kinship nomenclature, and myths, rituals, and folktales. They interpret cultural variations in these data as the working out of the central processing mechanism in different cultural milieus. Unlike general psychologists who see the sociocultural environment as "noise" that needs to be eliminated in order to observe the central processing mechanism at work, anthropologists view the sociocultural environment as expressing the contours of the central processing mechanism and the constraints under which it labors—that is their explanation for the persistence over time of these environments. Subscribing to the psychic unity of humankind, psychological anthropologists view intercultural variability as little more than rather superficial differences between a fairly limited number of possible ways of life.

Even in this wider field of sameness through diversity, it is rather surprising that psychological anthropologists should subscribe to the notion of human psychic unity (see Shore 1999, 29). Yet today, shorn of its social Darwinist associations and its racist implications, many seem to accept it tacitly, even if they do not assert it explicitly. At the same time, as they aspire to unity they maintain that cultural relativism is a fundamental principle of the discipline. As Shore has remarked, "Anthropologists have typically defended cultural difference as a defining human characteristic while repeatedly affirming their faith in humankind's psychic unity, usually without noting the apparent tensions between these two views" (1996, 15).

This reticence to reevaluate the psychic unity of humankind is especially surprising when one considers Franz Boas's significant work distinguishing between race and culture, along with his nuanced thinking on the subject and his stature in the field. Boas did begin to change the field. He was interested in trying to understand the degree to which human psychological processes were flexible and variable. In his 1909 lecture at Clark University, "Psychological Problems in Anthropology," he stated, "The fundamental problem on which all anthropological inquiry must be founded relates to the mental equipment of the various races of man. Are all the races of mankind equally endowed, or do material differences exist?" And then he goes to say, "The final answer to this question has not been given but . . . the composite picture of the mental characteristics of one race would presumably not coincide with the composite picture of the mental characteristics of another race. The evidence that has been brought forward does not justify us, however, in claiming that the characteristics of one race would be an advance over those of another, although they would be different" ([1909] 1974, 243). Boas later qualifies his statements by suggesting, "It would seem, therefore, that the weight of the evidence is, on the whole, in favor of an essential similarity of mental endowment in different races, with the probability of variations in the type of mental characteristics" ([1909] 1974, 244). In discussing these mental characteristics further, he makes the point that these characteristics, while they may "depend to a slight extent upon hereditary individual and racial ability," they are more likely to "be determined by the habitual reactions of the society to which the individual belongs" (244). In drawing this distinction between mental endowments and mental characteristics, he is doing what he did later when he distinguished between race and culture: He is suggesting that the former are inherited traits while the latter are the result of the shaping of cultural traditions. It is intriguing that, in articulating this difference, he appears to be anticipating the thinking within cultural psychology today about what it is that we humans share in terms of our minds and mental processes and what it is that separates us.

Cultural Psychology and the Essays in Universalism

The essays in *Universalism without Uniformity* draw in their own ways from these intellectual traditions of psychology (especially cross-cultural psychology) and anthropology (especially psychological anthropology). Some of the authors explicitly identify themselves as cultural psychologists and their work as cultural psychology, while others identify most explicitly as following one of these other intellectual traditions, even as they also engage with cultural psychology issues. Labels matter, but beyond their differences the authors in this volume believe that cultural psychology is still "in the air" today, as Michael Cole claimed it was a quarter century ago, and that it will be an important approach in coming years. Historically, views on the centrality of the field of cultural psychology have waxed and waned over time. Markus and Kitayama (1992) were optimistic about cultural psychology's chances of becoming part of academic establishments and felt that even then cultural psychology was coming into its own as a field of study. Michael Cole also believed that culture would in the future be a central part of all psychological study, but he placed its emergence within a broader and more cynical historical frame. Cole believed that cultural psychology was garnering academic attention "because the intellectual impulses associated with positivism and the Eurocentric world order with which they coincided have proven inadequate to understanding the world in the late 20th century" (1991, 439). He felt its popularity was due to a social sentiment in the United States and Europe that was based on "the implosion of European imperialism as former colonial peoples flood Europe and the United States" (1991, 439). Although the ramifications of imperialism were not necessarily going to end any time soon, Cole was deeply skeptical about the possibility that cultural psychology could become institutionalized and compete with departments of general psychology that have deep roots in today's modern industrialized societies.

Twenty-five years later, it appears that Markus, Kitayama, and Cole have all been accurate to some extent in their predictions. Cultural psychology has indeed taken off, and in a big way, as more and more young academics and activists are realizing the need to understand the relationship between society and mind as foundational to lived experience. In an increasingly multicultural world, full of the movements of recreational travel, voluntary migration, and refugee resettlements, Cole's view with its promise of culture's place in psychological study still holds. But disciplinary commitments are hard to break through, as young scholars seek to emulate the structural confines of their traditions and older scholars recreate past successes. Miller (this volume) points to the curious fact that references to culture in handbooks on psychology have even declined over the last few decades, and hardly any academic appointments are available to psychologists interested exclusively in cultural issues. And although the contributors to this volume are neither naive nor sanguine about the challenges that confront cultural psychology institutionally and as a school of thought, they do believe that the discipline, with its emphasis on the need to integrate anthropological and psychological approaches to better understand human behavior and motivation, addresses the questions that arise in a complicated and globalized world in a thoughtful and reasoned way. The essays in this book can therefore play a substantial role in enabling social scientists to interpret these complex realities, as they work to transcend the often unexamined, and perhaps unintended, ethnocentrism that characterizes social and psychological theorizing today.

It is through the theoretical tensions in these issues— culture's role in experience and how to best go about finding it, the ways that these findings may tell us something about the diversity and similarity of the human mind—that this book centrally engages with some of the important questions of culture and psychology today. In addition to the disciplinary traditions that the various authors draw from are related differences in the degree to which each author subscribes to the idea of psychological pluralism and the theoretical and methodological approaches they take demonstrate this. In a continuum that stretches from psychic unity to psychological diversity, some of the authors are more oriented toward and supportive of a greater degree of uniformity, or a greater degree of psychic unity, than others, who tend to think that psychological pluralism is the order of the day, and that, perhaps, cultures should be studied as incommensurable wholes. Within their diversity of positions in theoretical and methodological approaches, each of the essays in this book demonstrates a central commitment to psychological plurality as part of, rather than unnecessary to, the shared human experience. We have arranged the essays here around the kinds of problems that these different perspectives can help to solve. The first two parts of the book focus on particular psychological experiences, in particular cultural communities, and on how their expressions in one place may inform our understanding of the phenomenon around the world. The third part examines expressions of psychological diversity in practice that find themselves in political ideological clashes with the global community.

Robert LeVine opens the volume with his chapter "Challenging Developmental Doctrines through Cross-Cultural Research." He does so in order to introduce how the contested ideas of universalism without the uniformity can be taken up through the kinds of cultural psychological approach in each of the essays, through a demonstration of how the study of culture in mind relates to our understanding of the developing human being. Making the case that ideal patterns in child development are not singular but plural, and showing some of the debates that have emerged in the child development literature from the time of Margaret Mead and Jean Piaget to the present day, LeVine shows how a cultural psychological perspective has come to be an essential part of how we understand not just child development but the entire experience of what it means to be human.

LeVine's introductory chapter is followed by three chapters that together offer a theoretical framework on the interdisciplinary views of the field of cultural psychology. Drawing from psychological and anthropological perspectives, the essays in this section demonstrate what doing interdisciplinary research on culture and mind in the social sciences does and can look like. In each chapter some of the difficult challenges as well as the promising possibilities are addressed for the kinds of interdisciplinary attempts promoted in this book. In chapter 2, "'How Cultural Psychology Can Help Us See 'Divinity' in a Secular World," Haidt and Rozin elaborate on the emic–etic problem that often plagues cross-cultural psychology, suggesting that categories developed in Western moral psychology are inadequate not only when studying morality in non-Western cultures but also in the West, for instance among religious and conservative people in the United States. In chapter 3, "Beyond Universal Taxonomic Frameworks in Cultural Social Psychology," Miller explores the issues surrounding cultural psychology's current popularity within mainstream psychology, advocating for but also warning of the continual need to challenge universal taxonomic frameworks that tend to be insensitive to the dynamic nature of cultural processes and to the context dependency of psychological phenomena. D'Andrade, in chapter 4, wraps up the introductory section in "From Value to Lifeworld," as he points to discrepancies between cross-national value surveys that find universal value patterns and ethnographic research that suggests the opposite, and reconciles them in two ways—one, by addressing the problems in what gets counted as what and, two, by examining differences between personal values and values institutionalized in the lifeworlds of modern societies.

Following these interdisciplinary, barrier-breaking introductory chapters, the essays of part 2, "One Mind, Many Mentalities," delve into psychological experience and its construction within particular cultural communities. These chapters focus especially on the experience of emotion and emotion processing, addressing through them the significant and related patterns of thought and behavior that are implicated when we feel. Although some psychologists have argued for universal mechanisms of human emotion (e.g., Ekman 1972, 1992), following a long line of inquiry into the relationship between physiological experiences and their felt expression (James 1884; Cannon 1927; Schachter and Singer 1962), anthropologists have increasingly questioned these assumptions, highlighting instead social construction (Lutz and White 1986) and affective movement (Gregg and Seigworth 2010; Tompkins 1963). Yet as the cross-cultural psychologist Jeanne Tsai has pointed out, however, "Although most theories acknowledge that cultural and temperamental factors shape affective states, few, if any, specify how" (Tsai 2007, 251). The chapters in this section approach these issues through attention to both physiological and social influences, emphasizing the mechanisms of emotion's interpersonal, culturally influenced construction through religious orientations, relational models, and aesthetics. In chapter 5, "'Kama Muta' or 'Being Moved by Love': A Bootstrapping Approach to the Ontology and Epistemology of an Emotion," Fiske, Schubert, and Seibt claim that basic relational models give rise to social emotions, and that thus social emotions may be discrete categories, rather than dimensionally structured. In making this argument, they are arguing in favor of an emotion that is universally experienced, *kama muta*. Approaching the study of the emotions from a slightly different perspective, Cassaniti, in chapter 6, "Unsettling Basic States: New Directions in the Cross-Cultural Study of Emotion," makes use of affective experience in a Buddhist community in Thailand to think through state versus componential approaches to emotion and argues for the need to abandon discrete-state ideas in favor of componential elaboration. And Menon, in chapter 7, "*Rasa* and the Cultural Shaping of Human Consciousness," argues that *rasa*, a concept unique to Hindu aesthetics, is experienced both in the gut and as the transcendental bliss of final liberation. Together the chapters argue for a theoretical approach to human emotions that emphasizes the cultural and historical shaping of emotional experience.

In chapter 8, "The Socialization of Social Trust: Cultural Pluralism in Understanding Attachment and Trust in Children," Weisner argues against a single normative maturational model for conceptualizing well-being in development and suggests developing contextually variable models that are based on cultural pluralism and elaborate how children are socialized to experience and display trust. And in chapter 9, "An Attachment-Theoretical Approach to Religious Cognition," Nuckolls elaborates on the relevance of attachment theory to the development of religion, a theoretical stance that tends to affirm psychic unity and diverges, in some important ways, from Weisner's analysis in the previous chapter.

The five chapters of part 3, "Implications of Psychological Pluralism for a Multicultural World," turn to a demonstration of the ways in which recent research in cultural psychology contributes to the study of personal functioning in particular interpersonal environments as it relates to conflicts that this functioning can encounter when members of a particular cultural community find themselves at odds with a larger dominant society. The chapters focus especially on contested issues of moral personhood, female genital surgeries, and mental health practices around the world, and in doing so highlight the multicultural reality of living within a world of "universalism without uniformity." In chapter 10, "Accultura-tion, Assimilation, and the 'View from Manywheres' in the Hmong Dias-pora," Hickman draws out a Hmong theory of moral personhood and its variations in Thai and US Hmong communities, in order to argue for an important relationship between culturally variable models of personhood and moral thinking. Aware of the tension that exists between liberalism and multiculturalism yet recognizing that ethnic divergences in human functioning go deep, Hickman's chapter and the next two approach con-temporary problems through the perspective of cultural pluralism. In fo-cusing on the nature of tolerance within cultural pluralism, Hota shows in chapter 11, "Vexed Tolerance: Cultural Psychology on Multiculturalism," how recent attempts to address tolerance in engagement with moral dif-ferences reveals the potential for inconsistencies in attempts to combine liberalism with multicultural ideologies. And in chapter 12, "Equality, Not Special Protection: Multiculturalism, Feminism, and Female Circumcision in Western Liberal Democracies," Ahmadu tackles the contentious issue of female circumcision, paying particular attention to second-wave feminist views that this cultural practice is where liberal democracies must draw the line against multiculturalism.

The final two chapters of part 3 examine the culturally variable nature of healthy mental functioning. What does it mean to be a healthy person, they ask, with a healthy, functioning mind? What does it mean, on the other hand, to be mentally unhealthy, or mentally "disordered"? And, most important, how do these ideas about mental health and disorder vary and become contested cross-culturally, both on their own and in their relation-ship to other ideologies about what it means to be well? The American Psy-chiatric Association's *Diagnostic and Statistical Manual of Mental Disorders* (the *DSM*) has long stood as psychology's standard for recognizing and la-beling mental distress, both in the United States and elsewhere (Stein et al. 2010), but there is little in it in the way of cultural variation of health and distress within it. Culturally oriented psychologists and anthropologists are increasingly pointing to the ways that mental health is crafted within, rather than without, culture (Luhrmann and Marrow 2016; Watters 2010; Wilkinson and Kleinman, 2016). Leading scholars in the field of health and culture thus emphasize cultural psychology's contributions to the study of mental health as constructed in and through cultural communi-ties. In doing so they dislodge the idea of a healthy, universal normal mind and plant mental health firmly in the shifting tides of personal interactions with unique social histories. In chapter 13, "Cultural Psychology and the Globalization of Western Psychiatric Practices," Horton argues that cultural psychological perspectives have been critical in providing a counterweight to the globalizing tendencies in psychiatric discourses and practices. And in chapter 14, "Toward a Cultural Psychology of Trauma and Trauma-Related Disorders," Good and DelVecchio-Good explore the cultural psychology of trauma-related disorders suffered by people in postconflict Aceh, Indonesia, thereby reframing the debate between universalist and culturally relativist arguments about the nature of psychiatric categories, and focusing attention on psychocultural processes.

Richard Shweder offers a final chapter, "The Risky Cartography of Drawing Moral Maps: With Special Reference to Economic Inequality and Sex-Selective Abortion." In this essay, Shweder illustrates the value of a cultural psychology of morality approach to comparison through two examples of moral mapping, as he develops the ongoing cultural and psychological study of "personal functioning in particular interpersonal worlds" (1991, 76). Taken together, the essays of *Universalism without Uniformity* speak through their multiple perspectives to issues of self, health, and emotion that are today confronting people living on our planet. Although the ways and means by which they do so vary from essay to essay, the issues addressed through the authors' shared insight that culture matters in the way that our minds work will be of vital importance in the future of social science research. They help to show how our contextual psychological orientations matter in the multiple cultures in which we all find ourselves today.

References

Berry, John W. 2014. "Multiculturalism: Psychological Perspectives." In *Multiculturalism Question: Debating Identity in 21st Century Canada*, edited by Jack Jedwab, 225–40. Kingston, Canada: School of Policy Studies, Queen's University.

Boas, Franz. [1909] 1974. "Psychological Problems in Anthropology." In *A Franz Boas Reader*, edited by George W. Stocking. Chicago: University of Chicago Press.

Bock, Philip. 1999. *Rethinking Psychological Anthropology: Continuity and Change in Human Action*. Long Grove, IL: Waveland.

Bruner, Jerome. 1990. *Acts of Meaning: The Jerusalem-Harvard Lecture*. Cambridge, MA: Harvard University Press.

———. 1999. Foreword to *Culture in Mind* by Bradd Shore. New York: Oxford University Press.

Cannon, Walter. 1927. "The James-Lange Theory of Emotions: A Critical Examination and an Alternative Theory." *American Journal of Psychology* 39: 106–124.

Cole, Michael. 1971. *The Cultural Context of Learning and Thinking: An Exploration in Experimental Anthropology*. New York: Basic Books.

———. 1991. "On Cultural Psychology." *American Anthropologist* 93 (2): 335–439.

———. 1996. *Cultural Psychology: A Once and Future Discipline*. Cambridge, MA: Harvard University Press.

Ekman, Paul 1972. "Universals and Cultural Differences in Facial Expressions of Emotions." In *Nebraska Symposium on Motivation*, edited by J Cole, 207–83. Lincoln: University of Nebraska Press.

———. 1992. "An Argument for Basic Emotions." *Cognition and Emotion* 6 (3–4) 169–200.

Fish, Jeffrey. 2000. "What Anthropology Can Do for Psychology: Facing Physics Envy, Ethnocentrism, and a Belief in 'Race.'" *American Anthropologist* 102 (3): 552–63.

Fukuyama, Francis. 1989. "The End of History?" *The National Interest* 16: 3–18.

Geertz, Clifford. 1973. *The Interpretation of Cultures*. New York: Basic Books.

Irvine, Judith T., ed. 1994. *Edward Sapir: The Psychology of Culture; A Course of Lectures*. Berlin: Mouton de Gruyter.

James, William. 1884. "II—What Is an Emotion?" *Mind* IX (34), 188–205.

Luhrmann, Tanya, and Jocelyn Marrow, eds. 2016. *Our Most Troubling Madness: Schizophrenia across Cultures*. Los Angeles: University of California Press.

Lutz, Catherine and Geoffrey White. 1986. "The Anthropology of Emotions." *Annual Review of Anthropology* 15: 405–36.

Markus, Hazel, and Shinobu Kitayama. 1991. "Culture and the Self: Implications for Cognition, Emotion, and Motivation." *Psychological Review* 98 (2): 224–53.

———. 1992. "The What, Why and How of Cultural Psychology: A Review of Shweder's Thinking through Cultures." *Psychological Inquiry* 3 (4): 357–64.

Markus, Hazel, Shinobu Kitayama, and Rachel Heiman. 1996. "Culture and 'Basic' Psychological Principles." In *Social Psychology: Handbook of Basic Principles*, edited by Edward Higgins and Arie Kruglanski, 857–913. New York: Guilford.

Matsumoto, David. 2001. "Culture and Emotion." In *Handbook of Culture and Psychology*, edited by D. Matsumoto, 171–94. New York: Oxford University Press.

Mead, Margaret. 1974. *Ruth Benedict: A Humanist in Anthropology*. New York: Columbia University Press.

Miller, Joan. 1994. "Cultural Diversity in the Morality of Caring: Individually Oriented versus Duty-Based Interpersonal Moral Codes." *Cross-Cultural Research* 28 (1): 3–39.

———. 1997. "Theoretical Issues in Cultural Psychology." In *Cross-Cultural Psychology: Theory and Method*, edited by John W. Berry, Ype H. Poortinga, and Janak Pandey, 85—128, Boston, MA: Allyn and Bacon

———. 1999. "Cultural Psychology: Implications for Basic Psychological Theory." *Psychological Science* 10 (2): 85–91.

Nisbett, Richard. 2004. *The Geography of Thought: How Asians and Westerners Think Differently . . . and Why*. New York: Free Press.

Nisbett, Richard E., Kaiping Peng, Incheol Choi, and Ara Norenzayan. 2001. "Culture and Systems of Thought: Holistic versus Analytic Cognition." *Psychological Review* 108 (2): 291–310.

Ratner, Carl. 2008. *Cross-Cultural Psychology and Indigenous Psychology*. New York: Nova Science.

Ratner, Carl, and Lumei Hui. 2003. "Theoretical and Methodological Problems in Cross-Cultural Psychology." *Journal for the Theory of Social Behaviour* 33 (1): 67–94.

Schachter, Stanley, and Jerome Singer. 1962 "Cognitive, Social and Physiological Determinants of Emotional State." *Psychological Review* 379–399.

Shweder, Richard. 1991. *Thinking through Cultures*. Cambridge, MA: Harvard University Press.

———. 1996. "True Ethnography: The Lore, the Law and the Lure." In *Ethnography and Human Development: Context and Meaning in Social Inquiry*, edited by Richard Jessor, Anne Colby, and Richard Shweder, 15–52. Chicago: University of Chicago Press.

———. 1999. "Why Cultural Psychology?" *Ethos* 27 (1): 62–73.

———. 2003. *Why Do Men Barbecue? Recipes for Cultural Psychology.* Cambridge, MA: Harvard University Press.

Shweder, Richard, and Maria Sullivan. 1993. "Cultural Psychology: Who Needs It?" *Annual Review of Psychology* 44: 497–523.

Shweder, Richard A., Jacqueline Goodnow, Giyoo Hatano, Robert Levine, H. Markus, and Peggy Miller. 2006. "The Cultural Psychology of Development: One Mind, Many Mentalities." In *Handbook of Child Psychology* (6th ed.), edited by William Damon. New York: Wiley.

Shore, Bradd. 1999. *Culture in Mind.* New York: Oxford University Press.

Spiro, Melford. 1984. "Some Reflections on Cultural Determinism and Relativism with Special Reference to Emotion and Reason." In *Culture Theory: Essays on Mind, Self, and Emotion,* edited by Richard A. Shweder and Robert A. LeVine, 323–46. Cambridge: Cambridge University Press.

Stein, Dan J., Katharine Phillips, Derek Bolton, K. W. Fulford, John Sadler, and Kenneth Kendler. 2010. "What Is a Mental/Psychiatric Disorder? From DSM-IV to DSM-V." *Psychological Medicine* 40 (11): 1759–65.

Valsiner, Jaan. 2014a. *Oxford Handbook of Culture and Psychology.* New York: Oxford University Press.

———. 2014b. *An Invitation to Cultural Psychology.* London: Sage.

Watters, Ethan 2010. *Crazy Like Us: The Globalization of the American Psyche.* New York: Simon and Schuster.

Werker, Janet. 1989. "Becoming a Native Listener." *American Scientist* 77: 54–59.

Wertsch, James. 1991. *Voices of the Mind.* Cambridge, MA: Harvard University Press.

———. 1992. "Keys to Cultural Psychology." *Culture, Medicine, and Psychiatry* 16 (3): 273–80.

———. 1995. "Sociocultural Research in the Copyright Age." *Culture and Psychology* 1: 81–102.

Whiting, John W. M. 1978. Review, *American Ethnologist* (5) 2: 389–90

Whiting, John W. M., and Irwin Child. 1953. *Child Training and Personality.* New Haven, CT: Yale University Press

Wilkinson, Iain, and Arthur Kleinman. 2016. *A Passion for Society: How We Think about Suffering.* Vol. 35. Berkeley: University of California Press.

PART ONE

Breaking Down Barriers through the Study of Culture in the Study of Mind

ONE

Challenging Developmental Doctrines through Cross-Cultural Research

ROBERT A. LEVINE

Harvard University
Graduate School of Education

If our nervous system as evolved through natural selection provides the universal hardware of human behavior, and our cultures—as historically transmitted—supply its variable software, then psychology should offer a conception of the interactions through which children develop according to the divergent standards of human cultures. That there are many standards rather than one is a basic assumption in approaches to child development, supported by a large and growing body of evidence that anthropologists have accumulated. But psychologists have long been tempted to treat development as singular rather than plural.

G. Stanley Hall, a founder of child psychology, gave us the concept of adolescence (in 1904) but grounded it in the theory that ontogeny recapitulates phylogeny. The behaviorists claimed that the reinforcement principle could account for all behavioral outcomes. Jean Piaget's ([1951] 1962); Flavell 1963) ambitious and comprehensive genetic epistemology assumed that the course of cognitive development in all humans could be generated from observations of children in Geneva during the early and middle twentieth century. Lev Vygotsky's ([1934] 1962) theoretical formulations correcting Piaget opened the door to social influences but assumed them to be those that improve children's development by pushing it toward goals prespecified by progressive social theory.

All these theorists thought it was possible to construct a model of development that could fit the human species as a whole largely on the basis of evidence about children in a particular place at a particular time. From the perspective of cultural psychology and psychological anthropology in the twenty-first century, this assumption is naive. A better assumption might be that of Karl Popper's (1963) falsificationism, that scientific knowledge consists of those conjectures that have survived falsification by empirical evidence; science is constantly evolving as new evidence falsifies old conjectures. Child psychology, in trying to imagine the complex processes through which an infant becomes an adult in terms of behavior and mental development, is necessarily conjectural, but its conjectures should be subjected to a sturdy process of winnowing in which some generalizations survive to be recognized as (provisional) knowledge (Campbell 1974).

For most child psychologists, that winnowing process was provided by the laboratory experiment. They followed a pattern established during the behaviorist ascendancy in US psychology, roughly 1935–1960, when "the laws of learning" that applied to vertebrates in general were thought to be established through controlled experiments with albino rats that had been deprived of food for twenty-two hours. Psychologists from the 1960s onward conducted experiments with human children in which background factors were held constant so that the outcomes from factors manipulated by the experimenter could be detected. Thus, when Piaget's observational assessments of children's thought were subjected to experiments in the United States, the initial focus was on whether experimental conditions could accelerate children's age-linked mastery of tasks, falsifying Piaget's static portrait of age-linked stages. Then there was examination of whether the correlations among diverse abilities posited by his structural theory would hold up in empirical testing. The structural theory was declared dead at the Minnesota Symposium on Child Psychology in 1979 by John Flavell (published in 1982), who had done more than anyone to interest US psychologists in Piaget's work some fifteen years earlier (Flavell 1963). This was a triumph of falsification through the laboratory experiment.

For developmentalists less imbued with the standards of the *Journal of Experimental Psychology*, the "natural experiments" of Patricia M. Greenfield (1966) comparing schooled and unschooled children among the Wolof of Senegal and Douglass Price-Williams (1962) on the Tiv in Nigeria provided more convincing evidence to critique Piagetian theory. Greenfield's study of Wolof children strongly suggested that Piaget's conservation task results in Geneva depended on experience in Western schools rather than simply reflecting an inherent developmental sequence—an issue that could not be investigated in Geneva or anywhere else where schooling was universal. But for child psychologists inspired by a scientific ideal derived from the laboratory experiments of I. P. Pavlov and E. L. Thorndike rather than Darwin's field research, her discovery was too exotic, too sociological, to be taken as seriously as it should have been.

In anthropology at the time there was one place where an anthropological application of the conjecture-and-refutation model of science held sway: in John W. M. Whiting's research group at Harvard. Whiting had tested hypotheses derived from Freud's theory of psychosexual development in ethnographic reports from seventy-five cultures and found support for only some of them (Whiting and Child 1953). His students in seminar were urged to offer their own conjectures for explaining a given body of comparative data and suggestions for testing their conjectures against the cross-cultural evidence. The assumptions were that variations at the cross-cultural level could provide powerful, nonexperimental, evidence for and against developmental conjectures, and that generalizations based only on Western evidence were nothing more than speculations. For those of us trained in that research group, including several authors in this volume (Richard A. Shweder, Roy G. D'Andrade, Thomas Weisner, and me), the provisional character of monocultural findings was a fundamental methodological principle.

The Hausa Study

In 1968 I planned a long-term study of child development among the Hausa of northwestern Nigeria that had two parts: (a) exploring through ethnographic observations the social and cultural contexts of parents, infants, and children in a Hausa community; and (b) a program of replicating Western studies of developmental topics ranging from infant attachment to cognitive development with Hausa children in their natural social settings. If the studies, carried out by Nigerian university students in a child development training program, showed findings differing from those with Western children, the contextual data would help to explain why and might provide explanations making sense of the results in the Hausa context.

In the infant studies, Sarah LeVine observed mothers and babies in homes according to a schedule designed to assess conditions specified by Mary D. S. Ainsworth's Baltimore research (Ainsworth, Blehar, Waters, and Wall 1978).

In the cognitive development research, Douglass Price-Williams and I designed assessments based on Piaget's ([1928] 1968) early work in Geneva on the judgment and reasoning of the child (LeVine and Price-Williams 1974). We studied fifty-three Hausa children four to eleven years old; many had never been to school. (Our assistants gained their compliance in the assessment situation by letting them hear their voices on a tape recorder.) We adapted Piaget's questions to fit the family environments of the Hausa, in which people live in walled compounds that often contain several families. The results showed that as children get older they become more able to say how others in the compound are related to each other instead of simply how each is related to the child—consistent with Piaget's model of development from an egocentric to a relativistic perspective. And this was correlated (controlling for age) with left-right reversibility, that is, a child's ability to know that her right hand is on the "same" side as the left hand of the person facing her—supporting Piaget's structural theory of cognitive development.

At the same time, however, there were signs of environmental influence: Children tended to define the Hausa word for grandmother (*kaka*) as mother's mother, reflecting the salience of the maternal grandmother, who typically lives in a different community, as the most likely primary caretaker when a child is ready for weaning. And the Hausa customs of name-avoidance and social distance from certain categories of kin living in the compound also were reflected in the children's responses, suggesting *enculturation* of the growing child. Thus we could argue that a simple interview procedure focused on kinship could reveal the child's developmental status in Piagetian terms, her acquisition of the local culture, and her personal experience in that cultural environment. Unfortunately, political conditions related to the Biafran civil war did not permit us to continue the research beyond the first year. But there are other bodies of data collected at the same time, and with my new colleague Richard A. Shweder, I published another article on the dream concepts of Hausa children (Shweder and LeVine 1975).

We were of course following in the footsteps of Margaret Mead, both in testing developmental conjectures with anthropological evidence and in some cases showing the culture-bound nature of Piaget's findings. Mead (1928) had used her Samoan observations to challenge the universality of adolescent turmoil posited by G. Stanley Hall, and despite the much later attack by Derek Freeman (1983), her conclusions from that study about the culture-specific nature of adolescence still stand today. Her 1928 book *Coming of Age in Samoa* was revolutionary in demonstrating not only that development could vary across cultures but also that anthropological observations could be used to refute conjectures offered by Western psychologists. When she conducted fieldwork among the Manus of Melanesia a few years later, Mead examined how some of Piaget's ideas hold up in that society. She found that the "animism" of Manus children *increased* with age, instead of decreasing as Piaget had found among children in Geneva, in accordance with their respective cultural environments, suggesting that what psychologists treat as "development" may also be "enculturation."

Mead's article on the Manus was published in 1932, more than thirty years before Piaget's work became a recognized research topic among US psychologists, and for reasons that remain unclear, it appeared in the *Journal of the Royal Anthropological Institute*, where psychologists would be unlikely to read it. Perhaps this reflected Mead's increasing alienation from the field of child psychology. But in 1973, when I was asked to contribute an article to a special issue of the (then) new journal *Ethos* dedicated to Margaret Mead and focused on "the processes of cultural transmission," I asked Shweder if he would collaborate in writing up the data from the study of Hausa children's dream concepts, another replication of a Piaget study in Geneva, which Lawrence A. Kohlberg (1969) had replicated in Chicago. The article was largely written by Shweder when I was in Kenya, and it became "Dream Concepts of Hausa Children: A Critique of the 'Doctrine of Invariant Sequence' in Cognitive Development," published in *Ethos* in 1975 and then in a separate volume edited by Theodore Schwartz (1976), *Socialization as Cultural Communication: Development of a Theme in the Work of Margaret Mead*.

With the proliferation of psychologists and the growth of psychology departments and child development training programs in the United States during the 1960s, child development research had become "multiparadigmatic," Sheldon White's (2001) polite term for "chaotic." Researchers had been freed from having to pretend they were exploring how the laws of learning handed down from the rat lab applied to children in Iowa City. But child psychology lacked a consensus on theory and method, and there were only a few like Greenfield and Michael Cole who were doing cross-cultural studies. The field as a whole was disorderly but exciting, as psychological researchers freshly considered what to make of immature human beings. If there was a new mainstream, it was the study of human cognitive development from infancy through adolescence. Released from the constraints of behavior theory with its animal models, child development researchers nevertheless tended toward grandiose universalism, casually extrapolating from small-scale US studies to humans in general.

In this context, Kohlberg had formulated his own ambitious "cognitive-developmental approach" for David Goslin's 1969 volume, *Handbook of Socialization Theory and Research*. It was based on Piaget but emphasized certain aspects of that theory, including a "doctrine of invariant sequence" as well as presenting new evidence. Focusing on that doctrine, Shweder argued that the Hausa data did not support the notion of invariance or Kohlberg's "inner logic" in the sequence through which Hausa children, as they grew older, shifted from thinking that dreams were external perceptions to understanding them as private fantasies. Some Hausa children, though not all, seemed to be affected in their beliefs by the experience of sleeping with others in the family, that is, they thought the others could see their dreams. Shweder's raising of doubts about the Kohlberg doctrine of invariant sequence from African data forecast his later critiques of developmental doctrines and constituted a model for such critiques, in two respects:

First, though an anthropologist, Shweder approached Kohlberg's doctrine as an insider to developmental psychology, with which he was fully conversant. Unlike those anthropologists who are reluctant to criticize work outside their own discipline, or on the other hand, simply dismiss it, he launched an informed critique. The interdisciplinary training he and I had with the Whitings assumed that you learned the field you were criticizing, whatever the discipline, and Rick automatically took that approach in cutting psychological universalism down to size.

Second, in the Hausa article Shweder finds and disputes the philosophical core of Kohlberg's position—that developmental changes reflect logical necessity, the order of which *could not* be reversed—as he shows how the Hausa data suggest otherwise. This identification of a philosophical issue underlying a developmental position is characteristic of Shweder's later critiques as well, giving them power and providing a standard for argumentation in this field. Cross-cultural evidence is important not only because it may contradict misguided universalism in contemporary psychology but also because it addresses age-old philosophical problems with empirical evidence that promises new and more fundamental understanding. Anthropologists are, as Shweder has often argued, exploring problems that were raised by philosophers centuries ago but using our enhanced knowledge of human variation to solve them. That may be particularly true in cultural psychology and psychological anthropology, which restore to social science the psychological perspective that anthropologists have all too often excluded from their vision, while also keeping cultural variation in view.

Forty Years Later: Cross-Cultural Research in the Child Development Field

By now, cross-cultural studies are established as a specialty within the child development field but are not yet considered necessary for constructing theories or testing their validity. It may be that fewer developmental psychologists nowadays than in the 1970s make universalistic claims that need to be shot down, partly because they avoid theorizing altogether. It is clear, however, that developmental psychologists like Patricia Greenfield, Barbara Rogoff, Michael Cole, Mark Bornstein, Heidi Keller, Jonathan Tudge, and Pamela Cole have, through their own cross-cultural research, advocacy, and theoretical formulations, had a real impact on child development research. Yet the need for critique through cross-cultural falsification remains. In writings aimed at the general public, claims that a behavior found in US residents is rooted in evolution and the brain are regularly used to set aside the need to replicate a study in diverse cultural settings. As animal experiments once represented the gold standard, enabling researchers to ignore cross-cultural evidence on child development, so advances in evolutionary biology and neuroscience have now taken that transcendent place. If development is largely a matter of human evolution and the brain, why should we worry about childhood environments in the non-Western world?

One answer is that more than 90 percent of children are being raised in that world (UN Population Division 2012), including high-income, urbanized, and Western-educated people like the Japanese, whose child-rearing practices differ radically from ours (see Rothbaum et al. 2000). US children, even Western children as a whole, represent a smaller part of the human species than ever. To ignore the possibilities for refuting conjectural extrapolations from the easily observed few to the remote and amazingly varied many makes less sense than ever, as recognized by *Child Development*, the journal of the Society for Research in Child Development (SRCD) and the premier journal in child psychology, in their November 2014 announcement of a "New Sociocultural Policy":

> As developmental science becomes more global, and the role of context in human development becomes more evidenced, it is necessary that reports in *Child Development* provide, aside from gender and age of participants, an indication of the unique characteristics of the sample and the "socioeconomic and cultural place" to (sic) which their findings originate. (Society for Research in Child Development 2014)

This is surely welcome, though at least forty years late, and it does not mention using the context in interpreting findings from the children sampled. But as if to illustrate the need for the new policy, the journal published an article on children's teleology by Konika Banerjee and Paul Bloom (2015), in which the specific backgrounds of the thirty-four child subjects in the Yale database and at a children's museum are not provided, the relevant anthropological literature is not reviewed, and children are reported to be more teleological in their responses than adults. Though the main conclusion is that the "area is ripe for additional investigation," we are led to believe that the early emergence of a bias for teleology in children is not due to their parents' belief in God or other supernatural beings. There is no recommendation that the study should be replicated in populations more saturated with theological purpose than New Haven residents (Bengali Hindus, Hasidic Jews?) for potential refutation of this idea, or that its narrowly framed challenge to the cultural acquisition concept of children's teleology should be explored across cultures. In other words, we are back to considering some of the same issues that Mead confronted in Piaget in 1932 and that Shweder identified in Kohlberg in 1975—without the kind of cultural information that would help us resolve them. Good luck to the editors of *Child Development* with their new sociocultural policy. They need to catch up with the knowledge and sophistication represented by this book.

References

Ainsworth, Mary D. Salter, Mary C. Blehar, Everett Waters, and Sally Wall. 1978. *Patterns of Attachment: A Psychological Study of the Strange Situation*. Hillsdale, NJ: Lawrence Erlbaum.

Banerjee, Konika, and Paul Bloom. 2015. "'Everything Happens for a Reason': Children's Beliefs about Purpose in Life Events." *Child Development* 86 (2): 503–18.

Campbell, Donald. 1974. "Evolutionary Epistemology." In *The Philosophy of Karl Popper*, edited by Paul Schilpp, 413–63. LaSalle, IL: Open Court.

Flavell, John. 1963. *The Developmental Psychology of Jean Piaget*. Princeton, NJ: D. Van Nostrand.

———. 1982. "On Cognitive Development." *Child Development* 53 (1): 1–10.

Freeman, Derek. 1983. *Margaret Mead and Samoa: The Making and Unmaking of an Anthropological Myth*. Cambridge, MA: Harvard University Press.

Greenfield, Patricia M. 1966. "On Culture and Conservation." In *Studies in Cognitive Growth*, edited by Jerome Bruner, Rose Oliver, and Patricia Greenfield, 225–56. New York, NY: Wiley and Sons.

Hall, G. Stanley. (1904) 1969. *Adolescence*. New York, NY: Arno Press.

Kohlberg, Lawrence. 1969. "Stage and Sequence: The Cognitive-Developmental Approach to Socialization." In *Handbook of Socialization Theory and Research*, edited by David Goslin, 347–480. Skokie, IL: Rand McNally.

LeVine, Robert A., and Douglas Price-Williams. 1974. "Children's Kinship Concepts: Cognitive Development and Early Experience among the Hausa." *Ethnology* 13 (1): 25–44.

Mead, Margaret. 1928. *Coming of Age in Samoa*. New York: William Morrow.

———. 1932. "An Investigation of the Thought of Primitive Children, with Special Reference to Animism." *Journal of the Royal Anthropological Institute* 62: 173–90.

Piaget, Jean. (1922) 1969. *The Language and Thought of the Child*. Cleveland, OH: Meridian.

———. (1928) 1968. *Judgment and Reasoning in the Child*. Totowa, NJ: Littlefield, Adams.

———. (1951) 1962. *Play, Dreams and Imitation in Childhood*. New York, NY: W. W. Norton.

Popper, Karl. 1963. *Conjectures and Refutations: The Growth of Scientific Knowledge*. London, UK: Routledge and Kegan Paul.

Price-Williams, Douglas. 1962. "Abstract and Concrete Modes of Classification in a Primitive Society." *British Journal of Educational Psychology* 32: 50–61.

Rothbaum, Fred, Martha Pott, Hiroshi Azuma, Kazuo Miyake, and John Weisz. 2000. "The Development of Close Relationships in Japan and the United States: Paths of Symbiotic Harmony and Generative Tension." *Child Development* 71 (5): 1121–42.

Shweder, Richard A., and Robert A. LeVine. 1975. "Dream Concepts of Hausa Children: A Critique of the 'Doctrine of Invariant Sequence' in Cognitive Development." In *Socialization as Cultural Communication: Development of a Theme in the Work of Margaret Mead*, edited by Theodore Schwartz. Berkeley, CA: University of California Press.

Society for Research in Child Development. 2014. "New Sociocultural Policy." www.srcd .org/sites/default/files/documents/sociocultural_policy.pdf.

United Nations Population Division. 2012. *World Population Prospects*. https://esa.un.org/ unpd/wpp/.

Vygotsky, Lev. (1934) 1962. *Thought and Language*. Cambridge, MA: MIT Press.

White, Sheldon H. 2001. *Developmental Psychology as a Human Enterprise*. Heinz Werner Lecture Series. Worcester, MA: Clark University Press.

Whiting, John W. M., and Irvin L. Child. 1953. *Child Training and Personality: A Cross-Cultural Study*. New Haven, CT: Yale University Press.

TWO

How Cultural Psychology Can Help Us See "Divinity" in a Secular World

JONATHAN HAIDT

New York University
Stern School of Business

PAUL ROZIN

University of Pennsylvania
Department of Psychology

Among the best metaphors ever offered to illustrate the limits of human understanding is the story of Flatland, a short novel by the English mathematician Edwin Abbot, published in 1884. Flatland is a two-dimensional world inhabited by two-dimensional geometric figures. One day the protagonist—a square—is visited by a sphere. But when a three-dimensional sphere intersects with Flatland, all that is visible to the square is a circle. The sphere tries to explain the idea of a third dimension to the square, but the square simply cannot understand what the sphere means when he says that he came from "up" or "above" Flatland.

Finally, the sphere yanks the square up out of flatland and into the third dimension. The square is now able to look "down" on his world and see it all at once. He can see inside all the houses of the inhabitants, and even inside their bodies. The experience is terrifying and disorienting. Perhaps you can empathize if you imagine being yanked into the fourth dimension—time—and seeing the birth, life, and death of each person you look at, all at once.

But there's a gentler and more accessible way to share the square's experience: read cultural psychology and then do cultural psychological research. Many of us who came to cultural psychology from ordinary Western psychology experienced feelings of disorientation and wonder.[1] We had to alter and expand our mental categories.

In this essay we describe the ways that our thinking about morality changed in response to Richard Shweder's writings about morality, and in particular his description of the "ethics of divinity." We first describe Shweder's theory of the "three ethics" of moral discourse and explain why the theory was so important for moral psychology. We then show how useful the ethics of divinity has been for understanding some puzzles about sexual morality, bioethical controversies, and the US culture war more generally. We close with an endorsement of moral pluralism.

Three Selves and Three Ethics

Shweder's three ethics were first mentioned in a short section of a short article that was a reply to another article in the journal *Child Development*. Shweder (1990) described a standoff he had with his six-year-old daughter when she had refused, late on a Saturday morning, his request that she change out of her pajamas. He found himself unable to back up his request with any sort of moral justification as long as he was confined to the dominant language of moral discourse for secular westerners, which grounds moral appeals in concepts of harm, rights, and justice. But on the basis of his many years of ethnographic work in Orissa, India, he knew that there were other ways of thinking and speaking about morality. He then described three moral codes as follows: "A distinction needs to be drawn between moral arguments based on appeals to harm, rights, and justice (code 1) versus moral arguments based on appeals to duty, hierarchy, and interdependency (code 2) versus moral arguments based on appeals to natural order, sacred order, tradition, sin, and personal sanctity (code 3)" (2065).

The three moral codes arise, he said, because there are (at least) three ways to think about the self, each of which has implications for how selves should behave:

> Code 1 moral discourse focuses on the individual as a preference structure with autonomy to make free choices. Code 2 moral discourse focuses on the person as part of a community, an attendant at court with a position or station or role that is intimately connected to the self. Code 3 moral discourse focuses on the self as a spiritual entity and protects that spiritual essence from acts (e.g., eating slaughtered animals) that are degrading or disproportionate to our spiritual nature. (2065)

This idea, tucked away in an obscure commentary, eventually grew into a major challenge to the cognitive developmental theorists who dominated moral psychology at the time. As Shweder said in that essay (2062): "I think it is one of the problems with moral development research that Turiel, Kohlberg, Piaget, and many other Western social theorists have tended to define the moral domain in terms of their own code 1 moral reasoning."

Shweder, Much, Mahapatra, and Park (1997, 138) greatly expanded the description of the three ethics, based in part on a cluster analysis of the massive dataset that was first reported in Shweder, Mahapatra, and Miller (1987). Here is their longer description of the ethics of divinity:

> Presupposed by the ethics of divinity is a conceptualization of the self as a spiritual entity connected to some sacred or natural order of things and as a responsible bearer of a legacy that is elevated and divine. Those who regulate their life within the terms of an "ethics of divinity" do not want to do anything, such as eating the flesh of a slaughtered animal, that is incommensurate with the nature of the spirit that joins the self to the divine ground of all things.

The actions (taken from Shweder et al. 1987) that best exemplified violations of the ethics of divinity in Orissa mostly involved failing to observe food, sex, and hygienic taboos, for example, having a family member who eats beef or dog, a man entering a temple the day after his son was born (while the man is still thought to carry "birth pollution"), a woman who sleeps in the same bed as her husband while menstruating, a brother and sister who get married and have children. In Chicago, of course, most of these actions (other than incest and dog-eating) were not considered to be violations, and people rarely talked in ways that could be coded as the ethics of divinity.

The ethics of divinity is so easy to see in Hindu religious practice, but it can be found readily in many religions and holy books. In the Hebrew Bible the same logic is widespread: bodily processes and body products must be kept separate from holy objects and places. In the book of Leviticus, for example, it is said that when a women gives birth to a boy, "she shall continue in the blood of purification three and thirty days; she shall touch no hallowed thing, nor come into the sanctuary, until the days of her purification be fulfilled" (Leviticus 12:4; If she gives birth to a girl, the time periods are doubled).

Similar concerns can be found in many ethnographies: A large percentage of the moral regulations found in many cultures concern what people can and cannot touch or eat, or with whom and how they may have sexual relations. (See Douglas 1966; Meigs 1984; Tambiah 1969.) Many of these rules are not absolute prohibitions, for one cannot prohibit defecation, menstruation, and sexual intercourse. Rather, the underlying logic seems to be that people have a dual nature, including a spiritual self or soul, which makes contact with the divine at prescribed times (as during prayer), and a material self with a carnal nature and physical body whose needs also must be met. (See Bloom 2004 on how human beings—even atheists—are "natural born dualists.") Rules of "purity and pollution" guide people in managing those two contradictory parts of themselves.

When described in this way, the ethics of divinity might seem to be a relic of traditional religious societies, all of which lacked running water, tampons, and other modern conveniences that would allow people to manage their biological "necessities" efficiently and privately. A secular social scientist might therefore expect that the ethics of divinity fades away as societies become wealthy and technologically sophisticated. Indeed, several authors have found that the moral domain becomes "thinner," converging on the ethics of autonomy, as societies become WEIRDer (that is, more Western, Educated, Industrialized, Rich, and Democratic; Henrich, Heine, and Norenzayan 2010).

So is the ethics of divinity of interest merely as a historical relic or anthropological curiosity? Do people still think and talk using an ethics of divinity in WEIRD cultures? Does having the ethics of divinity in our conceptual toolkit help us to see things we would not otherwise be able to see, as when the square was lifted out of flatland and into the third dimension? We—Haidt and Rozin—believe so, and we'll try to show you a few new things now.

Sexual Morality

Much of the US culture war since the 1960s has pitted what we might call sexual libertarians against sexual conservatives. The libertarian ethos is the ethics of autonomy, which rests on John Stuart Mill's harm principle: "The only purpose for which power can be rightfully exercised over any member of a civilized community, against his will, is to prevent harm to others. His own good, either physical or moral, is not sufficient warrant" (Mill [1859] 2003). Sexual libertarians often cannot understand why anyone would object to anyone else's private sexual behavior. They see chastity not as a virtue but as a form of sexism or domination.

But social conservatives draw on a long history of thinking about sexuality that is, clearly, conducted in terms of the ethics of divinity. Evangelical pastor Rick Warren (2002) opened his mega-best-seller *The Purpose Driven*

Life with this line: "It's not all about you." He forcefully rejected the notion of self that Shweder had said underlies the ethics of autonomy—"a preference structure with autonomy to make free choices." In its place, Warren and other evangelicals refer to this line from 1 Corinthians (6:19–20): "Do you not know that your body is a temple of the Holy Spirit, who is in you, whom you have received from God? . . . Therefore honor God with your body." This is one particular cultural example of the notion of self, presupposed by the ethics of divinity.

The ethics of divinity helps to explain why nearly all US states used to have sodomy laws, why many still do, and why these issues and laws are still morally and politically divisive today. Haidt and Hersh (2001) interviewed US liberals and conservatives about three kinds of sexual acts: homosexual sex, unusual forms of masturbation (involving a teddy bear, or the willing participation of one's dog), and consensual incest between an adult brother and sister. They found no difference in the moralization of incest (an act that is often construed as having a female victim), but conservatives were more condemning of the other sexual acts, particularly homosexual sex.

When participants' justifications were coded in terms of Shweder's three ethics, large differences were found. Liberals spoke overwhelmingly in the ethics of autonomy and made hardly any use of the ethics of community or divinity. The idea of the self as a preference structure is shown in this justification of gay sex: "Everybody can do whatever they want. I'm not going to say anything about it at all."

Conservatives, however, did not see human beings exclusively as preference structures who should be allowed to fulfill their desires. They used all three ethics. As one participant put it, allowing gay marriage would "allow anybody to do whatever they want, like voting for a slippery slope, voting to do whatever." Such moral chaos would "lead to corruptions of the system, and it undermines the whole institution of marriage." Another participant, discussing masturbation, said "It's a sin because it distances ourselves from God." This idea is unintelligible if you do not understand the ethics of divinity.

It's important to note that conservatives used the ethics of autonomy more often (69 percent of all codable utterances) than the other two ethics combined (35 percent community, 26 percent divinity). They are, after all, US college students talking about ethics in a secular setting—a psychology study. But their many efforts to point to victims of consensual sexual practices do not mean that concerns about harm actually drove their thinking. Rather, they seem to have begun with emotional reactions and moral intuitions of condemnation, and then they struggled to justify their reactions using the ethics of autonomy. Conservatives were more likely than liberals to become morally dumbfounded—committed to a moral position but unable to justify it. As one conservative woman said, after condemning homosexual sex: "Well, I just, I don't know, I don't think that's, I guess [long pause], I don't really [laughter] think of these things much, so I don't really know but, I don't know, I just [long pause], um."

Against this backdrop, we can now better understand Immanuel Kant's struggle to justify his condemnation of masturbation using only the ethics of autonomy:

> That such an unnatural use (and so misuse) of one's sexual attributes is a violation of one's duty to himself and is certainly in the highest degree opposed to morality strikes everyone upon his thinking of it. Furthermore, the thought of it is so revolting that even calling such a vice by its proper name is considered a kind of immorality. . . . However, it is not so easy to produce a rational demonstration of the inadmissibility of that unnatural use. (Kant [1797] 1996)

Trying to explain why harmless consensual sexual acts are so often moralized without understanding the ethics of divinity is like trying to explain earthquakes without understanding the theory of plate tectonics. It can't be done.

Bioethical Controversies

As with sexual morality, so with other controversial issues that involve the human body, such as abortion, cloning, and voluntary euthanasia. If a community (such as a left-leaning community of bioethicists) limits itself to the ethics of autonomy, then it will have great difficulty understanding why so many in the United States object to these practices. If you embrace Mill's harm principle, then the imperative to let people make their own choices, combined with compassionate or utilitarian concerns about harm reduction, will usually lead you to a simple resolution of most bioethical debates: allow people to choose whatever they think is best for themselves, and allow policies (such as voluntary euthanasia for terminally ill patients, or cloning oneself to produce fetal tissue that can help oneself) that will reduce suffering.

It was precisely this attitude—that everything should be allowed if people want it—that led ethicist Leon Kass to write one of the most famous lines in US bioethics. The year after the first successful cloning of a mammal (Dolly the sheep), Kass wrote

> Repugnance . . . revolts against the excesses of human willfulness, warning us not to transgress what is unspeakably profound. Indeed, in this age in which everything is held to be permissible so long as it is freely done, in which our given human nature no longer commands respect, in which our bodies are regarded as mere instruments of our autonomous rational wills, repugnance may be the only voice left that speaks up to defend the central core of our humanity. *Shallow are the souls that have forgotten how to shudder.* (Kass 1997, emphasis added)

As Shweder had proposed, the key is the underlying sense of self. Kass is not expressing simple disgust for a medical procedure. He is objecting to the loss of an older notion of the self as a "soul" that must respect certain limits. He is horrified at the arrogance and solipsism of modern selves that are little more than preference structures in search of gratification. He is offering a *cri de cœur* against the shrinking of US morality down to the ethics of autonomy.

Haidt and his colleagues later developed moral foundations theory to bridge evolutionary and cultural psychology (Haidt and Graham 2007; Haidt and Joseph 2004). The theory tried to identify the innate moral "taste receptors" that underlie Shweder's three ethics, resting the ethics of autonomy on the foundations of care/harm and fairness/cheating and resting the ethics of community on the foundations of loyalty/betrayal and authority/subversion. The ethics of divinity rested on the foundation of sanctity/degradation, which is closely related to the emotion of disgust and the mental process that we call contagion (Rozin, Haidt, and McCauley 2016; Rozin, Lowery, Imada, and Haidt 1999).

Using moral foundations theory, Koleva et al. (2012) examined moral judgments about bioethical controversies. They analyzed the moral judgments made by nearly six thousand US respondents on a variety of "culture war" issues on a survey at YourMorals.org. These respondents also had completed the Moral Foundations Questionnaire, a thirty-item survey that gives each participant a score on each of the five moral foundations just described. This allowed the researchers to examine which foundations were the best predictors of condemnation across a wide range of issues, after controlling for several other variables (including age, gender, education, and ideology on a liberal-to-conservative scale) in a regression analysis.

The care foundation turned out to be by far the best predictor of people's attitudes toward medical testing on animals. People who condemned such testing on the culture war survey also expressed the strongest endorsement of care and compassion on the Moral Foundations Questionnaire. But on nearly every other item that involved matters of life and death, sexuality, or the body, the sanctity foundation was the best predictor. Those issues included gay marriage, abortion, voluntary euthanasia, cloning, having a child outside of marriage, and using pornography. The regression coefficients for sanctity scores were usually about as big as (and sometimes bigger than) the coefficient for ideology (liberal to conservative). Sanctity even predicted condemnation of a few actions that did not involve the body, including burning the US flag. Some people see sacredness inhering in objects, which must be protected; others think the flag is just a piece of cloth, which people (as preference structures) can do with as they like.

In other words: the US culture war is not just a battle between two teams of political elites who emit cues to their followers about what to think about policy issues. There is an underlying intuitive structure to the culture war. Those who feel some pull from the ethics of divinity are predisposed to joining the conservative side on bioethical controversies.

With regard to Kass's claim that the conservative side includes people who remember how to shudder, it is relevant that social conservatives have repeatedly been found to score higher on disgust sensitivity than do liberals and libertarians (Inbar, Pizarro, and Bloom 2009; Iyer et al. 2012). It is also relevant that violations of Shweder's ethics of divinity has been shown to have special linkage to disgust, whereas violations of autonomy and community show special linkages to anger and contempt, respectively (Rozin, Lowery, Imada, and Haidt 1999). Once again, you can't understand the full range of moral judgments and political identities in the United States without understanding Shweder's ethics of divinity.

Environmentalism

So far we have been arguing that social and religious conservatives still think and feel using an ethic of divinity, which has been largely bleached out of secular liberal subcultures in Western countries. But there are a few cases in which cultural ideals and practices on the left make more sense once you understand the ethics of divinity. This is particularly clear for some aspects of environmentalism.

One key to thinking about the psychology of divinity is that it always manifests itself in a rejection of purely utilitarian valuation. As the sociologist Robert Nisbet ([1966] 1993) put it when presenting "the sacred" as one of the most important concepts in sociology: "I use this word to refer to the totality of myth, ritual, sacrament, dogma, and the mores in human behavior; to the whole area of individual motivation and social organization that transcends the utilitarian or rational and draws its vitality from what Weber called 'charisma' and Simmel 'piety'" (121).

Concerns about environmental purity and pollution could certainly be powerful within a morality limited entirely to the ethics of autonomy. One could be very concerned about the harms caused to human beings and animals from the sheer tonnage of carcinogens, heavy metals, and endocrine disruptors that industrialized nations dump into the air, land, and water each year. One also could see such actions as harmful practices imposed by corporations on unwilling victims in violation of their rights.

But some people within the green or environmental movement seem to be motivated by concerns beyond what Nisbet called "utilitarian or rational." Pragmatic environmentalists who propose technological solutions to pollution and global warming, such as geoengineering or safer nuclear energy, rather than support reductions in energy consumption, are often attacked angrily, as though they had committed sacrilege against a "secular religion" (Pielke 2009). The writer Paul Kingsnorth was quoted in the *New York Times* as saying that such efforts are "repellant." Using more technology would, he said, further distort the proper relationship between humans and the natural world; it would be an abandonment of the principle that "nature has some intrinsic, inherent value beyond the instrumental" (Smith 2014). When thinking about economic activity with environmental consequences, some greens reject a notion of selves as preference structures who should be maximally free to do as they please. The human body may or may not be a temple, but the earth is often seen that way.

Frimer, Tell, and Motyl (2016) asked liberals and conservatives to discuss gay marriage and found the predictable result: liberal discourse focused almost entirely on fairness; conservatives in contrast drew heavily on concepts related to sanctity. They saw gay marriage as a desecration of marriage. But when the researchers asked these two groups to talk about the Keystone XL Pipeline—a giant pipeline that would bring crude oil from a very dirty energy source (tar sands) in Canada to the United States—the moral codes reversed. Now it was liberals who spoke about purity (e.g., the pipeline would spoil the "pristine condition of nature") and it was conservatives who talked about fairness and rights (e.g., "a business has the right to move forward with projects that are approved by officials"). Once again, we see that notions of selves as having rights (perhaps even businesses as selves) run up against notions of selves obligated to respect boundaries, maintain purity, and refrain from actions that are polluting or degrading. Shweder's ethics of divinity is used to construct arguments and guide understanding on the left, even if less frequently.

Nature and the concept of "natural" have become sacred or protected values (Baron and Spranca 1997; Tetlock et al. 2000) for many people in the United States. That is, violations of what is "natural" have come to be considered by some not simply as harmful, but as violations of the moral order. This is most apparent in attitudes toward the genetic engineering of plants and animals in the food supply. Using a nationally representative sample of people in the United States, Scott, Inbar, and Rozin (2016) found that roughly half of their sample were opposed to genetically modified organisms (GMOs). About 30 percent of these opponents treated the issue in a utilitarian way. In the judgment of these individuals, the potential harm to humans or the earth as a result of adopting GMOs outweigh the benefits. But 70 percent of the opponents refused to even consider cost–benefit analyses; they saw GMOs as a violation of the sacred order—the sanctity of nature. These divinity-motivated individuals were more likely to express disgust at GMOs and also were found to score higher on a measure of disgust sensitivity. Overall opposition to GMOs does not sort cleanly along the left–right divide; the fault line seems to run between the ethics of divinity and the ethics of autonomy.

Conclusion: The Triumph of Moral Pluralism

Lawrence Kohlberg was a moral monist. He asserted that "Virtue is ultimately one, not many, and it is always the same ideal form regardless of climate or culture. . . . The name of this ideal form is justice" (Kohlberg 1971, 232). Kohlberg's assertion may have been valid as a description of his own subculture—the secular US left (if we leave out some environmentalists). But Shweder's writings on morality—particularly on the ethics of divinity—opened up a line of empirical research that has led current moral psychology to a much more pluralist position. (See Graham et al. 2012; but see Gray, Schein, and Ward 2014 for a current monist argument.) This move was obviously necessary for cultural psychology, but it turns out to have been a crucial move for appreciating the diversity of morality even within a Western nation such as the United States. As we have shown, the morality of religious US citizens, conservatives in the United States, and some environmentalists simply cannot be understood without the ethics of divinity. Perhaps all of us have some ability to appreciate moral emotions and modes of moral discourse that are not our default or best-practiced ones. As Shweder wrote in 1991, about the power of cultural psychology in general: "Yet the conceptions held by others are available to us, in the sense that when we truly understand their conception of things we come to recognize *possibilities latent within our own rationality* . . . and those ways of conceiving of things become salient for us for the first time, or once again. In other words, there is no homogeneous 'backcloth' to our world. We are multiple from the start" (5). Like the square yanked out of flatland, cultural psychology is a constant reminder of our capacity for multiplicity.

Note

1. We both had the opportunity to do research in Bhubaneswar, the city in Odisha, India, where Shweder did much of his fieldwork. We were guided by Shweder, and by Usha Menon, who was a graduate student working with Shweder at the time. We are grateful to both for yanking us up out of flatland.

References

Abbott, Edwin A. (1884) 1952. *Flatland: A Romance of Many Dimensions*. 6th ed. New York: Dover.

Baron, Jonathan, and Mark Spranca. 1997. "Protected Values." *Organizational Behavior and Human Decision Processes* 70: 1–16.

Bloom, Paul. 2004. "Natural Born Dualists." *Edge*, http://edge.org/conversation/natural -born dualists.

Douglas, Mary. 1966. *Purity and Danger*. London: Routledge and Kegan Paul.

Frimer, Jeremy. A., Tell, Caitlin E., & Motyl, Matt. 2016. "Sacralizing Liberals and Fair-Minded Conservatives: Ideological Symmetry in the Moral Motives in the Culture War." *Analyses of Social Issues and Public Policy*. doi: 10.1111/asap.12127.

Graham, Jesse, Jonathan Haidt, Sena Koleva, Matt Motyl, Ravi Iyer, Sean Wojcik, and Peter H. Ditto. 2012. "Moral Foundations Theory: The Pragmatic Validity of Moral Pluralism." *Advances in Experimental Social Psychology* 47: 55–130.

Gray, Kurt, Chelsea Schein, and Adrian F. Ward. 2014. "Myth of Harmless Wrongs in Moral Cognition: Automatic Dyadic Completion from Sin to Suffering." *Journal of Experimental Psychology: General* 143: 1600–15.

Haidt, Jonathan, and Jesse Graham. 2007. "When Morality Opposes Justice: Conservatives Have Moral Intuitions That Liberals May Not Recognize." *Social Justice Research* 20: 98–116.

Haidt, Jonathan, and Matthew A. Hersh. 2001. "Sexual Morality: The Cultures and Reasons of Liberals and Conservatives." *Journal of Applied Social Psychology* 31: 191–221.

Haidt, Jonathan, and Craig Joseph. 2004. "Intuitive Ethics: How Innately Prepared Intuitions Generate Culturally Variable Virtues." *Daedalus* (Fall): 55–66.

Haidt, Jonathan, Silvia H. Koller, and Maria Dias. 1993. "Affect, Culture, and Morality, or Is It Wrong to Eat Your Dog?" *Journal of Personality and Social Psychology* 65: 613–28.

Henrich, Joseph, Steven J. Heine, and Ara Norenzayan. 2010. "The Weirdest People in the World?" *Behavioral and Brain Sciences* 33: 61–83.

Inbar, Yoel, David A. Pizarro, and Paul Bloom. 2009. "Conservatives Are More Easily Disgusted Than Liberals." *Cognition and Emotion* 23: 714–25.

Iyer R., S. Koleva, J. Graham, P. Ditto, and J. Haidt. 2012. "Understanding Libertarian Morality: The Psychological Dispositions of Self-Identified Libertarians." *PLoS ONE* 7 (8): e42366. doi: 10.1371/journal.pone.0042366.

Kant, Immanuel. (1797) 1996. *The Metaphysics of Morals*. Translated by M. Gregor. Cambridge: Cambridge University Press.

Kass, Leon R. 1997. "The Wisdom of Repugnance." *New Republic*, June 2, 17–26.

Kohlberg, Lawrence. 1971. "From Is to Ought: How to Commit the Naturalistic Fallacy and Get Away with It in the Study of Moral Development." In *Psychology and Genetic Epistemology*, edited by Theodore Mischel, 151–235. New York: Academic Press.

Koleva, Spassena P., Jesse Graham, Ravi Iyer, Peter H. Ditto, and Jonathan Haidt. 2012. "Tracing the Threads: How Five Moral Concerns (Especially Purity) Help Explain Culture War Attitudes." *Journal of Research in Personality* 46 (2): 184–94.

Meigs, Anna. 1984. *Food, Sex, and Pollution: A New Guinea Religion*. New Brunswick, NJ: Rutgers University Press.

Mill, John S. (1859) 2003. *On Liberty*. New Haven, CT: Yale University Press.

Nisbet, Robert A. (1966) 1993. *The Sociological Tradition*. 2nd ed. New Brunswick, NJ: Transaction.

Pielke, Roger. 2009. "Have You Stepped on a Secular Religion?" *Blogspot*, http://roger pielkejr.blogspot.com/2009/10/have-you-stepped-on-secular-religion.html.

Rozin, Paul, Jonathan Haidt, and Clark R. McCauley. 2016. "Disgust." In *Handbook of Emotions*, edited by M. Lewis, J. M. Haviland-Jones, and L. F. Barrett, 815–834. New York: Guilford.

Rozin, Paul, Laura Lowery, Sumio Imada, and Jonathan Haidt. 1999. "The CAD Triad Hypothesis: A Mapping between Three Moral Emotions (Contempt, Anger, Disgust) and Three Moral Codes (Community, Autonomy, Divinity)." *Journal of Personality and Social Psychology* 76: 574–86.

Scott, Sydney, Yoel Inbar, and Paul Rozin. 2016. "Evidence for Absolute Moral Opposition to Genetically Modified Food in the United States." *Perspectives on Psychological Science*, 11: 315–24.

Shweder, Richard A. 1990. "In Defense of Moral Realism: Reply to Gabennesch." *Child Development* 61: 2060–67.

———. 1991. *Thinking through Cultures: Expeditions in Cultural Psychology*. Cambridge, MA: Harvard University Press.

Shweder, Richard A., Manamohan Mahapatra, and Joan G. Miller. 1987. "Culture and Moral Development." In *The Emergence of Morality in Young Children*, edited by Jerome Kagan and Sharon Lamb, 1–83. Chicago: University of Chicago Press.

Shweder, Richard A., Nancy C. Much, Manamohan Mahapatra, and Lawrence Park. 1997. "The 'Big Three' of Morality (Autonomy, Community, and Divinity), and the 'Big Three' Explanations of Suffering." In *Morality and Health*, edited by Allan M. Brandt and Paul Rozin, 119–69. New York: Routledge.

Smith, Daniel. 2014. "It's the End of the World as We Know It . . . and He Feels Fine." *New York Times Magazine*, http://www.nytimes.com/2014/04/20/magazine/its-the -end-of-the-world-as-we-know-it-and-he-feels-fine.html.

Tambiah, Stanley J. 1969. "Animals Are Good to Think and Good to Prohibit." *Ethnology* 8 (4): 423–59.

Tetlock, Philip E., Orie Kristel, Beth Elson, Melanie Green, and Jennifer Lerner. 2000. "The Psychology of the Unthinkable: Taboo Trade-offs, Forbidden Base Rates, and Heretical Counterfactuals." *Journal of Personality and Social Psychology* 78 (5): 853–70.

Warren, Rick. 2002. *The Purpose Driven Life: What on Earth Am I Here For?* Grand Rapids, MI: Zondervan.

THREE

Beyond Universal Taxonomic Frameworks in Cultural Social Psychology

JOAN G. MILLER

New School for Social Research
Department of Psychology

Interest in cultural work in psychology has increased in recent years. Signs of this shift may be seen in the growing number of culturally based studies that have been conducted in psychology as well as in institutional changes that involve giving greater attention to culture. For example, the American Psychological Society, which is the premier organization for scientific research in psychology, changed its name in 2005 to the Association for Psychological Science, in part to recognize its goal of becoming more internationally inclusive, and it held its first international meeting ever in 2015. Even with this growth in visibility, however, cultural work has not had as much of an impact on the discipline as might have been anticipated. For example, in Higgins and Kruglanski's (1996) handbook on basic principles of social psychology, the only citations for culture referred to pages within the single chapter on cultural psychology by Markus, Kitayama, and Heiman (1996), and in the revised edition of this handbook issued ten years later (Higgins and Kruglanski 2007), references to culture occur virtually exclusively in a chapter on culture by Chiu and Hong (2007) and in a chapter on social identity and self-regulation by Oyserman (2007). With the exception of a one-page citation, no reference is made to culture in the twelve handbook chapters devoted to the cognitive system, despite the chapters in this section addressing topics such as causal explanation and principles of social judgment, on which extensive cultural research has been conducted. In another example, a perusal of current academic job openings in psychology reveals a proliferation of openings for neuroscientists in such new subareas as developmental neuroscience, cognitive neuroscience, and social neuroscience, but academic job openings in the area of culture are not only far fewer in number but entail primarily openings for psychologists working on cultural diversity, not basic psychological theory.

The present chapter presents a critical appraisal of work in the social psychological tradition of cultural psychology, a tradition of work focused on culturally broadening basic psychological theory. The argument is made that work in this tradition has achieved only partial success in realizing its goals. Whereas this limited success stems largely from ongoing resistance to cultural approaches within the mainstream discipline, it arguably also reflects the adoption of research strategies that have diminished the cultural sensitivity of the work being undertaken and that, in many respects, have facilitated the cooptation of cultural work by mainstream psychological perspectives, rather than the transformation of mainstream perspectives.

In the first section of this chapter, I discuss the premises and goals of work in cultural psychology in general, making clear its interdisciplinary nature and methodological heterogeneity, and identify the type of contemporary work being undertaken in the social psychological tradition of cultural psychology. In the second section, I review some of the long-standing assumptions within mainstream psychology that contribute to its downplaying of the importance of culture. In the third section, I present a brief overview of cultural research that I and my colleagues have undertaken on interpersonal morality, with the work shown not only to highlight ways psychological theory needs to be culturally broadened but to underscore the importance of context sensitivity in cultural research. Finally, in the concluding section, I underscore respects in which the limited context sensitivity and explicit embrace of mainstream premises that characterize much of the work in cultural social psychology have constrained the theoretical impact of this work in culturally broadening psychology and I identify ways to move toward overcoming these limitations.

Assumptions and Diverse Traditions of Cultural Psychology

The perspective of cultural psychology is defined by its view of culture and psychology as mutually constitutive. In this view, psychological functioning is understood to depend on cultural mediation, as individuals participate in and come to be affected by, as well as to create and transform the meanings and practices of the cultural communities in which they participate. It is this assumption of psychological and cultural processes as mutually entailed—and not the type of methodology adopted—that is central to cultural psychology. Thus, for example, whether an approach employs qualitative or quantitative methods or comparative or single culture analysis does not distinguish whether the approach may be considered as cultural psychology. Whereas Shweder et al. (2006) have advocated the adoption of research agendas in cultural psychology that center on elucidating custom complexes located in specific cultural settings and that make use of ethnography and other qualitative methodologies, that approach is not considered an integral part of work in cultural psychology. Thus, for example, the distinction between cross-cultural and cultural psychology is not a matter of whether explicit comparison is part of a research project or whether research employs empirically based psychological methods. Rather, the distinction rests in whether culture and psychology are treated as independent phenomena or as mutually constituted and in whether or not psychic unity is assumed.

The theoretical grounding of cultural psychology stems from a recognition of the essential role of culture in completion of the self, an insight that has been termed the incompleteness thesis (Geertz 1973; Shweder 1990; Wertsch 1999). Individuals are viewed not only as developing in specific culturally and historically situated environments and utilizing culturally and historically specific tools, but as carrying with them, in their language and cultural meaning systems, socially shared assumptions through which experience is both interpreted and created. This assumption of the interdependence of psychological and cultural processes represents the core idea of cultural psychology. Notably, the term *cultural psychology* was coined by theorists to convey the insight that psychological and cultural processes are inseparable—that is, that psychological processes need to be understood as always grounded in particular social-cultural-historical contexts that influence their form, just as cultural communities depend for their existence on particular communities of intentional agents. These considerations then lead to the expectation that qualitative differences in modes of psychological functioning may be observed among individuals from cultural communities characterized by different sociocultural meanings and practices. In this way, as pointed out in this volume's chapter by Menon and Cassaniti, work in cultural psychology challenges the premise of psychic unity that has long dominated work in psychology, even as it does not deny the possibility of universals existing in psychological functioning.

Whereas work in cultural psychology tends to share the premise that cultural and psychological processes are inherently interdependent, this work is characterized by diverse traditions that have somewhat contrasting agendas, not all of which even explicitly adopt the label of "cultural psychology." Thus, for example, the early seminal volume *Culture Theory: Essays on Mind, Self and Emotion*, edited by Shweder and LeVine (1984), included a set of articles by anthropologists and sociolinguists that instantiated these basic ideas of cultural psychology, even without introducing the term *cultural psychology*, as it was in later work by Shweder (e.g., Shweder 1990). Also, one sees in early handbook chapters on this emerging perspective (e.g., Miller 1994a, 1997; Shweder et al. 2006) how cultural psychology crosses disciplinary boundaries and includes a range of distinctive theoretical positions, including notably the sociocultural-historical perspective of theorists such as Cole, Rogoff, and Vertsch (e.g., Cole 1996), as well as work in medical anthropology, as seen in the chapter by Good and DelVecchio in this volume.

In the present essay, my attention centers on work in the social psychological tradition of cultural psychology. Much of the work in this tradition has not been affected by the type of anthropologically informed approach represented in the present volume. Rather, it has drawn inspiration largely from an influential paper by Markus and Kitayama (1991) that introduced some of the central ideas and agenda of cultural psychology to mainstream social psychology. The paper articulated the idea of the mutual constitution of culture and self and presented a research agenda focused on identifying cultural variation in basic psychological processes in such areas as cognition, motivation, and emotion.

Whereas the social psychological tradition of cultural work differs from most of the work presented in the present volume, it constitutes presently one of the dominant traditions of contemporary empirical work in cultural psychology, with numerous handbook chapters and edited volumes attesting to its scope (e.g., Fiske, Kitayama, Markus, and Nisbett 1998; Kitayama and Cohen 2007). This work has adopted the methods of the mainstream discipline, with its emphasis on quantitative methods and explicit comparison. It also is premised on the assumption that an effective way of culturally broadening psychology is to undertake research that meets the methodological standards of the mainstream discipline and thus can be published in leading journals where it stands to have the greatest impact on the field of psychology.

Assumptions Contributing to Downplaying of Culture in Mainstream Psychology

Although accounts of the history of psychology (e.g., Jahoda 1993) have pointed to culture being given more or less emphasis during different historical periods, cultural work has tended overall to remain in a peripheral role in the discipline over time. Reasons for this downplaying of cultural work may be seen in the core theoretical assumptions and goals of the discipline of psychology. It is these overall theoretical assumptions and goals that work in cultural psychology has sought to challenge.

Dualistic Models of Explanation

The dominant explanatory framework in mainstream psychology is dualistic, giving weight to features in the environment and in the person. The framework assumes a realistic view of situations as presenting one most accurate or most veridical structure. No consideration is given to cultural meanings and practices as implicated in the structuring of situations or in defining what constitutes objective knowledge, and thus as a consideration integral to all psychological theory. To illustrate, for example, within work in social psychology, explanatory emphasis is given to features of the person and of the situation (e.g., Ross and Nisbett 1991). From this perspective, evidence that cultures emphasize contrasting meanings and practices is assimilated to an individual difference dimension and is not seen as implying that there is a need to take into account cultural meanings and practices in psychological explanation.

Natural Science Ideals of Explanation

The dominant model adopted by mainstream psychology is one that treats the discovery of universals as the fundamental goal of psychological science and that privileges natural science models of explanation. From this perspective, whereas variation in cultural meanings and practices is acknowledged, they are downplayed as the mere content on which psychological processes operate and as having no implications for basic psychological theory. (See, for example, discussion of this "Platonic" image in general psychology as discussed in Shweder 1990.) Malpass (1988) illustrates this devaluation of culture in dismissing cultural variation in meanings and practices as extraneous content that needs to be held constant or controlled in psychological explanation: "Cultural differences are trivial because they are at the wrong level of abstraction, and stand as 'medium' rather than 'thing' in relation to the objects of study. The readily observable differences among cultural groups are probably superficial and represent little if any differences at the level of psychological processes" (31). From this perspective, the insight from cultural psychology that basic psychological processes in many cases are culturally variable in that they depend on meanings and practices that are socioculturally and historically contingent is dismissed as a sign that the psychological phenomenon under consideration is not yet fully understood.

In adopting a natural science model of psychological explanation, mainstream psychological views embrace the criteria of parsimony and predictive power as the hallmarks of explanation. As the social psychologists Higgins and Kruglanski (1996) articulate this view of scientific inquiry in psychology:

> A discovery of lawful principles governing a realm of phenomena is a fundamental objective of scientific research. . . . A useful scientific analysis needs to probe beneath the surface. In other words, it needs to get away from the "phenotypic" manifestations and strive to unearth the "genotypes" that may lurk beneath . . . probing beneath surface similarities and differences to discover deep underlying structures. (vii)

A sign of this fascination with natural-science models of explanation may be seen in the exponential increase in the number of psychological studies incorporating neuroscience approaches since the introduction of functional-neuroimaging techniques in the early 1990s. As Kagan (2007) explains, this dramatic embrace of neuroscience within contemporary psychology stems, in large part, from the "American attraction to material causes and the certainty they promise" (367). In contrast to the continuing lukewarm reception to cultural approaches within mainstream psychology, neuroscience is coming increasingly to dominate the discipline and to be embraced as the future of the field.

Context in Research on Culture and Interpersonal Morality

In this section a brief overview is presented of a program of cultural research that I and my colleagues have undertaken on interpersonal morality. This overview serves to illustrate ways research in cultural social psychology may serve to challenge the universalism of existing psychological theory while embodying sensitivity to context.

Work in mainstream psychology assumes that morality is universal, with this universality framed in terms of a morality both of caring and of justice. In terms of caring, Gilligan (1982) argued for a morality of caring that differs from the morality of justice, with females seen as emphasizing a morality of caring more than males do—a claim of gender difference that was challenged in later research (e.g., Walker 1991). Although Gilligan's theory identified an important conceptual limitation of views of morality framed as justice alone, the model itself was formulated in terms of psychological universals, with caring assumed to take the same basic form regardless of cultural setting. Likewise, the domain perspective of Turiel (1983, 2002), which represents the currently dominant psychological model of moral development, reflects a universalism in which morality is identified with issues of justice and rights (e.g., Turiel 1998). In this view, matters of interpersonal morality are assumed to be reducible to universal concerns with justice and individual rights (Turiel 2002). It was this downplaying of culture in theories of morality that prompted my cultural examination of interpersonal morality (Miller 1994b).

In a series of cross-cultural studies involving European American and Hindu Indian populations (for a review, see Miller 2007), my colleagues and I found evidence of a moral outlook grounded in ideas of dharma as prominent among Hindu Indians, which contrasts with a more individualistic interpersonal outlook prominent among European Americans. The nature of these cultural differences in interpersonal morality are illustrated in open-ended responses given by European American and Hindu Indian respondents to the case of an adult son not looking after his elderly parents in his own home (Miller and Luthar 1989). Appraising such behavior as the son's failure to perform his moral duty, an Indian respondent argued: "It's a son's duty—birth duty—to take care of his parents . . . even from the simple philosophy of give and take, the son has no business to ask his father to go away. Even if the parents had not exerted so much for the son, still he is expected to have a certain responsibility toward his parents" (Miller and Luthar 1989, 253). In contrast, a US respondent stressed the importance of individual decision making in categorizing the behavior as a matter of personal choice: "It's up to the individual to decide. It's duty to the parents versus one's own independence and, I guess, one's self interest. . . . It wasn't a life and death situation and their needs were being taken care of. Beyond that it's a personal choice." Whereas the response of the US participant reflects a voluntaristic view of interpersonal responsibility, which resembles the caring responses reported by Gilligan (1982), that given by the Indian respondent reflects a more obligatory view.

In subsequent experimental research we explored the boundaries of this cultural difference. For example, in an investigation that compared situations in which an individual refrained from providing low-cost help, we observed that no cultural differences occurred in the case of situations involving meeting life-threatening needs, with both US and Indian respondents agreeing on the moral responsibility to help (Miller, Bersoff, and Harwood 1990). US respondents, however, more frequently than Indian respondents characterized helping as a matter of personal choice in non-life-threatening-need situations, with this difference greater as the need for help decreased and the role relationship became more remote. To give another example, we observed no cultural differences between US respondents and Indian respondents in the tendency to view the moral obligation of a parent to care for their young child as unaffected by closeness felt for the child (Miller and Bersoff 1998). US respondents maintained, however, that there was less responsibility to help friends and siblings in affectively distant than in affectively close relationships, whereas Indians' views that there is a moral responsibility to be responsive to the needs of friends and siblings was unaffected by affective closeness.

In our research, we have also worked to contextualize our findings by considering the implications of the moral outlooks that we observed for motivation and social support. In pursuing these questions, we have examined ways moral outlooks are sustained by related psychological tendencies and cultural practices.

One of the unanswered questions raised by our work on morality is the psychological viability of the outlooks on morality that we documented as characterizing European American as compared with Hindu Indian outlooks. The emphasis on personal choice that we observed among European Americans is congruent with claims made about the nature of agency in self-determination theory (Deci and Ryan 1987). The overt emphasis placed on role-related duty that we observed among Hindu Indians, however, in giving less scope for individual freedom of choice, might be interpreted either as suggesting that individuals maintain a less developed sense of agency or that forms of agency exist that do not involve a sense of perceived choice. Drawing these types of implications, in fact, various cultural theorists have argued that collectivist cultures emphasize community at the expense of agency (e.g., Triandis 1995) or that choice is not implicated in the forms of agency emphasized in collectivist cultures (e.g., Iyengar and Lepper 1999).

In a series of studies comparing views of helping family and friends (Miller, Das, and Chakravarthy 2001), we observed that, in maintaining a more monistic outlook on duty than do Americans (Marriott 1990), Indians experience role-related duties to be responsive to the needs of family and friends in an agentic way. Thus, our findings indicated that whereas US respondents associated less satisfaction and choice with helping friends in situations in which the helping was strongly rather than only weakly socially expected, Indian respondents associated high levels of satisfaction and choice with helping friends in both types of situations. The emphasis placed on moral duty by Indians, such findings imply, is subjectively experienced as integrated with one's sense of self rather than experienced as in opposition to it.

A related unanswered question stemming from our work on morality concerns the extent to which our findings may imply a psychologically implausible selfless stance and contradict findings observed among other collectivist cultural groups. Although our research points to contextual boundaries on the role-related responsibilities experienced by Indians, it nonetheless provides evidence of a broader sense of role-related duty among Indians than among Americans and thus might imply that Indians maintain a stance that is discrepant from what is known about the self-serving aspects of human motivation. Also, our studies on morality appear incongruent with recent claims made in studies comparing East Asians and European Americans that collectivist populations experience greater discomfort in social support than do individualistic populations (e.g., Taylor et al. 2004).

In recent research that included Indian, Japanese, and European American cultural groups, however, we demonstrated that Indians place a greater emphasis on communal norms in family and friend relationships than do both European Americans and Japanese (Miller, Akiyama, and Kapadia 2017), and that this type of communal stance emphasized by Indians is associated with greater comfort in social support than that observed among both European Americans and Japanese. We also demonstrated that Japanese report greater discomfort in social support not only than European Americans, as found by Taylor and her colleagues, but also than Indians. Our research implies that the strong sense of moral duty observed among Indians is not purely altruistic or one-sided but rather involves mutual responsiveness, with individuals not only expected to be responsive to the needs of family and friends but expecting that family and friends will be responsive, in turn, to them in times of need (see also Miller et al. 2014). In pointing to contrasting outlooks among Japanese and Indian populations, this work also highlights limitations of global views of culture based on the individualism–collectivism dichotomy.

In sum, whereas our program of research in this area does not attain the anthropological richness achieved by ethnographic approaches, as is seen in the recently published research by Menon (2013) conducted among women in Bhubaneswar, it illustrates the potential to bring at least some of the insights of anthropological approaches into research within the social psychological tradition of cultural psychology. The work that my colleagues and I have conducted involves explicit comparison, adopts quantitative methods, and is published in mainstream psychology journals. Yet it also draws on insights into the cultures under consideration attained through analysis of the open-ended responses of our informants about their real-life experiences, the conduct of fieldwork, and collaboration with members of the cultural communities being reported. Avoiding standardized scale measures that embody taxonomic frameworks and that lack cultural sensitivity, the research takes into account the contextual dependence of psychological processes.

Recent Trajectory and Future Challenges of Cultural Social Psychology

Before concluding, I wish to discuss ways that the tradition of work in cultural social psychology has developed and the challenges that it faces. With its widespread embrace of the individualism–collectivism dichotomy and of models of culture based on individual differences, this recent work has become readily assimilated into mainstream psychology; but I argue that this stance has come with limited cultural sensitivity and ultimately a diminished theoretical impact in contributing to the cultural broadening of the discipline.

In one of the most influential papers in cultural social psychology, as well one of the most widely cited articles in all of psychology, Markus and Kitayama (1991) advanced the argument not only that basic psychological processes are culturally grounded and take culturally variable forms, but that the variation is based on two culturally variable forms of self—the independent and the interdependent self. In introducing this construct, these psychologists and other major cultural psychologists arguing for East–West differences in cultural views of self (e.g., Nisbett, Peng, Choi, and Norenzayan 2001) reintroduced, under a different label, the individualism–collectivism dichotomy that had dominated work in cross-cultural psychology (e.g., Triandis 1995). With the subsequent rapid development of psychological scale measures of independent–interdependence (Singelis 1994), the dichotomy quickly became instantiated as an individual difference variable tapping modes of self-construal—a move that accelerated the distinction catching on in mainstream psychology. It meant not only that culture could easily be empirically measured in etic rather than experience-near or emic terms, but that psychologists could engage in cultural research without the need to gain any in-depth understanding of cultural outlooks beyond their own.

As work inspired by the individualism–collectivism dimension has come to dominate work in cultural social psychology, however, it has arguably neutralized some of the work's potential to challenge mainstream psychological viewpoints. In forwarding a dichotomous framework for representing cultural differences, researchers in cultural social psychology have embraced the goal of mainstream psychology of reducing apparent complexity into underlying simplicity in order to achieve parsimony and predictive power. In treating culture as an individual difference dimension of self-construal, cultural psychologists also have adopted the dualistic person-situation frameworks that characterize mainstream social psychology. Culture no longer becomes a consideration that, through its patterns of practices and shared meanings, must be considered as affecting contextual and person factors, but rather culture is treated as itself an individual difference dimension.

To illustrate this type of mainstreaming of work in cultural social psychology in the domain of morality, consideration may be given to ways Shweder's argument for extending morality to include issues of divinity (e.g., Shweder, Much, Mahapatra, and Park 1997) became assimilated to an etic individual difference. Whereas Shweder and his colleagues pointed to concerns with divinity as a type of abstract consideration that characterizes moral outlooks universally, they grounded their discussion of this moral code in ethnographic observations of specific Hindu Indian cultural outlooks and practices among residents of Bhubaneswar. As embraced in mainstream social psychological work on culture, however, this insight about the existence of abstract moralities of autonomy, community, and divinity has become reified into a five-category taxonomy of limited cultural sensitivity. For example, Graham and his colleagues (Graham et al. 2011) developed the Moral Foundations Questionnaire (MFQ) as an individual-difference self-report scale measure to tap what they portrayed as the "full range of moral concerns" (366) that includes not only those found in non-Western cultures but in religious practices and among political conservatives. Adopting a goal similar to that of cross-cultural psychology, in which an assumed universal psychological theory is tested to assess cultural variation in the relative emphasis it is given, the MFQ is used to tap cultural differences in the relative emphasis given to the five basic moral dimensions of harm–care, fairness–reciprocity, ingroup–loyalty, authority–respect, and purity–sanctity.

The cultural sensitivity of the MFQ is limited, however, with constructs tapped by a limited number of scale items phrased in etic terms. The five-category taxonomy and importantly the associated individual-difference scale measure have stimulated interest in the topic of morality within social psychology. But work informed by the five-category taxonomy does not challenge the long-standing assumption of universalism that characterizes the major models of moral development within psychology (e.g., Kohlberg 1981; Turiel 1983). Whereas the research of my colleagues and me points to qualitative cultural variation in moralities of caring, as discussed, no evidence of such variation is evident in the constructs and scale items of the MFQ, which approaches issues of caring in terms of universal concerns with harm–caring and assesses caring with a single decontextualized scale item on compassion (to wit, "compassion for those who are suffering is the most crucial virtue"; Graham et al. 2011, 385).

Conclusions

Cultural work in social psychology has achieved marked success in terms of its growing visibility and influence in the discipline of psychology, but it faces a crossroads in its future development. As has been argued here, as cultural social psychology has come nominally to be more widely accepted in mainstream traditions of psychology, its theoretical vision has become diluted and it is facing growing charges of having developed into a perspective associated with the stereotyping of cultural variation (see Buchtel 2014). It is crucial to increase the context-sensitivity of cultural research and to become cognizant of ways the embrace of mainstream psychological premises and methods represents a mixed blessing in promoting the acceptance of cultural work at the cost of reducing the power of that work to culturally broaden psychological theory.

It is important to take into account the fact that all research involves tradeoffs, and the present argument does not advocate either that all research in cultural psychology should embrace a focus on in-depth analysis of single cultural practices or that the embrace of the methods of mainstream psychology, such as quantification or comparison, is inherently problematic. Whereas there is inevitably distortion introduced in the explicit comparisons found in social psychological approaches to cultural psychology, there are also limitations in the explanatory force of single case studies. Also, whereas a focus on quantification can in cases limit understanding, ethnographic work entails biases as well. It must be recognized that the methodological strategies of mainstream psychology are not invariably limiting but have features, such as methodological control and attention to implicit aspects of cognition that can make valuable contributions. Cultural social psychology, like other traditions of cultural psychology, has great promise with its agenda of making psychological theory more culturally grounded and less parochial. To achieve its agenda, however, it is important for investigators to work to gain deeper understandings of the cultural meanings and practices emphasized in the cultural communities that they study and to go beyond the adoption of essentializing taxonomic frameworks—an application of effort that can benefit from making greater contact with anthropological traditions of work in cultural psychology as emphasized in this volume.

References

Buchtel, Emma. 2014. "Cultural Sensitivity or Cultural Stereotyping? Positive and Negative Effects of a Cultural Psychology Class." *International Journal of Intercultural Relations* 39: 40–52.

Chiu, Chi-yue, and Ying-yi Hong. 2007. "Cultural Processes: Basic Principles." In *Social Psychology: Handbook of Basic Principles* (2nd ed.), edited by Arie Kruglanki and Tory Higgins, 807–25. New York: Guilford.

Cole, Michael. 1996. *Cultural Psychology: A Once and Future Discipline.* Cambridge, MA: Harvard University Press.

Deci, Edward, and Richard Ryan. 1987. "The Support of Autonomy and the Control of Behavior." In *"Integrating Personality and Social Psychology." Special issue, Journal of Personality and Social Psychology* 53 (6): 1024–37.

Fiske, Alan, Shinobu Kitayama, Hazel Markus, and Richard Nisbett. 1998. "The Cultural Matrix of Social Psychology." In *The Handbook of Social Psychology* (4th ed.; 2 vols.), edited by Daniel Gilbert, Susan Fiske and Gardner Lindzey, 2: 915–81. Boston, MA: McGraw-Hill.

Geertz, Clifford. 1973. *The Interpretation of Cultures.* New York: Basic Books.

Gilligan, Carol. 1982. *In a Different Voice: Psychological Theory and Women's Development.* Cambridge, MA: Harvard University Press.

Graham, Jesse, Brian Nosek, Jonathan Haidt, Ravi Iyer, Spassena Koleva, and Peter Ditto. 2011. "Mapping the Moral Domain." *Journal of Personality and Social Psychology* 101 (2): 366–85.

Higgins, Tory, and Arie Kruglanski. 1996. *Social Psychology: Handbook of Basic Principles.* New York: Guilford.

———. 2007. *Social Psychology; Handbook of Basic Principles.* 2nd ed. New York: Guilford.

Iyengar, Sheena, and Mark Lepper. 1999. "Rethinking the Value of Choice: A Cultural Perspective on Intrinsic Motivation." *Journal of Personality and Social Psychology* 76 (3): 349–66.

Jahoda, Gustav. 1993. *Crossroads between Culture and Mind: Continuities and Change in Theories of Human Nature.* Cambridge, MA: Harvard University Press.

Kagan, Jerome. 2007. "A Trio of Concerns." *Perspectives on Psychological Science* 2 (4): 361–76.

Kitayama, Shinobu, and Dov Cohen, eds. 2007. *Handbook of Cultural Psychology.* New York: Guilford.

Kohlberg, Lawrence. 1981. *The Philosophy of Moral Development: Moral Stages and the Idea of Justice.* Vol. 1. New York: Harper and Row.

Malpass, Roy. 1988. "Why Not Cross-Cultural Psychology? A Characterization of Some Mainstream Views." In *The Cross-Cultural Challenge to Social Psychology: Cross-Cultural*

Research and Methodology Series, edited by Michael Bond, 29–35. Thousand Oaks, CA: Sage.

Markus, Hazel, and Shinobu Kitayama. 1991. "Culture and the Self: Implications for Cognition, Emotion, and Motivation." *Psychological Review* 98 (2): 224–53.

Markus, Hazel, Shinobu Kitayama, and Rachel Heiman. 1996. "Culture and 'Basic' Psychological Principles." In *Social Psychology: Handbook of Basic Principles*, edited by Tory Higgins and Arie Kruglanski, 857–913. New York: Guilford.

Marriott, Marriott. ed. 1990. *India through Hindu Categories*. New Delhi: Sage.

Menon, Usha. 2013. *Women, Wellbeing, and the Ethics of Domesticity in an Odia Hindu Temple Town*. New Delhi: Springer.

Miller, Joan. 1994a. "Cultural Psychology: Bridging Disciplinary Boundaries in Understanding the Cultural Grounding of Self." In *Handbook of Psychological Anthropology*, edited by Philip Bock, 139–70. Westport, CT: Greenwood.

———. 1994b. "Cultural Diversity in the Morality of Caring: Individually Oriented versus Duty-Based Interpersonal Moral Codes." *Cross-Cultural Research* 28 (1): 3–39.

———. 1997. "Theoretical Issues in Cultural Psychology." In *Handbook of Cross-Cultural Psychology* (2nd ed.). *Vol. 1, Theory and Method*, edited by John Berry, Ype Poortinga, and Janak Pandey, 85–128. Boston, MA: Allyn and Bacon.

———. 2007. "Cultural Psychology of Moral Development." In *Handbook of Cultural Psychology*, edited by Shinobu Kitayama and Dov Cohen, 477–99. New York: Guilford.

Miller, Joan, Hiroko Akiyama, and Shagufa Kapadia. 2017. "Cultural Variation in Communal versus Exchange Norms: Implications for Comfort in Social Support." *Journal of Personality and Social Psychology*.

Miller, Joan, and David Bersoff. 1998. "The Role of Liking in Perceptions of the Moral Responsibility to Help: A Cultural Perspective." *Journal of Experimental Social Psychology*, 34 (5): 443–69.

Miller, Joan, David Bersoff, and Robin Harwood. 1990. "Perceptions of Social Responsibilities in India and in the United States: Moral Imperatives or Personal Decisions?" *Journal of Personality and Social Psychology* 58 (1): 33–47.

Miller, Joan, Chloe Bland, Malin Källberg-Shroff, Chiung-Yi Tseng, Jazmin Montes-George, Katelin Ryan, Rekha Das, and Sharmista Chakravarthy. 2014. "Culture and the Role of Exchange versus Communal Norms in Friendship." *Journal of Experimental Social Psychology* 53: 79–93.

Miller, Joan, Rekha Das, and Sharmista Chakravarthy. 2011. "Culture and the Role of Choice in Agency." *Journal of Personality and Social Psychology* 101 (1): 46–61.

Miller, Joan, and Sunanda Luthar. 1989. "Issues of Interpersonal Responsibility and Accountability: A Comparison of Indians' and Americans' Moral Judgments." *Social Cognition* 7 (3): 237–61.

Oyserman, Daphna. 2007. "Social Identity and Self-Regulation." In *Social Psychology: Handbook of Basic Principles* (2nd ed.), edited by Tory Higgins and Arie Kruglanski, 432–53. New York: Guilford.

Nisbett, Richard, Kaipeng Peng, Incheol Choi, and Ara Norenzayan. 2001. "Culture and Systems of Thought: Holistic versus Analytic Cognition. *Psychological Review* 108 (2): 291–310.

Ross, Lee, and Richard Nisbett, 1991. *The Person and the Situation: Perspectives of Social Psychology*. New York: McGraw-Hill.

Shweder, Richard. 1990. "Cultural Psychology—What Is It?" In *Cultural Psychology: Essays on Comparative Human Development*, edited by James Stigler, Gilbert Herdt, and Richard Shweder, 27–66. New York: Cambridge University Press.

Shweder, Richard, Jacqueline Goodnow, Giyoo Hatano, Robert LeVine, Hazel Markus, and Peggy Miller. 2006. "The Cultural Psychology of Development: One Mind, Many Mentalities." In *Handbook of Child Psychology*, edited by William Damon, 716–92. Hoboken, NJ: Wiley.

Shweder, Richard, and Robert LeVine. 1984. *Culture Theory: Essays on Mind, Self, and Emotion*. Cambridge, UK: Cambridge University Press.

Shweder, Richard, Nancy Much, Manmohan Mahapatra, and Lawrence Park. 1997. "The 'Big Three' of Morality (Autonomy, Community, Divinity) and the 'Big Three' Explanations of Suffering." In *Morality and Health*, edited by Allan Brandt and Paul Rozin, 119–69. New York: Routledge.

Singelis, Theodore. 1994. "The Measurement of Independent and Interdependent Self-Construals." *Personality and Social Psychology Bulletin* 20 (5): 580–91.

Taylor, Shelley, David Sherman, Heejung Kim, Johanna Jarcho, Kaori Takagi, and Melissa Dunagan. 2004. "Culture and Social Support: Who Seeks It and Why?" *Journal of Personality and Social Psychology* 87 (3): 354–62.

Triandis, Harry. 1995. *Individualism and Collectivism*. Boulder, CO: Westview.

Turiel, Elliot 1983. *The Development of Social Knowledge: Morality and Convention*. Cambridge: Cambridge University Press.

———. 1998. "The Development of Morality." In *Handbook of Child Psychology (4 vols.)*, edited by Richard Lerner. Vol. 3, *Social, Emotional, and Personality Development*, edited by Nancy Eisenberg, 863–92. New York: Wiley.

———. 2002. *The Culture of Morality: Social Development, Context, and Conflict*. New York: Cambridge University Press.

Walker, Lawrence. 1991. "Sex Differences in Moral Reasoning." In *Handbook of Moral Behavior and Development (3 vols.)*, edited by William Kurtines and Jacob Gewirtz. Vol. 2, *Research*, 333–64. Hillsdale, NJ: Lawrence Erlbaum.

Wertsch, James. 1999. "Sociocultural Research in the Copyright Age." In *Lev Vygotsky: Critical Assessments: Future Directions* (4 vols.), edited by Peter Lloyd and Charles Fernyhough, 4:144–63. Florence, KY: Taylor and Francis.

FOUR

From Value to Lifeworld

ROY D'ANDRADE

University of Connecticut
Department of Anthropology

Values is an essentializing concept, the formulation of a strong causal force within the human psyche. Despite the agreed importance of values, however, the grand attempt of the Five Culture Study in the 1950s to use Florence Kluckhohn's (1950) framework to describe and compare Zuni, Navaho, Spanish American, Texan, and Mormon values is generally thought to have been an interesting failure. As far as I know, Edmonson, Roberts, Romney, Strodbeck, Vogt, and the other project researchers never returned to the study of values after publication of the Five Culture material. As Ethel Albert (1967) pointed out in her introduction to *The People of Rimrock*, no solution had been found to the basic methodological problems involved in measuring values cross-culturally.

A similar situation occurred in psychology and sociology. Despite the theoretical importance of values in Parsons (1964) and Allport (1960), systematic quantitative study of values was rare before the 1980s, one of the few being a work by Milton Rokeach (1967), who developed a thirty-six-item value questionnaire in which respondents rated on Likert scales how strongly they endorsed his value items. In 1975 Francesca Cancian carried out a methodologically innovative study of values among the Tzotzil of Chiapas. In the 1980s Shalom Schwartz, a social psychologist, added twenty-two items to the Rokeach list. For more than two decades Schwartz (2002) asked seventy-five thousand respondents in two hundred samples taken from sixty-seven nations to rate his fifty-eight value items as "guiding principles in my life." Using smallest-space analysis (a nonmetric multidimensional scaling procedure) to map the relations between items, two dimensions were found to be effective and satisfactory for these data. The two dimensions were unlabeled, although Schwartz did develop labeled clusters on the basis of the proximity of items in the space (see table 4.3 for Schwartz's labeled clusters).

It seemed likely to me in 1995 that more interesting and finer-grained results than Schwartz's clusters could be obtained if a larger number of items and more powerful techniques such as principal components analysis were used. My research began by developing a pool of almost a thousand potential items from past questionnaires and articles on values. Finally 328 items were selected by three judges. American (sample 210), Japanese (nonstudent sample 61, student sample 205), and Vietnamese American (sample 248) respondents were asked to rate the 328 items in their native languages. Translation and back translation of the questionnaires were carried out, and after some adjustments, satisfactory correspondence in meaning was achieved. The rating frame "How important to you are the following" was selected from more than twenty other frames (e.g., "Is ____ connected to your major life goals," "How good is ____," etc.) on the basis of high principal component loadings and translatability (D'Andrade 2008, table 3.2 and table 3.3, 17–19).

When the data from the three cultures was analyzed, it was a surprise to discover that the cultures displayed almost identical *dimensions* for the first three components (D'Andrade 2008, chapters 2 and 3). My labels for the three dimensions are *Individualism versus Collectivism*, *Altruism versus Self-Interest*, and *Industry versus Leisure*. The highest and lowest six items on each dimension or principal component are presented in table 4.2. Graphing the items on the first two dimensions results in a circumplex that is almost identical to the smallest-space analysis that Schwartz (2002) carried out (see D'Andrade 2008, 40 and 42).

An important point needs to be stressed about these value dimensions. Although in this study the principal components are strong and consistent enough to be quite interpretable, in fact the first three components account for only slightly more than 10 percent of the variance. The average intercorrelation between all the value items on the same pole of the same dimension (e.g., all the *individualism* items on the individualism versus

Table 4.1 Rating frame used in comparative study of values across three cultures

How important to you are the following?	Not at all	A little	Moderately	Quite a bit	Extremely
1. Having peace and quiet	0	1	2	3	4
2. Being one of the elite	0	1	2	3	4
3. Doing what God wants me to	0	1	2	3	4

Table 4.2 Highest and lowest six items on the three dimensions: Individualism vs. collectivism, altruism vs. self-interest, and industry vs. relaxation

Individualism	Loadings	Collectivism	Loadings
Trying out new things	0.45	Preserving the family name	0.45
Listening to music	0.45	Defending my country	−0.46
Sexual freedom	0.43	Fulfilling family obligations	−0.43
Living in a different country	0.42	Raising children	−0.41
Living a life of adventure	0.42	Maintaining old traditions	−0.40
Being open to change	0.41	Being religious	−0.38
Altruism	Loadings	Self-interest	Loadings
Protecting the environment	0.50	Having social status	−0.59
Treating people equally	0.49	Having great wealth	−0.52
The elimination of racism	0.46	Making a good profit	−0.52
Living in harmony with nature	0.45	Being one of the elite	−0.51
Protection of minority rights	0.42	Owning a good stereo, car, house	−0.51
Maintaining the environment	0.42	Not being poor	−0.50
Industry	Loadings	Relaxation	Loadings
Science	0.44	Sleeping	−0.35
Having self-discipline	0.37	Having someone to care for me	−0.28
Social planning	0.37	Having love	−0.28
Thinking up ways of doing things	0.36	Watching TV	−0.28
Good leadership	0.34	Eating in restaurants	−0.28
Being prepared	0.34	Taking it easy	−0.27

Principal component analysis of combined ipsatized data, top and bottom six items from each component selected

collectivism dimension) is slightly less than 0.10! It would be a mistake to think that the items on any pole of one of these dimensions are strongly connected. The value dimensions have only a weak degree of *entitativity*, as Don Campbell (1958) would have said.

Most important, not only were the dimensions for all three cultures virtually the same, the *ratings of value items* for all three cultures were almost identical. A similar finding was reported by Schwartz and Bardi (2001). Schwartz and Bardi grouped the fifty-six Schwartz items into ten clusters on the basis of similar meanings (see table 4.3). To determine the *value profile* of these clusters, they averaged together the ratings of all items across all samples for each cluster. They then correlated this profile with the cluster means for each society. The results were consistent across types of samples and regions of the world. Schwartz's sample included more than thirty thousand respondents with translations of the Schwartz value survey into thirty-nine languages. For example, the mean *r* for national representative

Table 4.3 Comparison between Schwartz value data and American, Japanese, and Vietnamese data

Schwartz clusters with specific items	American, Japanese, and Vietnamese clusters with matching items
Cluster mean	Cluster mean
1.2 *benevolence*	1.2 *benevolence*
Helpful	Taking care of others
Honoring parents and elders	Having deep respect for parents, grandparents
Honest	Being honest and genuine
0.9 *self-direction*	1.2 *self-direction*
Creativity	Taking care of others
Independent	Having deep respect for parents, grandparents
Curious	Being interested in many things
Choosing own goals	Choosing my own goals
0.8 *universalism*	0.7 *universalism*
Broad-minded	Accepting people as they are
Wisdom	Gaining experience and wisdom from suffering
Social justice	Working for social justice
A world at peace	Treating people equally
A world of beauty	Enjoying the beauty of nature
Unity with nature	Living in harmony with nature
0.6 *security*	0.3 *security*
Family security	Fulfilling family obligations
National security	Defending my country
Social order	Law and order
A world at peace	Treating people equally
A world of beauty	Enjoying the beauty of nature
Unity with nature	Living in harmony with nature
0.5 *conformity*	0.6 *conformity*
Obedient	Being obedient
Politeness	Being polite and well-mannered
Self-discipline	Holding myself to high standards
Honoring parents, grandparents	Having deep respect for parents, grandparents
0.1 *achievement*	−0.3 *achievement*
Successful	Being a success
Capable	Being competent
Ambitious	Being ambitious
Influential	Being important
−0.4 *hedonism*	0.2 *hedonism*
Pleasure	Having erotic pleasure
Enjoying life	Enjoying life
−0.9 *tradition*	−1.1 *tradition*
Humble	Respecting authority
Accepting my portion in life	Accepting one's fate
Devout	Having religious faith
Respect for tradition	Maintaining old traditions
Moderate	Being careful, avoiding unnecessary risks

(*continued*)

Table 4.3 (*continued*)

Schwartz clusters with specific items	American, Japanese, and Vietnamese clusters with matching items
Cluster mean	Cluster mean
−1.1 *stimulation*	−1.0 *stimulation*
Daring	Taking risks
A varied life	Traveling to new places
An exciting life	Living a life of adventure
−1.8 *power*	−1.7 *power*
Social power	Being one of the elite
Authority	Having authority over others
Wealth	Having great wealth
Preserving my public image	Having others thinks well of me

r between means for Schwartz clusters and 3 culture clusters = 0.95

samples and the value profile was .92. Correlations of this size are not typical for most cultural data. Table 4.3 compares the three culture data with the Schwartz and Bardi data, matching the items from the Schwartz and Bardi clusters with the most comparable items from the D'Andrade (2008) data. In most cases the matches are quite close. (The means have been normalized to *z* scores for both samples to facilitate comparison.) The level of agreement is very high; the cluster means correlate at the .95 level. These results are an impressive demonstration of the universality of this pancultural value profile, which shows a high evaluation of treating others well and being self-directed and universalistic and a lower evaluation of tradition, stimulation, and power.

These similarities between values of different cultures create severe problems on a number of levels. On the *empirical* level, the results contradict decades of ethnographic research. On a *methodological* level, the results from survey questionnaires are different from the results of participant observation, leaving uncertainty in the choice of methods. On the *theoretical* level, if every society's values are almost identical to those of every other society, there would seem to be little to cause or sustain the notion of cultural difference. The finding of strong value similarity between societies seems very implausible. But that is what these data show.

What Counts as What

One partial resolution of this puzzle can be illustrated using the work of Fujita and Sano (1988). Fujita and Sano videotaped both Japanese and US preschoolers and their teachers. The videotapes were made in two day-care centers; one in a suburb of Tokyo, the other in a city in Wisconsin. Fujita and Sano showed videotapes of the Japanese school to the US teachers and videotapes of the US school to the Japanese teachers. Both the US and Japanese teachers were strongly impressed, and not favorably, by the differences between the schools. Thus, although the values are similar and the general ideas about children are similar, the response of each group to the videos of the other group is shock at how different and wrongheaded the other group is. But if the values are similar, where does the sense that the values of the two preschools are different come from? Why did the US and Japanese teachers criticize each other so harshly?

One answer to this question lies in the linkage between norms and values. *A norm is a rule about what one should do*, while *a value consists of the criteria by which things are judged to be good or bad* (Maltseva 2012). The norms in each of the two preschools show noticeable differences although the high-level goals of each preschool are similar: both sets of teachers want to care for the child and help it to become a successful adult. In a US preschool teachers believe their constant verbal directions and explanations best help the child learn and grow up. In a Japanese preschool teachers believe letting the child decide in its own way and at its own time best helps the child learn and grow up. The value is the same but differences in specific beliefs about what makes for effective teaching in preschool makes it seem to both that the other culture does not value maturity or independence.

The point, once made, is obvious. Most values are relatively abstract schemas and very different actions can be framed as fulfilling or not fulfilling them. Each culture makes its own interpretive linkage about which values apply to which norms. The differences between the US and Japanese day-care centers are, I believe, typical of the differences to be found when comparing cultural practices from different cultures. The big differences are not in high-level values, but in the interpretation of what counts as what.

Rick Shweder (2012) presents a striking example of how cultural meanings can give moral value to actions. He explains, for example, why the apparently innocent action of a man eating a chicken counts as a serious moral failure among Hindu Brahmans if done after the death of the man's father. This is because they believe the soul of the departed, although desiring to detach itself from the corpse and begin its transmigratory journey, is trapped by the death pollution that emanates from the dead body. It is the duty of the son to help the soul escape from the corpse by staying pure and thereby absorbing as much of the father's pollution as possible in his own body. Chicken is a "hot food," and to keep one's body pure one should eat only "cool foods." Through this complex linkage of norms, actions, and beliefs, eating chicken after one's father's death *counts as* doing harm to one's father.

Institutionally Based Values

Another of the surprising findings of the D'Andrade (2008) study was that the Japanese data *did not* display the expected high level of collective values. The collectivist reputation of the Japanese is based on extensive ethnographic work (Benedict 1945, Dore 1978, Lebra 1976, Nakane 1970, Oyserman et al. 2002; Traweek 2009). It is well documented that Japanese social groups—university departments, business, schools—display strong solidarity and group cohesion with social control. In this study, however, the Japanese scored only slightly higher than the Americans on *collectivism*. This contradiction between ethnographic data and questionnaire data cannot easily be accounted for by some discrepancy between the Japanese and the Americans in *what counts as what*. A better alternative solution is to postulate that there are two different kinds of values; *personal* values and *cultural* values (Kitayama 2002). Such a distinction could explain the differences between the personal values found on the Japanese questionnaire and cultural values described in Japanese ethnography. But this raises a question. It is hard enough to find out what someone's personal values are. How can one find out in a systematic way when a respondent gives a term a high value whether the respondent is rating *personal* values or *cultural* values?

My approach has been to define *cultural values* as values that are *institutionalized* and that may be more or less internalized (Spiro 1987). Take the role of the *doctor* as an example. If one is a *doctor*, then one *should* have the competencies of a *doctor* and care about the things that *doctors should* care about. A *value is institutionalized in a role* if there are understood norms that sanction role behavior that meet (or do not meet) this value criterion. Doctors are supposed to value helping patients, not just earning money. Using this definition of an institutionalized value, a questionnaire was developed to identify US values institutionalized in various roles.

A sample of sixty undergraduates was given questionnaires to judge forty-three value items for thirteen roles (*doctor, employee, teacher, business person, student, governor, father, mother, son, daughter, friend, lover, self*). Questionnaires were organized so that every role was evaluated on all value

Table 4.4 Circle the number that corresponds to how *important* each item is to being a *doctor*

	Not at All	A Little	Moderately	Quite a Bit	Extremely
1. Being careful	0	1	2	3	4
2. Being respectful	0	1	2	3	4
3. Doing what God wants me to	0	1	2	3	4

items by twenty respondents. Although the sample was small, the average alpha for each role was .97. Typically, judgments about established cultural understandings do not require large samples because of the strong homogenizing effects of cultural consensus (Romney, Moore, and Rusch 1997).

The forty-three value items divided into two groups, those values that were generally the same across all roles versus those that were generally different across different roles. The value items that tended to be the same across all roles were *be responsible, be honest, persevere to overcome difficulties, treat others well, have self-control, be independent and self-reliant, work hard,* and *be knowledgeable.* These values were equally high for occupational roles (*business person, governor, employee, doctor, teacher, student*) and for the self-and-intimate roles (*friend, lover, daughter, son, mother, father, self*) (D'Andrade 2008, 131–32). These values have a Puritan flavor: high on *altruism* and *industriousness.* Be a good person and be self-directing and competent no matter what your role—*sister* or *governor.*

Of the forty-three items, one can identify some that were generally the same across roles. To portray the complex relations between values and roles, *correspondence analysis* (Weller and Romney 1990) was applied to these data. Correspondence analysis is similar to principal components analysis, but unlike principal components, it places both the row variables and the column variables in the same space. Originally developed for the analysis of contingency tables of frequency data, it has been used effectively on a wide variety of data (Greenacre 1993; Romney et al. 1997). The results are presented in figure 4.1.

In figure 4.1 roles are printed in capital letters and value items are in lowercase. Both the *individualism–collectivism* and *altruism–self-interest* dimensions are apparent and emerged without rotation. From the graph it can be seen that SELF falls close to the center of the graph, indicating that respondents placed themselves neutrally with respect to the two dimensions. The values of being both *individualistic* and *altruistic* are perceived as important for the roles of LOVER and FRIEND, while being *collectivistic*

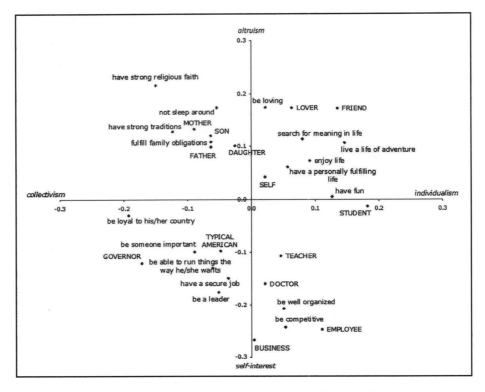

4.1. Correspondence analysis of roles and selected value items: US data

and *altruistic* are important for the roles of FATHER, MOTHER, SON, and DAUGHTER. Being *self-interested* is described as important for the TYPICAL AMERICAN, and both *collectivism* and *self-interest* are important for the role of GOVERNOR. Being almost purely *self-interested* is important for a BUSINESS PERSON, and the both *self-interest* and *individualism* are important for the roles of EMPLOYEE, TEACHER, and DOCTOR.

Chains of institutionalized values linked together by *what counts as what* can be quite long. April Leininger, in studying US Vietnamese families, found a culturally explicit and strongly institutionalized chain of culturally valued goals that count as the appropriate ways of reaching the highly valued top-level Vietnamese value of having a successful family (Leininger 2001). Thus:

study => get A's => get into good college =>
get into good professional school => get a high-paying,
high-status job => have a successful family (59)

An Organization of Cultural Values

The questionnaire described earlier attempted to find the values that are important to holding various roles. But values are embedded in many institutions besides roles, including rituals, laws, conventions, myths, art, and games, among others. Because the number of institutions in any society is huge (Searle 1995), if cultural values are to be studied, some systematic way of grouping institutions needs to be formulated. One perspective for grouping institutions is through the concept of the *lifeworld*. A lifeworld is an intersubjectively shared world, transparent to its members, full of meaning and consequence. Phenomenologists—Cicourel (1995), Garfinkel (1967), and Schultz (1967) for example—treat the lifeworld as the world of everyday ordinary life that is pervasively intersubjective and socially constructed, without which communication would be impossible. A family, for example, is a lifeworld that has its own action systems consisting of things people in the family do, its own material culture, collective representations, norms, institutions, and roles and social network. The major institutions of families are the kinship roles based upon the institutions of marriage and descent. The norms that apply to these roles change as the members of the family grow and age but retain core values of love, care, and intimacy (Quinn 2005).

The world of US family life contrasts sharply with the lifeworld of the typical US business office. A striking example of the home–office difference can be seen in comparing the trading floor of a large investment bank with a US family. Michael Lewis's (2010) book *Liar's Poker* contains a striking description of the trading floor of Salomon Brothers, a Wall Street investment bank in the 1980s. Salomon Brothers was divided into two departments; equities (stocks) and bonds. A series of governmental regulations in the 1980s changed the selling and buying of bonds from a relatively sedate activity to a high-stakes rapid market involving truly huge amounts of money, and in which the conditions of uncertainty created much risk. Bond traders came to glorify risk taking, along with the development of aggressive interpersonal competition and ruthless, cutthroat behavior. According to Lewis, the top traders in the bank engaged in huge bets on the movement of bond and stock prices, consumed gross amounts of food and drink, bullied lesser traders, swore constantly, and frightened the personnel assigned to assist them. This lifeworld glorified risk taking and the personal accumulation of wealth. Salomon Brothers in the 1980s is an extreme example, but business lifeworlds are generally alike in having a hierarchical set of roles (various levels of bosses and workers) with rewards based on values of minimizing costs and maximizing profits as well evaluating the skill, efficacy, responsibility on which the business depends.

How Many Lifeworlds in a Society?

What is unclear is how fine the classification of lifeworlds should be. Very fine lifeworld discriminations would make every family different from every other family, and even different from itself every few years (Nuckolls, this volume). On the other hand, less differentiated lifeworld categories would distinguish only between the strikingly different lifeworlds in a society. For example, there is some agreement that for many societies *kinship, religion, politics,* and the *economy* are distinctive enough to often require separate chapters in an ethnography.

The construct *lifeworlds*, as defined here, differs from that of Habermas (1984) or Schutz. For them the lifeworld concept focuses on the total *background* (Searle 1995), which is necessary for human communication, while in this chapter *lifeworlds* are treated *as an interconnected functioning complex of values, practices, norms, sanctions, institutions, and representations intersubjectively shared by a recognized collectivity.* Lifeworlds depend on cultural worlds held within the collectivity of some society. The lifeworlds of a modern society are much more numerous than the lifeworlds of a tribal society. For example, Allen Johnson, who worked among the Matsigenka of the Amazon (Johnson 2003), found a simple family-based society that had no chiefs or big men, no priests or shamans, no neighborhood- or territory-based roles, no clans or lineages. The family is practically the only lifeworld among the Matsigenka (Johnson, personal communication). The chapter in this book by Haidt and Rozin points out how deep the battle can be between lifeworlds of those who hold to the ethics of divinity and the lifeworlds of those who hold to the ethics of autonomy.

Civil Society, the Covering Lifeworld

This raises the question about whether in a modern society there is a lifeworld that corresponds in some way to the *whole society*. It would be impossible to describe all the lifeworlds of US society—business worlds, military worlds, legal worlds, neighborhood worlds, educational worlds, and so on. Such an ethnography would run to hundreds of thousands of pages. But there remains the question of whether, for a modern society, there is a covering lifeworld that includes almost everyone in a society, even if the roles, norms, practices, and the rest that apply to the full collectivity are relatively small in number. Jeffrey Alexander (2006) argues that there is such a lifeworld, which he calls *civil society*. For Alexander, US civil society is a *sphere* of actions, institutions and ideas, values and norms that the typical individual in US society knows and assumes that other people know. Intersubjectivity includes mutual knowledge of a variety of topics—current national political issues, current facts about war and peace, current candidates for political office, major sporting events, reported disasters, issues of public debt and finance, status and relations between ethnic and racial groups, positions of various religions on moral and spiritual matters, and so on. This information is provided by the media such as newspapers, television, and radio, but also by interpersonal contacts such as family, friends, respected others, for example. In a modern society this huge and constantly shifting mass of information is presented continually and redundantly to the average citizen.

Civil society contains a loosely defined role structure: *citizen, voter, pundit, media consumer, activist, public official, reporter, columnist, publicist, spin doctor,* and others. Most of these roles involve the production, consumption, and evaluation of information about the society. Alexander (2006) presents a comprehensive analysis of the binary discourse code used in civil society in which claims and counterclaims are made in a logic of *responsibility* versus *irresponsibility*. *Irresponsibility* covers a multitude of sins— *misuse of funds, stupidity, theft, lying, cheating, being biased, being immature, lack of moral sense, incompetence,* and a myriad of related ways of failing civil society. Alexander calls this lifeworld a *sphere* of society. Alexander gives "markets, states, parties, churches and sects, families and patriarchies, and groupings formed by ethnic, racial, and regional ties" (Alexander 2007) as other examples of spheres of modern society.

Lifeworld Colonization

Most people seem able to move from one lifeworld to another without even noticing that they have moved from one set of values to another. This nonawareness is aided by the fact that some values are important in both lifeworlds. Being responsible and being honest, for example, are salient across a wide variety of lifeworlds, as indicated by the results of the questionnaire described earlier. But sometimes people experience strong conflict when different values are salient in different lifeworlds. Michael Lewis (2010), for example, writes about how hard it was for him to make an advantageous sale in the trader's lifeworld when he had to *not* divulge to his buyer how bad the bonds he was recommending really were. He soon left his job as a bond trader with a strong feeling of relief and some lasting guilt.

Lewis's personal dilemma is not the only way conflicts in values come about. Another striking form of value conflict is when the values of one lifeworld *colonize* another lifeworld. The use of the term is borrowed here from Habermas. For Habermas, colonization occurs when an autonomous subsystem of the society makes its way into a lifeworld from the outside, "like colonial masters coming into a tribal society" (Habermas 1984, 2, 355). The term is used here to refer to a situation in which some value, central in one lifeworld, begins to become more dominant in a different lifeworld. For example, in the United States the value of acting in accordance with the business morality of making decision primarily on the basis of the "bottom line" partially colonizes other lifeworlds such as the lifeworld of higher education.

Such lifeworld colonization can be very upsetting. It is most distressing to US and European academics when the administration of a university begins to shift its primary decision from achieving academic excellence to purely monetary considerations such as maximizing the number of undergraduate enrollments. Around the world these conflicts are not rare. In the now defunct Soviet society the great colonizing value was the value of helping the Communist party, which was supposed to trump family or business values. In much of the Middle East the great colonizing values are Muslim religious values, which the people of many Middle Eastern countries believe should trump family, business, and national and political values. In Italy it is said that family relationships trump business relationships and even lawfulness. One can see the Mafia as an example in which fellow criminals are ritually incorporated as family.

Summary

The study of values is complex. Even given a robust method for assessing values, a number of complexities arise: A value may have a high rating only because it *counts as* some other value, linked to it by cultural understandings, or it may be a cultural value that everyone says is a wonderful thing, but this value is not internalized, only institutionalized, which paradoxically may make achievement of the value less admirable, and contribute less to self-esteem. A value may be in the process of colonizing a lifeworld and be the center of a dispute within the lifeworld being colonized but be perfectly acceptable within the original lifeworld from which it came. Values are not different from other social science terms, which show similar sense shifting and ambiguity.

References

Albert, Ethel. 1967. "Introduction." In *People of Rimrock: A Study of Values in Five Cultures*, by Evon Vogt and Ethel Albert. Cambridge, MA: Harvard University Press.

Alexander, Jeffrey. 2006. *The Civil Sphere*. New York: Oxford University Press.

———. 2007. "On the Interpretation of the Civil Sphere." *Sociological Quarterly* 48 (4): 641–59.

Allport, Gordon W. 1960. *The Study of Value: A Scale for Measuring the Dominant Interests in Personality*. New York: Houghton Mifflin.

Benedict, Ruth. 1945. *The Chrysanthemum and the Sword*. New York: Houghton Mifflin.

Campbell, Donald. 1958. "Common Fate, Similarity, and Other Indices of the Status of Aggregate Persons as Social Entities." *Behavioral Science* 3 (1): 14–25.

Cancian, Francesca. 1975. *What Are the Norms?* New York: Cambridge University Press.

Cicourel, Aaron. 1995. *The Social Organization of Juvenile Justice*. New Brunswick, NJ: Transaction.

D'Andrade, Roy. 2008. *A Study of Personal and Cultural Values: American, Japanese, and Vietnamese*. New York: Palgrave Macmillan.

Dore, Ronald. 1978. *Shinohata: A Portrait of a Japanese Village*. New York: Pantheon.

Fujita, Mariko, and Toshiyuki Sano. 1988. "Children in American and Japanese Day-Care Centers." In *School and Society*, edited by Harry Trueba and Concha Delgado-Gaitan. New York: Praeger.

Garfinkel, Harold. 1967. *Studies in Ethnomethodology*. Upper Saddle River, NJ: Prentice Hall.

Greenacre, J. Michael. 1993. *Correspondence Analysis in Practice*. Cambridge, MA: Academic Press.

Habermas, Jürgen. 1984. *The Theory of Communicative Action*. 2 vols., translated by Thomas McCarthy. Boston: Beacon Press.

Johnson, Allen. 2003. *Families of the Forest*. Los Angeles: University of California Press.

Kitayama, Shinobu. 2002. "Culture and Basic Psychological Processes—Toward a System View of Culture: Comment on Oyserman et al." *Psychological Bulletin* 128 (1): 89–96.

Kluckhohn, Florence. 1950. Dominant and Substitute Profiles of Cultural Orientation: Their Significance for the Analysis of Social Stratification. *Social Forces* 28 (4): 376–93.

Lebra, Takei S. 1976. *Japanese Patterns of Behavior*. Honolulu: University of Hawaii Press.

Leininger, April. 2001. *Culture and Cognitive Psychodynamics in Vietnamese-American Families*. Unpublished PhD diss. San Diego, CA: University of California Press.

Lewis, Michael. 2010. *Liar's Poker*. New York: W. W. Norton.

Maltseva, Kateryna. 2012. "Social Support Predicts Perceived Cultural Salience of Prosocial Ideas but Not Normativeness of Prosocial Behavior." *Journal of Cognition and Culture* 12 (3–4): 223–64.

Nakane, Chie. 1970. *Japanese Society*. Vol. 4. Berkeley: University of California Press.

Oyserman, Daphna, Heather Coon, and Markus Kemmelmeier. 2002. "Rethinking Individualism and Collectivism: Evaluation of Theoretical Assumptions and Meta-analysis." *Psychological Bulletin*, 128 (1): 3–72.

Parsons, Talcott. 1964. *Social Structure and Personality*. New York: Free Press.

Quinn, Naomi, ed. 2005. *Finding Culture in Talk: A Collection of Methods*. New York: Palgrave Macmillan.

Rokeach, Milton 1967. "Authoritarianism Scales and Response Bias: Comment on Peabody's Paper." *Psychological Bulletin* 67 (5): 349–55.

———. 1988. *Research Value Survey*. Palo Alto, CA: Consulting Psychologists Press.

Romney, A. Kimball, Carmella C. Moore, and Craig D. Rusch. 1997. "Cultural Universals: Measuring the Semantic Structure of Emotion Terms in English and Japanese." *Proceedings of the National Academy of Sciences* 94 (10): 5489–94.

Schwartz, Shalom H. 2002. "Mapping and Interpreting Cultural Differences around the World." *In Comparing Cultures, Dimensions of Culture in a Comparative Perspective*, edited by Henk Vinken, Joseph Soeters, and Peter Esters. Leiden: Brill.

Schwartz, Shalom H., and Anat Bardi. 2001. "Value Hierarchies across Cultures: Taking a Similarities Perspective." *Journal of Cross Cultural Psychology* 32 (3): 268–90.

Schutz, Alfred. 1967. *Phenomenology of the Social World*. Evanston, IL: Northwestern University Press.

Searle, John R. 1995. *The Construction of Social Reality*. London: Allen Lane.

Shweder, Richard A. 2012. "Relativism and Universalism." In *A Companion to Moral Anthropology*, edited by Didier Fassin, 85–102. Somerset, NJ: Wiley.

Spiro, Melford E. 1987. *Culture and Human Nature*, edited by B. Kilborne and L. L. Langness. Chicago: University of Chicago Press.

Traweek, Sharon. 2009. *Beamtimes and Lifetimes*. Cambridge, MA: Harvard University Press.

Weller, Susan C., and A. Kimball Romney. 1990. *Metric Scaling: Correspondence Analysis*, Newbury Park, CA: Sage.

PART TWO

Psychological Processes across Culture: One Mind, Many Mentalities

Section 1
Emotion: A Multiplicity of Feeling

"Kama Muta" or "Being Moved by Love": A Bootstrapping Approach to the Ontology and Epistemology of an Emotion

ALAN P. FISKE

University of California at Los Angeles
Department of Anthropology

THOMAS SCHUBERT

University of Oslo
Department of Psychology

BEATE SEIBT

University of Oslo
Department of Psychology

In English, people speak of *being moved, touched,* or *overwhelmed with emotion,* having a *heart-warming, tear-jerking,* or *poignant experience,* feeling *nostalgia* or *sweet sorrow* and the *rapture* of divine love. People also have feelings evoked by cute babies or adorable kittens and feelings that occur when feeling one with nature or the cosmos—neither of which feelings has a clear and definite name in English. Three years ago we began exploring what seems to be the emotion common to these experiences. To avoid the ambiguity and unwanted connotations of vernacular terms varying across languages, we call this emotion *kama muta* (Sanskrit for "moved by love"). We also coin this scientific term because we think that people are not entirely consistent in their use of any vernacular term, so that sometimes, for example, a person speaks of being *moved* when they are feeling awe or sadness, not kama muta. And because we believe that people feel kama muta about kittens and the cosmos, without being able to give their feeling a name. Moreover, being *moved* denotes approximately the same set of experiences as *gǎn dòng* (Mandarin 感动), Malayan-Indonesian *ter-haru*, Estonian *olema puudutatud* and *olema liigutatud*—but not exactly. These vernacular lexemes are the best translations for each other but do not have precisely the same prototypes or fields of reference; so which term would we use? And although English speakers who say they are *moved, touched, overwhelmed with emotion*, having a *heart-warming, tear-jerking*, or *poignant experience*, feeling *nostalgia* or *sweet sorrow* and *rapture* usually are referring to the same emotion, each of these lexemes encompasses some relationship-specific and context-specific aspects of experiences; which English term would we select to denote the intersection of these terms? So we call the emotion we are studying "kama muta."

Our endeavor is based on the assumption, not undisputed in emotion research, that there exists a set of universal, evolutionarily prepared innate mechanisms for generating emotions. Those mechanisms, however, do not work in isolation but expect and require cultural completion (Fiske 2000). An emotional episode consists in a pattern of coordinated changes in physiology, affect, cognition, and behavior. We assume that such an episode can be categorized as an instance of an emotion when these coordinated changes have certain attributes, as we will detail. It is important to mention here already, that although cognitions and motivations vary greatly between emotional episodes and cultures, we believe that it is possible to diagnose certain core themes common to all episodes of a particular emotion. To do so, however, requires good knowledge of the culture where one investigates it, in order to recognize the specific cultural forms and underlying structures. Our empirical approach presented here is designed to collect evidence on one emotion. We will come back to the importance of cultural context and comparison at the end of the chapter.

We have found that kama muta is common and important in both everyday life and pivotal rituals across very diverse cultures. Yet it has rarely been studied or theorized, and the few scattered articles about it have not been linked. This gave us both the freedom and the challenge to determine whether kama muta is a distinct emotion in the sense just explained and if so to characterize its defining features, to discover what evokes it, to identify its motivational effects, and to illuminate its social relational functions. Moreover, we had to address head-on the question of whether linguistic labels and self-report are valid guides for identifying, delimiting, and classifying emotions. We had to decide how to deal with differences across languages in the meanings of lexemes denoting what may or may not be "the same" emotion—and in some languages, such as Hindi/Urdu, Bikol, and ancient Greek, the apparent absence of any specific corresponding lexeme.

Most crucially, we had to try to figure out valid methods for identifying instances of an emotion from self-reports of informants speaking different languages, from ethnographies and historical accounts, from classical texts, from observations and reports of others, and, of course, in the personal experiences of the three of us across a variety of occasions. In this chapter, we discuss our approach to these issues. Moreover, we tackle the issue of what aspects of kama muta are universal and what aspects differ across cultures.

Ontology and Epistemology of Emotions between Psychology and Culture, or Why We Need a Bootstrapping Approach

How can we know that an emotion "exists," consisting of some set of attributes, delimited by boundaries that distinguish it from other emotions and states, and with distinctive causes and consequences? Also, how do we know that you and I are experiencing, or have experienced on particular occasions, "the same" emotion? Indeed, how does a person know whether an emotion that she experienced today is the same as the emotion she experienced last week—and how do we know this about two emotional experiences of someone else? How can we identify the emotions represented in primary texts, ethnographies, and histories? How do we know whether people in different cultures or at different points in history have "the same" emotion? Or rather, in what respects will an emotion be the same across culture and history, and in what respects may it differ, yet still be recognized as the same species? Mastiffs and Maltese are both dogs. Tamil and Tumbuka are both languages. Orgasm in ancient Egypt and orgasm in contemporary Papua New Guinea are both orgasm—though participants' concepts and lexemes for sex differ, as do many aspects of their subjective experience of copulation and its social meanings. Are a seventh-century CE Indian worshiper's *bhakti* from being in love with Krishna and a contemporary Norwegian child's *rørt* from watching a Pixar movie both kama muta?

After pondering similar questions, in the third generation of their classic chapter on the cultural psychology of emotions, Shweder, Haidt, Horton, and Joseph (2008) concluded on a hopeful note: "It is one of the great marvels of life that across languages, cultures, and history, it is possible, with sufficient knowledge, effort, and insight, to truly understand the meanings of other people's emotions and mental states" (424). But they add that it is "one of the great ironies of life . . . that the process of understanding the consciousness of others can deceptively appear to be far easier than it really is" (425). This may be especially so because, as they also point out in that chapter, the affective, cognitive, and behavioral processes making up what we know as an emotion are fast, efficient, and largely automatic, giving emotions almost perceptionlike qualities, such that it becomes difficult to distinguish between the mere apprehension of an event and the emotional effects we feel from it.

How do we attain the sufficient knowledge and insight? The questions we have posed are epistemological questions, but they can be answered only with respect to ontological assumptions about what "an emotion" *is*.

The epistemology becomes especially complex when we posit that emotions are likely to be polythetic categories that must be characterized by a total "score" based on the total degree of presence of features from a weighted list.[1] For example, we might say that a person experiences emotion X if the person's total score is ≥ 10, where the score is the sum of the intensity of features from a list of eight, where each feature may be weighted differently. Perhaps crying might be weighted more than being choked up. The weight of a feature might be multiplied by its intensity, such that, for example, if a person is crying intensely, that would count more than if a person merely had moist eyes.

A valid ontology may require a more complex criterion: for example, we may want to say that a person is experiencing emotion X only if their total score is ≥ 10 *and* at least two of the first four features are present. Then no matter how intense features 5–8 are, this is not an instance of the emotion unless two of the first four are present. Or the score could be computed as an interaction such that crying, goosebumps, and a warm feeling in the chest occurring *together* might be given a score greater than the sum of the scores of the three components when they occur alone. Such an ontology—which we think is valid for emotions and many other psychosocial entities—is an epistemological challenge because when we start to investigate some phenomena that might constitute an emotion, we do not know a priori how to identify the features, let alone how to weight or combine them, and whether some of the features are crucial. Of course, this would not be an issue if the emotion were characterized by a unique facial expression or any other necessary and sufficient feature, but we do not believe this is necessarily true of kama muta (or perhaps any emotion). Note that although polythetic categories do not have necessary and sufficient features, they are definite and discrete—they do not have the fuzzy boundaries of Wittgensteinian family resemblances.

The epistemology of emotions is especially challenging if we acknowledge that a person experiencing an emotion, or an observer, may not be aware of a feature, may be dimly aware of a feature but not attend to it sufficiently to encode it as a meaningful aspect of experience in long-term memory, may interpret a feature as something else, may not be able to recall the feature as an aspect or instance of X, or may wish or need to report it as something else. That is, features of emotion X may go unnoticed, be forgotten, go unreported, or be reported as something else.

Yet inevitably, language is a primary source of evidence about others' emotions and a primary medium for remembering our own emotions. When studying people who are not present, and especially for people in the past, language is virtually the only means of knowing about others' emotions, though images, including art, may also be informative. Language is an inexact medium for representing emotions, their features, their eliciting circumstances, and their significance and consequences (S. Fiske 1995). Individuals use language differently on different occasions, and no two people use a language quite the same way. Dialects vary, as do local practices of language use. Moreover, lexemes do not directly correspond to emotions or their features in any direct one-to-one mapping. Moreover, a word or phrase in a given language may denote only a subset of the experiences of a given emotion or may encompass more than one emotion. The same problems of messy and uncertain correspondence that obtain for lexemes for emotions obtain for features of emotions. What counts as *to weep*? What counts as *pleurer*? Informants within and between cultures may have different ideas of what constitutes *tears* or *pleurer*, and hence differ in what they are reporting. Language is the primary lens for studying emotion, but it is a distorting lens, typically focusing too broadly or too narrowly, representing selectively or misrepresenting the shapes and colors we see through it. And of course to the extent that emotions, their features, their eliciting conditions, their moral implications, or their motivational affordances do not become encoded in declarative semantic or narrative memory, or are encoded in a distorted or inconsistent manner, explicit language will be an inadequate or even deceptive guide to emotions.

Furthermore, we can expect each language to filter or distort in distinct ways. Each language divides the space of emotions into more or less different categories—and it requires careful investigation to determine how different, and in what ways. A given language may lack any lexeme for emotion X, may subdivide X into a number of categories denoted by different lexemes, may have lexemes that denote specific combinations of emotion X with emotions Y or Z, or may have a lexeme that denotes either X or Y or some types of Z. This makes it challenging to compare emotion reports from different languages, or even from "the same" language spoken in different communities or at different times.

Moreover, each culture has its own folk psychology of emotions, its own emotional practices, and its own distinctive prescriptions for experiencing, communicating, and evoking emotions (Shweder et al. 2008).[2] This folk psychology—often explicit in articulate discourse and texts, always implicit in practices, motives, and evaluations—is associated with, but goes far beyond, the lexicon of the language. And it shapes self-report and others' reports of psychological states: people tend to notice and interpret experience though the filter of their ethnopsychology, to make inferences and judgments with reference to their ethnopsychology, and to construct memories and communicate to others through cultural schemas from their ethnopsychology. Experiences and their perception, recall, and report are always at least to some degree formulated *through* the perceiver's explicit or implicit ethnopsychology.

This is one of the reasons why we should not mistake people's theories of psychology for veridical accounts of how their minds work. People have very incomplete, inaccurate, and misleading understandings of their own and others' psychology. Only academic psychologists understand such mechanisms as Herrnstein's matching law, negativity bias, source memory errors, dissonance, et cetera. And many people think dreams predict the future. And of course people constantly engage in all sorts of habits, practices, and activities without knowing how they do them and sometimes without being fully aware *that* they do them at all. In short, informants' language, beliefs, and explanations may be informative in various respects, but they cannot be uncritically relied on as valid accounts of how their minds or social relations actually work.

Yet beliefs about psychology feed back to shape people's experience and, above all, their representations and understandings of their experience. Both experience and memory are active processes of construction; while much of the raw material is sometimes sensory, the builder is cultural, and the builder constructs experience and memory according to the plans provided by cultural ethnopsychology. So, among other biases, people notice, remember, report, and actively construct—invent, even—the aspects of experience they have words, concepts, and metaphors for, that they believe that people like them have, or should have, or are admired for having. Generally they are unaware of this ethnopsychological shaping of their experiences.

Every action, motive, sentiment, evaluation, or emotion is the product of interactions between evolved psychological proclivities and cultural transmissions, including but not limited to ethnopsychology. Moreover, humans being born so neotenous, with so much neural development still to occur after birth, most human capacities and habits emerge slowly, as the expression of genes interacts with the sociocultural environment. So we can never observe pure endogenous psychological proclivities that have not been shaped by culture. As a psychological proclivity develops, it is informed by the culture in which it emerges. Moreover, the aspects of emotion and action that have psychological roots and those that have cultural roots are not distinct: It's not that certain features are psychologically inherited while others are culturally inherited—all the features of an emotion are generated by the interaction of psychological and cultural processes. An emotion is thus a category whose defining features take on a variety of cultural forms, and one needs cultural knowledge to recognize the common core among these diverse forms.

By "psychology" we mean here the innate, biological, ontogenetically emergent aspect of human minds. By "culture" we mean whatever people become able to do, become disposed to do, or actually do, and whatever technologies, architectures, landscapes and environments they can use by virtue of participating in a particular social system. Though this is a productive metatheoretical heuristic contrast, practices or institutions result from complex combinations: There are no purely psychological actions, nor are there any purely cultural practices or institutions.

This means that deciphering the nature of psychology and the nature of culture go hand in hand. You simply cannot study one without studying the other (for a similar point, see Henrich, Heine, and Norenzayan 2010). In particular, if we want to study an emotion, we must compare and contrast that emotion across cultures. We need to know what is more or less the same across most cultures and what varies. We cannot discern the central tendencies (some of them resulting from psychology, some from common emergent cultural processes) without studying the population variance. That is, we cannot understand what an emotion *is* without collecting evidence about the emotion across a wide range of cultures. But this ineluctably brings us back to the starting point: In order to make broad comparisons of the emotion across a broad range of cultures, we have to recognize instances of that emotion in each culture (or be able to determine that it is absent in a culture). How do we recognize instances of the emotion (if there is actually an emotion there at all) when the emotion is a polythetic category? How do we recognize instances of the emotion when each culture has its own speech practices, its own folk psychology of emotions, its own emotional practices, and its own distinctive prescriptions for experiencing, communicating, and evoking the emotion? How do we recognize instances of the emotion when it is not likely that any language has a lexeme that precisely, specifically, and distinctively identifies an entity that comprises the whole emotion and nothing but the emotion? How do we deal with various cultural practices and norms about attribution, disclosure, gossip, or confabulation about mental states?

The study of emotions thus presents an inevitable conundrum. We believe one, and probably the only, solution to it is to use a bootstrapping approach. The basis of the proposed bootstrapping approach is broad observation and comparison, from which one hopes to inductively construct an orienting theory. Obviously, previous psychological, anthropological, and biological theorizing and evidence must be carefully examined. The theory must explain the features of the emotion that define the phenomenon. Moreover, the theory should explain the functions of the emotion, hence the conditions under which it is likely to be evoked, its implications, and its consequences. Ultimately, the theory must explain why and how the emotion is at the same time psychologically *and* culturally evoked, oriented, and informed. Equipped with such a theoretical starting point, researchers can compare self-report and observation, connect psychology to culture, seek to identify empirical patterns, and generate and test hypotheses. Crucially, a bootstrapping process will entail many iterations of refinement and falsification in different cultures (Shweder 2014).

A Bootstrapping Approach to Kama Muta

So how are we studying the emotion which we call kama muta? We have interviewed native speakers and scholars of a number of languages, either asking for translations of the English lexemes, or starting with a description of the prototypical situations evoking kama muta, and describing the prototypical bodily sensations or manifestations. In most cases, our interviewees readily reported lexemes that seemed apt. In French, the principal terms for this emotion are *émouvoir* and *toucher*, with approximately the same literal meanings as their English cognates. Likewise, the Spanish is *estar conmovido*; similarly, the Portuguese is *comovido* (*comover*), and the Italian *commuovere/commozione* (*commuoversi*); all these literally mean "be moving with"). The corresponding German, Dutch, and Norwegian terms—*bewegt sein, gerührt sein; bewogen zijn, ontroerd zijn, geraakt zijn*; and *bli beveget* or *bli rørt*—all mean "be stirred" (as a liquid is swirled or mixed) or "be moved." In Russian, the closest term is быть растроганным (*byt' rastrogannym*, literally, "be touched").

In the Uralic language family we find similar terms. In Estonian, people say *olema puudutatud* (literally "be touched") and *olema liigutatud* ("be moved"), as well as *olema hingepõhjani liigutatud* ("to be moved to the bottom of one's soul") and *olema pisarateni liigutatud* ("to be moved to tears").

Similarly, in Finnish, "moving" is *liikuttava* and "moved" is *liikuttunut*; a term for this emotion when it is more intense is *koskettaa*, "to touch" and *koskettava*, "touching"; again, these words have the literal physical meanings of their English glosses. In Hungarian, there is *megérintett* (literally, to "move"), and *megérint* (literally, "to touch").

In Mandarin, it's *gǎn dòng* 感动; literally, "to feel movement"); Korean and Japanese use the same characters with the same general meaning. The Indonesian words are *terharu* and *keharuan* (a cousin of compassion and pity; Shaver, Murdaya, and Fraley 2001). *Terharu* seems to have no other nonemotional, physical meaning, but *tersentuh* means "touched" both literally and metaphorically.

These terms in these respective languages and others definitely have substantially overlapping denotations, though their meanings are not identical. That congruence increases our confidence about the ontological status of kama muta. Our confidence is bolstered by the fact that in many of the languages we have explored, the words for kama muta have literal meanings of passive physical motion or passive physical touch.[3]

But, one might ask, how do we know that these lexemes actually *do* denote instances that are mostly kama muta? There are two bases for these translations. First, very similar, well-delineated, and particular situations evoke the emotion most commonly denoted by each of the terms. For example, when we show the same videos to US, Norwegian, Israeli, Portuguese, and Chinese participants, they use the terms we have identified and report corresponding physical sensations. We also find these sensations reported in ancient texts. Our approach thus decomposes the emotion into several components and compares these components across cultures, both to see whether they are the same or different and to see whether they are linked together in the same or different manner. Various theorists have put forward different lists of components of emotion. Shweder et al. (2008) advocated investigating the following components: (1) somatic experience, (2) affective phenomenology, (3) environmental determinants, and (4) whether they are seen as significant, (5) normative social appraisal of experiencing or expressing the emotion, (6) impact on self-management, (7) communication and symbolization of the experience including facial and postural expression, (8) social management by others. To this point in our essay, we have covered components 1, 2, and 3 of this list. In what follows, we will add more evidence about them and also about component 7.

One important aspect of our bootstrapping approach is that we strive to use theoretically grounded analyses of the relational determinants of kama muta. People experience kama muta when a communal sharing relationship is suddenly intensified. A communal sharing relationship is a relationship in which the participants feel one with each other: Their motives, actions, and thoughts are oriented toward something they have in common, some common essence. Thus they feel love, solidarity, identity, compassion, kindness, devotion to each other (Fiske 1991 2004). More formally, communal sharing is an equivalence relation.

Our analysis of the situational determinants suggests that kama muta occurs when people who feel communal sharing have been separated and reunite; when their relationship has been problematic and they connect again, restoring the communal sharing; when the communal sharing has been dormant and is revived; or when they ardently seek communal sharing and the bond is suddenly fully realized. Intriguingly, a person experiences kama muta when she herself suddenly feels intensified communal sharing; when she suddenly appreciates someone who displays intensified communal sharing toward her (for example, by an extraordinary act of care, kindness, generosity, or self-sacrifice for her); or when she observes suddenly intensified communal sharing between third parties—even strangers or fictional characters (for example, a soldier reunited with his family). The fact that kama muta can be generated by intensification of communal sharing initiated in the first, second, or third person is a notable feature.

When a person very strongly experiences kama muta, the experience exhibits some of the following sensations or signs:

1   A feeling, often a warm sensation, sometimes one of expansion, at the surface of the center of the chest over the sternum
2   Moist eyes, tears, or weeping
3   Goosebumps, chills, shivers, piloerection (horripilation—hair standing up)
4   Putting one or both hands over the center of the chest
5   Choked-up throat, often more or less inhibiting phonation such that one speaks in what linguists call a "creaky voice"
6   An utterance indicative of tenderness or joyous pleasure and excitement vocables, such as English "Awww (how cute)," African and the Middle Eastern ululation, in some cultures melodic weeping, the adulatory screams when adored musicians appear or begin to play a "moving" song
7   Possibly, right afterward, a feeling of buoyancy, exhilaration, or security

Each of these sensations or signs may occur to any degree, depending on the intensity of kama muta, but in the most common, mild, everyday experiences of kama muta, many or most people neither feel nor exhibit any of them.

Note that any one of these sensations and signs can occur in emotions very different from kama muta: tears when experiencing pain, fear, or grief; goosebumps or chills when frightened or when something eerie occurs; warmth in the chest in embarrassment or orgasm; choking up in fear or disgust. Tears may result from eye irritation, and goosebumps from low ambient temperature. What identifies kama muta is some combination of these features when they occur due to the sudden intensification of communal sharing.

Kama muta is short-lived, usually lasting no more than a minute or two, and often less. There are some texts that suggest that perhaps there are cultural practices or contexts that facilitate more enduring kama muta, but we do not have good evidence for this. Participating in a wedding or dance performance, watching a movie, or in certain rituals, however, people may experience kama muta repeatedly within a span of minutes or hours.

We are of course not the first ones to point out the significance, symptoms, and causes of this emotion. Eminent scholars have over the years repeatedly said that this emotion is underresearched and deserves more work.[4] One of the first to point it out was Claparède (1930), who described it very much along our lines, but curiously thought it had no motivational consequences for self-management or social behavior (we disagree). Later Frijda (1988), Panksepp (1995), Scherer and Zentner (2001), Konečni (2005), and Tan (2009) theorized on it. More recently, and perhaps sparked by the trend that people share "moving," "touching," "tear-jerking," and "heart-warming" clips that will "restore your faith in humanity" on social media sites, this emotion has attracted renewed interest (Benedek and Kaernbach 2011; Cova and Deonna 2014; Hanich, Wagner, Shah, Jacobsen, and Menninghaus 2014). Before we started our ethnological, historical, and experimental research, little was published in English-, French-, or German-language journals on non-Western variants of the emotion, with the exception of Tokaji (2003), who reported on it in Japanese culture.

Although there is a fair consensus on the affective and somatic components of what is typically labeled *being moved, être ému,* or *gam dong* (Mandarin 感動), theories diverge on the situational determinants. We emphasize (and indeed postulate) that kama muta is caused by sudden intensification of communal sharing, but Cova and Deonna (2014) identify affirmation of core values as the main determinant. In his description of the emotion elevation, Haidt (2003) noted that "the popular press and Oprah Winfrey talk about [elevation] . . . as being touched, moved, or inspired" (281), thus equating elevation and being moved. Indeed, in a study testing whether elevation leads to altruistic behavior, Schnall, Roper, and

Fessler (2010) used self-reports of being moved as an index of elevation. Haidt (2003) proposed that elevation is caused by observing virtuous acts and constitutes the affirmation of a purity virtue. It remains an open question whether these diverging views mirror various emphases on different aspects of the same environmental condition (in the sense of Shweder et al. 2008's point 4), or whether one has more explanatory power, as they have not been empirically tested against each other or studied across a range of cultures.

Although we have only limited data relevant to the matter, we are inclined to believe that kama muta has specific motivational consequences reflected in certain attitudes. When individuals experience kama muta from the intensification of a relationship in which they are engaged, they seem to become more committed to the relationship: they feel more loving, more closely connected, more ready to make sacrifices for the other, and more devoted to maintaining the relationship. And whether they experience kama muta from intensification of a relationship that they themselves are engaged in or one that they observe, the emotion seems to dispose people to be open to new communal sharing relationships, to renew dormant communal sharing relationships, and to deepen or repair existing communal sharing relationships. People sometimes report that after a kama muta experience, they want to find someone to hug. Kama muta makes people more loving, kinder, and more charitable (Schnall et al. 2010; Strick, Bruin, de Ruiter, and Jonckers 2015). People often respond with kama muta when they observe or hear of other's kama muta, which may partially explain why crying makes observers want to care for, help, and share with the crying and weeping individual (Balsters, Krahmer, Sweets, and Vingerhoets 2013; Hendriks, Croon, and Vingerhoets 2008; Hendriks and Vingerhoets 2006), especially their own infants (e.g., Wiesenfeld and Klorman 1978).

The motivational effect and function of kama muta is likely to be specific to communal sharing: feeling kama muta probably does not make people diffusely "prosocial." We predict that it specifically affords enhancement of communal sharing relationships, with less effect—perhaps no effect—on authority ranking, equality matching, or market pricing relationships. That is a prediction, however, that needs to be tested, again comparing various cultures.

We think that the precise function of kama muta is to evoke commitment and devotion to communal sharing. Humans are extraordinarily dependent on communal sharing relationships for their fitness (and psychological wellbeing). But people have communal sharing relationships of various importance with different people, and not all communal sharing relationships are worth great investment. People must be discriminating but wholehearted in committing and showing commitment to the communal sharing relationships that matter to them. The adaptive function of kama muta is to enhance communal sharing motivation when there is new information about the prospects for the relationship indicating that the expected value of the relationship has suddenly increased. Likewise, observing others' communal sharing intensification is informative about the potential of communal sharing in one's own networks.

In short, kama muta typically has the following features, which we can use to identify instances:

1 It occurs when people are engaged in or observe the sudden intensification of communal sharing.

2 When kama muta is strongly felt, people feel or display a combination of some or all of the sensations and signs listed earlier. Kama muta is especially indicated when the sensations or signs include those high on that list (e.g., weeping is more indicative than hand moved to the chest). We can be most confident in recognizing kama muta when a *combination* of these sensations or signs occur simultaneously—the more signs or sensations, the more confident we can be.

3 People refer to their experience using lexemes whose primary meaning is "passively being moved, touched, or stirred" or translations of these.

4 The feeling is primarily positive: people tend to seek to experience or re-experience it.

5 When initiated by the first or second person, people feel a stronger, more enduring commitment to the intensified communal sharing relationship.

6 The person is diffusely more open to and more motivated to engage in communal sharing with others, for example, by being more caring and compassionate.

7 People experiencing kama muta want to share it with others: they want to give it to others, and like to experience it together with others.

8 People who witness kama muta are typically disposed to suddenly intensify their communal sharing relationships with the persons exhibiting kama muta, or sometimes with others, and hence themselves tend to experience secondary kama muta.

We believe the sudden intensification is a necessary feature. But because kama muta may be a polythetic category, we do not assume a priori that any of the other features are necessary or that any set of them is sufficient. We cannot yet specify the weighting function that defines kama muta, but heuristically, we weight them in the order listed. As a general research strategy, when we observe any of these, we start looking for the others, because we think they are features of the same emotional entity, kama muta. At the same time, we are attentively eager to discover and illuminate cultural variations in the particulars of each of these features. And having identified a great many cultural practices, institutions, roles, narratives, and artifacts whose psychosocial function is to evoke kama muta and exploit its motivational and behavioral outcomes, we are constantly looking for more.

Initial Quantitative Studies

To study kama muta, we are collecting convergent evidence from ethnological and historical materials, ancient and more recent texts, participant-observation miniethnographies focused on key practices, interviews, diary self-reports Internet blogs and videos, and experiments using self-report responses to controlled stimuli (see our lab page: www.kamamutalab.org).

Our first laboratory research question was whether indeed people experience kama muta when communal relationships intensify. We therefore searched for and selected videos from the Internet that were described as "moving," "touching," "heart-warming," or "tear-evoking." We pretested each of them with a small group of researchers and students and retained for the study those that evoked the emotion strongly in a majority of us. We then presented these videos to large samples of US residents recruited through the online platform Amazon Mechanical Turk, and Norwegian, Portuguese, Israeli, and Chinese participants recruited through word of mouth and subject pools (Seibt et al., forthcoming). Participants were asked to watch at least two such videos (they could watch up to ten), reporting on the extent to which they were *touched or moved* (or *rørt* in Norwegian, and corresponding terms in Portuguese, Hebrew, and Mandarin) by the videos, indicating which bodily symptoms they observed in themselves and rating the videos on five appraisal dimensions. We conducted a number of such studies with partially overlapping videos and with the same appraisal questions. The main hypothesis to test was that the more participants indicated that "characters in the video got closer to each other"—our operationalization of observing intensified communal sharing—the more kama muta they experienced from the video. Our results showed consistent, significant, and sizable relations, (a) between the communal sharing appraisal and being moved, (b) between self-reported bodily symptoms of weeping and goosebumps and being moved, and (c) between these bodily symptoms and the communal sharing appraisal. In sum, we found covariation among the three pillars of our analysis: intensified communal sharing, lexemes referencing being moved or touched, bodily symptoms of weeping and chills, along with a positive tone (people like the experience).

These data provide support for our bootstrapped hypotheses, but they also demonstrate how skillful the producers of many of our videos are: By combining real footage or performances by actors, often music, and sometimes voiceover, within two minutes these clips cause many of our participants to weep and have other kama muta sensations. Although the emotional impact of these clips is impressive, this impact also poses a problem for our analysis, as these stimuli are quite complex, and we are asking participants to provide a summary appraisal of an entire two-minute clip *after* watching it. To overcome this problem, a second research strategy consisted in asking US participants to report on only one judgment but do so continuously over time *while* watching a clip. Some participants were asked to continuously report real-time changes in their experiences of being moved as they watched each clip. Other participants were asked to report changes in closeness among the protagonists of the movie, while still other samples reported sadness, or goosebumps, or happiness. Averaging each set of participants' reports on a given judgment, we generated time curves for each variable, which we then cross-correlated with each other at each point in time. Then we compared the curves to the events in the movie.

We observed extraordinarily strong moment-to-moment relations between reported feelings of being moved and observed closeness: the magnitude of each predicted the other across moments. Happiness also tends to temporally covary with being moved, but not always; sadness only sometimes covaries with kama muta. This demonstrates the distinctness of kama muta. Goosebumps occur with strong intensifications of kama muta, but also at other points, which corroborates our earlier observation that this physiological symptom is not unique to kama muta. One set of participants' reports of tears at a given moment strongly predicted the other sets of participants feeling *moved or touched* and judgments that the protagonists were close (Schubert, Zickfeld, Seibt, and Fiske 2016).

Our second research question addresses the assumption that kama muta can be experienced as a first-, second-, or third-person experience. To study this question, we asked research participants in Norway to report daily on whether they had felt *rørt*, and to categorize and describe the eliciting event. Our data suggested that our participants remembered experiencing kama muta fairly frequently, on average two times per week, that during these everyday personal experiences, the same main bodily symptoms occur as when watching the videos, and that about half the experiences reported are first- or second-person, the other half third-person experiences in which they observed a sudden intensification of communal sharing. In this study we found that it was not easy to clearly distinguish between first- and second-person kama muta because often it is not clear whether the first or second person initiated the sudden increase in the feeling of communal sharing between them.

We also asked online participants in the United States to recall an episode in which they cried or shed a tear because of something positive. As we had expected, the episodes participants reported were predominantly kama muta experiences, and they indicated greatly feeling moved and touched during the episode. We content analyzed the episodes and found that about two-thirds were first- or second-person events. Again, the degree of closeness predicted how moved or touched participants indicated feeling (Seibt, Schubert, Zickfeld, and Fiske 2017).

At the same time, we have been exploring ethnographies, histories, and texts for accounts of kama muta in diverse cultures and historical epochs. These sources generally tell us relatively little about the experiences of individuals but often illuminate sociocultural institutions, practices, schemas, ideals, and linguistic genres in which kama muta is quite salient. Kama muta appears in cultures in all regions of the world, at all levels of social and technical complexity, and in all the major periods in history. Of course we do not know whether kama muta is present in individual experience or in socioculturally structured institutions, practices, schemas, ideals, or linguistic genres in *all* cultures. One methodological issue is at the same time an intriguing discovery: kama muta does not seem to have clear, definite, distinct, or salient lexical representation in some languages, such as Turkish, Hebrew, Bikol, Classical Greek, and Hindi-Urdu. Yet people definitely seem to experience kama muta in these cultures, and indeed accounts of kama muta events are prominent in the *Odyssey* and in classical Sanskrit and Pali texts that have been translated and widely read by Hindus and Buddhists.

In many cultures there are major rituals that seem to consistently evoke strong kama muta or structure its performance according to the situation. One intriguing aspect of this ritualization is that cultural models for the performance of kama muta apparently afford its experience: People evidently frequently tend to *feel* kama muta when they participate in or observe rituals that are supposed to evoke it, or when they are expected to perform it. For example, in quite a number of widespread cultures men or especially women are prescriptively expected to weep with kama muta at reunions, peace ceremonies, or funerals. For example, Andaman Islanders and people in several Amazonian cultures weep at reunions; Tupinamba women of north coastal Brazil wept when welcoming guests—even complete strangers (Urban 1988). When people weep in accord with their culturally valued practices, the evidence suggests that they commonly feel kama muta: The weeping, highly structured in a culture- and situation-specific manner, quickly elicits kama muta in the weepers and in their audience, who often start weeping. Among many examples is the weeping of Shia Muslims in Muharram commemorations of the martyrdom of Hussain ibn Ali at Karbala in 680 CE. Shia informants say that they often get goosebumps as they weep and pound their chests. Western informants evidently often feel kama muta when they are expected to at weddings.

In many cultures kama muta weeping is culturally elaborated into melodic forms, sometimes containing isolated words, and sometimes poetic lyrics. Such laments are extraordinarily effective in evoking kama muta in performers and listeners. There is only a short space between such laments and modern blues, country and western, and many other genres of popular songs. Perhaps singing in general is to some extent an outgrowth of these genres of melodic and lyrical weeping. Informants tell us that performing and listening to music can sometimes evoke intense kama muta.

In many cultures of Africa both south and north of the Sahara, as well as in the Levant, women ululate in a wide range of situations that correspond to the situations in which Western informants commonly report strong kama muta experiences, and which apparently involve sudden intensification of communal sharing. This suggests the intriguing hypothesis that ululating is a culturally evolved and diffused performance of kama muta.

Naturally, there are cultural models for who should feel or perform kama muta in what situations. One of the most striking is that of western desert Bedouins analyzed by Abu-Lughod (1986), where people are proudly stoic, imperturbable, and fiercely autonomous in public, even in the face of great disappointment or loss. Yet in private, with immediate family and close friends, both men and women recite poignant verses declaring their neediness, longing, despair, and unrequired love—which often evokes kama muta in listeners, who may be moved to help. In Papua New Guinea, Kaluli men dress up in beautiful feather and leaf costumes and come to the men's longhouse in another community to perform a *gisaro* (Schieffelin 1976). In the torch-lit night, they slowly dance while singing songs they have composed that allude to places that remind their hosts of loved ones who have died. When a host man is moved to tears by these memories, he then becomes enraged, grabs a torch, and severely burns the singer—who continues dancing and singing unperturbed. The burner then fervently hugs the singer and soon departs, weeping. Then the cycle continues with more burning of the same and subsequent dancers. The next morning, the dancers give their hosts ample gifts to compensate them for the sorrows they inflicted. Kaluli are deeply moved by these *gisaro* songs, regularly seek and create the experience, admire the burned dancers for the poignancy of their songs, and recite the new songs and comment on them extensively. For the Kaluli, the only performance more moving than *gisaro* is one of their five forms of weeping in which women cry in a manner that evokes the songs of the birds who embody the mournful spirits of dead children pleading for nurturance (Feld 1990).

Kama muta is pivotal to major strains of Hinduism, Buddhism, Christianity, and Islam. When devotees abruptly encounter or recall the extraordinary kindness, compassion, and love of the deity, a prophet, a saint, or a guru, and especially when devotees experience a sudden sense of deep loving union with the deity, they experience kama muta—sometimes overwhelmingly. These experiences are represented in holy texts and reported by contemporary worshipers. One might speculate that the profound experience of kama muta was and remains a major appeal crucial to the endurance and diffusion of the world religions. In contrast to devotees of these mystical personal-experience-based religious practices, followers of the strands of these religions that are more oriented to theological doctrine—to the declarative semantics of their religion—may be much less prone to experience kama muta in their religious practices.

Our initial ethnological, historical, and textual research already has made it clear that many cultures have evolved institutions, practices, and symbolic genres whose effect and function is to evoke kama muta. Conversely, it seems likely that these cultural forms have been propagated *because* they resonate with the psychological proclivity for kama muta: People respond to, remember, and reenact stories and practices that evoke kama muta, leading to their ritualization and institutionalization. Indeed, we suspect that beyond its centrality in religion and ritual, kama muta is crucial to the creation, resonance, and diffusion of many forms of poetry, song, music, oral narratives, theater, short stories and novels, television and movie drama, news, and social media (regarding narratives, see Fiske,

Schubert, and Seibt 2017). People also evoke kama muta strategically in oratory and marketing, and it seems to be a key attraction of addiction-recovery meetings and other kinds of support groups.

Emotions are shaped by psychology—the innate, biological, ontogenetically emergent aspect of human minds and bodies—and by culture—acquired through participating in a particular social system, with its languages, relationships, institutions, technologies, norms, religions, and practices. With such a model, we position ourselves between theorists who assume that basic emotions are natural kinds and theorists who see them as constructs that are completely constructed by cultures and devoid of any evolved adaptive structure beyond core affect, arousal, and an approach–avoidance dimension. (For a discussion, see Gross and Barrett 2011; Lindquist 2013.) Kama muta is fundamentally generated and oriented by the social relationships in which it emerges—like all other social and moral emotions (Fiske 2002, 2010). Because the fundamental forms of social relationships are necessarily implemented in culture-specific and context-particular implementations (Fiske 2000), we can identify a social emotion only by observing and comparing it across diverse cultures and contexts. This is what we are doing in our bootstrapping approach to kama muta. Kama muta theory explains the functions of kama muta, hence the conditions under which it is likely to be evoked, its manifestations, and its consequences. Using this bootstrapping approach enables researchers to address the epistemological question strategically: We can identify the emotion syndrome only by comparing across many cultures and contexts, searching for the co-occurrence of a certain social relational experience, characteristic sensations, specific motives, distinctive actions, a particular valance, and named (if it is named at all) by certain metaphors. In any particular social relational context in any particular culture at any point in history, we may not find all these features. But when several of them co-occur, including most of the important features, we are looking at a cultural realization of a universal emotion.

Notes

1. *DSM* diagnoses are formulated somewhat like this.
2. See, for instance, the insightful account Cassaniti (this volume) gives of the Thai Buddhist folk theory of emotionality.
3. The identification of these terms requires corroboration; we invite readers to comment on them, as well as suggesting corresponding lexemes in other languages.

One way to share translations is to post them online at https://www.facebook.com/beingmoved.

4.   In the first text on social psychology, McDougall (1919) described seven primary emotions, one of which, "the tender emotion," closely corresponds to kama muta.

References

Abu-Lughod, Lila. 1986. *Veiled Sentiments: Honor and Poetry in a Bedouin Society*. Berkeley: University of California Press.

Balsters, Martin, Emiel Krahmer, Marc Swerts, and Ad Vingerhoets. 2013. "Emotional Tears Facilitate the Recognition of Sadness and the Perceived Need for Social Support." *Evolutionary Psychology* 11 (1): 148–58.

Benedek, Mathias, and Christian Kaernbach. 2011. "Physiological Correlates and Emotional Specificity of Human Piloerection." *Biological Psychology* 86 (3): 320–29.

Claparède, Édouard. 1930. "L'émotion 'pure.'" *Extrait des Archives de Psychologie* 22: 333–47.

Cova, Florian, and Julien Deonna. 2014. "Being Moved." *Philosophical Studies* 169 (3) 447–66.

Feld, Stephen. 1990. *Sound and Sentiment: Birds, Weeping, Poetics, and Song in Kaluli Expression*. 2nd ed. Philadelphia: University of Pennsylvania Press.

Fiske, Alan P. 1991. *Structures of Social Life: The Four Elementary Forms of Human Relations*. New York: Free Press.

———. 2000. "Complementarity Theory: Why Human Social Capacities Evolved to Require Cultural Complements." *Personality and Social Psychology Review* 4 (1): 76–94.

———. 2002. "Moral Emotions Provide the Self-Control Needed to Sustain Social Relationships." *Self and Identity* 1: 169–75.

———. 2004. "Relational Models Theory 2.0." In *Relational Models Theory: A Contemporary Overview*, edited by Nick Haslam, 3–25. Mahwah, NJ: Lawrence Erlbaum.

———. 2010. "Dispassionate Heuristic Rationality Fails to Sustain Social Relationships." In *Language, Interaction and Frontotemporal Dementia: Reverse Engineering the Social Brain*, edited by Andrea Mates, Lisa Mikesell, and Michael Sean Smith, 199–241. Oakville, CT: Equinox.

Fiske, Alan Page, Thomas W. Schubert, and Beate Seibt. Forthcoming. "The Best Loved Story of All Time: Overcoming All Obstacles to Be Reunited, Evoking Kama Muta." *Evolutionary Studies in Imaginative Culture*.

Fiske, Susan. T. 1995. "Words! Words! Words! Confronting the Problem of Observer and Self Reports." In *Personality Research, Methods, and Theory: A Festschrift Honoring Donald W. Fiske*, edited by Patrick E. Shrout and Susan T. Fiske, 221–40. Hillsdale, NJ: Lawrence Erlbaum.

Frijda, Nico H. 1988. "The Laws of Emotion." *American Psychologist* 43 (5): 349–58.

Gross, James J., and Lisa Feldman Barrett. 2011. "Emotion Generation and Emotion Regulation: One or Two Depends on Your Point of View." *Emotion Review* 3 (1): 8–16.

Haidt, Jonathan. 2003. "The Moral Emotions." In *Handbook of Affective Sciences*, edited by Richard J. Davidson, Klaus R. Scherer, and H. Hill Goldsmith, 852–70. New York: Oxford University Press.

Hanich, Julian, Valentin Wagner, Mira Shah, Thomas Jacobsen, and Winifred Menninghaus. 2014. "Why We Like to Watch Sad Films. The Pleasure of Being Moved in Aesthetic Experiences." *Psychology of Aesthetics, Creativity, and the Arts* 8 (2): 130–43.

Hendriks, Michelle C., Marcel A. Croon, and Ad Vingerhoets. 2008. "Social Reactions to Adult Crying: The Help-Soliciting Function of Tears." *Journal of Social Psychology* 148 (1): 22–42.

Hendriks, Michelle C., and Ad Vingerhoets. 2006. "Social Messages of Crying Faces: Their Influence on Anticipated Person Perception, Emotions and Behavioural Responses." *Cognition and Emotion* 20 (6): 878–86.

Henrich, Joseph, Steven J. Heine, and Ara Norenzayan. 2010. "The Weirdest People in the World?" *Behavioral and Brain Sciences* 33 (2–3): 61–135.

Konečni, Vladimir J. 2005. "The Aesthetic Trinity: Awe, Being Moved, Thrills." *Bulletin of Psychology and the Arts* 5 (2): 27–44.

Lindquist, Kristen A. 2013. "Emotions Emerge from More Basic Psychological Ingredients: A Modern Psychological Constructionist Model." *Emotion Review* 5 (4): 356–68.

McDougall, William. 1919. *An Introduction to Social Psychology.* 14th ed. London: Methuen. Reprinted 2001 by Batoche Books, Kitchener, Ontario. http://socserv2.socsci .mcmaster.ca/~econ/ugcm/3ll3/mcdougall/socialpsych.pdf.

Panksepp, Jaak. 1995. "The Emotional Sources of 'Chills' Induced by Music." *Music Perception* 13 (2): 171–207.

Scherer, Klaus R., and Marcel R. Zentner. 2001. "Emotional Effects of Music: Production Rules." In *Music and Emotion: Theory and Research,* edited by Patrick N. Juslin and John A. Sloboda, 361–92. New York: Oxford University Press.

Schieffelin, Edward L. 1976. *The Sorrow of the Lonely and the Burning of the Dancers.* New York: St. Martin's Press.

Schnall, Simone, Jean Roper, and Daniel M.T. Fessler. 2010. "Elevation Leads to Altruistic Behavior." *Psychological Science* 21 (3): 315–320. doi: 10.1177/0956797609359882.

Schubert, Thomas W., Janis H. Zickfeld, Beate Seibt, and Alan Page Fiske. 2016. "Moment-to-Moment Changes in Feeling Moved Match Changes in Closeness, Tears, Goosebumps, and Warmth: Time Series Analyses." *Cognition and Emotion.* http://dx.doi.org/10.1080/02699931.2016.1268998.

Seibt, Beate, Thomas W. Schubert, Janis H. Zickfeld, and Alan Page Fiske. 2017. "Kama Muta: A Social Relations Model of Being Moved." *Emotion.*

Seibt, Beate, Thomas W. Schubert, Janis H. Zickfeld, Lei Zhu, Patricia Arriaga, Cláudia Simão, Ravit Nussinson, and Alan Page Fiske. Forthcoming. "Kama Muta: Similar Emotional Responses to Touching Videos across the US, Norway, China, Israel, and Portugal." Manuscript submitted for publication.

Shaver, Phillip R., Upekkha Murdaya, and R. Chris Fraley. 2001. "Structure of the Indonesian Emotion Lexicon." *Asian Journal of Social Psychology* 4 (3): 201–24. doi: 10.1111/1467-839X.00086.

Shweder, Richard A. 2014. "The Tower of Appraisals: Trying to Make Sense of the One Big Thing." *Emotion Review* 6 (4): 322–24.

Shweder, Richard A., Jonathan Haidt, Randall Horton, and Craig Joseph. 2008. "The Cultural Psychology of the Emotions: Ancient and Renewed." In *Handbook of Emotions* (3rd ed.), edited by Michael Lewis, Jeannette M Haviland-Jones, and Lisa Feldman Barrett, 409–27. New York: Guilford.

Strick, Madelijn, Hanka Bruin, Linde de Ruiter, and Wouter Jonkers. 2015. "Striking the Right Chord: Moving Music Increases Psychological Transportation and Behavioral Intentions." *Journal of Experimental Psychology: Applied* 21 (1): 57–72.

Tan, Ed S. 2009. "Being Moved." In *Companion to Emotion and the Affective Sciences, edited by* David Sander and Klaus Scherer, 74. Oxford: Oxford University Press.

Tokaji, Akihiko. 2003. "Research for Determinant Factors and Features of Emotional Responses to 'Kandoh' (the State of Being Emotionally Moved)." *Japanese Psychological Research* 45 (4): 235–49.

Urban, Greg. 1988. "Ritual Wailing in Amerindian Brazil." *American Anthropologist* 90 (2): 385–400. http://www.jstor.org/stable/677959.

Wiesenfeld, A. R., and Klorman, R. (1978). "The Mother's Psychophysiological Reactions to Contrasting Affective Expressions by Her Own and an Unfamiliar Infant." *Developmental Psychology* 14: 294–304.

SIX

Unsettling Basic States: New Directions in the Cross-Cultural Study of Emotion

JULIA L. CASSANITI

Washington State University
Department of Anthropology

Scholars have long sought sets of universal basic emotions.[1] Those with cross-cultural inclinations tend to ask people in diverse settings to fit images of emotional faces to predetermined emotion words and make subsequent claims for some degree of universal commensurability. Anthropologists who study emotion reveal the complex workings of local theories of emotion in practice. They rarely make cross-cultural comparisons, and when they do they tackle the issue of apparent differences by assuming some kind of universal emotions and see how these "basic emotions"[2] are expressed differently through the scripts of cultural management, for the most part leaving the black box of the human psyche untouched. These disciplinary boundaries mirror to some extent the physical boundaries between an individual and the social group; psychologists address the internal workings of the mind and anthropologists address the external workings of society. On neither side can a full or adequate theory of human emotion develop, however, because on the psychological side the maneuvering of forced-choice tasks and prompts derived from English-language terms have shown that apparent similarity is found only when outside categories are imposed on a group of people, and on the anthropological side the scripts and mediums of expression obfuscate broad claims about the mind. Usually emotion is reported as fairly unproblematically referring to things like anger, sadness, happiness, and the like, with some cross-cultural psychologists, cultural psychologists, and psychological anthropologists then proceeding to tear apart the illusion of universality in these emotional states or argue for their connection to other, less famous and non-English emotion terms. What is often left in the wake of this deconstructive work, however, is a fairly disordered group of affective, dimensional, and componential parts that are then reassembled in various ways to fit various emotion states. Even though the idea of uniform emotions across cultures is found in popular culture outlets and college psychology textbooks that relegate culture still for the most part to the side, the claim of basic emotions demonstrates neither universalism nor uniformity, and cultural influences in emotion construction are still poorly understood. As the affective psychologist Jeanne Tsai tells us, "Although most theories acknowledge that cultural and temperamental factors shape affective states, few, if any, specify how" (Tsai 2007, 251).

The cultural psychology tenet of universalism without uniformity suggests that we find difference within apparent similarity. But rather than claim that incommensurable differences in discrete emotion states suggest incommensurability in our capacity to connect emotionally with those of other cultural groups, it can present an understanding of that difference in a way that connects rather than distances us as human beings.

The Various Basic Emotions across Cultures

The most well-known cross-cultural emotion comparisons are those of Paul Ekman (1972, 1994), who asks whether facial expressions of emotions are universal, and concludes that for the most part they are.[3] Ekman et al. (1987; Ekman 1994) approach emotion as categorically discrete phenomena (such as sadness or anger), and ask people in different places around the world whether they can match a face to an emotion.

The second most well-known cross-cultural emotion comparison, and the most famous one that uses native emotion terms as an equal starting point for comparison, is that of Richard Shweder (1994, 2003; Shweder et al. 2010). Taking a cultural psychological approach, Shweder and colleagues analyzed a medieval Sanskrit text, the Rasādhyāya chapter of the Nāṭyaśāstra, for what are called the basic *rasa*, or emotions (Shweder et al. 2010). "In the Rasādhyāya," Shweder et al. tell us, "one finds a relatively elaborate account of the symbolic structures that give shape and meaning to a selected subset of mental experiences, which, because they have been privileged for local symbolic elaboration, have become transformed into mental experiences that people regard as "basic" in their particular culturally constituted world" (2010, 414).[4] Shweder et al. then compare these basic *rasa* to Ekman's (1992) famous list of nine emotions: anger, fear, sadness, happiness, surprise, disgust, interest, shame, and contempt.

Although there is some overlap (i.e., recognizability or potential "universality") between these texts, he concludes that there also is a great deal of dissimilarity, or nonuniformity. After trying to make sense of the emotion list of the Rasādhyāya by seeing whether it will fit with Ekman's list, and finding a lack of fit, Shweder et al. conclude that "any sense of easy familiarity [between Ekman's list and] the Sanskrit list is more apparent than real (412). . . . [I]n the end, most of the items cannot be easily mapped across the two lists without a good deal being lost in translation." (413)

Shweder's goal in drawing attention to the Rasādhyāya is to show by analogy that other cultural constructions of the basic emotions stand to similarly reveal some apparent but not across-the-board actual overlap with Ekman's Western list of emotions, and that comparing emotions on their own terms rather than as subsets of Western lists problematizes the claim of universal emotionality. Sticking to English-language emotion categorical prompts that gloss over differences make other emotions look like imperfect representations of those doing the imposing, and force rather than discover similarity. A cultural psychological approach to emotion, in contrast, seeks universality by breaking down emotions into component parts and approaching differences as well as similarities in the construction of emotion. It sees emotion as an experience rather than a discrete state of being. Shweder suggests eight components into which emotion is decomposable:[5] somatic experience (bodily sensation); affective phenomenology (evaluative metaphors used to describe feelings: pleasant, empty, calm, and so on); environmental determinants (what happened previously in association with the experience); appraisals of significance (the meaning assigned: as good, disrespectful, lasting, transformative, etc.); normative social appraisals (how others would evaluate the phenomena, including its public display); self-management (impulses to action: approach, disengage, celebrate, etc.); communication (social expression in the face, voice, posture, and action); and social management (the ways others act toward the experience: emulating, shunning, etc.). Approaching emotion as experience in this way allows for the analytic elaboration of parts of experience, to piece together local ties to cultural meanings.

The Flood of a Bee Sting

To learn about Buddhism and emotion in practice I have spent more than three years total in a small community in northern Thailand I call Mae Jaeng, studying the cultural psychology of everyday life. I had first gone to the field armed with ideas about the emotions, but I slowly realized that the emotions were not a locally salient unit of analysis. People did seem to feel what I took to be anger, sadness, and the host of other emotions that I could translate from the Thai terms or (less commonly) glimpse from facial expressions, but these basic emotions were rare and did not seem to capture the most interesting, or even essential, parts of affective experience.[6] I came across this feeling again and again in the field. One fairly simple example here can help demonstrate what I mean.

It was the rainy season, and the river that cut through the valley of the community I was living in in northern Thailand had flooded again. People living on the riverbanks were scrambling to move their belongings up to higher ground. My friend Aeh was one of them. I was sitting in the shop of our friend Sen, watching the rain outside, when Aeh came into the shop, soaking wet and laughing.

"Hey, you should see my house! It's totally flooded, the TV's about to get soaked." She and Sen chatted for a while, and she disappeared again out into the rain. Sen laughed and said to me, "her house floods every year."

What were Aeh's feeling at that moment when she was in the store? I felt a little perplexed when I tried to figure them out; the flood represented a loss of her possessions, or at the very least a loss of time and energy to clean it up, but she seemed almost happy about it. She may have had one overarching emotion (e.g., worry), or a mix of a set of emotions (e.g., worry with some degree of anger, sadness, and surprise), but somehow none of these captures the emotional experience she was going through. If anything, judging from her face, her speech, her actions, she was happy. But the river flooding was not a fun event, and it was even regular enough to not be terribly exciting. I wanted to know how she felt, but to do that I needed to understand how emotion works in her cultural community. I wanted to understand the human connection I felt to her right then, without resorting to assumptions that her feelings fit with my categories or relying on empathy as a feeling connection. Finding out what she really felt could not be captured in one or a set of English emotion words, or even a set of Thai words, but then again I did not know all the Thai words, and I did not want to rule out the possibility that it could.

In the course of doing fieldwork I was informally collecting what I had thought of as emotion terms, from *dii-jai* (happy) and *sao* (sad) to more common but less easily translatable ones like *chuey* (ok) and *sabai* (comfortable). To flesh out and deepen my list, as a means through which to access the emotional experiences of people, or how Aeh felt when her house flooded, I decided to collect emotion terms more explicitly. I asked people to create their own list of basic emotions, much like the list in Ekman's work or Shweder's Rasādhyāya. But I immediately encountered a problem: because no one in the town speaks English and there is no clear word for emotion in Thai I was not even sure what I was asking about. Was I looking for words to describe *arom* (for "mood"), or that described *kwam ruu suuk* ("feelings," referring to the skin as well as the mind), or—what? In response to questions about these, I was told things like "a good mood" (*arom dii*) or "a not pleasant feeling" (*my sabai jai*). Responses emphasized an affective valence (e.g., positive or negative feelings), but there was not a clear list of robust emotion terms to be found.[7]

"Emotion?!" Ajarn Somwang, a philosophy and Buddhist studies professor at Chiang Mai University, scoffed when I went to his office and asked him to tell me about emotion in Thailand: "Emotion is just a fancy Western psychological term. They study 'emotion' down the hall," he said, pointing to the psychology wing of the social sciences building, where I had an office at the time, and was familiar with the Western-oriented reconstructions of psychological studies. "It has nothing to do with Thai life or Buddhism." When I pressed him further, arguing that certainly Buddhist people in Thailand have experiences that I could call emotional, he said, "well, I mean I guess we could think of emotion as a kind of perception, feeling . . . from karma, from intention . . . through the contact of the heart with the mood. This contact is part of the creation of karma and the continuation of life, which is suffering."[8] He told me that the Pali term *vedanā* (feelings) come closest in meaning. *Vedanā* is one of the *khandha* (or "aggregates") that makes up the feeling of being a person in Buddhist thought, along with the other four *khandha* of form, perception, mental formations, and consciousness. *Vedanā* refers to feelings, but not to emotion. This distinction is made explicitly in the "Contemplation of Feeling: The Discourse-Grouping on the Feelings," a commentary on the Saṃyutta Nikāya 22 sutta of the Theravada canon: "It should be first made clear that, in Buddhist psychology, "feeling" (Pali: *vedanā*) is the bare sensation noted as pleasant, unpleasant (painful) and neutral (indifferent). Hence, it should not be confused with *emotion* which, though arising from the basic feeling, adds to it likes or dislikes of varying intensity, as well as other thought processes" (Nyanaponika Thera 2013).[9] If I asked people in Mae Jaeng to tell me about the various kinds of *vedanā*, however, the question would appear confusing, for two reasons: (1) as part of an elaborated religious theory, *vedanā* is not normally extracted and integrated within other more colloquial terms for moods and feelings, and (2) such an extraction would, as with moods and feelings, fail to tell us about "kinds" of feeling, because *vedanā* is not understood to exist that way. Instead of relating discrete states of feelings that we might then call emotions, we need to see how ideas about emotionality fit within a broader moral causal ontology in Thailand and analyze emotional experience as part of this wider interpretive scheme of cultural meanings.

From these conversations and books on Buddhist thought I drew together a Thai Buddhist theory on emotion. In general there are three kinds of feelings in Buddhist thought: pleasant feelings (or "joy," *sukha*), unpleasant feelings (or "pain," *dukkha*), or neutral feelings (neither pleasant nor unpleasant, *adukkham-asukham*). The perspective of pleasant, unpleasant, and neutral aligns much better to the empirical data I collected on emotion in Thailand, both from informal observations and from formally generated lists. A Buddhist theory of emotionality at its center combines sensations with a preference (a craving, really) for that sensation to stay or go away. In the middle of this process is the heart of feelings: feeling is thought to arise from sensation; that feeling is constituted affectively as positive, negative, or neutral. People (unenlightened people, that is) then attach to that feeling and wish for it to stay or go away, but because everything is impermanent (*anicca*)[10] and part of a cyclical wheel of dependent origination (*paticca-samuppada*), this wish will always be unfulfilled and will cause suffering. It is that craving and clinging to a feeling of pleasant or unpleasantness associated with a sensation that, in Buddhist theory, creates what we might then call emotion, but it is emotion only in the sense that it is built up from feelings and cravings; it is not differentiated at all as states that occur to a person and are then managed. This is the moralized intentionality that underscores emotion in a Buddhist model; the clinging and craving to something that, according to the Buddhist perspective of impermanence, will never stay the same and causes suffering and perpetuates the cycle of continuous rebirths. The Buddhist goal, then, is to remain unattached to a feeling, and, hence, to not craft it into an emotion.[11]

There are variations on this model in practice. A monk at a monastery of the famous Thai Buddhist monk scholar Buddhadasa Bhikkhu once explained it to me this way: "Let's say a bee stings you. It causes a sensation, an unpleasant sensation. You could say 'oh, a bee stung me,' and leave it at that, or you could become attached to wanting that sensation to go away, and you start to feel upset—'angry' even if you must name it, but it's based on an illusion, a clinging." Most of the process of an emotional experience in this perspective is oriented around not attaching to a feeling of pleasure or pain, because such attachment breeds suffering. A Thai friend who had recently moved to the United States said in English, when I asked him to explain emotionality in Thai for me, that he could not, and instead told me this: "*Kwam ruu suk* (feeling) is the outcome of the mood, but it's not emotion. You feel *vedanā*, okay, and you do not want to get stuck on that feeling. You do not elaborate it and fixate it and turn it into what in English you call emotion, because it makes your feelings attached to it and you're stuck in your mind, and that's not good." He went on, "That's why it's difficult for me sometimes here in America; I smile all the time and laugh, you do that and people in Thailand will understand you, but here they don't. Something happens, there's nothing you can do, you have to just accept it, it happens so fast, it's not a long drawn out thing, you laugh, it's okay. . . . I don't know, it just happens. I wonder why!"

When Aeh laughed at her house being flooded that day in the rainy season she was probably not thinking about an elaborate theory of emotion in Buddhist thought. She was no doubt familiar, however, with its perspective on sensation, feeling, attachment, and suffering, as she, like most others in Thailand, chant Buddhist chants at night that refer to it and hear monks speak regularly at weekly monastery events. It is, like models of emotionality everywhere, less an overt and more an implicitly felt orientation to feelings. She did not feel *good* about the flood, which was what seemed to be the case from her appearance and demeanor, and even her verbal analysis of the situation ("it's fine!") did not point to her being upset. A US folk theory of emotionality as a hydraulic process (using a metaphor of pressure and the private interior psyche [Luhrmann 2001]) might suggest that she was keeping her "real" or "private" inner feelings hidden when she was laughing about the flood; but such a model of discrete basic states would miss out on the ways that emotions are crafted rather than simply contained or managed. A theory that points to feelings as carrying valence, but not necessarily fully formed emotion, is part of Aeh's own local cultural psychology of emotionality. What Aeh was doing in genuinely laughing at the flood was, in effect, practicing detachment of a felt sensation (say, of displeasure) at the flood from turning into an emotion (such as sadness or anger). The "sting" of the flood was not physical, per se, but it represented something that her mind and body made contact with, and in Buddhist theories of perception it can be thought of in a similar sense. Aeh was, I think, in the process of crafting an emotional orientation to not let the flood bother her, not as management of her "real" emotions of sorrow or anger but as an integral part of her psyche. She may have been able to label her emotional demeanor with a state-based emotion if I had pushed her to, but the more interesting part of her emotional experience is in that process of crafting rather than regulating feelings. She did not talk to me at length about how she felt at that moment, but the Thai Buddhist model of emotionality helps to explain how she felt.

This Thai Buddhist model of emotion looks different from a Western model, not just in terms of a list of basic emotions, but as an attitude about emotionality more broadly. It emphasizes feelings (described as positive, negative, or neutral) that are then more or less elaborated into emotion, rather than robust discrete emotion states that occur and then are managed.[12]

A Componential Model of Emotion for Thai Buddhist Emotionality

I am confident that what we call emotion is experienced quite differently in a Thai Buddhist context than in a US academic setting.[13] More than that, I am confident that emotion is not necessarily a useful term to think with for this community. A goal of both anthropology and psychology is to understand how we humans share certain characteristics, as well as how we differ. A cultural psychological approach addresses this problem of similarity and difference by asking how we can reconcile a Thai Buddhist model with that of Western models of emotionality. Rather than claim that an emotional experience of a Thai Buddhist person is "really" the same as that of, say, a US university student, and rather than say the two are "really" different, we can use cultural psychological perspectives on emotion to deconstruct an experience and understand the universalism without the uniformity. And rather than narrow in on "an emotion," which would carry with it a host of assumptions about emotions as states that may not be warranted, we can break down an experience and integrate it with a lived, actual experience like Aeh's that is connected to a local way of thinking about emotionality within larger frameworks of morality, ontology, and causation. I would suggest that we can do this through the componential model that Shweder and colleagues have offered for comparison of discrete emotions. Within Shweder's model lie aspects of the Buddhist model, and also of new and emerging theories of emotionality within the psychological sciences. Some aspects of emotionality will be highlighted more than others; no component has the same relevance in each time and place. Shweder has suggested that in order to understand emotional life in a cultural community we need to do more than just describe feelings and their symbolic representations; we need to link it to local moral causal ontologies of meaning.

Anthropological ethnographies of emotion usually end here, with a model of emotionality drawn out as practiced in a particular cultural community. Such ethnographies of emotion call attention to particular local emotions and emotion complexes (e.g., Bedouin *hasham* as embedded within ideas about modesty and honor (Abu-Lughod 1986) or Inuit *ningaq* as connected to reason and temper (Briggs 1970)). Culturally included psychologists and psychological anthropologists take these local emotions and emotion complexes and compare them with each other and with English-language emotions: They ask how Bedouin *hasham* (Abu-Lughod 1986) is related to and yet experientially distinct from *honor* in the US South (Cohen and Nisbett 1996), for example; or how Inuit *ningaq* and Ilongot *tiget* (M. Rosaldo 1980) compare to each other and to a US experience of *anger*. They ask how the Odia Hindu *lajja* (Shweder 2003) and Balanese *lek* (Geertz 1973) are similar to and different from shyness; or how Ilongot rage at loss may be quite differently felt than its closest English language equivalent of grief (R. Rosaldo 1984). It is through such comparisons that componential models of emotion become especially useful, but it is not the only way they are useful. Like the particular emotions of the Rasādhyāya, a componential model helps to understand similarity and difference without privileging one emotion or the other as the real one, the others being less objectively articulated cultural elaborations.

Universalism without the Uniformity

Addressing emotionality through various components can help to appreciate variation not just in "an" emotion, but in the idea of emotionality itself, and I think that this is where its legacy and its promise lie. The problem with componential models as they are usually applied is that they do not go far enough in critiquing the idea of emotional states. In using a componential model of emotions one could still compare emotions as discrete states broken "at the joints," "natural kinds," as it were, that are experienced however variously in different ways in different places. That a componential model can break emotional experience into discrete states, however, does not mean that it should, or that it must. It does not suggest inherently that each component is a part that together makes up the emotion; that is, each component is not a piece of the real thing that is an emotion. Facing squarely the finding that emotion does not exist in Thailand (and may also not exist in other places and times), at least not the same way it exists as a given entity in US ethnopsychological models, means dismantling emotion and putting emotional experience back together again as a conglomeration of components that can be constructed but not objectified or essentialized as existing apart from the various pieces. Such a perspective aligns with a Buddhist model of emotion, and of the person more broadly, because of the teaching of the five *khandha*, or aggregates, that Ajarn Somwang was implying when he told me about feelings: as parts that only look like they make up a whole.

Analyzing how components within a componential model of emotion work at a metalevel in particular cultural contexts reveals attitudes about emotionality that serve as interpretive schemes tied to moral causal ontologies that would otherwise be missed in a discrete-state-based approach. Each aspect of Shweder's componential list (addressing somatic experience, affective phenomenology, environmental determinants, appraisals of significance, normative social appraisals, self-management, communication, and social management) allows for elaboration, but some components may be more or less elaborated in different cultural contexts. The affective phenomenology of positive and negative feelings in a Thai Buddhist context, for example, helps to make sense of Aeh's and others' experiences without resorting to a universalizing uniformity or a radical relativism.

In a Thai Buddhist context affective phenomenology is especially elaborated. The quality of feelings of pleasantness or discomfort, warmth or coolness, heaviness or lightness, and so on may be a universal quality of emotionality, but it is one that is developed differently in different cultural contexts. The pleasant–unpleasant dichotomy of feelings captured in the Thai *kwam ruu suk* and the Pali Buddhist Thai *vedanā* through the lens of a cultural elaboration on the affective phenomenology of emotionality helps to make sense of emotional experience as part of a broader, shared human practice.

What is shared cross-culturally, then, are not emotion states revealed through a fog of culture but aspects of emotionality that are differently elaborated in different times and places. Such a perspective allows for a study of emotion that moves beyond basic states, and approaches the cultural psychology aspiration of understanding universalism without the uniformity.

Notes

1. The most famous list of supposedly cross-culturally universal ones consists of six (or nine) basic, discrete human emotions, drawn from Paul Ekman's (1972; Ekman and Davidson 1992) research on facial expression: anger, disgust, fear, happiness, sadness, and surprise (and sometimes interest, shame, and contempt). (For an extended critique of Ekman's work, see Russell 1994.) Other social scientists and philosophers have compiled their own lists: Descartes declared our basic emotions as wonder, love, joy, desire, hate, and sadness (in Panksepp 1982); Watson suggests

just fear, rage, and sexual activity (1924); Izard proposes surprise, enjoyment, interest, disgust, shame, distress, fear, contempt, and anger; and Plutchik claims surprise, acceptance, desire, fear, rage, panic, and disgust. Each list implies to some extent that emotions are "natural kinds," similarly felt across time and place but sometimes masked or regulated (Gross 1998) according to personal and cultural norms.

2.   The idea of "basic" or "natural" emotions implies that an emotion is a categorically discrete phenomenon (such as sadness or anger) and can be isolated apart from another emotion, cutting "nature at its joints." Work in this perspective both for general and cultural psychology has attempted to find out what these "basic" emotions might be. See Fiske, Schubert, and Seibt (this volume) for an alternative thesis to the one put forward here. Fiske et al. make use of much of the same cultural psychology evidence to suggest that there *are* universal discrete emotions, and that emotions do exist as "natural kinds."

3.   Although Ekman does not always explicitly make the claim that consistency in the recognition of facial expressions implies consistency in emotion itself, the implications of his work have been taken to suggest as much. The idea of emotion being revealed in the face has a long history: among many others, Aristotle and Darwin both advocated it. As Barrett (2006) writes in her review of the study of emotions as natural kinds, "By referring to a set of facial movements as an expression, Darwin implied that there is an internal emotional state that seeks an outlet in behavior" (37). See also Matsumoto and Willingham 2009 for more theories of emotion as discrete states communicated through facial expression.

4.   The Rasādhyāya suggests the following nine basic emotions, or *rasa*: sexual passion, love, or delight (rati); amusement, laughter, humor, or mirth (hāsa); sorrow (śoka); anger (krodha); fear or terror (bhaya); perseverance, energy, dynamic energy, or heroism (utsāha); disgust or disillusion (jugupsā); amusement, wonder, astonishment, or amazement (vismaya); serenity or calm (sama).

5.   Other emotion theorists have made similar component lists: Tanya Luhrmann has suggested six components: feeling, physiology, facial expression, display rules, appraisals (primary and secondary), and representations (2006, 355). See Mesquita and Frijda (1992) and Scherer (2000) for others. The list here draws from Shweder 1994, reconstructed in Shweder et al. 2010.

6.   Even this sense of (un)easy familiarity was difficult. As Ekman says of his work, "It has not been easy to obtain adequate translations in every language even for the six or seven emotion words we have used in our studies" (1994, 271). If so, how can they be basic? This may be because at least to some extent the discrete labels we put on our emotions are reflective of the language we use (Wierzbicka 1992). For a more detailed analysis of the problem of emotion terms in Thai see Yimngam, Premchaisawadi, and Kreesuradej (2009) and Moore (2006). Yimngam et al. attempts to reconcile a list of emotion terms compiled by the Royal Thai Institute with those gathered from informants, but found little commensurability between them. Moore compiled Thai words with the term *jai* (for heart) in them, which suggests some aspect of emotionality, and found over 700; this emphasis on the heart as part of (rather than states of) emotionality may be a useful way to think about emotional experience in Thailand.

7.   The problem I am pointing to here may be generalizable to other attempts to collect emotion terms across cultural contexts more broadly. It seems that one obvious way to avoid the ethnocentrism implicit in Ekman's emotions is to find locally generated lists and see how common *those* are cross-culturally, in terms of facial recogni-

tion or through other measures. But if even the idea of emotion itself may not be a human universal (in terms of existing as a shared phenomenon) such a project is not practical, and this may be the reason as much as the uniforming momentum of psychology is why such work has not been done.

8. Ajarn Somwang went on to explain this link: "There are three kinds of moods related to karma: kusala, a-kusala, and abiyakata. Abiyakata moods are moods without intention, and are known as 'the feeling of enlightenment. You can't get the good or bad karma without mood. The Buddha can act without intention, with abiyakata, but regular people can't (Dr. Somwang Kaewsufong, Chiang Mai University, December 8, 2009, personal communication). The connection of feeling to karma is significant and is one of the main differences between Buddhist theories of karma and those of other South Asian religions (where Shweder 2003 bases his discussions of karma in his work on morality and emotion). In the Theravada Buddhist country of Thailand, karma (in Thai *kam*, based on the Pali *kamma* and etymologically related to the better-known Sanskrit rendering *karma*) accumulates not through action but through intention (Keyes and Valentine 1983) and not the action itself, as in Hinduism or Jainism (Krishan 1997; O'Flaherty 1980).

9. Feeling, in that sense, is one of the five aggregates or groups of existence *(khandha)*, constituting what is conventionally called "a person" (Bhāra Sutta, SN 22.22, translated from the Pali by Nyanaponika Thera 2013).

10. Impermanence (anicca) is one of what is known as the Three Characteristics of (unenlightened) existence, along with nonself (anattā) and nonsatisfactoriness (dukkha). For more on impermanence in practice in Thailand, see Cassaniti 2006, 2015. For more on dependent origination, see Buddhadasa (1992). For more on these ideas in general Buddhist philosophy, see Rahula (1974) and Swearer and Buddhadasa (1989).

11. De Silva (2000) draws a model of emotion in a Theravada Buddhist context similar to the one I have laid out here: "With the emergence of craving and grasping, we discern the transition from the state of a feeling into the experience of an emotion" (40).

12. The Theravada studies scholar Padmasiri De Silva points to difference (i.e., nonuniformity) in emotion when he says, "This ethical and spiritual dimension that cuts across the analysis of feeling, making subtle distinctions between different qualitative levels of pleasure, is of course something alien to modern western psychology" (2000, 41). I flesh out this Thai Buddhist model of emotionality more fully in Cassaniti (2014, 2015).

13. See Cassaniti (2002, 2006, 2014) and Cassaniti and Luhrmann (2011).

References

Abu-Lughod, Lila. 1986. *Veiled Sentiments: Honor and Poetry in a Bedouin Society*. Berkeley: University of California Press.

Barrett, Lisa. Feldman. 2006. "Are Emotions Natural Kinds?" *Perspectives on Psychological Science* 1 (1): 28–58.

Buddhadasa Bhikkhu, 1992. *Paticcasamuppada: Practical Dependent Origination*. Nonthaburi, Thailand: Vuddhidhamma Fund.

Briggs, Jean L. 1970. *Never in Anger: Portrait of an Eskimo Family*. Cambridge, MA: Harvard University Press.

Cassaniti, Julia. 2002. "Meditation at the Mall." *Seeds of Peace: Journal of Engaged Buddhism and Asian Issues* 18 (2): 25–26.

———. 2006. "Toward a Cultural Psychology of Impermanence in Thailand." *Ethos* 34: 58–88.

———. 2014. "Moralizing Emotion: A Breakdown in Thailand." Special issue, *Anthropological Theory* 14 (3): 280–300.

———. 2015. *Living Buddhism: Mind, Self, and Emotion in a Thai Community*. Ithaca: Cornell University Press.

Cassaniti, Julia, and Tanya Luhrmann. 2011. "Encountering the Supernatural: A Phenomenological Account of Mind." *Religion and Society* 2: 37–53.

Cohen, Dov, and Richard E. Nisbett. 1996. "Field Experiments Examining the Culture of Honor: The Role of Institutions in Perpetuating Norms about Violence." *Personality and Social Psychology Bulletin* 23 (11): 1188–99.

De Silva, Padmasiri. 2000. *An Introduction to Buddhist Psychology*. Landham, MD: Rowman & Littlefield.

Ekman, Paul. 1972. Universals and Cultural Differences in Facial Expression of Emotion. In *Nebraska Symposium on Motivation*, edited by J. K. Cole, 207–83. Lincoln: University of Nebraska Press.

———. 1992. "An Argument for Basic Emotions." *Cognition and Emotion* 6 (3–4): 169–200.

———. 1994. "Strong Evidence for Universals in Facial Expressions: A Reply to Russell's Mistaken Critique." *Psychological Bulletin* 115: 268–87.

Ekman, Paul, and Richard J. Davidson., eds. 1994. *The Nature of Emotion: Fundamental Questions*. New York: Oxford University Press.

Ekman, Paul, Wallace V. Friesen, Maureen O'Sullivan, Anthony Chan, Irene Diacoyanni-Tarlatzis, Karl Heider, Rainer Krause, William Ayhan LeCompte, Tom Pitcairn, Pio E. Ricci-Bitti, Klause Scherer, Masatoshi Tomita, and Athanase Tzavaras. 1987. "Universals and Cultural Differences in the Judgments of Facial Expressions of Emotion." *Journal of Personality and Social Psychology* 53: 712–17.

Geertz, Clifford. 1973. *The Interpretation of Culture*. New York: Basic Books.

Gross, James J. 1998. "The Emerging Field of Emotion Regulation: An Integrative Review." *Review of General Psychology* 2: 271–99.

Izard, Carroll. 2013. *Human Emotions*. New York: Springer.

Keyes, Charles F., and Daniel E. Valentine. 1983. *Karma: An Anthropological Inquiry*. Berkeley: University of California Press.

Krishan, Yuvraj. 1997. *The Doctrine of Karma: Its Origin and Development in Brahmanical, Buddhist, and Jaina Traditions*. Delhi: Banarsidass.

Luhrmann, Tanya. 2001. *Of Two Minds: An Anthropologist Looks at American Psychiatry*. New York: Vintage.

———. 2006. "Subjectivity." *Anthropological Theory* 6 (3): 345–61.

Matsumoto, David, and Bob Willingham. 2009. "Spontaneous Facial Expressions of Emotion of Congenitally and Noncongenitally Blind Individuals." *Journal of Personality and Social Psychology* 96 (1): 1.

Mesquita, Batja, and Nico Frijda. 1992. "Cultural Variations in Emotions: A Review." *Psychological Bulletin* 112: 179–204.

Moore, Christopher. 2006. *Heart Talk*. Bangkok: Heaven Lake Press.

Nyanaponika, Thera, trans. 2013. *Contemplation of Feeling: The Discourse-Grouping on the Feelings*. Access to Insight. http://www.accesstoinsight.org/lib/authors/nyanaponika/wheel303.html.

O'Flaherty, Wendy Doniger. 1980. *Karma and Rebirth in Classical Indian Traditions*. Berkeley: University of California Press,

Panksepp, Jaak. 1982. "Toward a General Psychobiological Theory of Emotions." *Behavioral and Brain Sciences* 5 (03), 407–22.

Plutchik, Robert. 1984. "Emotions: A General Psychoevolutionary Theory." *Approaches to Emotion*, 197–219.

Rahula, Walpola. 1974. *What the Buddha Taught*. New York: Grove.

Rosaldo, Michelle Zimbalist. 1980. *Knowledge and Passion*. Vol. 4. Cambridge University Press.

Rosaldo, Renato I. 1984. "Grief and a Headhunter' s Rage: On the Cultural Force of Emotions. In *Text, Play, and Story: The Construction and Reconstruction of Self and Society*, edited by S. Plattner and E. Bruner, 78–95. Washington, DC: American Ethnologist.

Russell, James A. 1994. "Is There Universal Recognition of Emotion from Facial Expression? A Review of the Cross-Cultural Studies." *Psychological Bulletin* 115: 102–41.

Scherer, Klaus. 2000. "Psychological Models of Emotion." *The Neuropsychology of Emotion* 137 (3), 137–62.

Shweder, Richard. 1994. '"You're Not Sick, You're Just in Love': Emotion as an Interpretive System." In *The Nature of Emotion*, edited by P. Ekman and R. Davidson, 32–44. Oxford: Oxford University Press.

———. 2003. *Why Do Men Barbeque? Recipes for Cultural Psychology*. Cambridge, MA: Harvard University Press.

Shweder, Richard, Jonathan Haidt, Randall Horton, Craig Joseph. 2010. "The Cultural Psychology of the Emotions: Ancient and Renewed." In *The Handbook of Emotions*, edited by Michael Lewis, 409–27. New York: Guilford.

Swearer, Donald K., and Bhikkhu Buddhadasa. 1989. *Me and Mine: Selected Essays of Bhikkhu Buddhadasa*. Albany, NY: SUNY Press.

Thanissaro, Bhikkhu, trans. 2001. "Bhāra Sutta: The Burden" (SN 22.22). *Access to Insight*, http://www.accesstoinsight.org/tipitaka/sn/sn22/sn22.022.than.html.

Tsai, Jeanne. 2007. "Ideal Affect: Cultural Causes and Behavioral Consequences." *Perspectives on Psychological Science* 2: 242–59.

Watson John B. 1924. *Behaviorism*. New York: People's Institute.

Wierzbicka, Anna. 1992. *Semantics, Culture, and Cognition: Universal Human Concepts in Culture-Specific Configurations*. London: Oxford University Press.

Yimngam, Sukanya, Wichian Premchaisawadi, and Worapoj Kreesuradej. 2009. "Thai Emotion Words Analysis." In *Eighth International Symposium on Natural Language Processing*, IEEE, 211–15.

SEVEN

Rasa and the Cultural Shaping of Human Consciousness

USHA MENON

Drexel University
Department of Anthropology

Introduction

I have always marveled at the popularity of Bollywood films both in India and abroad—and, as I write this essay, I wonder whether the *Natya Sastra*, the ancient Hindu treatise on dramaturgy, and *rasa*, the Hindu aesthetic concept, are, perhaps, the key to understanding its popularity. Let me elaborate on what *rasa* is supposed to be.

The aesthetic concept *rasa* and the theory of the emotions associated with it were first formulated by the sage Bharata in the *Natya Sastra* sometime between 200 BC and AD 200 (de Bary 1958), and later commented on and interpreted by several scholars—most notably in the tenth and eleventh century by Abhinavagupta, the Kashmiri Saivite philosopher (see Gnoli 1956). Although this central connection with the performing arts has continued down the ages, *rasa*, as I hope to demonstrate in this chapter, has far broader implications because it is a cultural concept that both shapes and is shaped by Hindu[1] ways of thinking both within and outside the world of aesthetics.

It is noteworthy that although the partaking of *rasa* as a spectator to a theatrical performance, or as the reader of a poem, enables the partaker to transform herself, enables her to savor the bliss (*ananda*) that comes with final liberation (*moksa*), its underlying referent is invariably food and cooking. The *Natya Sastra* uses verbs like *carvana* (chewing or masticating), *āsvādana* (tasting) and *rasanna* (relishing) to describe the *rasa* experience—clear references to the gastronomic aspects of emotional experiencing (Thampi 1965). *Rasa* is, thus, an emotional distillate that is experienced, as

Richard Schechner, the well-known authority on the performing arts, says, "in the gut" (2003, 356)—clearly underscoring Hindu thinking about the unity of body and mind.

The concept of *rasa* also qualifies as a mentality in the Shwederian sense (see Shweder et al. 1998) because it encapsulates a range of Hindu values and understandings about the manifest world and beyond. The core meanings attached to *rasa* are revealed in gastronomy, in emotional functioning and even in Hindu doctrines of soteriology; in other words, as "the symbolic inheritance" of Hindus, *rasa* has left "its generalized mark on many domains" (Shweder et al., 1998, 727–28) of Hindu life. Through exploring these various meanings of *rasa* and their implications for motivation and action, this chapter will explicate the multiple ways in which culture and psyche make each other up (Shweder 1999; Shweder et al. 1998) in this cultural world.

The present chapter is based on both textual analysis and ethnographic data. As far as texts go, apart from the *Natya Sastra*, I also will be referring to the *Caraka Samhita* and the *Susruta Samhita*, ancient medical treatises that discuss *rasa* and its role in maintaining good health and ensuring longevity. As for ethnographic data, those on Hindu gastronomy and Hindu soteriology are part of a much larger body of material that I collected during my fieldwork in the temple town of Bhubaneswar in the eastern Indian state of Odisha, although the data on Hindu aesthetics and *rasa* are the result of a more recent research collaboration between Ahalya Hejmadi, a psychologist, and myself. Eager to understand the concept of *rasa* from the vantage point of a performing artist, Hejmadi and I developed a questionnaire that she then used to interview thirteen Odissi dancers, eight women and five men, Odissi being the classical dance form indigenous to Odisha.

Hindu Traditions and the *Rasa* Theory of the Emotions

Hinduism, an amalgamation of several related yet distinct ancient traditions that go back more than four thousand years, encompasses great diversity in beliefs and practices. Considered by many scholars to be both a way of life and a highly organized social and religious system (Flood 1996; Zaehner 1966), it lacks a single historical founder and possesses no single unified set of beliefs, no centralized authority, and no bureaucratic structures. Instead, what Hindus share is a worldview—a set of metaphysical and philosophical concepts orienting them to life and the world. Many Hindus believe that *samsāra*, the never-ending cycle of rebirth and redeath, binds all living creatures; that maintaining *dharma*, in the sense of upholding order in this world, is a worthy human goal; that *karma*, an impersonal calculus of good and bad actions undertaken over past and present lives, decides one's present and future life circumstances; and that the ultimate goal of all humans should be to break out of *samsāra* and achieve *moksa* or final liberation.

For many Hindus, the human mind (*manas*), an organ that both thinks and feels, is material—composed, it is believed, of the subtlest of matter. According to the highly influential Samkhya-Yoga school of philosophy, the mind emerges only after both *buddhi* (higher intellect) and *ahankara* (sense of "I" or ego) develop. Many Hindus also claim that there are four states of consciousness ranging from the waking to a transcendental fourth state, each ranked according to its perception of reality. The normal waking state (*jagriti*), in which our senses perceive the world and rational thought occurs, is considered to be the lowest state of consciousness because the self is incoherent and fragmented (Klostermaier 2008, 105); dreaming (*svapna*) is thought to be higher than wakefulness because the self is neither bound by the laws of logic nor constrained by the limitations of space and time; and dreamless sleep (*susupti*) is still higher because in this state all aspects of the self are unified. The highest state of consciousness, however, is the fourth state or *turiya*. This state cannot be described in empirical terms because it is "pure awareness, consciousness of consciousness, complete emancipation from all limitations which the body imposed on the self. The 'Fourth State' is the true nature of the Self—immortal, blissful, independent" (Klostermaier 2008, 105–6).

Although the goal of *moksa* remains distant for most Hindus, it is still thought possible to savor the transcendental bliss (*ānanda*) associated with it through self-refinement, through cultivating the self by exercising self-control and self-discipline. And this is where the *rasa* theory influences the emotional life of many modern Hindus. It does so by suggesting that through cultivating an aesthetic sensibility one can savor the *rasa*s of various emotions and thereby transport oneself into the fourth state of consciousness or *turiya* for however brief a time and experience the divine bliss associated with *moksa*.

The *rasa* theory states that there are eight (or nine) basic, enduring emotions (*sthāyi bhāva*), and thirty-three transitory and subordinate emotions (*vyābhicari bhāva*) [*bhāva* implying "emotion," "feeling," "being," "existence']. The eight basic emotions are sexual passion (*rati*), mirth or amusement (*hāsa*), sorrow (*soka*), anger (*krodha*), fear (*bhaya*), dynamic energy or perseverance (*utsāha*), disgust (*jugupsā*), wonder or amazement (*vismaya*), and a ninth (added some centuries later), serenity (*sama*). It is important to note that the *Natya Sastra* identifies these basic emotions as enduring because they are assumed to be a "set of inherited, instinctual propensities" (Thampi 1965, 76)—innate and therefore universal characteristics of the human mind. While this list of basic emotions is interesting in and of itself for what it says about the cultural underpinnings of this world, each of these emotions is also said to have its own flavor, its own *rasa*; thus, the basic emotion, sexual passion, has eroticism (*srngāra rasa*) as its *rasa*, while sorrow's *rasa* is compassion (*karunā*).

Bharata and later commentators sought to understand the relationship between the eight or nine basic and enduring emotions and their *rasa*s. How was the flavor of sorrow, when witnessed as part of a dramatic performance, different from the direct experience of sorrow? They concluded that the experience of *rasa* and the direct experience of the emotion are incommensurable. They maintained that the main purpose of the arts—whether dance, drama, or poetry—is to enable performers and spectators to cultivate an aesthetic sensibility in order to transcend the humdrum concerns of the workaday world and taste the flavor—the *rasa*—of the various emotions. Tasting the flavor of emotions in this way was, and still is, thought of as an opportunity to apprehend the essence of ultimate reality, to experience, as I said earlier, the divine bliss of *moksa*.

Cultural Psychology, *Rasa* Theory, and the Study of the Emotions

Shweder's seminal work on the cultural psychology of the emotions (Shweder 1992) uses the *Natya Sastra* and its *rasa* theory as a "useful intellectual pole star" (418) with which to begin the discussion. As he outlines it, the research agenda in this field revolves around four basic questions. The first has to do with trying to understand why a particular culture identifies an experience as an emotional one rather than as something else. The second documents the various emotions that are salient in a particular culture and examines the cultural meanings attached to each of them. The third assesses the degree to which people in different cultures experience events in their lives emotionally rather than somatically. And the fourth explores the ways in which a people learn, both consciously and unconsciously, the emotional meanings that are salient and significant in their culture.

In this research agenda, the *rasa* theory has a particular relevance for several reasons. A very significant one is that the theory with its list of eight or nine enduring emotions and thirty-three transitory emotions and its focus on the various ways in which emotional experiences unfold clearly answers the first two of the four questions that constitute cultural psychology's research agenda—and does so in ways that are curiously similar to the way contemporary cultural psychologists do their research. Thus, this ancient Hindu theory also assumes that "implicit symbolic structures give shape and meaning" (Shweder 1992, 425) to emotional experience. Although cultural psychologists decompose an emotional experience into its constituent narrative slots (the taxonomic, the ecological, the semantic, the communicative, the social regulation, and the self-management), the *rasa* theory talks of stimulus (*vibhava*), involuntary reactions involving the face and the body (*anubhava*), and voluntary reactions including action tendencies and mental states (*vyabhicari bhava*). The *Natya Sastra* pays detailed attention to how setting, character, voice, posture, action, facial expression, and physiological response can be used to represent the emotions for the most compelling dramatic effect (Dimock 1974), for evoking the most potent emotional response from the spectators. Clearly, ancient Hindu philosophers of the emotions thought of emotional experiences holistically; as being composed of constituent elements; as having causes, consequences, and associated features. From their perspective, when the constituent elements come together, they arouse and bring into consciousness the *sthāyi bhāva*s, inherent elements of the human psyche, that lead then to experiencing the appropriate *rasa*s.

In addition, the interpretive scripts associated with three of these basic emotions—anger, fear, and sorrow—appear to be "genuinely familiar, in the sense of possessing an equivalent shape and meaning" (Shweder 1992, 421). The same cannot be said for the other six emotions that, on closer examination, appear to be less, rather than more, familiar. Apart from these six emotions and their interpretive scripts appearing unfamiliar and strange, it is an open question whether contemporary cultural psychologists would even classify them as emotions. As Shweder observes, they are likely to consider some of these Hindu emotion terms—sexual passion or perseverance, for instance—to be motives or states of mind or "nonemotional feelings" rather than emotions (Shweder 1992).

Furthermore, there is the distinction that Hindu theorists of the emotions draw between primary basic emotions (sexual passion, anger, perseverance, and disgust) and secondary basic emotions (amusement, wonder, sorrow, and fear)—a distinction that does not make much sense to a non-Hindu. Hindus, however, make this distinction because they see a connection between these primary basic emotions and the four aims of life as defined in Hindu traditions—*kama*, *artha*, *dharma*, and *moksa*. Thus, sexual passion is associated with *kama* (attachment), anger with *artha* (self-assertion, material gain), perseverance with *dharma* (righteousness, ethical conduct) and disgust with worldly affairs with *moksa* (liberation). As Shweder (1992) remarks, it appears that this ancient theory of the emotions assumes "a special theory of morality and human motivation, and a specific way of life" (423). And he is absolutely correct: the *rasa* theory does assume that morality is a this-worldly concern, that liberation can be achieved only through self-transformation, and that experiencing *rasa* is transformative because it transports one to *turiya*, the fourth and highest state of consciousness, when one can savor, even if only fleetingly, the bliss of liberation. Little wonder then that, despite an initial thrill of familiarity, the *rasa* theory of the emotions seems rather distant from contemporary Western folk and academic concerns and assumptions about emotions and emotional functioning.

What Then Is *Rasa*?

The term *rasa* has a range of meanings associated with it. The Indologist Monier Williams, for instance, includes all of the following: "sap, juice, water, milk, liquor, nectar, poison, mercury, relish, taste, savor, the prime or finest part of anything" (http://www.sanskrit-lexicon.uni-koeln.de/monier/) in his list. The general consensus is that the conventional meanings of *rasa* are "juice, flavor, taste"; at the same time, there is a widely shared understanding that *rasa* also stands, in some fundamental sense, for "essence, the essence of everything, the essence of the universe itself" (Thampi 1965, 76).

Despite these various meanings attached to *rasa*, several commentators note that when speaking specifically of aesthetics and the arts, there is no accurate English gloss for *rasa*. It is more than aesthetic pleasure because it signifies both artistic production and aesthetic perception, appreciation, and consumption (see Thampi 1965). As Thampi points out, Bharata uses the seed => tree => fruit metaphor to describe this concept. *Rasa*, as an aesthetic experience, is thus an inclusive term, melting distinctions between subject and object and assuming a continuity of experience beginning with artistic creativity and ending with the performer(s) and the audience tasting and savoring the artistic product with delight (Thampi 1965). In order for this to happen, Bharata and later commentators emphasize the necessity of distancing and objectification; they acknowledge that much of the raw material for artistic creativity comes from personal experiences, but for such creativity to have relevance, for it to be something more than the unique details of an artist's autobiography, for it to be appreciated and consumed by an audience, requires distancing.

The process of distancing and objectification is known as *sādhāranikarana* (generalizing, universalizing, or transpersonalizing [Thampi 1965, 78]). It requires removing personal details and replacing them with, to quote T. S. Eliot, "objective correlatives," that is, "a set of objects, a situation, a chain of events which shall be the formula of that *particular* emotion; such that when the external facts, which must terminate in sensory experience, are given, the emotion is immediately evoked (Eliot 1950, 124–25, emphasis in original). Hindu theorists of the emotions seem to agree with Eliot because they too argue for such replacement so that a personal experience loses its particularity and becomes universal, a part of collective human experience, and, therefore, potentially accessible to all.

For this reason, Bharata and later commentators describe aesthetic emotional experiences as nonordinary—*alaukika*. They claim that people can relish such experiences only when they relate to them vicariously, in nonordinary, distant ways. When emotions are experienced directly, the immediacy of this experiencing confuses people so that they can neither discern the characteristics of an emotion nor identify its components. Ancient Hindu philosophers are at pains, then, to distinguish between the experiencing of emotions in our workaday lives and the "emotional content of the aesthetic experience" (Thampi 1965, 77). The everyday experience of emotions involves reacting to them and expressing these reactions in culturally appropriate ways. In sharp contrast, although aesthetic experiences should, and do, affect the mind, they do not move a person to action; more important, because these experiences occur at a remove, people do more than simply undergo the emotions—they observe and savor their particular *rasa*s.

Stylization

The distancing and objectification just described has other cultural significances as well. It evokes the importance of stylization in all forms of Hindu art—drama, dance, poetry, painting, sculpture, and even architecture. In fact, stylization is an essential aspect of such art. If one excludes works produced in the post-Independence era, realism or naturalism have never been important movements in Hindu art. Instead, as Kinsley (1993) reminds us, the purpose of art has always been—and to a great extent, is, even today—to embellish, to represent nature not as it is but as it should ideally be. From the Hindu perspective, "there is nothing desirable about unrefined nature, either in its human or non-human aspects. . . . The function of much of Hindu art is to express a world that has been perfected by a civilized people or a world that faithfully reflects a divine model" (Kinsley 1993, 68). In a telling illustration of this preference for the idealistic, the sanctum sanctorum (*garbhagriha*) in Hindu temples is always a square or rectangular structure because a circle is seen as a natural shape, and therefore, by definition, unrefined.

This emphasis on stylization reveals the Hindu view of the relationship between nature and culture. Hindus categorically privilege culture over nature, believing that the goal of human existence is to perfect oneself as a cultural artifact through subjecting natural processes and natural impulses to cultural reshaping. Such cultural reshaping involves performing daily ablutions (*nitya karma*) meticulously, participating in refining and transformative life-cycle rituals (*samskaras*), and exercising self-control and self-discipline in all aspects of one's life (Menon 2002, 2013).[2] From a Hindu perspective, then, the path to transcendence requires human beings to transform themselves into cultural artifacts that become as perfect as possible through self-discipline and self-cultivation.

Rasa as Gastronomic Experience

As Khare (1992) has remarked, "Food in India is never merely a material substance of ingestion, nor only a transactional commodity. It is synonymous with life and all its goals, including the subtlest and the highest" (1). And one can see these attitudes about food exemplified in the meticulous care with which Odia Hindus of the temple town of Bhubaneswar prepare and consume their meals. First, the foods prepared in any household have to match the physical properties and moral qualities of its members (Marriott 1976; Menon 2013); thus, for those temple town Brahmans who claim to have descended from families that migrated during the thirteenth and fourteenth centuries from north India, the right diet is a bland, vegetarian one in which boiled foods and the products of the cow (milk, cottage cheese, yogurt, and clarified butter [*ghee*]) predominate. Second, given Ayurveda's proscription of raw foods because of their unsuitability for the human digestive system, cooking in the temple town involves the total transformation of all the raw ingredients used. Thus, the slow simmering characteristic of cooking here serves to make the salt, spices, and other condiments penetrate the raw items completely in order to ensure their total transformation. One way of interpreting this style of cooking is to see it as a way of removing all natural grossness and impurity from the original raw materials—another example of the Hindu emphasis on refining the natural through the cultural process of cooking. It is not surprising that such total cooking results in flavors that were originally separate in their raw state becoming fully blended and unified and so "when one eats properly transformed food, one is, in fact, eating flavor . . . flavor or *rasa* reigns supreme" (Seneviratne 1992, 190).

And this concern about flavor or *rasa* can also be seen in the typical meal that is served in the households of the temple town. Rice is the central part of every meal and the vegetarian or nonvegetarian dishes that accompany the boiled rice are thought of less as foods in their own right and more as aids that add flavors to the consumption of rice. In a typical meal, the flavors, colors, and consistencies of the accompanying dishes are in equilibrium: spicy and mild, cream-colored and reddish-brown, smooth and textured, hot and cold,[3] thick and thin. The idea is that the composite experience of seeing, smelling, touching, and tasting the various flavors, colors, and consistencies of these foods is inherently pleasurable—akin to the pleasure one enjoys as a spectator to an aesthetic performance in which a range of emotions is expressed through words, gestures, and facial expressions (*abhinaya*).

In keeping, then, with this Hindu understanding of food and cooking, the *Natya Sastra*'s evocative description of *rasa* as the relish with which diners at a sumptuous banquet enjoy their food is more than mere metaphor. The text explicitly links the *rasa* of aesthetic experience to the *rasa* produced through eating. Furthermore, gastronomic and aesthetic experiences also are thought to be similar in that both involve all the senses. Thus, when Schechner says, "Rasa is flavor, taste, the sensation one gets when perceived, brought within reach, touched, taken into the mouth, chewed, mixed, savored, and swallowed. . . . Rasa is sensuous, proximate, experiential. . . . Food is actively taken into the body, becomes part of the body, works from the inside. What was outside is transformed into what is inside" (2003, 337), he is talking of eating food but he could as well be talking of aesthetic experiences.[4]

Apart from the *Natya Sastra*, classical medical treatises like the *Caraka Samhita* (dating to around the first and second centuries CE) and the *Susruta Samhita* (dating to around the fourth century CE) elaborate on this gastronomic understanding of *rasa*. These texts, concerned with maintaining health and ensuring longevity, describe the human body as being constituted of seven essences: flavor (*rasa*), blood (*rakta*), flesh (*mamsa*), fat (*medas*), bone (*asthi*), marrow (*majja*), and semen (*sukra*) (Ray and Gupta

1965; Ray, Gupta, and Roy 1980; Seneviratne 1992). These seven essences are in constant flux but as long as they are in equilibrium with each other good health is maintained. According to these texts, the digestive fires of the stomach cook the food one has eaten intracorporeally producing first *rasa*, the essence that sustains life, and then the other substances (*dhātus*) that maintain the organic integrity of the body.[5]

With respect to cooking and eating, then, *rasa* is the essential distillate that maintains life; and with respect to aesthetic experiences, *rasa* is the distillate that allows the person with a cultivated aesthetic sensibility to partake of divine bliss. These are clearly analogous experiences although happening on two different planes—the concrete, physical one of eating and savoring food and the more refined, more ephemeral one of savoring eternal bliss. This deliberate interweaving of experiences happening on different planes reflects, once again, Hindu thinking about nature and culture not as separate, dichotomous categories but rather as interpenetrating ones: "culture is enclosed in nature, nature is reworked in culture, so that we cannot tell the difference" (Ramanujan 1990, 50).

It merits reiterating that while Hindus certainly privilege culture over nature, they do not deny the body; instead, they recognize that while embodiment undoubtedly makes us part of nature, it also provides us with the wherewithal to rework that nature and refine it into a cultural artifact. On a related note, while discussing the intricacies of *vipassana* meditation in Theravada Buddhism, the renowned religious scholar Huston Smith says, "The body may be the site of our bondage, but it is also the means of our extrication" (Smith and Novak 2003, 80). I think many Hindus share this understanding about the body and its potential for transformation through cultural reworking. From this perspective, it is not surprising that Hindus experience *rasa* "in the gut" (Schechner 2003, 356) *and* as transcendental bliss (*ananda*).

The Significance of the Acontextuality of *Rasa*

From a Hindu perspective, the most striking feature about *rasa* is its acontextuality. In aesthetics, this acontextuality is achieved through universalization or "transpersonalization" (Thampi 1965, 78)—the stripping off of particularities through adopting formulaic postures, gestures and facial expressions and, thereby, bringing to life emotions that are embedded in the subconscious minds of all the participants (see Fiske, Schubert, and Seibt in this volume for a discussion of *kama muta*, an emotional experience they interpret as universal). Such acontextuality goes against the grain of Hindu thought because, typically, a concern for contextuality pervades Hindu thinking (Ramanujan 1990), both in textual exegeses on subjects like *karma* and *dharma*, as well as in the way ordinary Hindus talk about everyday events and experiences. As Ramanujan has pointed out, however, there are some Hindu concepts—*moksa* in the four aims of life, *sannyasa*[6] in the four phases of life, and *bhakti*[7] in the three paths to liberation, to name just three—that go against this "inexorable contextuality" (1990, 54). Ramanujan explains the presence of such acontextual concepts within the Hindu system by saying that many cultures have "underbellies" that hold ideas and notions that resist or push against prevailing ideologies. He is, of course, correct in saying that cultures are far from being consistent wholes, but I think these acontextual Hindu concepts represent more than a cultural "underbelly."

As anyone who is familiar with Hindu India knows, these concepts—*moksa*, *sannyasa*, and *bhakti*—far from being marginal, are central to the Hindu worldview—a centrality that points to the enormous cultural value and significance that many Hindus attach to renunciation and world-denying tendencies. It is thus more than likely that the acontextuality of *rasa*, *sannyasa*, *bhakti*, and *moksa* exemplifies the tension that exists between world-denying tendencies and world-affirming impulses within Hindu traditions—a tension that is one of the more distinctive features of these traditions (Kinsley 1993; Zaehner 1966).

What do *bhakti*, *sannyasa*, and *moksa* have in common? First, they are all about the individual qua individual—not as part of a group. Dumont (1965) has identified the renouncer (*sannyasi*) as the only true individual in Hindu India; all others, who live in society, according to indigenous definitions of personhood, are composite entities made up of heterogeneous elements and essences, "dividual and divisible" (Marriott 1976, 111). And second, all these concepts reference the world beyond, they speak to the transcendental. The Hindu moral code is best described as goal-based, the goal being either that of upholding sociomoral order (*dharma* in a sociocosmic sense) or that of achieving *moksa* (Menon 2010). The three acontextual concepts being discussed here—*bhakti*, *sannyasa*, and *moksa*—are about the goal itself or about the self-centered quest for it. *Bhakti* or unswerving devotion to one's chosen god or goddess charts the path to achieving *moksa*; *sannyasa* stands for radical renunciation of this world and its entanglements and the hope of achieving *moksa*; and, *moksa* itself represents breaking out of the never-ending cycle of rebirths and redeaths.

Rasa is similar to these three concepts—the only difference being that the experience of *rasa* is fleeting. But it, too, is focused on an individual's solitary quest to achieve transcendence. One relishes *rasa* only when one experiences the emotion vicariously, through nonattachment to the direct experience of the emotion. In addition, one relishes *rasa* by actively cultivating one's aesthetic sensibility through self-control and self-discipline. Self-refinement emerging through the exercise of self-discipline is an extraordinarily important Hindu value, part of Hindu morality (Ingalls 1957; Menon 2010, 2013). The concept of *rasa* is, therefore, intimately tied to Hindu ideas of self-transformation, enlightenment, transcendence, and finally liberation (Paranjpe 2009).

And here the data that Ahalya Hejmadi and I gathered in 2013 become particularly relevant. Seeking to understand the *rasa* experience from the vantage point of the performing artists themselves, we developed a questionnaire and Hejmadi conducted the interviews. These data are, as yet, neither fully analyzed nor written up—but it is still possible to hear contemporary voices echoing meanings and understandings that were first elaborated in the *Natya Sastra*. Being a classically trained Odissi dancer herself, Hejmadi had unrestricted access to her professional peers. She spoke to thirteen dancers and, although this may appear to be a small sample it is not, because professional exponents of Odissi—both teachers and performers—who are established and well-respected by their peers number no more than a few dozen.

What is truly noteworthy of the data we gathered is the consistency with which the dancers speak about their experience of *rasa* and its transformative effects. Whether discussing the self-discipline required for proficiency in their chosen field, or the transcendence of the *rasa* experience or its potential for self-transformation, these highly articulate artists speak with one voice. Thus, when emphasizing the importance of unremitting practice and the discipline it engenders, they recite, without exception, a particular verse from the *Natya Sastra*: *jato hasta, tato drishti, jato drishti tato mano, jato mana, tata bhava, jato bhava, tato rasa* (where the hand is, the eye follows; where the eye is, the mind follows, where the mind is, the feeling follows; where the feeling is, the *rasa* follows) to explain the relationship between unswerving self-discipline and the experience of *rasa*, with *hasta* or hand being the synecdoche for discipline (*sadhana*). And when talking about the transcendence of the *rasa* experience, they again echo each other. In this context, a forty-four-year-old female *guru* says, "We rise to become more than ourselves . . . you see the oneness of yourself with the universe, you transcend the boundaries of your body . . . you then may cry in the joy of this realization"; while a male teacher in his early fifties describes the *rasa* experience in the following words: "You are not yourself, you are eternal and unbound, you achieve *shanta* (serenity), you can attain *moksa*. It is a different level of being . . . time is rhythm but this rhythm is the rhythm of the universe, not something measured by this clock or that calendar." And finally, when talking of the *rasa* experience's potential for self-transformation, the young wife of a guru and herself a famous exponent of Odissi talks of "the dancer as becoming a changed person . . . one starts observing and experiencing the world differently. In everything one feels the presence of divine vibrations and sees divine brightness everywhere."

Equally important, these dancers also interpret the intense bliss that one experiences when enjoying *rasa* as empirical evidence of transcendental space beyond the mundane world with its messy and emotional entanglements. As a twenty-nine-year-old female dancer says, "All life is *maya* (illusion). So when you experience and appreciate *rasa*, you are appreciating *maya* and understanding it for what it is . . . that is the higher realization you achieve—that the meaning of life lies beyond." Thus, the *rasa* experience underscores the Hindu idea that the world around us is ultimately illusory and that the really real lies beyond it.

Finally, what do the *rasa* theory and the larger cultural-psychological project of studying the emotions have in common? The short answer would be "Not a lot"—because despite an apparent similarity in focus, they are two very different intellectual enterprises, holding very different assumptions and having very different goals (see Cassaniti in this volume for the Thai Buddhist theory of emotionality). In cultural psychology, one assumes that an emotional experience is a cultural construction and one examines it in all its immediacy for what it can tell us about the human psyche and variations in psychological functioning. In contrast, the *rasa* theory, focused on the ultimate goal of liberation, discusses the "emotional content of the aesthetic experience" (Thampi 1965, 77)—not the emotional experience.

Cultural psychologists investigate the cultural particularities of emotional experiences. And it is not surprising that in the last three or four decades, research within cultural psychology has amassed empirical evidence that advances the case not for the psychic unity of humans but rather for psychological pluralism. The *Natya Sastra*, however, has a more universalist approach. Despite seeming so modern in its understanding that implicit symbolic structures shape and form emotional experiences, it views the domain of emotions and emotional functioning quite differently. It is part of that corpus of Hindu sacred literature that concerns itself with the self-transformation necessary to achieve what it sees as the universally relevant goal of liberation from *samsara*, the never-ending cycle of rebirths and redeaths. The *Natya Sastra*'s purpose, therefore, is to explore a particular area of human experience—that of emotional functioning—so as to delineate a path to *moksa*. It emphasizes not the personal and particular but the transformation of the personal and the particular into the transpersonal and the universal.

And very preliminary findings from the study that Hejmadi and I are currently doing seem to suggest that for Hindu artists raised in a world in which self-discipline and self-refinement are culturally validated practices and the quest for transcendence is an unspoken yet well-understood goal of life, participating in aesthetic performances does enable them to experience *rasa*, and enter *turiya*—the fourth state of consciousness (although of the thirteen, only two actually used this term). Whether spectators of such performances also share in the *rasa* experience is a subject that has not, to the best of my knowledge, been explored—but there is some credible anecdotal evidence to suggest that they do (see Macaulay 2014; Paranjpe 2009).

And then there are the Bollywood movies that I mentioned at the beginning of this chapter. How does one explain their mass appeal to audiences not just in India but around the world? Sophisticated critics dismiss the typical Bollywood blockbuster as a *"masala"* movie with the requisite number of songs, dances, and fights; they complain about its formulaic nature, its lack of character development, and the absence of any serious discussion of social situations and human predicaments. But perhaps the secret of Bollywood's success lies precisely in what is derided the most about it—its adherence to formulaic plots. Perhaps this is twentieth-century *sadharanikarana* or transpersonalization as delineated in the *Natya Sastra*; and perhaps such transpersonalization does strike a chord in the hearts and minds of Hindu and some non-Hindu audiences leading them to savor *rasa* and experience utter delight. Again, this is no more than a cursory mention of possible dramaturgical connections between Bollywood movies and the *Natya Sastra*; clearly this is an issue that deserves to be explored seriously and systematically.

Conclusion

Shweder et al. have invited cultural psychologists "to address the question of whether a particular cultural community has a characteristic mentality (e.g., the Protestant mentality), which leaves its generalized mark on many domains in that community, thereby making, for example, Protestant economics, Protestant religion, and Protestant family life more like each other than like a parallel natural domain in another cultural community" (1998, 728). From this understanding of a mentality and from the discussion of *rasa* presented in this chapter, I think one can conclude that this concept does shape and leave its mark on various domains in Hindu life. Thus, the preparation and eating of food, participating in aesthetic experiences, and working toward achieving *moksa* can be seen as analogous processes, each occurring on different planes but all having something to do with *rasa*. Thus, when speaking of food, the digestive fires that burn within the human body cook the food intracorporeally, transforming it first into *rasa*, the essence that maintains life, and then into the other substances that maintain bodily integrity. With respect to aesthetic experiences, through participating in performative events, partakers savor the *rasa* that is distilled from experiencing the various *sthāyi bhāva*s and thereby experience transcendental bliss. And the very experience of such *rasa* is thought to demonstrate the existence of a transcendental space beyond the mundane world we inhabit—the space that those who achieve *moksa* would attain.

The *Natya Sastra*, therefore, is best thought of as a cultural artifact, a text that reflects the values and concerns of a particular cultural world. More important, it makes certain universal claims about the human psyche. There is, of course, no way of demonstrating with any degree of confidence whether the human psyche is as the *Natya Sastra* describes it to be; the Natya Sastra's claims reminds me of Freudian theory about the architecture of the brain—they resonate with those who belong to the same cultural world but rarely beyond. The *Natya Sastra* seems to be saying that as humans living in this world we are culturally particular beings but there is a universal aspect to all human existence, one that grapples with the ultimate meaning of life. And with respect to this aspect, the *Natya Sastra*, quite understandably, suggests a very culturally particular path—cultivate the ability to experience *rasa*, it says, because doing so will take one a long way toward achieving liberation, the ultimate goal of life as defined by Hindu ways of thinking.

Notes

1. In this essay, when I use the term "Hindu" to classify ideas, customs, and practices, I am primarily referring to high culture, i.e., Brahmanical traditions, those followed by the Brahmans, the caste having the highest ritual status, who constitute roughly 3 percent of India's population. I do not want to make unwarranted generalizations and I am well aware that other castes follow their own customary practices that resemble but are not identical with Brahmanical practices.

2. Thus, Hindu women are thought to embody *sakti* (energy/power) (Reynolds 1980) because they share their gendered anatomy with Devi, the Great Goddess of Hinduism. Embodying that energy and power does not, in and of itself, guarantee the ability to influence and exercise authority in socially and culturally meaningful ways. For that to happen, a woman has to refine her natural *sakti* into moral energy and power, *dharmik sakti*, through self-control and self-discipline, through surrendering her sense of self ("self" here implying "ego'), and through giving service to others (*seva*) (Menon 2002, 2013). Thus, for naturally powerful women to become truly potent and generative, they have to refine the *sakti* immanent in them through culturally prescribed actions—only then does it become intense, awesome, and overpowering.

3. Indigenous designations of "hot" and "cold" have less to do with the temperatures of the food and more to do with their ability to excite the senses. Thus, meat, fish, onions, and garlic are typically thought of as "hot" foods.

4. Thus, partaking in an aesthetic performance is supposed to be a holistic experience in which, ideally, all the senses are involved—seeing and hearing certainly, but also smelling, and perhaps even touching and tasting. Traditionally, performances are most often "open-air events, organized on the level ground, on a platform stage or as a mobile processional spectacle" (Awasthi 1974, 36). The distance between performers and audience is minimal—a closeness that is further heightened by the use of dramatic devices such as a performer being both a character and the narrator, and having performers address the audience directly or in asides. The skill of the performers is reflected in the way they are able to transform one space into many places and in their "nonrealistic and metaphysical use of time" (Awasthi 1974, 36). And finally, audience participation expressed in epithets and sounds of appreciation are integral elements of these performances—again, pointing to the interdependent and reciprocal nature of the performative events.

5. Food is essential for another reason: the mere ingestion of food stimulates the digestive fires, keeps them burning, and thereby maintains life. When digestive fires burn brightly, the person is healthy, when they burn low, the person is diseased, and when they go out, the person dies.

6. Hindu traditions have formulated an ideal life course for upper-caste men. This life course consists of four phases: *brahmacharya* or celibate student, *grihastha* or householder, *vanaprastha* or forest-dweller, and *sannyasa* or renouncer. In this scheme, the fully relational householder and the arelational renouncer are the more important phases, the celibate student being a preparatory phase training a young man to become a householder, and the forest-dweller phase being transitional phase marking the time between being in the world and outside it.

7. Soteriologically speaking, Hindus have available three possible paths to achieving *moksa* or liberation: *jnana marga* or the path of knowledge, *karma marga* or the path of work, and *bhakti marga* or the path of unswerving devotion.

References

Awasthi, Suresh. 1974. "The Scenography of the Traditional Theater in India." *Drama Review* 18 (4), 36–46.

De Bary, W. Theodore. 1958. *Sources of Indian Tradition*. New York: Columbia University Press.

Dimock, Edward C. 1974. *The Literatures of India, an Introduction*. Chicago: University of Chicago Press.

Dumont, Louis. 1965. "The Functional Equivalent of the Individual in Caste Society." *Contributions to Indian Sociology* 8: 85–99.

Eliot, T. S. 1950. "Hamlet and His Problems." In *Selected Essays*, 124–25. New York: Harcourt, Brace and World.

Flood, Gavin. 1996. *An Introduction to Hinduism*. Cambridge: Cambridge University Press.

Gnoli, Raniero. 1956. *The Aesthetic Experience According to Abhinavagupta*. Rome: Istituto Italiano per Il Medio ed Estremo Oriente.

Ingalls, David H. H. 1957. "Dharma and Moksa." *Philosophy East and West* 7 (1/2): 41–48.

Khare, Rajendra S. 1992. "Introduction." In *The Eternal Food: Gastronomic Ideas and Experiences of Hindus and Buddhists*, edited by Rajendra S. Khare, 1–27. Albany, NY: SUNY Press.

Kinsley, David. 1993. *Hinduism, a Cultural Account*. Upper Saddle River, NJ: Prentice Hall.

Klostermaier, Klaus. 2007. *Hinduism, a Beginner's Guide*. London: Oneworld.

Macaulay, Alastair. 2014. "Casting an Elaborate Rhythmic Spell." http://www.nytimes .com/2014/12/27/arts/kathakali-dance-in-india-with-the-locals.html.

Marriott, McKim. 1976. "Hindu Transactions: Diversity without Dualism." In *Transaction and Meaning: Directions in the Anthropology of Exchange and Symbolic Behavior*, edited by Brian Kapferer, 109–42. Philadelphia: Institute for the Study of Human Issues.

Menon, Usha. 2002. "Making *Sakti*: Controlling (Natural) Impurity for Female (Cultural) Power." *Ethos* 30 (2–3): 154–74.

———. 2010. "Dharma and Re-envisioning the Hindu Moral Code" in *Psychology and Psychoanalysis* (Vol XIII, Part 3), edited by Girishwar Misra, 877–913. Project of History of Indian Science, Philosophy and Culture. Delhi: Centre for Studies in Civilizations.

———. 2013. *Women, Wellbeing, and the Ethics of Domesticity in an Odia Hindu Temple Town*. New Delhi: Springer.

Monier-Williams, Monier. 2008. *English–Sanskrit Dictionary*, http://www.sanskrit-lexicon .uni-koeln.de/monier/.

Paranjpe, Anand. 2009. "In Defence of an Indian Approach to the Psychology of Emotion." *Psychological Studies* 54: 3–22.

Ramanujan, A. K. 1990. "Is There an Indian Way of Thinking?" In *India through Hindu Categories*, edited by McKim Marriott, 41–58. New Delhi: Sage.

Ray, Priyadaranjan, and Hirendra N. Gupta. 1965. *Caraka Samhita*. New Delhi: National Institute of Sciences.

Ray, Priyadaranjan, Hirendra N. Gupta, and Mira Roy. 1980. *Susruta Samhita*. New Delhi: Indian National Science Academy.

Reynolds, Holly 1980. "The Auspicious Married Woman." In *The Powers of Tamil Women*, edited by Susan S. Wadley, 35–60. Syracuse, NY: Maxwell School of Citizenship and Public Affairs.

Schechner, Richard C. 2003. *Performance Theory*. New York: Routledge.

Seneviratne, Herbert L. 1992. "Food Essence and the Essence of Experience." In *The Eternal Food: Gastronomic Ideas and Experiences of Hindus and Buddhists*, edited by Rajendra S. Khare, 179–200. Albany, NY: SUNY Press.

Shweder, Richard A. 1992. "The Cultural Psychology of the Emotions." In *Handbook of the Emotions*, edited by Michael Lewis and Jeannette Haviland, 417–31. New York: Guilford.

———. 1999. "Why Cultural Psychology?" *Ethos* 27 (1): 62–73.

Shweder, Richard A., Jacqueline Goodnow, Giyoo Hatano, Robert LeVine, Hazel Markus, and Peggy Miller. 1998. "The Cultural Psychology of Development: One Mind, Many Mentalities." In *Handbook of Child Psychology*, edited by William Damon and Richard Lerner, 716–92. Hoboken, NJ: Wiley.

Smith, Huston, and Philip Novak. 2003. *Buddhism: A Concise Introduction*. New York: HarperOne.

Thampi, G. B. Mohan. 1965. "'Rasa' as Aesthetic Experience." *Journal of Aesthetics and Art Criticism* 24 (1): 75–80.

Zaehner, Robert C. 1966. *Hinduism*. Oxford: Oxford University Press.

Section 2
Intersubjectivity: Social Trust, Interpersonal Attachment, and Agency

The Socialization of Social Trust: Cultural Pluralism in Understanding Attachment and Trust in Children

THOMAS S. WEISNER

University of California at Los Angeles
Departments of Psychiatry and Anthropology

Introduction: Social Trust and Attachment

Research at the intersection of culture and psychology brackets in the cultural learning environments of the communities and people we are studying (Edwards and Bloch 2010; Worthman 2010). It privileges the experiences, beliefs, practices, and goals that are alive in that social world. Of course, comparisons across cultural communities depend on the presumptions of human universals and a common human nature as well. Hence, common biological hardware, constrained variation in cultural ecologies and family systems, and diverse local communities all are relevant in the study of human development. Attachment systems provide an important example of the value of understanding these universal processes in cultural context. Attachment systems around the world have universal features, but with enormous diversity, not uniformity, in their contexts, practices, cultural meanings, and outcomes (Shweder, 2012).

The study of attachment in developmental science has typically been used to claim the universality of social orienting mechanisms, with powerful evolutionary antecedents. The claim is that at least some behavioral processes are similar across societies, and that the attachment system and outcomes are broadly similar as well. In their review chapter, for example, Mesman, van IJzendoorn, and Sagi-Schwartz (2016, 809) conclude that

the available cross-cultural studies have not refuted the bold conjectures of attachment theory about the universality of attachment, the normativity of secure attachment, the link between sensitive caregiving and attachment security, and the competent child outcomes of secure attachment. In fact, taken as a whole, the studies are remarkably consistent with the theory. Until further notice, attachment theory may therefore claim cross-cultural validity.

The measures used and conceptual framework for thinking about attachment have become standardized, and it is this literature using standard methods and designs that Mesman et al. review. (They do not review the extensive ethnographic literature describing attachment, caretaking, and security, for example.) This standardization, of course, can improve systematic comparative research. At the same time, however, reliance on exclusively standard measurement out of cultural context can lead to a false or overgeneralized conclusion that attachment beliefs, behaviors, and outcomes are highly similar across communities. Attachment research is an important field that includes universalism—both a universal mechanism (the attachment-sensitive period in children and the stress-buffering roles of privileged caretakers) and a likely universal developmental goal (security, safety, buffering of stress)—but where there is far less uniformity and far more diversity and pluralism than is claimed in most developmental research on these topics.

Mesman et al. (2016) make a strong claim for the universality of attachment theory and processes, yet at the same time strongly support and recognize the importance of cultural-contextual approaches to attachment: "Attachment theory without contextual components is as difficult to conceive of as attachment theory without a universalistic perspective" (808). They recognize the significance of multiple care and attachment figures, acknowledge variations in the applicability of constructs like "sensitive caregiving," recognize the variety of modalities through which caregiver responsiveness is expressed, and encourage more studies of the important influence of socioeconomic circumstances in particular. With regard to the limited number of diverse, cross-cultural samples, they see clearly that with respect to socioeconomic, ethnic, religious, and other variation around the world, "the current cross-cultural database is almost absurdly small compared to the domain that should be covered" (809). So the awareness of these issues is a part of the attachment research field, yet these concerns are not widely recognized or even admitted, and the implications not often appreciated or acted on in literature reviews, theory, research design, and sampling frames. Popular and journalist versions of "attachment parenting," attachment theory, and its clinical implications are even more remarkably unaware of these criticisms (for example, see Murphy 2017).

I will describe several lines of evidence and conceptualizations of children and developmental processes that challenge the conventional, universalistic understanding of attachment, further modify strong claims about the universality and cross-cultural validity of attachment theory and processes, and suggest ways to encourage pluralist and contextual research in this field. First, there does appear to be a sensitive period in development, with an onset around nine or ten months of age, when infants begin to show preference for their most frequent caregivers and avoid and show fear toward others. Certain caregivers are usually more preferred or privileged and can reduce child distress. The sensitive period for a positive emotional response to these most frequent caregivers, however, is not the only evolved mechanism children use to learn about safety and security in their environment and who can reduce distress. There are many such mechanisms, and children use them to capture social and cultural and linguistic information of all kinds. Children are prepared to seek information from the environment about what is safe, dangerous, and advantageous in that child's world in many ways, not only through the specific attachment-sensitive-period mechanism. Why, then, are all these learning mechanisms and the cultural learning environment around children they learn within, not fully included in understanding attachment?

Second, plural caretaking was likely favored in the past and is still today the favored form of care in most of the world. What would have been selected for in the environment of evolutionary adaptation: exclusive socioemotional attachment to the single maternal caretaker, or plural attachments to several caregivers that provided socially distributed care, attention, safety, and security? The selection for socially distributed multiple care is much more likely. Because of the high mortality and harsh, unpredictable, and variable environments that children and caregivers faced throughout our history and still face today, the likely alternative then and still today would be multiple, socially distributed, diverse care (Weisner 2005).

Third, although there clearly are universal processes at work during the attachment period, "all we can ever observe is the particular attachment behaviors that have been organized by what a particular culture expects from and gives to infants" (Gaskins 2013, 59). Greater use of mixed methods, integrating both these local and universal maturational models, should drive attention to local context and cultural diversity in attachment research (Weisner 2014). The methods used to describe, measure, and assess attachment nonetheless continue to be very narrowly defined. Making it a routine practice in research to place a child and caregivers into their local cultural ecology, and bracketing that context fully into the description and analysis of attachment and security, would put to empirical test conclusions of uniformity across the remarkably diverse contexts children are in. Local adaptation of standard measures also will add value to descriptions and measurement validity. Mixed methods arguably should be the default for a research program on attachment. Inclusion of diverse samples, and careful attention to cross-cultural evidence, should be as well.

Finally, there is an inevitable moral valence when using terms such as *secure attachment, sensitive parenting,* or *attuned caregiving and behaviors.* These labels (secure, sensitive, attuned), regardless of the reasons they may have been chosen in the past, are not appropriate, because their opposites inevitably end up being assigned to the non-Euro-American world or to those less educated and resource-advantaged within a country (LeVine and Miller 1990). How can it be justified to characterize individuals, families, and entire cultures and ethnic groups or social classes as insecure, insensitive, and unattuned, without careful attention to *why* caregivers and children are acting as they are and what their opportunities, constraints, and beliefs and goals are in their local environments and communities?

Evolution Prepared Children to Gather Information from the Environment Using Many Learning Mechanisms, Not Only the Attachment Response

The attachment response in infancy is a sensitive period in development, for parents and children alike. It is a mechanism ensuring the orientation of infants and young children to significant social others in their world. A key function of the attachment system is to *guide the child into social learning* through the special influence of their attachment figures, as well as regulating child stress. Consider, however, the nineteen other putative evolved mechanisms that lead to preparedness for the acquisition of social and cultural knowledge proposed by Melvin Konner (2010, 720, table 29.3), in his encyclopedic study of the evolution of childhood. He describes four broad categories of evolved learning, attentional, and emotional/motivational mechanisms in children, and the evolved capacities that are involved in the acquisition of culture. He calls them the cultural acquisition devices: *reactive processes in the cultural surround* (such as classical conditioning, or social facilitation due to reduced inhibition, or instrumental or intentional conditioning); *social learning* (such as scaffolding, mimicry, imitation, direct instruction); *emotional/affective learning processes* (attachment learning appears here, along with positive or negative identification, emotional management and learning through rituals and scripts); and *symbolic processes* (cognitive modeling, schema learning, narrative and thematic meaning systems). The behavioral expression of security and trust in relationships in community context are influenced by *all twenty of these*—including, but hardly limited to or dominated by, attachment processes. The attachment *system* is the unit for study, and it includes these multiple mechanisms and resources for psychobiological regulation and learning.

Hence evolution has ensured that children enculturate to the local world of their caregivers, families, and communities through multiple mechanisms in many different ways—not by relying exclusively or primarily on a single mechanism such as attachment responsiveness (Super and Harkness 1999). The emotional processes of attachment, seen as an evolved mechanism to recruit the child to orient to its primary caregivers, are in conversation with all the other mechanisms. How do all these learning processes form a choir in each local cultural community and in each family situation, a choir with many different songs and lyrics in many different and wonderful cultural idioms, all contributing to the goals and moral directions for life desired in that community, with various scripts for producing a secure and sufficiently trusting person? This surely is an understudied and undertheorized question in the field of attachment.

Attachment processes depend substantially on all these cultural acquisition device mechanisms. Yet how can it be that attachment, as but one of a putative twenty such evolved mechanisms for enculturation, is so disproportionately foregrounded, when so many other mechanisms certainly also have evolved to ensure social learning, stress regulation, and child survival in the context of social relationships? Furthermore, what evidence is there, since there are these nineteen other mechanisms, that early attachment-sensitive periods and child and caregiver preparedness would be uniquely efficacious, in comparison with all the others?

Human communities do not rely on just one of these twenty mechanisms over and above all the others for ensuring a sense of security and social relatedness, either in the development in individual psychological attachment or recognition of social group affiliation. Furthermore, many of these learning capacities come on line right around the same times in infancy and early childhood as the preference for familiar persons and the attachment system. Gaskins points out, for example, that the attachment system matures at about the same time as "locomotion, differentiation between familiar people and strangers, increased memory (including object permanence in the real world), and understanding and sharing attention and [the recognition of others' goals and] intentions" (Gaskins 2013, 58). There may well be an underlying, universal "interactional instinct" to affiliate with others in general, a propensity in infancy and early childhood to imitate and model others and seek out verbal as well as nonverbal cues (Joaquin and Schumann 2013).

It also is clearly untrue that cultural groups overwhelmingly respond to and emphasize the dyadic attachment relationship with a single caregiver over all other ways of socializing emotional security and stress reduction. The research question should rather be framed as, How do the many cultural acquisition devices interrelate to produce a sense of relational trust and security in children in diverse cultural learning environments around the world? As Carlson and Harwood (2014) put it in a recent chapter, "the precursors of healthy attachment relationships are not specific, individual behaviors on the part of isolated caregivers, but rather systems of supports that nurture the development of caregivers who are able to successfully protect and socialize their children" (27). As Johow and Voland (2014, 40) argued on the basis of their work on evolutionary anthropology, "If the child has to cope with varying conditions, then conditional development strategies that are able to react to the respective ecological conditions are superior to an inflexible behavior pattern."

Further, these local ecologies produce patterns of lower attention to infants and young children as well as increased attention. For instance, Lancy (2014) reviewed some two hundred ethnographic studies that described beliefs, practices, and ecologies around the world related to infant care and parenting. He described the ecological and other conditions that encourage many communities to maintain a degree of emotional distance from their young children, not necessarily continuous closeness: "Six factors emerged from the survey that militate against or temper the attention paid to infants. These are as follows: high infant mortality rate and chronic illness; the mother's vulnerability; alloparenting and fostering; dysfunctional families; neglect because the infant is unwanted or on probation; abandonment and infanticide; and a utilitarian view of offspring" (70). Hence not showing high degrees of "attuned" and "sensitive" behaviors (as defined by middle-class Western presumptions and associated measurement scales) would be appropriate parenting, because keeping some emotional distance fits with the local environment, parental beliefs, and/or mortality threats children and parents face.

Caregiving behaviors of course differ, sometimes dramatically, around the world (Broch 1990; Keller 2013; Quinn and Mageo 2013a). For example, some cultural communities want young children to show emotional and behavioral calmness and attentional focus when around kin other than their mother, and even around strangers, as Keller and Otto (2009) describe for the Nso in Cameroon. This pattern occurs widely in sub-Saharan Africa and elsewhere (LeVine et al. 1994). In many communities, caretakers are anticipating the likelihood of children becoming distressed, and the goal is to minimize the distress that the child shows by interacting with the child before overt stress is shown (by the child crying, for example), while in other communities the child shows distress first and then caretakers respond. Both are common patterns that are each believed in many communities to lead to the child's security, social competence, improved self-regulation and greater independence.

Cultural goals regarding the display of emotional expression thus vary widely. Children are encouraged to be calm among the Nso; to be socially active and accepting of many other people and caregivers among the Beng (Gottlieb 2004); quiet, respectful, and close to sibling caregivers among the Gusii (LeVine et al. 1994) and Abaluyia (Weisner 1997); lively and "vivace" among Italian families (Axia and Weisner 2002); displaying symbiotic harmony in relationships with anticipatory empathy and relational understanding of others in Japan (Rothbaum et al. 2000); encouraging shared care with multiple and deep emotional attachments to joint family households in North India (Seymour 1999, 2004); and displaying verbal, outgoing, responsive, "independent," and "exploratory" responsiveness (described as parental "concerted cultivation") for many US middle-class families (Lareau 2003). This means that good, appropriate parenting—attuned and sensitive parenting—is not attuned only to the child at hand focused on that child's moment-to-moment interactional needs. *Good, sensitive, security-enhancing parenting is attuned to the cultural expectations for emotional display, and the kind of person and life goals desired, as well as to the particular child at a given moment.*

Socially Distributed Care and Multiple Attachments

Socially distributed childcare and multiple attachments are common, in addition to or instead of monomatric dyadic care with a privileged secure base of a single caregiver. Socially distributed caregivers include siblings, cousins, aunts and grandparents, hired caretakers, and others, along with parents. Multiple caretaking emphasizes less intense affective and maternal ties in favor of relationship nets spread among many people. Learning how to get and give support in such relational networks is part of learning how to survive in often harsh, uncertain, and impoverished circumstances for children around the world today and certainly in the past.

Crittenden and Marlowe (2013, 72) point out that "flexibility in childcare patterning [alloparenting and multiple care] and subsistence behavior would permit a hominin mother to thrive in any ecological setting, a characteristic highlighting human behavioral diversity." To the extent that evidence from contemporary foraging societies allows reconstruction of past environments, "the pan-forager model of child care . . . involves a wide array of caregivers who routinely provide high-quality investment to infants and children" (73). A careful and detailed study of the Aka foragers in Cameroon, for example, revealed that children show attachment behaviors to multiple individuals in their close-knit community. Most children did not display strong reactions to their mothers' departure; and maternal sensitivity scores (measured by Aka mothers who scored as very responsive and sensitive to their infants) were not related to children's distress at departure. At the same time, children with more sensitive allomothers showed less fussing and crying during their mother's absence.

> Aka children . . . are integrated into the social fabric of Aka life from the moment of birth. It is more likely that multiple attachments form simultaneously rather than sequentially, as they do in Western populations, and children's expectations regarding who will care for and protect them is naturally more distributed. Thus, children's responses to separations and reunions will not fit Western models of child behavior. (Meehan and Hawks 2013, 108)

Sibling caretaking, a widespread feature of socially distributed care (Serpell, Sonnenschein, Baker, and Ganapathy 2002), is a very common context for understanding attachment, trust, and security for children throughout most of the world (Lancy 2014; Weisner 1996; Whiting and Edwards 1988). Sibling care promotes what Margaret Mead long ago called "pivot roles" in childhood, in which developmental pathways afford the child the roles of being taken care of and then becoming the caretaker of other children younger in age. This is an expectable and culturally valorized experience during development in many communities (Weisner and Gallimore 1977). Children learn all sides of receiving and providing nurturance, dominance, and responsibility tasks and roles while young. They recognize that the intimate attachments of caregiving can and will extend to non-care contexts and that such reciprocity is at the center of "socially distributed support" within a wide network of relationships. Children become adults with relational and attachment security different from, but no less socially competent and emotionally appropriate than, what might be a working model of a single-caregiver "secure base" that is then presumably generalized to others.

Many examples in the cross-cultural record show the connections between attachment security and socially distributed caretaking. For example, Gottlieb (2004; 2014) described the world of the Beng, in which strangers are not to be feared, and training across a wide range of social mechanisms is directed at the cultural goal of encouraging sociality and multiple caretaking, with the moral goal of valorizing community and extended kin ties. Religious beliefs, economic trade, and cultural history all influence why the Beng think about strangers, caregiving, and trust in these ways, and hence what secure attachment relations mean in their world.

Not only do multiple caregivers not place children at risk, they can offer advantages to the parent, child, and family, such as protecting against the consequences of maternal mortality or other health risks. For example, Gaskins recognizes the universal attachment processes from around nine to twelve months among the Yucatec Maya, but emphasizes the nonuniform expression of security and social trust. Gaskins (2013) summarizes the contrast between the presumption of single maternal dyadic care and the preponderance of multiple caretaking found around the world and in the West today: "by coming to place their trust in multiple people, they are more likely to generalize that the world is a benign and giving environment they should explore. . . . [and] with multiple partners, they have to develop a much more complex working model of social relations, since people's interactions with them are quite different based on personality, age, roles, status and so forth" (50).

Mageo also contrasts the cultural ideals of group care in Samoa and one-to-one bonding in the United States: "Samoans view secure group bonding and a willingness to serve elders as the ideal outcome of proper child rearing. In the middle-class Northwest [United States], a capacity for secure one-to-one bonding and a willingness to explore the environment are developmental ideals" (Mageo 2013, 209). These different cultural ideals regarding children's abilities direct widely varying practices around attachment. Mageo, like Lancy, also presents evidence on the widespread use of distancing practices by caregivers—such as ignoring children, explicitly pushing them away toward others, and physical or psychological punishment (in Samoa). In Mageo's view, a focus only on sensitivity, responsiveness, and providing succor and security is insufficient for understanding attachment in any community. She also points out that we have to study culturally organized attempts to detach, separate, punish, monitor negatively, criticize, and push away children through *detachment*.

The Murik are marine foragers in the mangrove regions of the Sepik River in Papua New Guinea, a complex and difficult ecology (Barlow 2013).

Understanding this cultural ecology is essential for understanding the meanings and practices surrounding culturally desirable forms of attachment, which include cultural goals of interdependence, respect for social and gender hierarchy and discipline, sibling caretaking, and the use of food as a reward:

> Murik child rearing develops and values both independence/autonomy and interdependence/identification with group(s). . . . The qualities of a "good" person are developed through cultural forms of discipline that shape attachment orientations. . . . For example, Murik punish sibling rivalry in older siblings in order to instill caregiving qualities that extend to all senior–junior relationships. . . . food and feeding are a crucial material basis for conveying and shaping the emotional commitments of attachment. Giving food expresses maternal caregiving, while going without food expresses feelings of separation and loss. . . . Attachment emotions and behaviors are differentiated by gender in cross-sex relationships and in romantic, marital ones. (Barlow 2013, 166–67)

The different cultural emphases given to goals of autonomy, interdependence, and dependence illustrated by these ethnographic studies of culturally organized attachment systems, the different ways stress is regulated (and by whom, particularly multiple caretakers), and different goals for organizing social learning are all recurring themes throughout cultural studies of attachment. All communities require some versions of autonomy, interdependence, and dependence, but the degree of cultural elaboration or suppression of one or another differs widely, as do the contexts, ages, genders, and other circumstances in which one or another is emphasized or required. Felt security and autonomy of the child, emerging out of a secure base from a dyadic relationship, is the presumptive universal outcome in conventional attachment theory, yet empirical studies abound with evidence of other attachment systems.

Nuckolls's chapter (in this volume), for example, points out the prevalence of duality and ambivalence in the emotional attachments to human and supernatural figures in his essay on religion: "Attachment theory suggests that humans develop opposed and competing tendencies, the one toward dependency and the other toward autonomy. . . . Ambivalence arises chiefly as a result of the developmentally natural assumption that childhood dependencies, formed in relation to primary caregivers, will continue forever" (see Nuckolls, this volume). Even using the standard attachment theory, the emotional experience of ambivalence (both wanting and not wanting something or someone) appears in religious beliefs, rather than a unitary independence and felt security.

Early language socialization in many communities also has a socio-centric pattern of practice and belief and a cultural goal that complements multiple caretaking systems. For example, Ochs and Izquierdo (2009) describe early socialization practices that orient the child outward toward others, in order to emphasize to children the importance of reading social cues and learning social responsibility. This is important for a child's sense of security and interactive competence, and a base for social trust. They describe communities (Matsigenka, in the Peruvian Amazon, and Samoa) in which socialization for "respectful awareness of and responsiveness to others' needs" and anticipation of the needs of others is learned early as a key component of emotional security and social belonging. In many African, Meso-American, and Pacific societies children learn at an early age their place in a complex social network, and adults orient the child to focus outward toward the community, not primarily to the parent, for how and when to respond appropriately and feel secure. Conversational skills, social positioning and referencing, attentional orienting, and prompting are key early sociolinguistic routines closely tied to sociocentric developmental training (Weisner 2011).

Finally, multiple caretaking itself depends on the fundamental and universal human cognitive ability to grasp the fact that others' minds are like our own—that is, the human capacity for intersubjective awareness of other minds and intentions, the capacity for joint attention, and engagement with others. Neither trust nor attachment nor sociality itself would exist, nor would any form of socially mediated attachment or sense of social security, absent these shared human social abilities. Hrdy (2009) proposes that this capacity for intersubjective awareness itself evolved along with joint care and alloparenting of offspring during human evolution. To share the care of children in a primate group, for example, requires this awareness. The mothers must have the capacity to grasp that the other mothers understand the nature of care and reciprocity, for example, just as the mother herself understands it. Hence it is likely that multiple attachments and shared caretaking evolved along with the capacity for intersubjective understanding. Security, as well as stress buffering (an important function of those privileged caretakers of a child), therefore, may have been achieved through sharing of childcare within a trusted social group, not primarily through dyadic attachment to a single primary caretaker. The adaptive advantage of ensuring security and trust may well have been multiple care-taking practices, not exclusive mother–child dyadic care.

Integrating Qualitative and Quantitative Methods in Attachment Research

Although cultural and ecological context clearly influence attachment processes and outcomes, measurement practices in the study of attachment remain remarkably narrow. The Strange Situation Procedure, the Q-Sort Attachment Interview, the Adult Attachment Interview, and similar measures are considered the gold standards for measurement. It is fair to say that absent these kinds of measures, or some newer equivalents, many would not say that "attachment security" had been measured at all. The ethnographic, fieldwork-based descriptions of attachment, caretaking, and managing child distress are very rich and provide essential new evidence (LeVine et al. 1994; Lancy 2008; Otto and Keller 2014; Quinn and Mageo 2013b). Incorporating these data into our evidence regarding attachment opens a marvelous additional source of understanding.

The world certainly is not linear or additive or decontextualized, though it sometimes can usefully be modeled as if it were (Weisner and Duncan 2014). For good *analytic* reasons, there can of course be scientific value in bracketing context out—to isolate specific behaviors in an experimental design to understand the attachment system, measured in an experiment or other structured interview, or questionnaire paradigm. But these analytic methods and research designs do not replace the importance of incorporating context. The items on the questionnaire or assessment procedures carry historical and contextual limitations in measurement. To then claim that the results can be interpreted absent equivalent scientific attention to diverse cultural contexts misses the value of the analytic approach and methods, which is to use systematic measures and designs, and then reinsert and interpret them in context.

In addition, social attachments to groups and to plural caregivers are unmeasured by scales that rely exclusively on individual dyadic psychological attachment measures. As David Lancy has pointed out from the ethnographic record, "social attachment, including attachment to collectives like the extended family and clan, is of far more importance in cultural models of human development than psychological attachment" (2014, 81). A widely shared goal in socialization beliefs described around the world is to ensure that children understand how to interpret and display appropriate *social trust* of others. Social trust requires the understanding of connections to kin and social groups, in addition to individual/dyadic attachments. These social group connections also deserve measurement in studies of the development of security and social trust.

The Valence and Moral Direction in Judgments of Attachment Security, Sensitive Caregiving, and Attuned Parenting

A number of authors who have examined the constructs of secure attachment in a wide range of other communities have directly critiqued the explicit moral or evaluative claim being made by arraying societies or mothers or children along a unilinear scale where the label "insecure" or "insensitive" (or avoidant or resistant or disorganized) or "not attuned to the child" anchors one end of the scale—especially where this is done without consideration of the threats, resources, and opportunities characterizing these communities and families (for discussions see, e.g., Gottlieb 2014; LeVine 2014; Quinn and Mageo 2013b; Scheper-Hughes 2014). Members of these communities have questioned this as well.

For instance, the exclusive use of unilineal scales to assess sensitivity and security is unjustified, absent rich contextual understanding of the contexts of care. Comparative assessments based on describing the ideal mother using standard questionnaire items about sensitive mothering are insufficient for capturing the nature and valence of parenting within the context of the world's diverse attachment systems. The concept of attunement, which is one of the components of secure-base attachment caretaking, is now recognized as only a part of a wide-ranging set of conditions that influence attachment—only one part of a nurturing ecocultural environment. Leaving aside chaotic or pathological circumstances (which surely are found in all communities and require additional assessment and appropriate intervention), attunement and sensitivity is a blend of contextually and behaviorally appropriate practices. And like measures claiming to assess children who are secure, scales claiming to assess sensitive or attuned caretaking include their unidimensional opposites: insecure or insensitive or not attuned, without putting such assessments into appropriate context. These terms classify communities that enjoy different ways of ensuring trust and social and emotional sensitivity as inherently lesser along whatever scales or assessment systems are used to define those other socialization patterns and the parents who follow them.

It is an instructive exercise, for example, to construct scales assessing interactional quality that are based on the desired characteristics of social and emotional interaction among mothers in a different cultural community (the Nso in Cameroon being one example) and then use both that scale and a Western scale to assess interactional "quality" or "sensitivity" (Yovsi, Kärtner, Keller, and Lohaus 2009). The German contrasting sample in the Yovsi et al. study has "low quality" interactions with young children using the Nso scale, for example, while the Nso are "lower in quality" using the Western scale. Actually, both communities have, on average, appropriate interactions that fit with their different scripts and goals, along with some components of the other caregiving script revealed in their interactions or questionnaire responses.

Similarly, attunement is not only an assessment at the scale of micro-interaction with an individual child. What kind of person a parent hopes to shape through caretaking their child, influences the behavioral patterns parents will be attuned to. Parents are attuned to their cultural learning environment, their family system (not only to that individual child at hand at a given moment), their cultural ecology and resources, and other circumstances that matter for sustaining their lives in their local community. There certainly are caregivers not as effectively attuned to this broader task as others in a cultural community, and differences in children's sense of social trust and cultural competence do result. The objection to the moral valence in the current terminology and assessment of security, attunement, or sensitivity in parenting is not that such evaluations cannot or should not be made between individuals, within a cultural group or across groups. It is that the contexts that matter for security, attunement, or sensitivity should be incorporated into such measurement descriptions and comparisons before, during, and after making them.

Conclusion

A sense of security and social trust is an important component of well-being, which cannot be only an individual assessment, but rather emerges from the engaged participation of a child in the cultural activities deemed desirable in that community, and the psychological experiences, including but not limited to the experience of stress reduction or security, produced by such participation. Whom should children trust and learn from, and how will they learn how to appropriately feel, show, and receive security, trust, and social competence? Diversity, not uniformity, in these socialization activities exists around the world. Incorporating this diversity into attachment theory, methods, and research designs will only improve our scientific understanding of attachment systems.

References

Axia, Vanna D., and Thomas S. Weisner. 2002. "Infant Stress Reactivity and Home Cultural Ecology of Italian Infants and Families." *Infant Behavior and Development* 25 (3): 255–68.

Barlow, Kathleen. 2013. "Attachment and Culture in Murik Society: Learning Autonomy and Interdependence through Kinship, Food, and Gender." In Quinn and Mageo, *Attachment Reconsidered*, 165–88.

Broch, Harald B. 1990. *Growing Up Agreeably: Bonerate Childhood Observed*. Honolulu: University of Hawaii Press.

Carlson, Vivian J., and Robin L. Harwood. 2014. "The Precursors of Attachment Security: Behavioral Systems and Culture." In Otto and Keller, *Different Faces of Attachment*, 278–303.

Crittenden, Alyssa N., and Frank Marlowe. 2013. "Cooperative Childcare among the Hadza: Situating Multiple Attachment in an Evolutionary Context." In Quinn and Mageo, *Attachment Reconsidered*, 67–84.

Edwards, Carolyn P., and Marianne Bloch. 2010. "The Whitings' Concepts of Culture and How They Have Fared in Contemporary Psychology and Anthropology." *Journal of Cross-Cultural Psychology* 41 (4): 485–98.

Gaskins, Suzanne. 2013. "The Puzzle of Attachment: Unscrambling Maturational and Cultural Contributions to the Development of Early Emotional Bonds." In Quinn and Mageo, *Attachment Reconsidered*, 33–64.

Gottlieb, Alma. 2004. *The Afterlife Is Where We Come From: The Culture of Infancy in West Africa*. Chicago: University of Chicago Press.

———. 2014. "Is It Time to Detach from Attachment Theory? Perspectives from the West African Rain Forest." In Otto and Keller, *Different Faces of Attachment*, 187–214.

Hrdy, Sarah B. 2009. *Mothers and Others: The Evolutionary Origins of Mutual Understanding*. Cambridge, MA: Harvard University Press.

Joaquin, Anna Dina L., and John H. Schumann, eds. 2013. *Exploring the Interactional Instinct (Foundations of Human Interaction)*. New York: Oxford University Press.

Johow, Johannes, and Eckart Voland. 2014. "Family Relations among Cooperative Breeders: Challenges and Offerings to Attachment Theory from Evolutionary Anthropology." In Otto and Keller, *Different Faces of Attachment*, 27–49.

Keller, Heidi. 2013. "Attachment and Culture." *Journal of Cross-Cultural Psychology* 44 (2): 175–94.

Keller, Heidi, and Hiltrud Otto. 2009. "The Cultural Socialization of Emotion Regulation during Infancy." *Journal of Cross-Cultural Psychology* 40 (6): 996–1011.

Konner, Melvin. 2010. *The Evolution of Childhood: Relationships, Emotion and Mind*. Cambridge, MA: Belknap.

Lancy, David F. 2008. *The Anthropology of Childhood: Cherubs, Chattel, Changelings*. Cambridge, MA: Cambridge University Press.

———. 2014. "'Babies Aren't Persons': A Survey of Delayed Personhood." In Otto and Keller, *Different Faces of Attachment*, 66–111.

Lareau, Annette. 2003. *Unequal Childhoods: Class, Race, and Family Life*. Berkeley: University of California Press.

LeVine, Robert A. 2014. "Attachment Theory as Cultural Ideology." In Otto and Keller, *Different Faces of Attachment*, 50–65.

LeVine, Robert A., Suzanne Dixon, Sarah Levine, Amy Richman, P. Herbert Leiderman, and Constance Keefer. 1994. *Child Care and Culture: Lessons from Africa*. Cambridge: Cambridge University Press.

LeVine, Robert A., and Patrice Miller. 1990. "Commentary on Special Topic Issue: Cross-Cultural Validity of Attachment Theory." *Human Development* 33: 73–80.

Mageo, Jeannette M. 2013. "Toward a Cultural Psychodynamics of Attachment: Samoa and US Comparisons." In Quinn and Mageo, *Attachment Reconsidered*, 191–214.

Meehan, Courtney L., and Sean Hawks. 2013. "Cooperative Breeding and Attachment among the Aka Foragers." In Quinn and Mageo, *Attachment Reconsidered*, 85–113.

Mesman, Judi, Marinus van IJzendoorn, Kazuko Behrens, Olga Alicia Carbonell, Rodrigo Cárcamo, Inbar Cohen-Paraira, Christian de la Harpe, and Hatice Ekmekci. 2015. "Is the Ideal Mother a Sensitive Mother? Beliefs about Early Childhood Parenting in Mothers across the Globe." *International Journal of Behavioral Development*. jbd.sagepub.com/content/early/2015/7/13/0165025415594030.

Mesman, Judi, Marinus H. van IJzendoorn, and A. Sagi-Schwartz. 2016. "Cross-Cultural Patterns of Attachment: Universal and Contextual Dimensions." In *Handbook of Attachment*, edited by Jude Cassidy and Philip Shaver, 790–815. New York: Guilford.

Murphy, Kate. 2017. "Yes, It's Your Parent's Fault," *New York Times*, January 7.

Ochs, Elinor, and Carolina Izquierdo. 2009. "Responsibility in Childhood: Three Developmental Trajectories." *Ethos* 37 (4): 391–413.

Otto, Hiltrud, and Heidi Keller. 2014. *Different Faces of Attachment: Cultural Variations on a Universal Human Need*. Cambridge: Cambridge University Press.

Quinn, Naomi, and Jeannette Mageo. 2013a. "Attachment and Culture: An Introduction." In Quinn and Mageo, *Attachment Reconsidered*, 3–32.

Quinn, Naomi, and Jeannette Mageo, eds. 2013b. *Attachment Reconsidered: Cultural Perspectives on a Western Theory*. New York: Palgrave Macmillan.

Rothbaum, Fred, Martha Pott, Hiroshi Azuma, Kazuo Miyake, and John Weisz. 2000. "The Development of Close Relationships in Japan and the United States: Paths of Symbiotic Harmony and Generative Tension." *Child Development* 71 (5): 1121–42.

Scheper-Hughes, Nancy. 2014. "Family Life as Bricolage–Reflections on Intimacy and Attachment in Death without Weeping." In Otto and Keller, *Different Faces of Attachment*, 230–62.

Serpell, Robert, Susan Sonnenschein, Linda Baker, and Hemlatha Ganapathy. 2002. "Intimate Culture of Families in the Early Socialization of Literacy." *Journal of Family Psychology* 16 (4), 391–405.

Seymour, Susan. 1999. *Women, Family, and Child Care in India: A World in Transition*. Cambridge: Cambridge University Press.

———. 2004. "Multiple Caretaking of Infants and Young Children: An Area in Critical Need of a Feminist Psychological Anthropology." *Ethos* 32 (4): 538–56.

Shweder, Richard A. 2012. "Relativism and Universalism." In *A Companion to Moral Anthropology*, edited by Didier Fassin, 85–102. New York: Wiley.

Super, Charles M., and Susan Harkness. 1999. "The Environment as Culture in Developmental Research." In *Measuring Environment across the Life Span: Emerging Methods and Concepts*, edited by Sarah L. Friedman and Theodore D. Wachs, 279–323. Washington, DC: American Psychological Association.

Weisner, Thomas S. 1996. "The 5–7 Transition as an Ecocultural Project." In *The Five to Seven Year Shift: The Age of Reason and Responsibility*, edited by Arnold J. Sameroff and Marshall M. Haith, 295–326. Chicago: University of Chicago Press.

———. 1997. "Support for Children and the African Family Crisis." In *African Families and the Crisis of Social Change,* edited by Thomas S. Weisner, Candice Bradley, and Philip L. Kilbride, 20–44. Westport, CT: Greenwood Press/Bergin and Garvey.

———. 2005. "Attachment as a Cultural and Ecological Problem with Pluralistic Solutions." *Human Development* 48 (1–2): 89–94.

———. 2011. "Culture." In *Social Development: Relationships in Infancy, Childhood and Adolescence, edited by* Marion K. Underwood and Lisa H. Rosen, 372–99. New York: Guilford.

———. 2014. "Why Qualitative and Ethnographic Methods Are Essential for Understanding Family Life." In *Emerging Methods in Family Research,* edited by Susan McHale, Paul Amato, and Alan Booth, 163–78. Dordrecht, Switz.: Springer.

Weisner, Thomas S., and Greg Duncan. 2014. "The World Isn't Linear or Additive or Decontextualized: Pluralism and Mixed Methods in Understanding the Effects of Anti-Poverty Programs on Children and Parenting." In *Societal Contexts of Child Development: Pathways of Influence and Implications for Practice and Policy,* edited by Elizabeth T. Gershoff, Rashmita S. Mistry, and Danielle A. Crosby, 124–38. New York: Oxford University Press.

Weisner, Thomas S., and Ronald Gallimore. 1977. "My Brother's Keeper: Child and Sibling Caretaking." *Current Anthropology* 18: 169–90.

Whiting, Beatrice, and Carolyn Edwards. 1988. *Children of Different Worlds: The Formation of Social Behavior.* Cambridge, MA: Harvard University Press.

Worthman, Carol M. 2010. "The Ecology of Human Development: Evolving Models for Cultural Psychology." *Journal of Cross-Cultural Psychology* 41 (4): 546–62.

Yovsi, Relindis D., Joscha Kärtner, Heidi Keller, and Arnold Lohaus. 2009. "Maternal Interactional Quality in Two Cultural Environments: German Middle Class and Cameroonian Rural Mothers." *Journal of Cross-Cultural Psychology* 40 (4): 701–7.

NINE

An Attachment-Theoretical Approach to Religious Cognition

CHARLES W. NUCKOLLS

Brigham Young University
Department of Anthropology

A variation on the theme of universalism is the question of where religious concepts come from. The "naturalness of religion" hypothesis, developed by Pascal Boyer and his colleagues, asserts that agency is part of a "security motivation system" (Boyer 2001; Boyer and Liénard 2006; Sørensen, Liénard, and Feeny 2006). It is a fundamental human adaptation to the detection of prey and predators. "Agents," in this view, become significant first and foremost as sources of opportunity or danger, and from this Boyer constructs a theory of religious representations that depends on the natural human tendency to detect agency. The superhuman entities universally posited by religion emerge from a psychologically inherent agency detection system that all humans share, and that, for reasons not entirely understood, detects agency even where there is none. The system is therefore said to be "hyperactive." Agency detection and the religious representations it gives rise to are products of evolutionary development; it is for this reason that Boyer calls his proposal the "naturalness of religion" hypothesis (Boyer 1994, 2001).

Gods and spirits can be (and often have been) perceived as predators that provoke fear and anxiety. Barrett (2004) describes the operation of "hyperactive agent detection" thus:

> Our evolutionary heritage is that of organisms that must deal with both predators and prey. In either situation, it is far more advantageous to overdetect agency than to underdetect it. The expense of false positives (seeing agents where there are none) is minimal, if we can abandon these misguided

intuitions quickly. In contrast, the cost of not detecting agents when they are actually around (either predator or prey), could be very high. (144)

But gods and spirits also can be seen as invisible partners with whom one can seek refuge, communicate, and exchange goods (Boyer 2001, 146– 50). What is distinctive is the fact that the communication with invisible partners is decoupled from the external social exchange and thus offers a space for learning both social and self-reflective skills against a stable background, constituted by the relation to the Invisible Other (2001, 149). In other words, the pervasiveness and persistence of notions of a personal God can be explained by the naturalness of the mental model of agency detection, which is operative below the threshold of reflection.

Although the Boyer hypothesis may be correct, the detection of agency is not, I shall argue, wholly concerned with primitive survival but with locating and relating to sources of emotional engagement, the most important survival "tool" for human beings because of the lengthy course of child development. *This is what children are primed to do, and that is what agency detection is for.* Agency detection, in other words, is an enabling device whose purpose is to create and maintain what Bowlby (1969, 1973, 1983) called "attachment." If the cognitive theory of religion proposed by Boyer depends on the detection of agency, then the kind of agency at issue is strongly implicated in (and may, indeed, be identical with) the development of emotional attachment. Cognitive theorists, however, generally neglect the relevance of attachment theory to the development of religion. This is not surprising. Psychodynamic perspectives are, for methodological reasons (e.g., Grunbaum 1984; Kazdin 1992) not well integrated within cognitive psychology.

This chapter will examine the nature of attachment, not as a supplement to, but as a core component of the cognitive theory of agency detection and religious representations. It will be shown that the agency/attachment system is a developmental process, shaped by the circumstances of human evolution (Bowlby 1969; Kirkpatrick 2005) but also subject to cultural variation, as Weisner (this volume) and others argue (Carlson and Hardwood 2014; Meehan and Hawks, 2014). It will be suggested that human attachment inevitably creates internal contradictions. These, I claim, are defining aspects of attachment itself, and to the extent attachment informs the representation of religious concepts, emotional oppositions are basic to religious representations of superhuman agencies.

Chief among these contradictions is the opposition between "dependence" and "independence"—the inevitable developmental opposition, as Millon and Davis (1994) point out, between the identification of others as opposed to the self as the primary source of emotional reinforcement. This opposition is "natural" but also irresolvable, and it therefore exists as a permanent source of tension in the human attachment system (see Nuckolls 1998; Strack 1999). The dynamics of unresolvable attachment goals have important implications for how we understand representations called "supernatural" or "divine."

My analysis suggests that intuitive ontologies, of the sort Boyer describes, become salient mainly insofar as they are implicated in the agency/attachment system. Their violation achieves memorability and transmissibility by virtue of their ability to refer or relate to fundamental oppositions in achieving or maintaining attachment. Just as Berlin and Kay ([1969] 1991) did not account for the salience of color categories by reducing them to so-called "basic" terms, so also Boyer does not account for construction of superhuman agencies by reducing their salience to basic ontological categories of perception and their violation. I do not deny that such violations play a role in category construction and mnemonic salience. Without considering the emotional correlates of this process, however, the Boyer hypothesis remains incomplete, reducing the development of religious categories to motivations born of the simple need to survive in a world of predators, or what Boyer and Liénard designate (in all capital letters) the "Potential Hazard Repertoire" (Boyer and Liénard 2006: 7).

Boyer and the Naturalness of Religion Hypothesis

The theory of mind Boyer posits consists of various component systems, such as "agency detection" and "contagion avoidance," whose adaptive significance follows from their role in survival and reproduction in a world of predators and prey. The easy plausibility of this argument springs from the special bias inherent in the Western normative view of the human condition, to wit, that humans live in a brutish predicament of nature and must develop strategic coping mechanisms or they will be killed. There is nothing novel here, of course. One finds it in the pages of *The Leviathan*. The problem arises when we reduce the development of cultural categories to crude survival algorithms, as if the human evolution were to be understood as a quest not to be eaten.

Even if Boyer is correct in reducing the postulation of superhuman agencies to primitive systems of survival, how many such systems are there? There are, or appear to be, as many systems as there need to be. In other words, Boyer's hypothesis proceeds by identifying the characteristics of religious intuitions and then positing a cognitive mechanism to generate it. Usually Boyer ends up naming these mechanisms and putting them in capital letters, endowing them with a thinglike status they would otherwise lack. Thus we are presented with a (potentially unlimited) number of "just-so" stories held together by speculations on their adaptive significance, construed in extremely narrow terms. One recalls the heyday of Wilsonian sociobiology, and the rush to explain everything—from the European handshake to Aztec ritual murder—as evolutionary adaptations of one sort or another. Masters's critique of behaviorist psychologists and their assertions about undifferentiated drives applies here, too (Masters 1989a, 1989b). To be sure, cognitivists do not speak of "drives," but in all but name the innate propensities they call "intuitive ontologies" function in the same way that drives were said to function. Usually this sort of theory building turns out to be anything but parsimonious.

Consider, for example, Boyer's explanation of spirits and ancestors. In his view, "spirits and ancestors would be seen by some as plausibly real because thoughts about them activate 'theory of mind' systems and agency-detection and contagion-avoidance and social exchange, etc." (2001, 3). For those who are counting, that is four systems, even before you get to the "etc." Boyer concludes that it would be futile to look for the single factor that causes religious belief: "the very fact that several systems are active is what causes 'belief'" (2001: 3–4). This is an assertion, however, not a theory, and there are three problems with it.

First, the fact that no single system is sufficient to "cause" belief means that the theory never has to put all its eggs in one basket. One sees the same rhetorical flavor in Konner's postulation of no less than twenty so-called "cultural acquisition devices" (Konner 2010, 720). Should one "system" be shown weak or insufficient, one is free to shift to others in an additive process that knows no end and possesses no constraints on the number of "just-so" stories it is free to invent. All we know is that the more the better, because, Boyer asserts (without evidence) that the number of systems activated is crucial to the generation of "belief." There is an irony here. Cognitivists typically dismiss Freud and psychoanalysis because of the reliance on clinical case studies, with their unverified assumptions about various generative mechanisms (id, ego, superego, etc.) in the unconscious. Boyer, however, has done exactly the same thing, with a theory of mind chock full of "devices," or what Lorenz (2007), in another context, called a "parliament of instincts," one for each purpose Boyer deems necessary to account for religious behavior.

Second, even if the number of systems activated is important, we do not know why particular systems seem to group themselves as they do. What is it about agency and social exchange that unites them, in most instances, in the constitution of belief? The proliferative (i.e., one thing on top of another) explanation Boyer posits is weak because it fails to pull these together according to a comprehensive logic. Boyer tells us that no single factor is sufficient, and that permits him to add to the pile without betting the whole game on any one factor. But this is a rhetorical convenience, not a theory, because there is no theoretical justification for the assumption that mental representations require numerous and unique processing systems. What if there *were* a unifying logic that would help us make sense, not just of the fact that there are many systems, but that only certain systems are critical?

The third problem is that of the indeterminacy of the agent (Pyysiäinen 2001) or what Atran (2002) and Tremlin (2006) call the "Mickey Mouse Problem." The problem is that there is no reason to attribute the properties Boyer describes exclusively to *religiously* postulated superhuman agents. In fact, the action system he describes and whose violations he says critically underpin the gods could just as easily be attributed to Mickey Mouse or domestic pets as to deities. My golden retriever, for example, possesses the minimally counterintuitive property of extrasensory perception—or so it always seems to me. Why does that not qualify as a religious proposition? Why are pet retrievers and Mickey Mouse not gods, at least for most people? As Tremlin points out, "Why do only certain counterintuitive representations provoke intense personal commitment and wind up the focus of psychologically and economically costly religious thought and practice?" (2006, 121–22). The fact is that they could, at least within Boyer's framework—a point that McCauley and Lawson were apparently driven to recognize in their frank acknowledgment that their work on religion might not be about religion at all. Consider this astounding disclaimer:

> On this view cheering at football games or marching at May Day is just as much a religious ritual as is sacrificing pigs to the ancestors. Perhaps this is so. In that case what we have, then, may not be a theory of religious ritual. Instead, it is only a theory about actions that individuals and groups perform within organized communities of people who possess conceptual schemes that include presuppositions about those actions' connections with the actions of agents who exhibit various counter-intuitive properties. (2002, 9)

Of course McCauley and Lawson, like other committed cognitivists, would like to preserve the claim that they are talking about religion. But they are prepared to "concede" that their theory might be even more important than that. Such modesty! But does not such a concession vitiate the theory of specific applicability, and empty the category of "religion" of distinctive features?

These are important difficulties. They can be solved by rendering cognitivist theory accessible to insight from the psychoanalytic study of the emotions. The problem of the emotions in the cognitivist construction of religion is acknowledged, here and there, by a few of those who define the cognitivist project (Pyysiäinen 2001; Tremlin 2006). It is a problem because even the most stridently cognitivist account is driven to acknowledge the existence of emotions and the fact that they appear to play some role in forming and maintaining religious beliefs. A theory that actually integrates them is yet to emerge. Like Tremlin (2006), we can conjure up the vaguely defined "limbic system" (the so-called "emotional brain") and assert that neurological mechanisms will be found to explain the most obviously emotional states associated with religion—mystical experiences and the like. But this is no more than an uncertain hope—an act of faith, even—and cannot be considered a satisfactory substitute for an empirically grounded hypothesis. As Kotter (2003) points out, the "limbic system" is too vague to serve as a scientific explanation or even a useful heuristic (see also Kotter and Stephan 1997). The cognitivist account cannot be said to have incorporated "the emotions" simply by invoking the semimystical properties of limbic brain structures (Isaacson 1992). Simply put, the cognitivist account promises more than it can deliver and constantly puts off to the future the day of reckoning when it must either integrate emotional dynamics or limit itself to the study of something no one in the real world would define as "religion."

Still, Boyer could be right in identifying agency detection as a primary cognitive skill humans possess from early infancy. But then, why should it be so? The cognitivists adopt the view that humans are social, and, in order to survive, must vigilantly scan the environment for intentional agents. My response does not so much challenge the instrumentalist view as to greatly expand it, because the most significant intentional agents are those to whom the child develops an attachment relationship. In other words, it is the *quality* of the agency and its internal dynamics—*not agency itself*—that is the determining factor. By "quality" I refer specifically to emotional attachment (Frye 1991). Here is the *place de rapprochement* we have been seeking: a place where cognitivist and attachment theoretical approaches can meet and mingle.

What Is Attachment Theory?

The theory is well known. Bowlby (1988) defined attachment as "any form of behavior that results in a person attaining or maintaining proximity to some other clearly identified individual who is conceived of as better able to cope with the world" (39). Given the opportunity, all normal human infants become attached to their primary caregivers, typically within the first eight months of life. In a series of experiments, Bowlby showed that attachment behavior emerges most strikingly "whenever the person is frightened, fatigued or sick, and is assuaged by comforting and caregiving" (Bowlby 1988 26–27). The existence of attachment, therefore, is revealed when the attachment figure is removed or otherwise unavailable.

Bowlby concluded that attachment to a primary caregiver (usually the mother) is essential when he observed that separation anxiety diminishes with the return of the attachment figure. Continued absence, however, could cause the development of character abnormalities and behavior problems. For example, the loss of the mother before age eleven predicts much greater vulnerability to depression than does the loss of the father. Likewise, Freeny and Noller (1990) discovered that avoidant adolescents—those diagnosed, that is, with the persistent tendency to avoid close social relationships—were more likely than secure adolescents to report childhood separations from their mothers.

On the basis of these, and similar, observations, attachment theory (e.g., Bowlby 1969, 1973, 1983; Bretherton 1985; Sroufe and Fleeson 1986) postulates that mental representations of self and others emerge from early relationships with caregivers. Representations act as schemata, templates, or heuristic guides. The structure and content of these cognitive-affective schemata influence (but do not wholly determine) expectations and feelings that characterize people's interpersonal relationships (Diamond and Blatt 1994; Hazen and Shaver 1994; Slade and Aber 1992) and they appear relatively stable over time (Elicker, Englund, and Sroufe 1992; Hazen and Shaver 1994; Main, Kaplan, and Cassidy 1985; Waters, Kondo-Ikemura, Posada, and Richters 1991).

Attachment and Human Evolution

Boyer and other cognitivists (e.g., Whitehouse 2000), however, generally neglect the relevance of attachment to the development of religion. To ground the cognitive theory of religious representations in evolutionary development, postulating a variety of predator-avoidance mechanisms, is not sufficient to account for our peculiar attentiveness to matters of agency. Attachment theory is needed, and the fact that it enjoys robust support from evolutionary theory should recommend it to Boyer and Whitehouse. Here are the reasons why. The first is what Simpson and Belsky (2008) call synchronized capabilities. Postpartum reactions of mothers appear to operate in a kind of psychosocial harmony with those of their newborn infants, facilitating the creation of mother–infant bonds. Systems that operate in this kind of synchronous fashion are often telltale signs of evolved adaptations.

Second, young children behave in ways that promote proximity between themselves and their attachment figures. Signaling (e.g., smiling), aversive behaviors (crying, screaming), and active behaviors (approaching, following) all serve the same function—to keep vulnerable infants in close proximity to their caregivers. In evolutionary terms, this makes sense, because death prior to reproduction is the first major threat to inclusive fitness, and the best way to avoid death is to maintain attachment to caregivers.

Third, selection pressures appear to have shaped the constitution of different phases of attachment, from the earliest period to adolescence. In the early phases, children exhibit strong preferences for one attachment figure, usually the mother, whose care and maintenance are crucial to infant survival. In evolutionary terms, this is what we would expect, because infants and mothers who forge stronger emotional bonds should, on average, have higher reproductive fitness. Later, children begin to see the world from the point of view of a wider array of interaction partners, and this permits them to incorporate the plans and desires of others into their decision making. Early in adolescence, overt manifestations of attachment with parents begin to diminish (Hinde 1976), and the principle functions of attachment are transferred from parents to peers and romantic partners as adolescents enter adulthood (Hazen and Shaver 1994). All these capabilities were most likely shaped by selection pressures, as Simpson and Belsky conclude:

> Infants (and mothers) who forged stronger emotion bonds should, on average, have had higher reproductive fitness. Young children who were motivated to maintain closer contact to their parents (and parents who encourages such tendencies) should have experienced better fitness. And individuals who successfully moved through each attachment stage and were able to "transfer" critical attachment functions from their parents to adult romantic partners should have experienced superior fitness. (2008, 135)

Naturally there are variations in attachment patterns that depend on social and ecological circumstances, just as Bowlby (1969) and Ainsworth,

Blehar, Waters, and Wall (1978) suggested. (See also Buss 1995; Cosmides and Tooby 1995, 1996.) The adaptive significance of attachment, however, has been accepted in evolutionary psychology, with important implications (one would think) for the development of religious constructs.

"Independence" and "Dependence" as Attachment Orientations

What I am calling "dependence" is the natural emotional correlate of early attachment, but as Margaret Mahler points out, all humans must eventually develop some degree of independence, if for no other reason than that primary attachment figures are no longer available as much or in the same form as they were in a child's infancy (Mahler 1979; see also Mahler 1968; Mahler, Pine, and Bergman 1975). But dependence desires continue because they are based on the attachment template formed in early childhood. Attachment involves the play of these opposing forces, as human beings seek to balance the desire for dependence and the desire for independence. For our purposes, the significance of this view is that it frames attachment as a dynamic relationship between motivational opposites, with consequences for all kinds of cultural constructs, including religion.

Most of the research to date strengthens the view that human development involves, as Shor and Sanville put it, "a dialectical spiral or helix which interweaves these two dimensions of development" (1978, 101). Much earlier, Adler (1956) talked about the balance between social interest and self-perfection and defined neurosis as the consequence of a distorted overemphasis on self-enhancement in the absence of sufficient social interest. And Freud himself pointed to the same tendencies, observing, in *Civilization and Its Discontents*, that "the development of the individual seems . . . to be a product of the interaction of two urges, the urge toward happiness, which we usually call "egoistic," and the urge toward union with others in the community, which we call "altruistic'" (Freud 1964, 140).

Like all dialectics, however, the relationship between dependence and independence is paradoxical, because it depends for its maintenance on two highly motivating but contradictory desires: the desires for independence and dependence (Nuckolls 1998). The term I use to describe this is "deep paradox." It refers to the universally cognizable repertoire of motivational contradictions that arise, naturally and inevitably, in the circumstances of normal human development. It therefore bears a resemblance to a stage in Piaget and Inhelder's (1969) theory of psychological development, wherein the balance between assimilation and accommodation breaks down under the weight of contradiction and is replaced by a new structure that resolves the contradiction, at least temporarily.

The Piagetian view, however, does not assume that the contradictions of earlier stages continue to be motivating. If they do, then they might employ the resources available to them in Boyer's supernatural imagination, finding representation through the domain assumptions of intuitive ontological concepts. To speculate: It might be the case that stages in the development of attachment succeed each other, just as Bowlby suggested, but it also might be the case, as Piaget and Inhelder (1969, 1973) showed, that developmental succession is prompted by the appearance of contradiction. A new developmental stage, however, does not resolve the contradiction that gives rise to it. In fact, the contradictions remain as resources out of which concepts and knowledge systems can be created. These could be thought of as a "repertoire of paradox." Developmental contradictions arise in the vicissitudes of attachment, and they continue to be available, much like perceptual categories, to be used when certain kinds of knowledge structures are developed.

Ontological Assumptions as Enabling Devices

What Boyer (2001) refers to as attention-grabbing phenomena, I believe, enable representation of deep paradox through ontological categories of perception. The paradox in this case is the opposition between basic attachment orientations, the one geared to dependence and the other to independence. In other words, the irresolvable contradiction at the core of human attachment contains, within itself, fundamentally counterintuitive expectations. One of these is the expectation that childhood dependencies will continue forever, in a condition in which full and complete attachment to a primary caregiver never changes or diminishes. The other is the expectation that personal autonomy—the "core self" as Pyysiäinen (2001) calls it—will develop as the experience of selfhood.

Although it is true that superhuman agencies systematically violate intuitive ontological assumptions—this point can be conceded—believers generally exhibit remarkably little interest in these characteristics. In Hindu South India, goddesses known in Telugu as *ammavallu* or "mothers" possess the ability to move objects at a distance, pass through solid objects, and variously manifest themselves as animals or human beings. One must elicit these characteristics from informants, however; they do not typically volunteer them, nor do they expound on them at any length, unless pressed by the foreign observer. The attitude is one of bored acknowledgment. On the other hand, when the conversation turns to the emotional qualities of the relationship between goddesses and believers, people become more animated. The goddesses are variously described as angry and vindictive, loving and nurturing. All these—both the negative and the positive—function as terms of endearment, because they refer to the emotional qualities of attachment—the attachment between superhuman agencies and adherents, with its basis in the contradictory and changing circumstances of childhood.

There are different ways to argue this point. One is to suggest that superhuman agents are reflections of early attachment relationships, so that, for example, the typically binary images of Hindu goddesses is explained as a result of split images of the Hindu mother (Nuckolls 1996). This point has been argued by Kakar (1981) and also by Kurtz (1993), Obeyesekere (1990), and Roland (1988). It is "natural" because mothering in South Asia is generally provided by many female caretakers, not just one, and because the mother herself (or, rather, her image in the mind of a child) is split between benevolent and malevolent halves. Thus one gets not just many goddesses, but forms of the same goddess that are nurturant and caring, on the one hand, and angry and rejecting, on the other (see Nuckolls 1996). Another possibility, suggested, indirectly, by Pyysiäinen (2001), is that Hindu goddesses become memorable by virtue of their intuition violations, but the relevant intuitions are emotional, not perceptual. The most "natural" emotional assumption, as it were, is that early childhood attachment, principally to the mother, will continue forever. This assumption is always violated in practice, however. One would not wish to suggest that autonomy is everywhere and always an ideal. Shweder has argued repeatedly that it is not. And as Markus and Kitayama (1991) have shown, collectivist cultures, like Japan, do not see individuation from the mother as necessarily leading to adult independence. On the contrary, the ideal is more often realized through transference and substitution, as Kurtz (1992) argued with reference to Hindu India, where extended kin relations (especially the mother's sisters) become nurturing others.

There is experimental evidence to support the contention that ambivalence about attachment plays a key role in religious experience. In a well-known study by Kirkpatrick and Shaver (1992), the authors investigated the contention that an individual's experience of a personal relationship with God functions in a way similar to a human relationship and can be considered an attachment. They hypothesized that from an attachment perspective, God (as a superior being) will act as a secure base for the believer. Kirkpatrick and Shaver found that participants with secure attachments perceived God as more loving, less controlling, and less distant than those with insecure attachment. They also scored highest on level of commitment to religion. Those with an avoidant attachment were most inclined toward agnosticism and individuals with an anxious/ambivalent attachment reported the highest incidence of speaking in tongues as well as the greatest proportion of atheists and individuals describing themselves as antireligious. The authors note that results for insecurely attached subjects appear to parallel the idea that the opposite of love is not hate but indifference, with anxious/ambivalent subjects tending toward being demonstratively religious or atheistic (ambivalent between these two extremes) and avoidant subjects being agnostic (indifference).

What is interesting about this is that whereas secure—that is, non-ambivalent—individuals demonstrated the highest level of religious commitment, they were not the most intensely religious. This category was occupied by those defined as ambivalent—those motivated by desires that are both independence- and dependence-oriented. This is exactly what my theory would predict. Intense ambivalence could either make one very religious or very antireligious. It is a category, therefore, of extremes. This is important because, although no religion depends on a majority of its adherents being ambivalent, it might depend on some being so. That is because a religion requires at least a few of its members to identify strongly with its central attachment figure—so much so that the person wishes to merge with the figure. Ambivalence of this sort corresponds to uncertainty and confusion about the sources of dependence and the need for independence. The paradox is never resolvable, a tension that all must feel, but one that a few people feel very intensely. These people are the "religious virtuosi" referred to by Weber (1963).

To take just one example, the Sri Lankan case studies of Obeyesekere (1981, 1990). Men and women who become ecstatic mediums, possessed by spirits and ancestors, typically experience a crisis earlier in life in which their desire for attachment to someone is counterbalanced by fear or hostility toward the same person. The crisis erupts when the other person dies, suddenly accentuating the conflict between opposing desires. The "dark night of the soul" that ensues threatens the individual with psychological collapse, but she recovers, usually by converting the ambivalence-laden memory of the attachment figure into a benign and protecting spirit. The conversion process is culturally sanctioned, and so the person ends up with a psychological defense that also is congruent with the culture's role categories.

A society does not require all, or even most, of its members to undergo culturally sanctioned transformation. Not everyone in Sri Lanka, after all, is an ecstatic medium. The few who do exist, however, play an essential role as culturally marked points of convergence, where powerful conflicts are represented and resolved. This is true in two ways. First, "religion" in Sri Lanka, including propositions about superhuman agencies, is partly defined in terms of possession experiences. Somebody has to undergo these experiences in order for the propositions about superhuman agencies to be considered relevant. Second, possession mediums represent in high relief the conflicts that, at a less intense level, the vast majority of people feel at the death of an attachment figure. Identification with the experiences of possession mediums is one way these people resolve such conflicts for themselves. My point here is that the question of "how religion works," to use Pyysiäinen's (2001) phrase, may depend both on intuitive principles that are widely shared and on the intense experiences of a few virtuosi, appearing only occasionally but often enough to act as embodiments of vital categories of experience. These individuals conform to Kirkpatrick and Shaver's definition of the "insecure" attached, that is, people who are ambivalent about the attachments they feel are (or were) primary. Always in the minority, such individuals are nevertheless essential, making ambivalence (about attachment) not only an interesting aspect of the system but essential to how it reproduces itself over time.

Conclusions

A fundamental polarity of interpersonal relatedness (dependence) and self-definition (independence) describes two major dimensions of attachment development. This polarity arises in the circumstances of normal human development and is a result of human attachment processes that begin very early in life. Later experiences violate the early "intuitive" assumption that attachment to a primary caregiver will continue forever. Religious propositions violate the violation, as it were, by constructing superman agents that not only preserve but enhance attachment. Attachment processes, however, are necessarily ambivalence-producing, and therefore religious propositions often end up being wildly contradictory. The deity who loves you is also the deity who smites you with boils for no reason. Why is that so?

Attachment theory suggests that humans develop opposed and competing tendencies, the one toward dependency and the other toward autonomy. This we have already seen. Ambivalence arises chiefly as a result of the developmentally natural assumption that childhood dependencies, formed in relation to primary caregivers, will continue forever. One consequence of this ambivalence is the construction of superhuman agencies as attachment figures one is both drawn to and repelled by. But like all ambivalences, this one is not recognized as generated within the self. Instead, it is projected outward, onto deistic attachment figures, where it becomes essentialized as a trait of the divine. The deity is memorable (and its tradition transmissible) because it simultaneously confirms and violates our expectations about dependency and autonomy.

Despite its explanatory power, the cognitivist strategy encounters difficulties on a number of fronts. One is that the theory of religion proposed by Boyer is more than a theory of religion. It is a theory of agency and attachment—whether Boyer wants it to be or not. Boyer and his colleagues are not so much wrong as misdirected: They identify the mechanisms of agency detection without taking into account their deeper emotional roots in early childhood. But it is also true that the theory is less than a theory of religion because it fails to take into account the most salient dimension of religious cognition, namely, the search for "good enough" attachment figures. Finally, the cognitivist account posits an evolutionary mechanism that is too narrowly utilitarian: Human beings are seen as calculating rational actors, full of needs and wants that they pursue in classical means-end fashion. Evolutionary theory has much to contribute, but without attention to the attachment-generating mechanisms all humans possess, and the way they are shaped and directed culturally, it cannot deliver the full measure of its potential to a dimension where attachment is clearly implicated: religious propositions about superhuman agencies.

References

Adler, Alfred. 1956. *The Individual Psychology of Alfred Adler*, edited by Heinz Ansbacher and Rowena Ansbacher. New York: Harper Torchbooks.

Ainsworth, Mary, Mary Blehar, Everett Waters, and Sally Wall. 1978. *Patterns of Attachment: A Psychological Study of the Strange Situation*. Hillsdale, NJ: Lawrence Erlbaum.

Atran, Scott. 2002. *In Gods We Trust*. Oxford: Oxford University Press.

Barrett, Justin. 2004. *Why Would Anyone Believe in God?* Walnut Creek, CA: Altamira Press.

Batson, Charles, Patricia Schoenrade, and Larry Ventis. 1993. *Religion and the Individual*. New York: Oxford University Press.

Berlin, Brent, and Paul Kay. [1969] 1991. *Basic Color Terms. Their Universality and Evolution*. Berkeley: University of California Press.

Bowlby, John. 1969. *Attachment and Loss. Vol. 1, Loss*. New York: Basic Books.

———. 1973. *Attachment and Loss. Vol. 2, Separation: Anxiety and Anger*. New York: Basic Books.

———. 1983. *Attachment and Loss. Vol. 3, Loss: Sadness and Depression.* New York: Basic Books.

———. 1988. *A Secure Base: Clinical Applications of Attachment Theory.* London: Routledge.

Boyer, Pascal. 1994. *The Naturalness of Religious Ideas: A Cognitive Theory of Religion.* Berkeley: University of California Press.

———. 2001. *Religion Explained.* New York: Basic Books.

Boyer, Pascal, and Pierre Liénard. 2006. "Why Ritualized Behavior? Precaution Systems and Action Parsing in Developmental, Pathological, and Cultural Rituals." *Behavioral and Brain Sciences* 29 (6): 635–41.

Bretherton, Inge. 1985. "Attachment Theory: Retrospect and Prospect." *Monographs of the Society for Research in Child Development* 50 (1–2): 3–35.

Buss, David M. 1995. "Evolutionary Psychology: A New Paradigm for Psychological Science." *Psychological Inquiry* 6 (1): 1–30.

Carlson, Vivian, and Robin Hardwood. 2014. "The Precursors of Attachment Security: Behavioral Systems and Culture." In *Different Faces of Attachment: Cultural Variations on a Universal Human Need*, edited by Hiltrud Otto and Heidi Keller, 278–306. Cambridge: Cambridge University Press.

Campbell, Donald. 1965. "Variation and Selective Retention in Socio-Cultural Evolution." In *Social Change in Developing Areas: A Reinterpretation of Evolutionary Theory*, edited by Herbert Barringer, George Blansten, and Raymond Mack. Cambridge, MA: Schenkman.

Cosmides, Leda, and John Tooby. 1995. "Cognitive Adaptations for Social Exchange." In *The Adapted Mind: Evolutionary Psychology and the Generation of Culture*, edited by Jerome Barkow, Leda Cosmides, and John Tooby, 163–228. New York: Oxford University Press.

———. 1996. "Are Humans Good Intuitive Statisticians after All? Rethinking Some Conclusions from the Literature on Judgment under Uncertainty." *Cognition* 58 (1): 1–73.

Diamond, Diana, and Sidney Blatt. 1994. "Internal Working Models of Attachment and Psychoanalytic Theories of the Representational World: A Comparison and Critique." In *Attachment in Adults: Clinical and Developmental Perspectives*, edited by Michael Sperling and William Berman, 72–97. New York: Guilford.

Elicker, J., M. England, and L. Sroufe. 1992. "Predicting Peer Competence and Peer Relationships in Childhood from Early Parent-Child Relationships." In *Family-Peer Relationships: Modes of Linkage*, edited by Ross Parke and Gary Ladd, 77–106. Hillsdale, NJ: Erlbaum.

Freeney, Judith, and Patricia Noller. 1990. "Attachment Style as a Predictor of Adult Romantic Relationships." *Journal of Personality and Social Psychology* 58 (2): 281–91.

Freud, Sigmund. 1964. *Civilization and Its Discontents.* London: Hogarth.

Frye, Douglas. 1991. "The Origins of Intention in Infancy." In *Children's Theories of Mind: Mental States and Social Understanding*, edited by Douglas Frye and Chris Moore, 15–38. Hillsdale, NJ: Lawrence Erlbaum.

Grunbaum, Adolf. 1984. *The Foundations of Psychoanalysis: A Philosophical Critique.* Berkeley: University of California Press.

Hazen, Cindy, and Philip Shaver. 1994. "Deeper into Attachment Theory." *Psychological Inquiry* 5 (1): 68–79.

Hinde, Robert. 1976. "On Describing Relationships." *Journal of Child Psychology and Psychiatry* 17 (1): 1–19.

Isaacson, Robert. 1992. "A Fuzzy Limbic System." *Behavioral Brain Research* 52 (2): 129–31.

Kakar, Sudhir. 1981. *The Inner World*. Delhi: Oxford University Press.

Kazdin Alan. 1992. "Child and Adolescent Dysfunction and Paths toward Maladjustment: Targets for Intervention." *Clinical Psychology Review* 12 (8): 795–817.

Kirkpatrick, Lee. 2005. *Attachment, Evolution, and the Psychology of Religion*. New York: Guilford.

Kirkpatrick, Lee, and Philip Shaver. 1992. "An Attachment-Theoretical Approach to Romantic Love and Religious Belief." *Personality and Social Psychology Bulletin* 18 (3): 266–75.

Konner, Melvin. 2010. *The Evolution of Childhood: Relationships, Emotion, and Mind*. Cambridge, MA: Belknap.

Kotter, Rolf. 2003. "Limbic System." In *Encyclopedia of the Neurological Sciences*, edited By Michael Aminoff and Robert Daroff. New York: Academic Press.

Kotter, Rolf, and Klass Stephan. 1997. "Useful or Helpful? The 'Limbic System' Concept." *Reviews in the Neuroscience* 8 (2): 139–45.

Kurtz, Stanley. 1992. *All the Mothers Are One*. New York: Columbia University Press.

Lawson, E. Thomas, and Robert McCauley. 1993. *Rethinking Religion: Connecting Cognition and Culture*. Cambridge: Cambridge University Press.

Lorenz, Konrad. 2007. *On Aggression*. New York: Taylor and Francis.

Mahler, Margaret. 1968. *On Human Symbiosis and the Vicissitudes of Individuation*. New York: International Universities Press.

———. 1979. *Selected Papers of Margaret S. Mahler*. New York: Jason Aronson.

Mahler, Margaret, Fred Pine, and Anni Bergman. 1975. *The Psychological Birth of the Human Infant*. New York: Basic Books.

Main, Mary, Nancy Kaplan, and Jude Cassidy. 1985. "Security in Infancy, Childhood, and Adulthood: A Move to the Level of Representation." *Monographs of the Society for Research in Child Development* 50 (1–2): 66–104.

Markus, Hazel, and Shinobu Kitayama. 1991. "Culture and the Self: Implications for Cognition, Emotion and Motivation." *Psychological Review* 98 (2): 224–53.

Masters, Roger D. 1989a. "Obligation and the New Naturalism." *Biology and Philosophy* 4 (1): 17–32.

———. 1989b. *The Nature of Politics*. New Haven, CT: Yale University Press.

McCauley, Robert, and Thomas Lawson. 2002. *Bringing Ritual to Mind*. Cambridge, UK: Cambridge University Press.

Meehan, Courtney, and Sean Hawks. 2014. "Maternal and Allomaternal Responsiveness: The Significance of Cooperative Caregiving in Attachment Theory." *Different Faces of Attachment*, edited by Hiltrud Otto and Heidi Keller, 113–40, Cambridge, UK: Cambridge University Press.

Millon, Theodore, and Davis, R. 1994. "Millon's Evolutionary Model of Normal and Abnormal Personality: Theory and Measures." In *Differentiating Normal and Abnormal Personality*, *edited by* Stephen Strack and Maurice Lorr, 79–113. New York: Springer.

Nuckolls, Charles. 1996. *The Cultural Dialectics of Knowledge and Desire*. Madison: University of Wisconsin Press.

———. 1998. *Culture: A Problem That Cannot Be Solved*. Madison: University of Wisconsin Press, 1998.

Obeyesekere, Gananath. 1981. *Medusa's Hair*. Chicago: University of Chicago Press.

———. 1990. *The Work of Culture*. Chicago: University of Chicago Press.

Piaget, Jean, and Barbel Inhelder. 1969. *The Psychology of the Child*. New York: Basic Books.

———. 1973. *Memory and Intelligence*. New York: Basic Books.

Pyysiäinen, Ilkka. 2001. *How Religion Works*. Leiden, Neth.: Brill.

Roland, Alan. 1988. *In Search of the Self in India and Japan*. Princeton, NJ: Princeton University Press.

Shor, Joel, and Jean Sanville. 1978. *Illusion in Loving: A Psychoanalytic View of the Evolution of Intimacy and Autonomy*. Los Angeles, CA: Double Helix.

Simpson, Jeffry A., and Jay Belsky. 2008. "Attachment Theory within a Modern Evolutionary Framework." In *Handbook of Attachment: Theory, Research, and Clinical Applications*

Sørensen, Jesper, Pierre Liénard, and Chelsea Feeny. 2006. "Agent and Instrument in Judgment of Ritual Efficacy." *Journal of Cognition and Culture* 6 (3): 463–82.

Sroufe, L. Alan, and June Fleeson. eds. 1986. *Attachment and the Construction of Relationships*. Hillsdale, NJ: Lawrence Erlbaum.

Strack, Stephen. 1999. "Millon's Normal Personality Styles and Dimensions." *Journal of Personality Assessment* 72 (3): 426–36.

Tremlin Todd. 2006. *Minds and Gods: The Cognitive Foundations of Religion*. Oxford: Oxford University Press.

Waters, Everett, Kiyomi Kondo-Ikemura, German Posada, and John Richters. 1991. "Learning to love: Mechanisms and milestones." In *Self-Processes and Development: The Minnesota Symposium on Child Psychology*, edited by Megan Gunnar and L. Alan Sroufe, 217–55. Hillsdale, NJ: Lawrence Erlbaum.

Weber, Max. 1963. *The Sociology of Religion*. Boston: Beacon Press.

Whitehouse, Harvey. 2000. *Arguments and Icons*. Oxford: Oxford University Press.

PART THREE

Implications of Psychological Pluralism for a Multicultural World: "Why Can't We All Just Get Along?"

Section 1
Challenges to the Modern Nation-State:
Globalization's Impact on Morality,
Identity, and the Person

Acculturation, Assimilation, and the "View from Manywheres" in the Hmong Diaspora[1]

JACOB R. HICKMAN

Brigham Young University
Department of Anthropology

Introduction

The Hmong diaspora provides an interesting social context to address questions about the cultural psychology[2] of migration. Although there are now significant populations of Hmong on five continents, the epicenter of the Hmong diaspora is southwestern China. From here Hmong began to emigrate in large numbers to the Southeast Asian peninsula during the nineteenth century. This diaspora was further globalized after the Second Indochinese war, which (beginning in 1975) displaced hundreds of thousands of Hmong refugees from Laos to camps in Thailand. Most of these Hmong refugees would eventually resettle in third-party countries such as the United States or France. Some of them, however, would resettle permanently in the Thai countryside in preexisting Hmong communities.[3] As a result of these divergent migration patterns, some families became transnational families almost overnight, as some members of the family stayed in Southeast Asia, while other relatives were resettled in places like Minnesota and California. These disparate resettlement circumstances provide a unique context for examining theoretical understandings of how distinct resettlement contexts play into the psychocultural adaptations of migrants.

In this chapter I employ data from a transnational comparison of Hmong refugee families spread across two locations—the Twin Cities, Minnesota, and a rural farming village in Northern Thailand. This analysis leads me to challenge some of the core assumptions in "acculturation" and "assimilation" scholarship that dominates our understanding of how migrants' lives change in the course of migration and resettlement. I argue that a "view from manywheres" (Shweder 2003, 6) analysis of these data forces us to consider the quality of change in migrants' moral outlooks, as opposed to presuming universal (and often ethnocentric) models of psychocultural change that force us to think about changes in migrants' lives in more linear, objectivist terms.

Acculturation and assimilation are dually psychological *and* social-cultural phenomena, which is why some of the most prominent theoretical frameworks have been developed in the disciplines of psychology, sociology, and anthropology to try to better understand the phenomena. Contemporary theoretical frameworks of acculturation and assimilation were developed in response to a unilineal conception of the process(es) of cultural change, from which migrants could supposedly be located somewhere on a spectrum from more-or-less X to more-or-less Y. As I will describe, however, even the nuances introduced into these frameworks do not account for the cultural realities that many Hmong migrant families face. The problem with these revised acculturation and assimilation frameworks is that they still rely on linear thinking, even if multilinear in nature.

Through an examination of ethnographic and discursive evidence, I argue that Hmong of both older and younger generations in my sample of transnational families are adapting their moral thinking to new social contexts, but that these patterns of intergenerational difference cannot be productively understood through the linear thinking inherent in current acculturation and assimilation models. Instead, I argue that an ethnographic life course perspective can provide a more adequate explanation of my findings and others. This alternative approach requires more culturally specific understandings of dominant modes of life course development as they intersect with distinct social contexts of development. In other words, a better understanding of the psychocultural adaptations of migrants requires a theory that is more attuned to cultural variations and intercultural interactions, such as how people negotiate and respond to conflicting cultural models. As opposed to a linear model, we need a model that takes seriously the possibilities of "universalism without the uniformity" (Shweder 2003, 30). As Usha Menon and Julia Cassaniti adeptly argue in the introductory chapter to this volume, and as the various contributions of this volume demonstrate, the "view from manywheres" approach provides a more defensible comparative theory for understanding psychological function across cultural contexts. In the case of migration research, however, the culturally comparative enterprise relies just as much on *within*-cases analyses as it does the traditional *between*-cases concerns. The "view from manywheres" allows one to view reality from figuratively different cultural places, but migrants *literally inhabit* new cultural places. This raises the question, How does their thinking change in the process? I provide an alternative framework for thinking about how Hmong moral thinking changes over the course of migration from one cultural context to a dramatically different one.

The Three Ethics Framework

With the concept of "universalism without the uniformity" Rick Shweder seeks to describe a minimalist notion of psychic unity that maintains the capability of accounting for deep cultural difference (Shweder 2003, 30). The Three Ethics formulation was developed by Shweder and colleagues (Shweder, Mahapatra, and Miller 1990; Shweder, Much, Mahapatra, and Park 2003) as an empirically grounded framework for understanding the "universalism without the uniformity" inherent in culturally various visions of morality and ethics. This was in particular response to the moral development literature (Kohlberg 1969, 1981, Kohlberg, Levine, and Hewer 1983), in which cultural difference in core psychological function was seen as relatively shallow, and cultural differences in moral development were therefore used to conclude that adults in some cultures tend to achieve lower levels of moral development than others. These moral development psychologists favored a stronger notion of psychological universalism (see Shweder 1990). The reach of Shweder, Mahapatra, and Miller's (1990) critique is beyond the scope of the present chapter (see Haidt and Rozin, this volume, for a more complete contextualization of this framework and how it affected moral psychology). What is critical here, however, is that the Three Ethics framework that came out of these critiques of the moral development literature allows for a depth of difference in moral thinking that was unthinkable in the stronger universalist framework. The Three Ethics framework allows for the possibility that culturally various— even competing—notions of "the good" might be mutually incommensurable, without concluding that one or the other is more rationally defensible or developmentally desirable. Hence the lack of uniformity. The Three Ethics framework is not a mere form of relativism, however, because it poses particular moral goods that are limited in scope and are potentially rationally accessible to any cultural framing of an ethical outlook. Herein lies the universalism. Culturally various visions of the good, then, may be understood as simply keying into rationally distinct moral principles in different arrangements or value hierarchies (Cassaniti and Hickman 2014; Wong 2014), whereas the moral development literature characterized any

moral outlook that failed to satisfy the rational demands of one particular ethic—liberal individualism—as morally deficient or underdeveloped.
Alternatively, Shweder and colleagues framed three ethics—autonomy,
community, and divinity—as candidates for universals, but in a theoretical
framework that did not require all of them to be expressed to their fullest
extent or even in the same way in different cultural contexts.

The universalism inherent in the Three Ethics approach allows for cross-
cultural comparison in the manifestation and distributions of these ethics,
while the lack of required uniformity allows one to do so without impe-
rializing some ethics at the expense of others. This framework inspired a
proliferation of research that used this framework to do comparative analyses on morality that simultaneously maintained ethnographic sensitivity to
deep cultural difference in manifestations of the good while still allowing
for a high degree of comparative validity. (See Haidt and Rozin, this volume; Jensen's 2015 edited volume of Three Ethics scholarship; Cassaniti
2014; Guerra and Giner-Sorolla 2007, 2010; Haidt, Koller, and Dias 1993,
Hickman 2011, Jensen 1995, 1998, 2009; Rozin, Lowery, Imada, and Haidt
1999; and Wong 2014, as just a few examples.)

The clear advantages of this framework for engaging in culturally comparative research on morality allow for particularly productive possibilities
when the actual phenomenon under study—migration—inherently deals
with people who physically move from one cultural space to another. My
intergenerational and transnational comparison of Hmong parents' and
children's moral discourse provides just such a case. The analysis of these
data requires a more nuanced vision of change over time that cannot be
adequately reconciled with the linear thinking inherent in acculturation
and assimilation theories, and the Three Ethics framework provides a critical piece to developing an alternative framework.

Beyond Three Ethics theory, a second important framework that I draw
from in this analysis is life course theory. Shweder and others (Jessor, Colby,
and Shweder 1996; Menon and Shweder 1998; Shweder 1998) have advocated for ethnographic perspectives that require us to deal with cultural
variations in developmental contexts of life course trajectories (not just in
terms of moral reasoning). Lene Jensen (2008, 2015) integrated the Three
Ethics framework back into a more explicitly developmental approach,
from which the original critique was hatched. I likewise adopt a life course
perspective that is sensitive to the cultural contexts of moral development
(which I also develop in Hickman 2011, 2014, 2016, and Hickman and
DiBianca Fasoli 2015). The phenomenon of interest here—moral thinking across two generations in two different resettlement locations of trans-

national families—requires me to deal with both developmental change and change that results from migration to a new location. In the present analysis I parse out these intergenerational and transnational trends in order to present data that provides an alternative to the core assumptions of two central theoretical frameworks in the (im-)migration literature—acculturation and assimilation.

A Comparison of Migrant Families in Two Distinct Locations

In previous research on health beliefs and practices (Hickman 2007), I found that Hmong who had resettled in Alaska were not holding out and preserving their traditional beliefs in the face of immense pressure to conform to a US biomedical system (including the older generation), which is the sense one gets from Anne Fadiman (1997) and the robust literature on Hmong health beliefs and practices in the United States. Neither were Hmong simply acculturating to the US system. Rather, the set of beliefs and practices that I documented among Hmong in Alaska demonstrated an altogether new, syncretic way of thinking about health and healing that could account for both spiritual and biomedical etiologies.

Sample

Expanding on these questions of psychocultural adaptation, I designed an intergenerational and transnationally comparative ethnographic study of moral thinking in Hmong families (Hickman 2011). These families all originated in Laos prior to 1975 and fled that country in the aftermath of America's Secret War in Laos—an important theater in the Second Indochinese War. As refugees, these families would spend a few years in either formal or informal refugee camps in Thailand before permanently resettling in Thailand or a third-party country of resettlement, such as the United States. Many families split, with part of a kin group resettling in the United States while their relatives remained permanently in Thailand. My comparative ethnographic analysis focused on families with close relatives in both locations, and I used several criteria to select participants in this comparative analysis that would minimize selection bias at the point of resettlement.[4] I selected refugee families with both a parent and child available for interviewing that I could track down for interviews in both countries, all of whom met criteria of relatedness in order to maximize comparative validity. This selection strategy ultimately resulted in a sample of nine paired-comparison families. Each family had one relative in the

older generation in each country of resettlement and one late adolescent/
emerging adult in each country—Thailand and the United States—for a
total of thirty-six participants (nine parent–child dyads in each country).[5]

The following analysis entails a comparison of the patterns of discourse utilizing the Three Ethics across generations and locations in this
intergenerational-transnational sample. In order to build on a rich enterprise of culturally comparative research on moral thinking that grew out
of Rick Shweder's work, I employed a vignette-driven approach (following Shweder, Mahapatra, and Miller 1990; Shweder et al. 2003) to supplement my person-centered interviews and ethnographic study of these families. Following the Hmong speech genre of moral story telling (see Briggs
1986), I discussed moral stories that I developed or adapted from my ethnography and discussed them with members of these families in a way that
would help me understand the core moral principles that each participant
brought to bear on the moral issue at hand. By comparatively analyzing
the intergenerational and transnational patterns of moral themes invoked
by my interlocutors in this sample of Hmong families, I am able to derive
some interesting conclusions about how the resettlement context affects
moral thinking across generations in these migrant families.[6] The subsequent analysis of this moral discourse focused on the coding of responses
to these vignettes under the rubric of the three ethics of autonomy, community, and divinity (using the coding strategy outlined in Jensen 2004,
2015), as these concepts have been shown to provide a good index of culturally varying modes of moral thinking.

Results

In further analyses of these data (Hickman 2011, 2016) I argue for a persistent life course trend among Hmong families in both locations of resettlement (the United States and Thailand). In both locations the younger
generation utilized moral reasoning that was based on an ethics of autonomy to a much greater extent than their parents did. The inverse is true
for community—the older generation relied on community-based ethics to
a much greater extent than their children. While acculturation researchers
would be quick to draw the conclusion that in the US sample this finding is consistent with an acculturation framework, I found the same trends
in Thailand, without any indication of significant differences *between*
countries. Given the dramatic differences in the social contexts of resettlement, and given the strikingly similar intergenerational differences found
across these different contexts, I argue that a life course perspective pro-

vides a more satisfactory explanation of these trends than an explanation based on acculturation or assimilation into the new social contexts. For the present chapter, however, I want to focus on what happens when multiple ethics—autonomy, community, and divinity—are utilized in a single mode of moral reasoning. Understanding the dynamics between ethics *within* individuals' moral discourse can reveal *how* they navigate competing moral ideas, including those they encounter in the course of migration. This discourse analysis more directly addresses claims and assumptions inherent in acculturation and assimilation frameworks.

Beyond looking at the mere distributions of the three ethics, DiBianca Fasoli and I (2015) have argued that researchers need to look at the *ways* in which these ethics interact with one another in the moral thinking of various people. Doing so, we argue, will reveal the very nature of distinct moral outlooks and help us better understand the dynamics contained therein. To this end, I will first analyze some examples of moral discourse that reveal two types of ethical interaction, which DiBianca Fasoli and I have termed *divergent* moral justifications and *parallel* moral justifications. Each represents a different way of integrating distinct lines of ethical thought into a line of moral reasoning.

Parallel justifications. I use the term *parallel justification* (following Hickman and DiBianca Fasoli 2015) to denote the ethical justifications in my interlocutors' discourse where multiple lines of moral discourse can be demonstrably represented as distinct rationales (e.g., autonomy and community) while also converging on the same ultimate moral judgment. In other words, they compound on one another in order to provide a more expansive rationale for a singular moral assessment. As an example of a parallel justification, one participant in the United States responded in the following way when presented with the following moral story:

> There was a Hmong businessman who knew of a particular place to buy goods at a very cheap price. He would purchase the goods and bring them to his village and sell them at a more expensive rate. He would sell them for the same price to kin and non-kin. When his relatives asked him where he bought the goods at such a low price, he refused to tell them, fearing that they would compete with him and potentially ruin his business. Is this person morally wrong in doing this?

After responding that the merchant in the story has made a moral transgression (*muaj kev txhaum*) in doing this, a middle-aged subsistence farmer living in northern Thailand goes on to explain (speaking Hmong, trans. below):

(1) It's a moral transgression (*txhaum*) because they sell

(2) it over there and they sell it at a cheap price—

(3) they sell it for a cheap price to *him*, and he takes

(4) it to sell over there and he sells it way above the

(5) customary (*kev cai*) price. They sell far beyond the

(6) customary price, then he must be morally wrong

(7) (*yuav tsum txhaum*) because he used them to make

(8) so much profit (*nws noj ntau heev*). He therefore

(9) must have fallen into moral transgression

(10) (*poob kev txhaum*).

In this instance my interlocutor responded that the moral transgression is found in the person's breaking with custom and tradition—*kev cai* (line 5) as it is glossed in Hmong. In other words, a merchant who does this would be in breach of the generally understood social contract that exists in the community not to do such things. The merchant would clearly be committing a transgression (lines 6–7) because of his wanton action of taking advantage of others despite the tradition. This reason clearly falls under the ethics of "community" in the Three Ethics framework. My interlocutor went on, however, to delineate additional reasons for why the merchant was wrong:

(11) [The merchant] will ultimately receive a just

(12) desert (*npam*). Some elders, they always chide,

(13) saying: Oh, you bought something cheap then you sell

(14) to us as expensive as this—so shameful (*txaj muag*).

(15) Well, if people's hearts are as crooked as this—then

(16) [that person] will receive a just desert (*raug npam*),

(17) [they] will—find themselves without any money . . .

(18) one's heart will not be well.

In this second justification, he keys into the notion of karmic just desert, or *npam* in Hmong (line 12). This term is etymologically derived from the Thai and Lao word for demerit, *bap*. Its use here is quite similar (although being adapted for a Hmong cosmology), for he is keying into a transcendent sense of divine justice, of which the heavens (*ntuj*) are understood to be the arbiter. This is a clear instance of divinity reasoning in the Three Ethics scheme. What is critical here is the way that these two lines of ethical thinking—community and divinity—work *together* toward the same moral judgment. Namely, they are both used to argue that the merchant should not engage in this behavior. This is the key aspect of parallel justifications that distinguishes it as a particular type of ethical co-occurrence.

Divergent justifications. DiBianca Fasoli and I have used the term *divergent moral justifications* to classify instances in which an individual seems to be conflicted about the ultimate moral judgment at hand, with different ethics pulling the individual's rationales in different directions. We argue that this can be characterized as a kind of moral-cognitive dissonance. As an example, consider responses to the following moral story by a young Hmong man living in the United States:

> A father and son lived together in their village. One day, the father committed a serious moral transgression that made him lose face and also made the son very embarrassed. The son decided to move to another village, and he changed both his given name and his clan name, so that no one would know whose son he is. Is a son that does this morally wrong?

My interlocutor initially responded (speaking English):

(1) If it's really something that person really believed

(2) in and—and they wanted to start afresh, then I would

(3) say it's not morally wrong by changing your name and

(4) trying to start anew. Which I think—that story was

(5) trying to say—that person was trying to start anew

(6) by distancing themselves from their parent.

He is clearly appealing to an ethics of autonomy in his first response to this vignette—namely the psychological welfare of the son and his right to seek a situation that suits him emotionally. However, he quickly countered with another line of reasoning that challenged the first, saying that the son is also wrong:

(7) because you're supposed to carry your parents'—

(8) um—honors and name. [He is wrong] because no

(9) matter what your parents do—for instance, um,

(10) my dad had some problem . . .

He went on to tell a story about how his father supposedly overcharged another clan for the brideprice in a past wedding that his father had a part in arranging about forty years ago. The son (the interviewee) had to eventually compensate for this by paying $600 after his father had passed away, despite having no firsthand knowledge of the supposed error. He told this story to make the point that children have an obligation to honor their parents' name and even rectify their mistakes after they pass away—appealing to a normative ethics of community. What is key here is that this line of reasoning (lines 7–10 and the subsequent story) actually contradicts the first line of autonomy reasoning (lines 1–6), pulling my interlocutor's moral judgments in different directions. Reinforcing the point, he manifested a significant degree of ambivalence about this story as he recounted it. He explained how he felt ambivalent about having to lose his own money and having to compensate for the problem created by the older generation when it was not in his personal interest, while at the same time he decided ultimately to concede because he wanted to honor his father's name and resolve the tension between the two clans. In sum, these divergent lines of ethical reasoning manifest a degree of what could be termed moral-cognitive dissonance, which is clearly distinct from *parallel* lines of ethical reasoning, which rather work together toward a singular moral judgment.

I discuss the developmental significance of this moral-cognitive dissonance elsewhere (see Hickman 2011 for an ethnographic description of the lives of these youth and an intergenerational and transnational comparison of patterns in moral discourse), but for the present it is sufficient to note that the youth in my sample did manifest higher levels of moral-cognitive dissonance than their parents did. Critically, these young Hmong were born right about the time that their parents resettled to the United States or Thailand as refugees from Laos. One explanation for moral ambivalence being more common among the younger generation, then, may be that they are struggling with competing moral principles offered by their parents and peers. In other words, they are dealing with the competing demands of Hmong moral models handed down to them by their parents and relatives *and* those that are more prevalent in US society (such as their non-Hmong peers) and more typical of US emerging adults in particular (see Jensen 1995). This is an important dynamic for understanding the moral worlds of these migrant youth, and it suggests a more complicated picture of the development of moral identity (see Hardy, Walker, Olsen, Woodbury, and Hickman 2014). Critically, this trend would be overlooked by an approach that stops at coding the mere presence of the three ethics in order to understand the distribution and does not analyze the dynamic of competing moral goods in the discourse. The key point here is that employing the Three Ethics framework within a cultural discourse analysis reveals a moral ambivalence that would otherwise be missed. The ways in which Hmong elders and youth deal with the demands of competing moral principles is revealing about *how* their moral outlooks can change during migration, and the precise dynamic that leads to changes in moral thinking.

To this end, we developed a codebook[7] to standardize the classification of divergent and parallel forms of interactions between two or more ethics in this corpus of moral discourse data. This coding system was applied to instances where my interlocutors brought multiple ethical concepts (autonomy, community, and divinity, using the Jensen 2004, 2015, coding manual) to bear on a single moral story in their moral discourse. This coding method provides at least one measure of the ways in which cultural models of morality interact with one another in the discourse of older and younger Hmong in these two countries. It is precisely this interaction *between* cultural models of morality that demonstrate a nonlinear model of change in moral thinking between the older and younger generations in these resettlement contexts.

Given the sample sizes, I conducted a Fisher's exact test (using Fisher-B software, see White 1995) on the relationship between generation (old and young) and each type of moral dynamic (divergent and parallel reasoning) for both countries combined (Thailand and the US), for each country separately, and for a three-way interaction between country, generation, and moral dynamic.

Table 10.1 gives the distribution of divergent and parallel justifications in the entire sample (both countries combined), separated out by generation. A Fisher's exact test of the pattern in table 10.1 revealed a one-tailed[8] p-value of .0000, suggesting that these overall intergenerational differences are larger than what one would expect from chance alone. Because the sample is the transnational, however, it is critical to analyze the patterns in each location. Fisher's exact one-tailed *p*-value for the intergenerational comparison of divergent versus parallel justifications was .0367 in Thailand (table 10.2) and .0005 in the United States (table 10.3).

The overall intergenerational trend (table 10.1) manifest in these patterns indicates that, when the younger generation in these families brought multiple, distinct lines of ethical reasoning to bear in their moral assessments, they were roughly equally divided between divergent and parallel forms of interaction in the lines of moral reasoning (autonomy, community, and divinity) that they employed in moral judgment. What this means is that, in the instances where my interlocutors in the younger generation drew on multiple ethical concepts, they had approximately a 58 percent likelihood of manifesting some form of moral-cognitive dissonance in their reasoning between these concepts. In these cases, the different moral models were pulling the person's moral judgment in different directions. For the older generation, on the other hand, when multiple ethical concepts were brought to bear on the moral judgment, they were

Table 10.1 Divergent and parallel justifications across generations (entire sample)

All	Divergent	Parallel	
Generation = Young	34	25	59
Generation = Old	11	43	54
	45	68	

Table 10.2 Divergent and parallel justifications across generations (Thailand)

Thailand	Divergent	Parallel	
Generation = Young	11	13	24
Generation = Old	4	19	23
	15	32	

Table 10.3 Divergent and parallel justifications across generations (United States)

United States	Divergent	Parallel	
Generation = Young	23	12	35
Generation = Old	7	24	31
	30	36	

much more likely to exhibit parallel forms of ethical justification. In other words, analyses of their moral discourse indicated that different lines of ethical reasoning were much more likely (80 percent) to bolster each other in their moral judgments with distinct, yet mutually supportive, lines of ethical reasoning.

Dividing these trends out by country of resettlement is even more revealing. The three-way Fisher's exact test revealed no three-way relationship between country of resettlement, generation, and type of ethical co-occurrence (the one-tailed p-value was .6631). One reason for this is that the older generation looks very similar on these measures in both countries. Overall for this generation, 20 percent of the instances where multiple ethics were utilized in their reasoning consisted of divergent justifications and 80 percent of instances of ethical co-occurrence consisted of parallel justifications. For the younger generation, however, there seems to be a trend toward a country effect (approaching statistical significance, the one-tailed p-value comparing youth in each country was .1057). For the younger generation in Thailand, 46 percent of instances of ethical co-occurrence were coded as divergent and 54 percent as parallel. For the younger generation in the United States, 66 percent of the instances of ethical co-occurrence were coded as divergent and only 34 percent as parallel. This indicates that Hmong youth in the US portion of the sample were predominantly expressing some form of moral-cognitive dissonance in their moral reasoning when multiple ethics were invoked. Hmong youth in Thailand expressed some degree of moral-cognitive dissonance, but as with their parents, it was more common for them to express multiple ethics in ways that built on one another than for them to be pulled in different directions by distinct moral rationales.

As DiBianca Fasoli and I (2015) have argued, the *types* of ethical co-occurrence are critical in considering culturally specific developmental stories or in understanding changes in moral thinking over time. In the present case, it is the *type* of interaction between these ethics in the two generations that I argue reveals an important intergenerational difference. Overall, the younger generation seems to be experiencing a larger degree of moral-cognitive dissonance in which they weigh distinct ethics in competition with one another as they are making moral judgments. The older generation, while using multiple ethics to the same degree, tend much more toward supporting the same moral judgment with multiple lines of reasoning. It also seems to be the case that this moral-cognitive dissonance is stronger with Hmong youth in the United States than in Thailand, although in both cases it is stronger in the younger generation than with their parents. The quality of this moral-cognitive dissonance or lack thereof is further bolstered by a rich ethnographic account of the lives of these youth and parents (Hickman 2011, 2016), and it points to the *ways* that migrants grapple with competing moral ideas. Critically, these intergenerational differences are not well accounted for under the linear assumptions inherent in the acculturation and assimilation literature. It is to these two frameworks that I now turn my attention.

The Problem

My evidence provides an empirical and theoretical critique of the two predominant frameworks for understanding the acculturation and assimilation of migrant groups into places like the United States. One of the frameworks is largely used by sociologists—segmented assimilation—and the other by psychologists—acculturation theory. Both of these frameworks were developed as more nuanced accounts of the ways that groups adapt to cultural and social circumstances in the communities where they resettle, in contrast with the unilinear understanding of acculturation that preceded them. Both models manifest similar problems in the core assumptions that underpin them—namely, linear thinking.

A Psychological Model of Acculturation and Assimilation

Both of the predominant models I address in this section were developed in reaction to an older, unidimensional conception of acculturation and assimilation as a process in which migrants or minorities supposedly move (or could be placed) on a linear continuum from their original cultural practices, beliefs, and values to an adoption of those of the majority in the host society where they live or resettle (Gordon 1964; Teske and Nelson 1974). Earlier critiques of theorizing this type of social change argued that acculturation and assimilation are not the same process, and neither acculturation nor assimilation is necessarily unidirectional (Teske and Nelson 1974). These earlier accounts nevertheless conceived of the process as ultimately constituting a unilineal continuum from one set of cultural practices and beliefs to another. Both psychologists and sociologists have responded to this simplistic model by adding further dimensions to the theory.

Critiquing the unidimensional model, John Berry (1970, 1980) formulated the foundation of what is now the predominant psychological model of acculturation. Berry argued that one must consider the orientation toward one's natal culture *and* the orientation toward the host or majority culture separately. They are two distinct orientations, and being high or low on one dimension is not mutually exclusive with being high or low on the other. In Berry's two-dimensional framework, migrants could be classified in terms of four types: highly bicultural (characterized by a high level of orientation toward both the culture of origin and the host culture), ethnically identified (high orientation toward natal culture, low orientation toward host culture), host-culture-identified (a low orientation toward the culture of origin and a high orientation toward the host culture), or low bicultural (a low orientation toward both the natal and host cultures; see also Felix-Ortiz, Newcomb, and Myers 1994; Nguyen 2009; Nguyen and von Eye 2002).

Berry's model has received a significant amount of attention and critique and has also formed the basis for how psychologists approach the concept of acculturation from both a psychometric standpoint and in other areas of psychological practice (for several examples, see Barry 2001; Berry, Phinney, Sam, and Vedder 2006; Lee and Green 2010; Nguyen 2009; Nguyen and von Eye 2002; Sam and Berry 2006; Schwartz, Unger, Zamboanga, and Szapocznik 2010; Weinreich 2009). Despite theoretical and methodological modifications that Berry's model incorporated, the central characteristic that remained was the assumption of linear movement. Berry elaborates on the older model by proposing two distinct dimensions on which one might move, but the model simply imposes one linear dimension on top of another. This results in a two-dimensional, but still linear, model. The two-dimensional model is reflected in the four types described earlier. Critically, these linear assumptions work quite well with the ways that these constructs are commonly operationalized and quantified in cross-cultural psychological research. That is, the common practice is to develop quantitative measures of the constructs, which inevitably leads to linear indices of the theorized construct. The result of this method is necessarily to place each research participant on a continuum of the *a priori* scale that is integral to the method. Berry's elaboration of the traditional unidimensional model of social change provided an important complication to our understanding of these processes, but the epistemological enterprise to which it has given rise still is limited to linear conceptions of psychosocial change for migrants. Alternative forms of psychocultural change, such as developing parallel moral rationales, divergent ethical justifications, or altogether new ways of thinking are incomprehensible in this model, despite how central such changes may be to the lived experience of actual migrants.

Segmented Assimilation in Sociology

In the sister discipline of sociology, a massive research enterprise has been built around another elaboration of the traditional unidimensional and linear conception of acculturation and assimilation. It has been pioneered primarily by Portes and Rumbaut (Portes, Fernández-Kelly, and Haller 2005, 2009; Portes and Rumbaut 2005; Portes and Zhou 1993; Rumbaut 1994, 1997). Their elaboration of the traditional model rests on the central point that there is no single sector of society into which migrants assimilate, and in fact assimilation is not always such a desirable end for migrant families.

Portes and Rumbaut theorize multiple "pathways" to assimilation with distinct endpoints. One of their more important contributions to sociological perspectives on migration includes the concept of downward assimilation, in which migrant youth adopt practices and socioeconomic lifeways characteristic of the US underclass. This may include countercultural practices such as gang activity and other socially deviant lifestyles. This model has a heavy socioeconomic emphasis and is based on large-scale sociological data sets. The model portrays three assimilative pathways that result from different social conditions such as family factors, social capital, and modes of incorporation. Each pathway leads to a different style of acculturation—full, selective, and dissonant. Dissonant acculturation is associated with downward assimilation, one of the key insights in their revised model (see "Paths of Mobility across Generations" in Portes and Rumbaut 2014, 280).

As with Berry's model, Rumbaut and Portes provide a wealth of interesting data and necessary complications of the traditional assimilationist framework. Also like Berry's model, however, segmented assimilation elaborates on the original formulation only by adding additional (linear) pathways to assimilation in the host society. The very concept of *pathways* is indicative of the extent to which segmented assimilation fundamentally maintains the linear thinking of the traditional model.

A Different Model

I want to draw attention to the fact that both of these predominant frameworks maintain the linear thinking of the traditional acculturation and assimilationist thinking of the midtwentieth-century models, even despite the multidimensional nature of each.[9] These models have been applied to explaining Hmong experiences of adaptation in the United States (Lee 2005;

Lee and Green 2010; Nguyen 2009). The fundamental limitations of these applications lay in the *a priori* assumption that Hmong must be engaged in some sort of linear movement on one of the possible pathways to integration in US society. Again, these limitations are deeply intertwined with the epistemological enterprises on which they were built. A sole employment of interval-level scales of measurement (e.g., Barry 2001, Nguyen and von Eye 2002) require conclusions of this sort, and indeed preclude nonlinear observations (ethnographic, discourse analysis, or otherwise) that might fall outside the purview of the theory. Rather than occupying the objectivist "view from nowhere" that one is forced into by this epistemological-ergo-ontological view, I argue that a "view from manywheres" allows one to see more interesting interactions in the moral worlds of Hmong migrant youth and adults.

Ultimately, what these models lack is an approach that is firmly grounded in person-centered ethnography while remaining open to the quantitative trends on which they largely base their conclusions.[10] Ultimately, we need to pay greater attention to the interplay between individual psychocultural dynamics and the more cultural-level models and social processes that impinge on them (Shweder 1995). This is precisely what my analysis of *parallel* and *divergent* justifications in ethical thinking do in the present analysis. By enabling us to see moral-cognitive dissonance across two generations of a sample of transnational families, we can start to get a better sense of the actual texture of how the moral worlds of these migrant youth and adults are actually changing.

The evidence on moral discourse among Hmong in Thailand and the United States points to the likelihood of a Hmong-specific cultural-developmental template (Jensen 2008, 2015) for how autonomy-, community-, and divinity-oriented thinking develops across the life course. The life course trend fits with ethnographic research on Hmong families and provides a much more satisfying explanation of the empirical data that I collected on intergenerational trends in moral thinking among Hmong families in two very different resettlement contexts—the urban US Midwest and a rural Hmong farming community in Thailand (Hickman 2011, 2016). As in my analysis of the syncretism of Hmong health beliefs in the United States (Hickman 2007), my argument here about the pervasiveness of a Hmong cultural-developmental template is not meant to suggest that no change is happening as a result of migration to US communities. At the same time, the types of changes that I document in my person-centered ethnography cannot be adequately characterized under the linear thinking inherent in the concepts of acculturation and assimilation as they are theorized in migration research in psychology and sociology. Rather than thinking about cultural movement along these supposedly (multi)linear continua, my ethnography suggests that a more nuanced and nonlinear understanding of how resettlement and migration affect moral thinking is needed. For instance, what becomes clear in the present data is the observation that moral-cognitive dissonance was strongest among the younger generation, and in the United States in particular.

Conclusion: Understanding Psychocultural Change in Resettlement

Something interesting is happening as Hmong navigate the moral worlds of a new society. Hmong youth (particularly in the United States) seem to be juggling these competing models in ways that lead to a higher degree of moral-cognitive dissonance, evidenced by their more frequent use of *divergent* moral justifications. Their parents, on the other hand, tend more often to assemble *parallel* rationales in ways that build community and divinity thinking together in a larger cultural view of the good (as in the example given previously). Inspired by the "view from manywheres," my approach attends to the particular ways in which these participants juggle competing cultural models—such as autonomy, community, and divinity, in all of their cultural embodiments—and to the ways that they develop rationales for making these ethics work together or against one another that acculturation and segmented assimilation frameworks cannot account for.

The value of understanding how resettlement contexts affect personhood and morality in different ways will contribute to a better overall understanding of how migration affects the lives of those who relocate. As moral thinking develops over the life course, the younger generations of Hmong migrants confront models that they themselves describe as "traditionally Hmong," intermixed with the circulating moral models in the macrosocial contexts where they have resettled—in this case the United States and Thailand. From the person-centered ethnographic perspective, what is really crucial here is the way that these competing cultural models (traditional and new) challenge one another or work together in the experiences of particular migrants. This space for negotiation becomes a complex one in which migrants come to make moral meaning in the midst of competing moral models. Although it is certainly the case that—aside from migration—there is an inherent complexity in how individuals navigate the ethical landscape of Hmong, US, and Thai societies themselves (the traditional focus of person-centered ethnographic scholarship), the migration context adds another dimension that must be accounted for in a person-centered analysis. I do not want to simplify the dynamics between nonmigrants and the cultural models they encounter, use, challenge, and so on, as if to essentialize US culture or Thai culture. (See D'Andrade in this volume for some of these complications between values and society.) But at the same time, I argue that the significant sociopolitical changes that Hmong have undergone in migrating from the highlands of Laos to a more urban US sociopolitical environment offers a comparatively complex context in which Hmong navigate quite disparate and previously unencountered cultural models of personhood and moral ideation.

As Hmong youth encounter moral models that challenge what they experience as traditional moral models, they quite often find themselves conflicted, and they express this moral-cognitive dissonance in the interviews that I conducted with them. Trying to force this ethical struggle into the linear assumptions of acculturation and assimilation as outlined herein would not allow one to see the nuance in the ways that Hmong youth struggle with competing cultural models as they seek to cultivate a moral outlook that makes sense of their complicated world. A more thorough ethnographic treatise is necessary in order to more fully understand these experiences (see Hickman 2016). But the present findings provide insights into two ways that Hmong deal with competing moral ideas—through developing *divergent* and *parallel* modes of moral justification—and the present analysis also suggests that the younger generation (particularly in the United States) tends more toward divergence. Further longitudinal research on the developmental process itself (this research deals primarily with cross-sectional data) would provide important insights into this process in migrant communities.

The discursive evidence on which I base my analyses (see Hickman 2011, 2014, Hickman and DiBianca Fasoli 2015) demonstrates that both prototypical "Hmong" and "American" models (as my interlocutors themselves often label them) come to bear on the moral reasoning of my Hmong interlocutors. The form in which they are dually employed cannot, however, be accounted for in the acculturation model of psychology, which forces an unrealistic linear and objectivist thinking onto the more complex reality that Hmong inhabit, as I have described in this chapter. Alternatively, the corpus of moral discourse and personal narratives that I have collected demonstrates at least some of the complexity of how these families navigate the experiences of resettlement in a new context.

The "view from manywheres" (Shweder 2003) argues against the objectivist ("the view from nowhere") stance that underpins the linear thinking inherent in the predominant models of acculturation and assimilation. Rather, the "view from manywheres" suggests that researchers dig more deeply into the lived experience of migrants, who may actually be living in different moral worlds that are incomprehensible to an "empty," or objectivist, view. The "view from manywheres" urges us to produce thick descriptions of those moral worlds in order to understand them in their own terms. In the present analysis I have provided some insights into the nature of these worlds and how these worlds might themselves be changing for these migrant families. Rather than striving for a linear, objectivist basis for comparative work such as this, we would be better off striving toward better, thicker descriptions of these worlds.

Viewing Hmong migration from "manywheres" allows one to see a quality in the change of moral thinking that escapes the confines of objectivist linear thinking. But it does so without rejecting the value of comparison. Understanding the ways that particular migrants navigate the landscape of competing ethical demands allows for a degree of psychic unity that makes such comparisons even possible—universalism—but without imposing an experience-distant model onto *how* those migrants come up with new moral lines of thinking—that is, universalism, but without the uniformity.

Notes

1. This chapter is based on work supported by a National Science Foundation Doctoral Dissertation Improvement Grant [No. BCS-0852593] and a grant from the Committee on South Asian Studies at the University of Chicago, as well as research funds from Brigham Young University.
2. One could likewise label my approach the "psychological anthropology" of migration, but I use "cultural psychology" in the spirit of this volume (see Menon and Cassaniti's introductory chapter to this volume). In doing so, I identify with the approach laid out by Shweder (1990), namely an ethnographically oriented discipline that takes the coconstitution of mind and culture seriously.
3. These previous Hmong villages in Thailand originated from the same migration patterns that led Hmong to Southeast Asia in waves of diasporic resettlement in the nineteenth century, which sent Hmong in large numbers to Vietnam, Laos, Thailand, and, to a more limited extent, Myanmar (Burma).
4. In Hickman (2011) I extensively document the reasons for resettlement and argue that the choices to go to the United States or stay in Thailand do not seem to have exerted a significant sampling bias in my group of participants. See pages 183–84 for a full description of the selection criteria, the migration histories of these families, and a more complete methodological account of how these families were chosen for inclusion in this study. The rigor of finding comparable families was paramount in this comparative project.
5. Age ranges for each subgroup included (in years): 45–85 for the Thailand older gen-

eration; 39–75 for the US older generation, 18–32 for the Thailand younger generation, and 18–23 for the US younger generation. One younger-generation person in the United States estimated his age as early thirties but because of disruptions during the war did not know his exact age, and he was integrated into a school cohort of biologically younger children when they resettled as refugees. Segments of one older generation interview in Thailand were excluded from this analysis for logistical reasons.

6. The full vignettes and follow-up questions are in Hickman 2011.

7. The full codebook used to make these determinations can be provided by the author. I would like to thank Mary Cook for all her hard work in helping me develop and employ this codebook in this analysis.

8. Fisher-B software (White 1995) provides one-tailed p-values only. However, there were not meaningful variations between one-tailed and two-tailed p-values, which I checked against alternative software that calculates one-way Fisher's exact statistics. Fisher-B also has the advantage of calculating a three-way Fisher's exact test. The calculation of one-way p-values is also less ambiguous (there are multiple methods for calculating two-tailed p-values), if less conservative. Further, it makes sense to consider one-tailed p-values for this analysis because life course theory would predict higher levels of divergence among the younger generation.

9. It is worth noting that acculturation and assimilation are not isomorphic concepts, and there are noted differences in the literature. Nevertheless, the similarities in linear thinking (despite the attempt by theorists in each camp to elaborate on the picture of acculturation/assimilation) pervade both theoretical approaches in similar ways. The similarities present similar issues when it comes to interpreting my empirical findings, and the two approaches are therefore treated together. For a discussion of the differences between the concepts of acculturation and assimilation, see Redfield, Linton, and Herskovits (1936), as well as Gans (2007).

10. Person-centered ethnography presents a particularly useful epistemological window into understanding how the experiences of migration and resettlement shape the subjectivities of migrants. Person-centered ethnography emphasizes the interplay and tensions between cultural models or schema and the idiosyncratic psychological processes of individuals who belong to the communities where these cultural models hold sway. As described by Levy and Hollan (1998, Hollan 2001), this methodology is particularly useful in grounding ethnographic analyses in the lived experiences of those whom we seek to understand and does not place too much theoretical weight on more "experience-distant" notions of culture or community, or, I would argue, multilinear models of psychological or demographic change (also see Shweder 1995).

References

Barry, Declan T. 2001. "Development of a New Scale for Measuring Acculturation: The East Asian Acculturation Measure (EAAM)." *Journal of Immigrant Health* 3 (4): 193–97.

Berry, John W. 1970. "Marginality, Stress and Ethnic Identification in an Acculturated Aboriginal Community." *Journal of Cross-Cultural Psychology* 1 (3): 239–52.

———. 1980. "Acculturation as Varieties of Adaptation." In *Acculturation: Theory, Models and Some New Findings*, edited by Amado M. Padilla, 9–25. Boulder, CO: Westview.

Berry, John W., Jean S. Phinney, David L. Sam, and Paul Vedder. 2006. "Immigrant Youth: Acculturation, Identity, and Adaptation." *Applied Psychology* 55 (3): 303–32.

Briggs, Charles. 1986. *Learning How to Ask: A Sociolinguistic Appraisal of the Role of the Interview in Social Science Research.* Cambridge: Cambridge University Press.

Cassaniti, Julia L. 2014. "Moralizing Emotion: A Breakdown in Thailand." *Anthropological Theory* 14 (3): 280–300.

Cassaniti, Julia L., and Jacob R. Hickman. 2014. "New Directions in the Anthropology of Morality." *Anthropological Theory* 14 (3): 251–62.

Fadiman, Anne. 1997. *The Spirit Catches You and You Fall Down.* New York: Farrar, Straus, and Giroux.

Felix-Ortiz, Maria, Michael D. Newcomb, and Hector Myers. 1994. "A Multidimensional Measure of Cultural Identity for Latino and Latina Adolescents." *Hispanic Journal of Behavioral Sciences* 16 (2): 99–115.

Gans, Herbert J. 2007. "Acculturation, Assimilation and Mobility." *Ethnic and Racial Studies* 30 (1): 152–64.

Gordon, Milton M. 1964. *Assimilation in American Life: The Role of Race, Religion, and National Origins.* Cary, NC: Oxford University Press.

Guerra, Valeschka, and R. Giner-Sorolla. 2007. "The Big Three of Morality in UK and Brazil: Differences and Similarities." Latin American Regional Congress of Cross-Cultural Psychology Conference Proceedings, Mexico City.

———. 2010. "The Community, Autonomy, and Divinity Scale (CADS): A New Tool for the Cross-Cultural Study of Morality." *Journal of Cross-Cultural Psychology* 41 (1): 35–50.

Haidt, Jonathan, Silvia Helene Koller, and Maria G. Dias. 1993. "Affect, Culture, and Morality, or Is It Wrong to Eat Your Dog?" *Journal of Personality and Social Psychology* 65 (4): 613–28.

Hardy, S. A., L. J. Walker, J. A. Olsen, R. D. Woodbury, and J. R. Hickman. 2014. "Moral Identity as Moral Ideal Self: Links to Adolescent Outcomes." *Developmental Psychology* 50 (1): 45–57.

Hickman, Jacob R. 2007. "Is It the Spirit or the Body? Syncretism of Health Beliefs among Hmong Immigrants to Alaska." *NAPA Bulletin (Annals of Anthropological Practice)* 27 (1): 176–95.

———. 2011. "Morality and Personhood in the Hmong Diaspora: A Person-Centered Ethnography of Migration and Resettlement." PhD diss., Department of Comparative Human Development, University of Chicago.

———. 2014. "Ancestral Personhood and Moral Justification." *Anthropological Theory* 14 (3): 317–35.

———. 2016. "Ancestral Pasts, Ancestral Futures: Morality and Personhood across Generations in the Hmong Diaspora." Unpublished book manuscript, accessed December 2016.

Hickman, Jacob R., and Allison DiBianca Fasoli. 2015. "The Dynamics of Ethical Co-occurrence in Hmong and American Evangelical Families: New Directions for Three Ethics Research." In Jensen, *Moral Development in a Global World*, 117–140.

Hollan, Douglas W. 2001. "Developments in Person-Centered Ethnography." In *The Psychology of Cultural Experience*, edited by Carmella C. Moore and Holly F. Matthews, 48–67. Cambridge, UK: Cambridge University Press.

Jensen, Lene Arnett. 1995. "Habits of the Heart Revisited: Autonomy, Community, and Divinity in Adults' Moral Language." *Qualitative Sociology* 18 (1): 71–86.

———. 1998. "Moral Divisions within Countries between Orthodoxy and Progressivism: India and the United States." *Journal for the Scientific Study of Religion* 37 (1): 90–107.

———. 2004. Coding Manual: Ethics of Autonomy, Community, and Divinity. Worcester, MA: Clark University.

———. 2008. "Through Two Lenses: A Cultural-Developmental Approach to Moral Reasoning." *Developmental Review* 28: 289–315.

———. 2009. "Conceptions of God and the Devil across the Lifespan: A Cultural-Developmental Study of Religious Liberals and Conservatives." *Journal for the Scientific Study of Religion* 48 (1): 121–45.

———, ed. 2015. *Moral Development in a Global World: Research from a Cultural Developmental Perspective*. Cambridge: Cambridge University Press.

Jessor, Richard, Anne Colby, and Richard A. Shweder. 1996. *Ethnography and Human Development: Context and Meaning in Social Inquiry. John D. and Catherine T. MacArthur Foundation Series on Mental Health and Development.* Chicago: University of Chicago Press.

Kohlberg, Lawrence. 1969. "Stage and Sequence: The Cognitive Development Approach to Socialization." In *Handbook of Socialization Theory and Research*, edited by David A. Goslin. Skokie, IL: Rand McNally.

———. 1981. *The Philosophy of Moral Development: Moral Stages and the Idea of Justice. Vol. 1, Essays on Moral Development.* San Francisco: Harper and Row.

Kohlberg, Lawrence, Charles Levine, and Alexandra Hewer. 1983. *Moral Stages: A Current Formulation and a Response to Critics.* Vol. 10 in *Contributions to Human Development*, edited by J. A. Meacham. New York: Karger.

Lee, John K., and Katherine Green. 2010. "Acculturation Processes of Hmong in Eastern Wisconsin." *Hmong Studies Journal* 11: 1–21.

Lee, Stacey J. 2005. *Up against Whiteness: Race, School, and Immigrant Youth.* New York: Teachers College Press.

Levy, Robert I., and Douglas W. Hollan. 1998. "Person-Centered Interviewing and Observation." In *Handbook of Methods in Cultural Anthropology*, edited by H. Russell Bernard, 333–64. Walnut Creek, CA: Altamira.

Menon, Usha, and Richard A. Shweder. 1998. "The Return of the White Man's Burden: The Moral Discourse of Anthropology and the Domestic Life of Hindu Women." In *Welcome to Middle Age! (And Other Cultural Fictions)*, edited by Richard A. Shweder, 139–88. Chicago: University of Chicago Press.

Nguyen, Huong H., and Alesander von Eye. 2002. "The Acculturation Scale for Vietnamese Adolescents (ASVA): A Didimensional Perspective." *International Journal of Behavioral Development* 26 (3): 202–13.

Nguyen, Jacqueline. 2009. "Acculturation, Autonomy, and Parent–Adolescent Relationships in Hmong Families." Phd diss., Educational Psychology, University of Wisconsin–Madison.

Portes, Alejandro, Patricia Fernández-Kelly, and William Haller. 2005. "Segmented Assimilation on the Ground: The New Second Generation in Early Adulthood." *Ethnic and Racial Studies* 28 (6): 1000–1040.

———. 2009. "The Adaptation of the Immigrant Second Generation in America: A Theoretical Overview and Recent Evidence." *Journal of Ethnic and Migration Studies* 35 (7): 1077–1104.

Portes, Alejandro, and Rubén G. Rumbaut. 2005. "Introduction: The Second Generation and the Children of Immigrants Longitudinal Study." *Ethnic and Racial Studies* 28 (6): 983–99.

———. 2014. *Immigrant America: A Portrait*. 4th ed. Berkeley: University of California Press.

Portes, Alejandro, and Min Zhou. 1993. "The New Second Generation: Segmented Assimilation and Its Variants." *Annals of the American Academy of Political and Social Science* 530 (1): 74–96.

Redfield, Robert, Ralph Linton, and Melville Herskovits. 1936. "Memorandum for the Study of Acculturation." *American Anthropologist* 38: 149–52.

Rozin, Paul, Laura Lowery, Sumio Imada, and Jonathan Haidt. 1999. "The CAD Triad Hypothesis: A Mapping between Big Three Moral Emotions (Contempt, Anger, Disgust) and Three Moral Codes (Community, Autonomy, Divinity)." *Journal of Personality and Social Psychology* 76 (4): 574–86.

Rumbaut, Rubén G. 1994. "The Crucible Within: Ethnic Identity, Self-Esteem, and Segmented Assimilation among Children of Immigrants." *International Migration Review* 28 (4): 748–94.

———. 1997. "Assimilation and Its Discontents: Between Rhetoric and Reality." *International Migration Review* 31 (4): 923–60.

Sam, David L., and John W. Berry, eds. 2006. *The Cambridge Handbook of Acculturation Psychology*. Cambridge, UK: Cambridge University Press.

Schwartz, Seth J., Jennifer B. Unger, Byron L. Zamboanga, and José Szapocznik. 2010. "Rethinking the Concept of Acculturation: Implications for Theory and Research." *American Psychologist* 65 (4): 237–51.

Shweder, Richard A. 1990. "Cultural Psychology: What Is It?" In *Cultural Psychology: Essays on Comparative Human Development*, edited by James W. Stigler, Richard A. Shweder, and Gilbert Herdt, 1–43. Cambridge: Cambridge University Press.

———. 1995. "The Confessions of a Methodological Individualist." *Culture and Psychology* 1: 115–22.

———. 1998. *Welcome to Middle Age! (And Other Cultural Fictions)*. John D. and Catherine T. MacArthur Foundation Series on Mental Health and Development. Studies on Successful Midlife Development. Chicago: University of Chicago Press.

———. 2003. *Why Do Men Barbecue? Recipes for Cultural Psychology*. Cambridge, MA: Harvard University Press.

Shweder, Richard A., Manomohan Mahapatra, and Joan G. Miller. 1990. "Culture and Moral Development." In *The Emergence of Morality in Young Children*, edited by Jerome Kagan and Sharon Lamb, 1–83. Chicago: University of Chicago Press.

Shweder, Richard A., Nancy C. Much, Manomohan Mahapatra, and Lawrence Park. 2003. "The 'Big Three' of Morality (Autonomy, Community and Divinity), and the 'Big Three' Explanations of Suffering." In *Why Do Men Barbecue? Recipes for Cultural Psychology*, edited by Richard A. Shweder, 74–133. Cambridge, MA: Harvard University Press.

Teske, Raymond H. C. Jr., and Bardin H. Nelson. 1974. "Acculturation and Assimilation: A Clarification." *American Ethnologist* 1 (2): 351–67.

Weinreich, Peter. 2009. "'Enculturation,' Not 'Acculturation': Conceptualising and Assessing Identity Processes in Migrant Communities." *International Journal of Intercultural Relations* 33 (2): 124–39.

White, Douglas R. 1995. "Fisher-B: A Program for Exact Significance Test for Two- and Three-Way Interaction Effects." *World Cultures* 8 (2): 33-36.

Wong, David B. 2014. "Integrating Philosophy with Anthropology in an Approach to Morality." *Anthropological Theory* 14 (3): 336–55.

ELEVEN

Vexed Tolerance: Cultural Psychology on Multiculturalism

PINKY HOTA

Smith College

Department of Anthropology

In order to concretely and tangibly convey the continued relevance of the word *culture* to undergraduate students, I assign Richard Shweder's essay "What about FGM?" in the Introduction to Cultural Anthropology class that I teach at Smith College. Postmodern critiques have made *culture* a rather contentious term within cultural anthropology. Indeed, I myself provocatively ask students to attend to their interest in "different cultures" as a kind of voyeurism, a desire to peep into the lives of exotic Others for the shock and thrill of encountering practices such as headhunting and cannibalism, removing them temporarily from their seemingly banal surrounds. I press them to ask where exactly culture is located and rendered visible. Is it in macro structures spun like Geertzian webs of significance by humanity itself, in which symbolic meanings generate a coherent cultural system that can then be made legible and analyzed? Or is it the case that culture is not a coherent, intelligible system? How do we understand culture as patterned yet plastic, discernable yet not fixed? Rather than attend to sociocultural rules, should we seek culture in contradictions—gaps between purported social rules and their myriad quotidian violations? Despite these provocations that seek precisely to unsettle students who come to anthropology because "they like learning about different cultures," I also wish to impress upon students the importance of meaningfully engaging with cultural differences. At a time when the culture concept has been so roundly critiqued and somewhat abandoned in contemporary anthropology, perhaps it is not all that surprising that I would turn to cultural psychology for a reading that would demonstrate, as Shweder (2002) would say, "why engaging with culture matters in the first place," to emphatically convey the risks of adopting a liberal worldview that would not only undermine but even seek the erasure of meaningful difference.

In a recent interview in which he reflects on his contributions to the field of cultural psychology, Shweder calls female genital mutilation "the practice that cannot be named" (Shweder 2013, 7), insisting that the mere act of naming female genital mutilation invariably and necessarily invokes a set of morally laden assumptions. On a campus such as Smith, gender politics tack back and forth between a plurality of feminisms. Some of these lay claim to a unitary category of women and call for shared cause among them (some might lump these under the label second-wave feminism). Others call for an attention to intersectionality (Crenshaw 1989)—the intersections of systems of discrimination such as gender and race—and also insist on understanding gender as a fluid rather than binary system but nevertheless rely on what Gayatri Chakravorty Spivak (1987) has called a "strategic essentialism" to advance a shared feminist agenda. In her essay in this volume, Fuambai Ahmadu states that a Shwederian cultural psychological analysis exposes second-wave feminism's blind spots in assessing female genital mutilation as merely another tactic of subordination of women in cultures that practice it. She goes on to suggest that Third Wave Feminism might have room for a more nuanced understanding of female genital mutilation and can recognize female circumcision as a tool through which women exercise subversive defiance within patriarchal societies. Despite the radical break that Ahmadu posits between second and third wave feminism in their capacities for a meaningful engagement with the gender politics of female genital mutilation, I wish to suggest that second and third wave feminism might both still grapple with liberal moral imperatives in equal measure and that the moral liberal feminist subject continues to linger within third wave feminism—a political subject who experiences doubt about female genital mutilation and its claims about asserting rather than negating culturally salient forms of female emancipation and gendered identity.

The persistent presence of liberal moral impulses and the moral feminist subject who experienced doubt were certainly evidenced in my discussions with my students at Smith. Though there is no unitary strand of feminist thought on campus, the discussion of female genital mutilation in the Smith classroom invoked several moral impulses distinctly liberal in their assumptions across a plural set of feminist positions. Several questions arose, particularly around how one could definitively ascertain consent and desire on part of the young women undergoing circumcision—whether it was peer pressure or a real choice—demonstrating the tenacity of the concept of free will at the core of the feminist liberal subject. A week later, a student stopped me after class to say that reading the article had destabilized her in her first few weeks of college. Having recently started college after attending a private school in Boston, she had chosen to come to a women's college because of her keen interest in women's rights and a desire to build a career as an activist. After reading the article, she now did not know what to think. On the one hand, she could not accept that female genital mutilation was not a patriarchal practice aimed at disciplining women's bodies and sexualities and had a visceral reaction to the very thought of women's bodies undergoing such "violence." On the other hand, she did not want to be a white liberal feminist who assumed that the West should impose its brand of feminism on women of color elsewhere "who did not know what was best for them." Shweder's analysis, she said, had made it clear that her visceral reaction to female genital mutilation was "more her problem than that of women undergoing the surgeries." She looked genuinely troubled, her neatly laid plans of a life devoted to women's activism disrupted as she experienced, in her words, at first a "kind of bind" and then later "almost a paralysis." The student articulated a gap between reasoned argument and moral sensibility—"Am I supposed to not have a response at all to anything anymore?" Her questions betrayed genuine anguish, suggesting that despite the appeals to reason made in the text, she had, in fact, experienced an embodied, visceral moral response that exceeded reason. This was a response that could not easily be resolved, a visceral rejection of the corporeal harms being done to bodies that she could only imagine as similar to hers in form, meaning, and subjective experience. It is this gap between liberal reason—we should be respectful of difference, we should not replicate a colonial viewpoint seeking the annihilation of "barbaric" practices—and a visceral embodied morality that forms the starting point of this essay.

Elizabeth Povinelli (2002) asserts that these contradictions and impasses between reason and an embodied morality of liberalism are Maussian total social facts, spanning economic, legal, political, and religious spheres in late liberal society, which reveal the tensions riddling ongoing projects of multiculturalism. These disjunctive moments, she says, are not merely barriers to multicultural success but rather constitute the very fabric of multiculturalism. Shweder's cultural psychological analysis of female genital mutilation consistently exposes these tensions and slippages between public reason and embodied morality too, which, as my student stated, made her experience a kind of paralysis upon reading the text. In this essay, taking cues from this gap between public reason and embodied morality, I set up a dialogue between two unlikely interlocutors—cultural psychological scholarship on multiculturalism represented in the work of Richard Shweder and his colleagues on the limits of tolerance in multiculturalism, and Elizabeth Povinelli's (2002) anthropological account of political conditions under late liberalism, in which she examines the practices of multicultural recognition among indigenous groups in contemporary Australia. Povinelli argues that the multicultural legacy of colonial practices has created conditions under which Australian indigenous social life is threatened, not by identifying with colonial powers, but instead by an insistent evaluation and recognition through difference, demanding that indigenous people identify with an impossible standard of authentic culture. Povinelli argues that this maintenance of difference is fundamental to recognition of minorities in multicultural regimes. The modalities of the maintenance, manufacturing, and contestation of difference within liberal multiculturalism, far from being invested in upholding an ethical commitment to difference, then serve only to reinforce the power of liberal regimes.

I refer to these scholarly works as unlikely interlocutors not only because Shweder's work on the cultural psychology of multiculturalism and Povinelli's work speak about liberalism and multicultural recognition by employing two distinct registers but also to acknowledge that these registers index epistemological worlds that might, at best, see each other as lacking common ground or at worst, be fundamentally at odds with one another. Povinelli might see a cultural psychological analysis of multiculturalism as attempting merely to translate difference rather than interrogate the very conditions under which difference is recognized and manufactured. An even more critical reading might see such an approach as a positivist attempt at reifying difference that is itself complicit in the maintenance of distinction as a necessary and ongoing project of liberal recognition. Cultural psychology might, in turn, despair of Povinelli's implicit postmodern distrust of culture as a unitary, intelligible, and coherent set of meanings, norms, and practices. Further, it might ask—if the recognition of difference in multiculturalism is always "cunning," what, if anything, lies outside such machinations of multicultural apparatus? To put it plainly, what are the alternatives to the pitfalls of the two poles represented by the erasure of difference and the recognition of difference? These are not small, inconsequential disagreements. Yet this essay argues that both Shweder's and Povinelli's arguments illustrate how cultural psychology and political anthropology converge in their ability to point to the same niggling, persistent refrains in multiculturalism's attempts to variously manage, mobilize, and bracket moral impulses that arise while encountering difference. By pointing to how Shweder and Povinelli both discuss difference and radical alterity, morality, and corporeal practices, this essay reveals how both cultural psychology and anthropology identify similar impasses and contradictions within liberal multiculturalism. In the past decade or so, scholarship investigating the relationship between moral and political formations has somewhat receded in the domain of cultural psychology, with most discussions limited specifically to practices lumped under female genital mutilation. Concomitantly, the connections between reconfigurations within moral reason and accompanying moral imperatives, as well as their implications for political liberal subject formation in (neo)liberal regimes, have gained traction in contemporary political anthropology (see, for instance, Fassin 2011; Muehlbach 2012; Ticktin 2011) with calls being made for a new "critical moral anthropology" (Fassin 2012, 1). By drawing out the similarities and differences between these two unlikely interlocutors on liberal multiculturalism, this essay aims to serve as a reminder of cultural psychology's precocious forays into illustrating the indispensability of attending to morality as a window onto political impulses, action, and subject formation. It is noteworthy that even in this volume, this essay and Ahmadu's are the sole contributions that primarily engage with the domain of the political, even though several essays richly illustrate the potential of cultural psychology to illuminate and nuance our understandings of moral life worlds and the politics within them. This essay is then also a call for a renewed and more expansive attention to the relationship between moral tensions and debates and political phenomena as objects of study within contemporary cultural psychology.

I also suggest that while Shweder's essay on female genital mutilation reveals the impasses of multiculturalism and the incommensurability of an ethical commitment to meaningful difference and liberal multiculturalism as moral-political order, cultural psychology's larger framing of debates about multiculturalism around questions of tolerance stops short of calling the analytic of tolerance itself into question. Finally, I end the essay with contributions of cultural psychology to thinking about difference in meaningful and tangible ways, particularly for the purposes of teaching young students the importance of engaging with cultural difference on its own terms.

Difference and Radical Alterity

In general, the purported facts about female circumcision go unquestioned, the moral implications of the case are thought to be obvious, and the mere query,

"What about FGM?" is presumed to function in and of itself as a knockdown argument against both cultural pluralism and any inclination toward tolerance.

—Shweder, "What about FGM," page 226

In his seminal essay "The Politics of Recognition" (Taylor and Gutmann 1994), philosopher Charles Taylor asserts that when it comes to the question of difference and "equal respect" in liberal orders, two kinds of political frameworks come to the fore. In the first framework, the principle of equal respect requires the treatment of all in the liberal order in a blindness to difference. This approach, Taylor reminds us, focuses on what is same in all. In the second, the liberal order has to recognize and foster particularity. Shweder alludes to the fact that such a supposedly fair and difference-blind society is inhuman in suppressing identities, critiquing its emphasis on a shared core of humanity that is outside or prior to culture that overlays it. Cultural psychology has been emphatic about there being no general psychological functioning to be abstracted as a universal, as the editors of this volume point out in their introductory remarks. As a corollary of this understanding, one might go as far as to say that the liberal subject is merely an abstraction because cultural psychology asserts there is no subjectivity that is outside culture—indeed, that culture and psyche "make each other up" (Shweder and Sullivan 1993).

For Povinelli, the question of difference is not merely one for the meaningful accounting of difference. Rather, the maintenance of difference is itself part of "cunning" of liberal recognition. Povinelli reminds us such a liberal multicultural recognition of difference hardly involves any real ethical commitment to understanding difference but rather merely becomes the very means through which liberalism continues to uphold itself as a meaningful framework.

Cultural psychology takes cultural difference as a *sui generis* barrier between liberal discourse law and the interests of communities and Povinelli's more critical approach asserts that cultural difference may itself be manufactured, made and remade through liberal orders. Both approaches, however, call for a substantive ethical commitment to understanding difference. Understanding difference is not merely a matter of legislation, it is necessarily a moral scheme. Moreover, as Povinelli shows, liberal multiculturalism invites citizens to take stances on how citizens can understand their experiences of the fundamental alterity of other moral orders. That is, it invites them to ascertain what is and should be the proper attitude to their own and others' feelings—how they should, ought, must act—that become the basis of distribution of rights, sympathy, and resources in national and global contexts (Povinelli 2002, 27). Therefore, it is not merely the case that liberal multiculturalism is threatened by other moral worlds but that it necessarily produces forms of multicultural citizenship through positioning one's own morality against those of others, which secures the basis of political distribution of rights and entitlements.

This section began with Shweder pointing out that even in the most reasoned debates about tolerance within multiculturalism, female genital mutilation is called upon as an ultimate weapon meant to throw multicultural tolerance into question. He suggests that the morals and affects engaged in female genital mutilation are so radically different, representing such a wholly radical alterity or otherness to the Western liberal subject, that they can arrest any conversation, immediately imposing limits on tolerance. Shweder uses this radical alterity as the starting point about his theorization about morality and multiculturalism because to him female genital mutilation's interpretation as radical alterity precisely display the vexed nature of what tolerance must encounter and meaningfully engage with. And so, Shweder indicates that although multicultural orders might routinely pay polite lip service to an acknowledgment of difference, moments of encountering radical alterity are those in which we can substantively and productively debate the limits of multicultural frameworks. Indeed, Povinelli (2002) herself brings up the fact that the partiality of multiculturalism finds "exemplary expression at the tip of the clitoris" (26) and that practices such as clitoridectomy have become the means through which a complex of affective reactions are invoked and a collective will that will not tolerate savagery among citizens. Encountering radical difference is productive of the formation of the liberal subject in the singular, echoed in Shweder's (1996) "principle of original multiplicity," which postulates that unexamined parts of a subject can be activated and brought into consciousness only by encountering the Other. But encountering radical difference also is productive of the formation of liberal multicultural subjects as citizens among whom collective political opinions are formed through such affectively charged processes.

Exposing the Gap between Public Reason and Moral Sensibility

But to reasonably debate the issue, we need first to discount, or at least bracket our own culturally shaped visceral reactions to the very thought of female genital alterations. If we don't, there will be no fair, informed and even-handed engagement with the voices of the many African women who think that an "eradication program" or a threat to withdraw foreign aid, or a prison sentence, or some other means of compulsion are not really appropriate responses to their valued way of life, and maybe more a measure of our brutality and barbarism than theirs.

—Shweder, "What about FGM," page 236

Povinelli (2002) is preoccupied with moments in which citizens of liberal multicultural regimes find themselves simultaneously obliged to their moral sense and to reason, and moments where the two are at odds with one another. She believes these instances to be productive of the social imaginaries and formations that form the basis of multicultural citizenship. It is in these moments of obligations that cannot be reconciled, when the ways of others continue to make us "sick," that liberal multiculturalism is exposed as partial and contested yet imperative. This is the sickness of liberal recognition for Povinelli—the discovery that "reasoning and affect are out of joint" (5). Subjects are repeatedly confronted with the imperative toward tolerance but cannot stop being deeply offended by the Other; indeed the presence of the Other makes them sick. Povinelli asserts that the power of liberal recognition comes not just from political discussion but from deeply ingrained moral sensibilities. She also points to moments when intellectual and performative aspects of liberal recognition work in concert but appeals to morality are deferred or because of the incommensurability of moral worlds. For instance, in legal settings, indigenous claimants can be legally persuasive if they narrate their beliefs and practices coherently, painting a picture of their "culture" rather than using the terms of morality, which fundamentally exposes the fact that multiculturalism relies consistently on the need to bracket questions of morality. This recourse to reason is what renders radical alterity into understandable difference, an enterprise Povinelli points out as inherent to the very practice of anthropology, and by extension any discipline that attempt to make "reasonable" other cultural worlds.

Shweder's (2002) cultural psychological approach too calls for reason but acknowledges a separation between reason and emotional-visceral reactions of morality, often expressed through a "yuck" response. He asserts that we should be aware that this experience of yuck can be wholly mutual, that our assumptions and practices may offend in equal measure but precisely does so to point out that while the Western yuck can be rationalized and even become encoded into law, the same is not true of those outside the Western formation. He acknowledges that the possibility of disjuncture between the two is what leads to the short-circuiting of reason:

These ethnographic reports are noteworthy because they suggest that instead of assuming that our own perceptions of beauty and disfigurement are universal and must be transcendental, we might want to consider the possibility that a real and astonishing cultural divide exists around the world in moral, emotional, aesthetic reactions to female genital surgeries. No doubt, of course, our own feelings of disgust, indignation, and anxiety about this topic are powerful and may be aroused easily and manipulated rhetorically with pictures (for example, of Third World surgical implements) or words (for example, labeling the activity torture or mutilation). If we want to understand the true character of this cultural divide in sensibilities, however, we need to bracket our initial (and automatic) emotional-visceral reactions and save any powerful conclusive feelings for the end of the argument, rather than have them color or short-circuit all objective analysis.

By pointing to a disjuncture between public reason and embodied moral response, Shweder asks that we bracket this feeling precisely because he is aware that the language of reason cannot access and explain the embodied moral response, which often serves as the basis of our evaluative frameworks as liberal subjects.

Corporeality

Physical spaces and semiotically mediated genres organized around "sex difference," "sex acts," "carnality," "sin" and so forth would entail new aspects of the world of the Arrente. New gendered and sexual subjects would be created through these organizing concepts and through the institutions that helped to cohere and reproduce them, as would be the space in which these subjects already interacted.

—Povinelli, *The Cunning of Recognition*, page 96

Shweder writes that in practices of female genital mutilation, a system of bodily aesthetics is enacted by circumcising groups, where the body is made beautiful to sight and touch through surgical alterations. Female genital mutilation genders the body, allowing bodies to occupy a proper gendered position in the context of the circumcising culture but also allows a particular salient matrix of gendered aesthetic beauty to be achieved. Shweder is emphatic about the fact that feminist critiques of female genital mutilation have included complaints about the purported suppression of women's sexuality in which the clitoris serves somewhat as an "ultimate symbol" of female emancipation, which insistently doubt self-reports of sexual pleasure among young circumcised women in Africa. Despite these women's protestations that they do indeed experience pleasure during sexual intercourse, such Western liberal feminist critiques have insisted that female genital mutilation is an attempt to police female sexuality. Shweder's cultural psychological analysis opens up possibilities that there may be no unitary female biological body that experiences sexual pleasure in the same way. Thus, cultural psychology reminds us that the way bodies experience pleasure and what constitutes pleasurable sexual experience are not biologically determined universals and that the bodily sensorium is always experienced within a cultural framework. Yet, as in the case of my students at Smith attempting to relate to the female genital mutilation experiences of young African women, when trying to access a particular embodied feeling state as a position from which to feel empathy for the Other, liberal multicultural citizens can access only what their own body might feel, insisting that "there could be no way" that these experiences were not traumatic and painful for these women. Shweder's drawing out of the corporeal aspects of the debate emphasizes that a bodily politics is important for understanding the impasse between reason and a true acknowledgment of difference. The mere naming, let alone discussion, of "the practice that cannot be named" invites us to imagine the bodily experience of women through our own embodied experiences, which Shweder implies will always result in a gap, for our bodily experiences cannot be translated across contexts. Shweder's cultural psychological approach to female genital mutilation then invites us to ask, What if one could not assume that women experienced their gendered body differently? And by implication, what if we could not assume that the category woman as a site of liberal claims could not be assumed as an ontological whole rooted in biological sameness?

For Povinelli too, the body and bodily practices become sites where a colonial history sows the seeds of multicultural difference and where radical alterity is made visible and debated. Through her examination of how ritual sex acts of the indigenous Arrente are discussed by British anthropologists Baldwin Spencer and Frank Gillen, who consistently sought to ascertain "why do they do what they do." Through a discussion of these barriers to reasoning and the challenges they posed, Povinelli charts how liberal discourse sought to make sex a distinct act and of sexuality as a form of identity, discernable in terms of Western understandings of sex and sexuality, which were fundamentally challenged by observations of the use of objects in sexual practices, group rather than dyadic sexual activity and the mixing of seemingly violent practices with pleasurable sex. As Spencer and Gillen attempted to make sense of these practices as such, they recursively returned to questions that cohered around whether the acts they had observed could be classified as sex and sexuality and akin to Western ideas of sex as a discrete domain cordoned off from ideas of community and religiosity. In so doing, they too began by assuming that the Arrente experienced their bodies in the same way as the Western white subject did, rather than considering possibilities such as those articulated by Povinelli: "What body, where and whose? Did the Arrente consider themselves as most intimately in their selves, their skins? Did the surface of the body separate them from the world or provide a sensuous medium of contact with it, a potential site of heightened mental and corporeal stimulation?" (105). Much like a Shwederian cultural psychology, Povinelli invites us to consider the limits of imagining the body of the Other in the same way that we imagine our own.

It is no accident that both Shweder and Povinelli theorize these insights about the impasses of liberal multiculturalism via discussions of corporeal and bodily practices. Bodily practices are particularly sites through which embodied visceral moral judgments are aroused, but also where appeals to a biological universalism are made. Everybody has a body, suggesting a universality of experience and a profound disconnect when that universalism is disrupted. The body is itself the means through which an embodied moral disgust is experienced, as articulated in Shweder's idea of the "mutual yuck" and Povinelli's assertion that "they cannot cease to make us sick." At the same time, both Shweder and Povinelli point to the niggling, persistent ways in which the body and bodily practices erect very particular barriers to fantasies of liberal sameness and consequently become charged sites of multicultural attempts to adjudicate between different behaviors indexing different moralities. Liberal subjects seeking to make moral sense of others in the liberal order in terms of their own corporeality are deeply, profoundly unsettled when corporeal differences make clear the incommensurability of moral frameworks that viscerally challenges their own. It becomes important to observe how universalizing impulses of liberalism consistently summon ideas of rights-bearing bodies that experience pleasure and suffering in biologically universal ways and find these assumptions challenged when bodily experiences are incommensurable, leading to moral disgust and political discomfort.

Tolerance

Tolerance is, as any vocabulary for recognizing and accommodating difference must be, a relativist theory of difference. Relativization, or perspectivism, ac-

knowledges that people can be different from oneself and yet not be inferior. . . .
[T]olerance is a relativist doctrine that seeks coexistence and moderation instead
of the imposition of one universalizing idea of virtue.

—Sarat, *The Micropolitics of Identity-Difference*, page 412

Both Shweder and his colleagues' cultural psychological approach and Povinelli's anthropological account point to the embodied, moral responses of liberal subjects that are irreconcilable with public reason and consequently resist narration. Yet the two frameworks also differ significantly, particularly in their approach to the notion of tolerance. In that sense, cultural psychology's approach to multiculturalism still attempts to recoup liberal multicultural imaginaries while seeking to make them more meaningfully accommodating of difference. By framing their interventions within the framework and language of tolerance, Shweder and colleagues point to the limits of tolerance but seek to revise, expand, and ultimately recoup it as a tool of liberal protection.

Povinelli is wary of this language of tolerance. Drawing on Michael Walzer's work *On Toleration* (1997), she insists that the language of tolerance points to the setting of limits on choice, in which theorists of liberal pluralism and multiculturalism urge us to set aside the intractable problems of multicultural politics and instead "begin with the doable." Jacques Derrida also emphasized a distrust of tolerance, pointing to its ties to sovereign reason. Reminding us that tolerance is embedded in a distinctly Christian framework, Derrida and Anidjar (2001) cast tolerance to be a paternalistic notion that mandated that the Other not be accepted as an equal but rather subordinated and certainly misinterpreted. In a recent excellent commentary on tolerance as a key word for thinking about bodies, and the body politic, Warwick Anderson (2014) asserts that in the late eighteenth century, *tolerance* had come to substitute the older *toleration* in the English language, meaning forbearance, patience, and indulgence of the opinions of others, echoing what Derrida might see as Christian motifs. Anderson also reminds us that for Derrida, tolerance was a "scrutinized hospitality, always under surveillance, parsimonious and protective of its sovereignty" (2003, 12), representing a "conditioned hospitality" that protected against the "wholly other." Pointing out that Derrida sought a system that harbored radical alterity, Anderson points out that the threshold of tolerance is the extreme limit of an organism's struggle to maintain its balance before total collapse.

In his contribution to *Engaging Cultural Differences*, Austin Sarat (2004) asserts that tolerance must necessarily engage moderation and relativity, and cultural psychology's emphasis on tolerance reveals that the liberal order is a framework that attempts to exercise moderation in some form but that it does not do so from a neutral position. As Derrida reminds us, the language of tolerance upholds the questioning and evaluative sovereign authority of liberal regimes. It essentially invites majority groups to tolerate difference but is fundamentally threatened by radical alterity, seemingly pushed to the point of collapse before it urges liberal subjects to engage in the tenuous bracketing of the visceral, embodied reactions to immoral Others. Moreover, as Povinelli points out, in the name of a meaningful accommodation of difference and the deployment of reason to expand the boundaries of tolerance, the project of liberalism hinges on the very manufacturing of difference for its maintenance. This is a dilemma not of tolerance of difference but of intolerance of assimilation, of sameness. Difference is reified, reproduced, and maintained through state and juridical processes, key tools of multicultural recognition, burdening Others with the maintenance of distinction as an ongoing project of making themselves intelligible as good multicultural subjects.

To illustrate the dangers of relying on a language of tolerance while discussing multiculturalism, I turn to an ethnographic context and a subject matter related to my own research—secularism as a program of multiculturalism in contemporary India. India is currently governed by a Hindu right wing government and debates about the rising intolerance toward religious minority communities have been receiving much attention in a climate of growing physical, verbal, and symbolic aggressions toward minorities. These aggressions have included the lynching of a Muslim man for suspected beef consumption by a Hindu mob and even the censure of public commentary lamenting a growing climate of intolerance. When asked to give an opinion on these developments, intellectuals such as Amartya Sen lamented the current state of affairs by relying on a long-standing idea of tolerance as tradition in Hindu India and insisted that most Hindus accept the food habits of those belonging to other groups and are "familiar and tolerant" of other people's religious beliefs (see Ghose 2016). Strikingly, this very same idea of tolerant Hindu majoritarian India was also invoked by aggressive political leaders belonging to the Hindu right wing to insist that despite being the only religion with natural and primary claims over the territory of the modern Indian state, Hinduism had been known for being more than tolerant, and perhaps even too accommodating of religious minorities who had run roughshod over its generosities (see, e.g., McCarthy 2014). Even ordinary citizens insisted that those who found

India intolerant were traitors who should leave the country at once and were ungrateful for the opportunities that minorities had in India, including prominent Muslim movie stars who have cult followings but were immediately rebuked for their statements expressing concern about violence toward minorities (see Sugen 2015). The popular actor Aamir Khan, who has been otherwise hailed for his commitment to social causes, expressed his "alarm" about these rising incidents of intolerance (see Pundir 2015). When he stated that his Hindu wife had contemplated leaving India fearing for the safety of their child, for that statement alone, ordinary Indians who had earlier hailed Khan's talent and celebrity immediately attacked him on social media and asked him to leave India. Others with some knowledge of the law went to the extent of filing First Information Reports against the actor under sections 153 (Wantonly giving provocation with intent to cause riot), 153A (Promoting enmity between different groups on grounds of religion, race, place of birth, residence, language, etc.), 153B (Imputations, assertions prejudicial to national-integration), and 154 (Sedition) of the Indian Penal Code (P.T.I. 2015). These developments revealed that Indian secularism as a multicultural order fundamentally rested on an idea of Hinduism as a majoritarian religion with a "rich" tradition of tolerance and plurality that had always "allowed" minorities to flourish because of its hospitality. The accompanying commentary reflected not only how the language of multicultural tolerance can be appropriated by the law as well as various factions to suit their agenda but that all these factions relied heavily on the notion of majoritarian tolerance as paternalistic benefaction in their deployments of Hindu tolerance. It also revealed how the Hindu right wing has successfully weaponized a script of tolerance in contemporary India such that mere suggestion that Hinduism's tolerance was to be questioned in some way invited the wrath not just of political hardliners but of ordinary citizens through whom Indian secularism as multicultural order was espoused, upheld, and enacted in quotidian ways. These developments chillingly echoed the themes that Derrida belabored in his criticism of tolerance as a "scrutinized hospitality, always under surveillance, parsimonious and protective of its sovereignty."

In drawing out connections and convergences between cultural psychological work on liberal multiculturalism and a critical anthropology of multicultural recognition, I have shown how they both point toward intractable tensions inherent in any project of multiculturalism. To conclude, I return to the student with whom this essay began. We may recall that reading Shweder's work on female genital mutilation made her doubt her neatly laid plans for a career in women's activism. This student's reaction to Shweder's "What about FGM?" reveals the potential of a cultural psychological approach to lay bare assumptions undergirding liberal human rights frameworks and imaginaries. Yet, as I have shown, cultural psychology's interventions are framed within the framework of tolerance and therefore stop short of pointing out that tolerance is not an equalizing acknowledgment of difference, but of a conditional, hierarchical, provisional acceptance. In a recent interview, Shweder asks whether it possible to be a robust cultural pluralist and a committed political liberal—a question he believes can be empirically answered by parsing out what forms of political liberalism are most compatible with a robust cultural pluralism. I would argue, however, that his question, as suggested in parts of his work on female genital mutilation, is also rhetorical, pointing to the possibility that liberal multiculturalism may have little to do with an ethical commitment to difference, and, in fact, may be irreconcilable with a robust cultural pluralism. Both Shweder and Povinelli do not provide an alternative to tolerance. This is not in the least because a multicultural framework that could accommodate radical alterity might, in fact, be an oxymoronic formulation.

At the outset, this essay suggested that cultural psychology is particularly well positioned to make greater forays into investigating the relationship between morality and politics. Although this analysis has pointed to the limitations of cultural psychology's reliance on a framework of tolerance in its study of multiculturalism, it also showcases its potential to reveal the immediate dangers of overlooking how cultural difference comes to bear on morality and politics. By framing the debate around the vexed nature of tolerance and concerning itself with the "doable," cultural psychology is unafraid to show the tangible ways in which overlooking culture can have serious ramifications and invites policymakers to reconsider the harms that can be done in the guise of upholding liberal values. No doubt, this engagement with the tangibility of culture is what made the issues of multiculturalism palpable and disconcerting to my student. Reading Shweder's essay on female genital mutilation made the risks of a glib multicultural accommodation of difference tangible and concrete for her, making her attend to the tensions within her as a liberal subject that Povinelli asserts to be total social facts of multiculturalism. At a time when anthropology has become afraid to use the word culture and shies away from political prescriptions, a Shwederian cultural psychological approach that begins with the doable can provide an important and immediate starting point for the examination of an unchecked "imperial liberalism"(Shweder 2002, 235).

References

Anderson, Warwick. 2014. "Tolerance." *Commonplaces: Itemizing the Technological Present.* http://somatosphere.net/2014/10/tolerance.html.

Crenshaw, Kimberlé. 1989. "Demarginalizing the Intersection of Race and Sex: A Black Feminist Critique of Antidiscrimination Doctrine, Feminist Theory and Antiracist Politics." *University of Chicago Legal Forum* 1989 (1): 139–67.

Derrida, Jacques. 2003. "Autoimmunity: Real and Symbolic Suicides" in *Philosophy in a Time of Terror: Dialogues with Jürgen Habermas and Jacques Derrida,* interviewed by Giovanna Borradori, 128. Chicago: University of Chicago Press.

Derrida, Jacques, and Gil Anidjar. 2001. *Acts of Religion.* New York: Routledge.

Fassin, Didier. 2011. *Humanitarian Reason: A Moral History of the Present.* Berkeley: University of California Press.

———. 2012. *A Companion to Moral Anthropology.* Boston: Wiley-Blackwell.

Ghose, Debobrat. 2016. "We Have Been Much Too Tolerant of Intolerance: Amartya Sen." *First Post,* http://www.firstpost.com/india/we-have-been-much-too-tolerant-of-intolerance-amartya-sen-2624688.html.

McCarthy, Julie. 2014. "In India, Hindu Nationalists Feel Their Moment Has Arrived." *Northwest Public Radio,* http://www.npr.org/sections/parallels/2014/08/26/343177139/in-india-hindu-nationalists-feel-their-moment-has-arrived.

Muehlebach, Andrea. 2012. *The Moral Neoliberal: Welfare and Citizenship in Italy.* Chicago: University of Chicago Press.

Povinelli, Elizabeth. 2002. *The Cunning of Recognition.* Durham, NC: Duke University Press.

P.T.I. 2015. "FIR against Aamir Khan, Wife Kiran Rao over Intolerance Remark." *The Hindu,* http://www.thehindu.com/news/national/fir-against-aamir-khan-wife-kiran-rao-over-intolerance-remark/article7949288.ece.

Pundir, Pallavi. 2015. "Aamir Khan on Intolerance: Kiran Asked Me if We Should Move Out of India." *Indian Express,* http://indianexpress.com/article/india/india-news-india/aamir-khan-joins-intolerance-debate-kiran-asked-if-we-should-move-out-of-india-rng-awards/.

Sarat, Austin. 2004. "*The Micropolitics of Identity-Difference: Recognition and Accommodation in Everyday Life.*" In Shweder, Minow, and Markus, *Engaging Cultural Differences,* 396–415.

Shweder, Richard A. 1996. "True Ethnography—The Lore, the Law, the Lure." In *Ethnography and Human Development,* edited by Richard Jessor, Anne Colby, and Richard A. Shweder. Chicago: University of Chicago Press

———. 2002. "*What about FGM?*" In Shweder, Minow, and Markus, *Engaging Cultural Differences,* 216–51.

Shweder, Richard A., Martha Minow, and Hazel Rose Markus. 2002. *Engaging Cultural Differences: The Multicultural Challenge in Liberal Democracies.* New York: Russell Sage Foundation.

Shweder, Richard A. 2013. "Robust Cultural Pluralism: An Interview with Professor Richard A. Shweder" (interview by Séamus A. Power). *Europe's Journal of Psychology* 9 (4): 671–86.

Shweder, Richard A., and Maria Sullivan. 1993. "Cultural Psychology: Who Needs It?" *Annual Review of Psychology* 44: 497–523.

Spivak, Gayatri C. 1987. *In Other Worlds: Essays in Cultural Politics.* Milton Park, Abingdon-on-Thames, UK: Taylor and Francis.

Sugden, Joanna. 2015. "The Intolerant Response to Aamir Khan's Intolerance Comments." *Wall Street Journal*, http://blogs.wsj.com/indiarealtime/2015/11/24/the-intolerant-response-to-aamir-khans-intolerance-comments/.

Taylor, Charles, and Amy Gutmann. 1994. *Multiculturalism: Examining the Politics of Recognition*. Princeton, NJ: Princeton University Press.

Ticktin, Miriam. 2011. *Casualties of Care: Immigration and the Politics of Humanitarianism in France*. Berkeley: University of California Press.

Walzer, Michael. 1997. *On Toleration*. Yale University Press.

TWELVE

Equality, Not Special Protection: Multiculturalism, Feminism, and Female Circumcision in Western Liberal Democracies

FUAMBAI AHMADU

I was twenty-three years old and a university graduate in Washington, DC, when, with great honor, I accepted my mother's request for her to "join" me into Bondo, the name of the women's "secret society" in Sierra Leone. My mother made the same offer to her younger sister, whom she had brought to the United States to raise with the rest of her children. My aunt, who was just a few years older than I, turned down my mother and her own mother graciously: "thanks but no thanks." My mother and I traveled with another, much older aunt, her fourteen-year-old daughter, and my eight-year-old sister (who were also at that time destined to be "sandene" or young initiates). Dubbed by today's global media as "vacation cutting," this Christmas holiday that I will never forget was a controversial journey that some other Western-born African girls have taken in previous decades.

Bondo female initiation involves what I refer to as female circumcision,[1] as part of the many rites that—to put it in an oversimplified way—transform girls into women (for a more nuanced discussion on the complexities and aesthetics of this process of transformation, see Ahmadu, in preparation; Boddy 1982, 1991; Boone 1986). According to the Sierra Leonean women I grew up among, female circumcision not only transforms girls into women but the operation beautifies the external genitalia, improves genital hygiene, and enhances female sexuality (Ahmadu 2009, 2009b; see also Boddy 1991 for the Sudan and El Guindi 2006 for Egypt). Today, this surgery is one of several types that are performed customarily among various groups of women mainly in Africa but also in parts of the Middle East, India, Indonesia, Malaysia, and South America.

These forms of female genital surgeries, performed predominantly by non-Western women, are called female genital mutilation by opponents who believe that the sole purpose of these operations is to advance men's control over women by diminishing women's sexual response in order to make them more passive and faithful in marriage (Abdalla 1982; Lightfoot-Klein 1989; UNICEF 2013).

If I were the same twenty-three-year-old today, however, I could go to my gynecologist's office where I currently reside in Bethesda, Maryland, and get a referral for a cosmetic surgeon to perform the same procedure I underwent in Sierra Leone. From what I have seen of the before and after pictures on the websites that advertise these female genital cosmetic surgeries, there are two perfectly anatomically comparable procedures that produce the same aesthetic appearance as WHO Type II Excision: labiaplasty (which involves the removal or trimming of labia minora) and clitoroplasty (which involves reduction of the structure and appearance of the external clitoral glans). These operations are legal, medically respected, and expensive (Braun 2005; Goodman 2011; Johnsdotter and Essen 2004). Western female genital cosmetic surgery is becoming more and more popular or "sexy" and is regularly featured in women's magazines, popular news outlets such as Huffington Post, reality shows, and many other forums. Typically, women who opt for these surgeries bring in photographs of what they view as perfectly sculptured vulvae that they see in men's porn magazines, such as *Playboy*. Interviews with these women reveal many of the same motives that I have heard Bondo women provide for female circumcision, "I feel cleaner, sexier . . . more sculpted!"

What then is the difference between my excision operation during my traditional rite of passage at the age of twenty-three in Sierra Leone and a similar cosmetic procedure I could easily obtain at an upscale US doctor's office if have the cash in hand? Some would argue that in both cases women are responding to patriarchal pressures and views of feminine beauty. This begs the question; why is the first case labeled as a threatening aberration and is a target for global eradication and criminalization and the second case is ignored as a normal, if controversial, cosmetic procedure that Western women can opt for freely? With this essay, I argue that the difference is preeminently about culture: In resituating female circumcision within a specific cultural context, the Kono of eastern Sierra Leone, and within a specific human body—my own—I reexamine the reasoning and implications of Susan Okin's question, "Is Multiculturalism Bad for Women" in terms of the equality of women in a multicultural liberal democracy, such as the United States (Okin 1999).

Group Rights versus Individual Rights

According to Okin (1999, 10), multiculturalism deals with "the claim, made in the context of basically liberal democracies, that minority cultures or ways of life are not sufficiently protected by the practice of ensuring the individual rights of their members and that as a consequence these should also be protected through special *group* rights or privileges." Okin goes on to argue against the rights of minority groups—particularly illiberal groups that violate their members' individual rights—to be "left alone" or to be accorded special privileges if their minority status endangers the culture's continued existence (11). In her view, these claims are inconsistent with the fundamental value of liberal democracies, individual freedom "which entails that group rights should not trump the individual rights of its members." Okin also criticizes defenders of multiculturalism who say these group rights should be restricted to groups that are internally liberal. In her view, feminists—"everyone, that is, who endorses the moral equality of men and women—should remain skeptical" (11).

In this essay, I argue against Okin's key assumptions and generalizations with regard to minority or immigrant groups that she states may not appear "illiberal" on the surface but in reality discriminate against the rights of women and girls. My purpose is not to necessarily defend or advocate for the type of multiculturalism that Okin criticizes (that insists on group rights trumping the rights of individuals in order to perpetuate the existence of a particular group) but to interrogate how interventions—in this case, specifically anti–female genital mutilation legislation and zero-tolerance policies—that are supposedly aimed at protecting individuals within minority groups end up discriminating against these same individuals vis-à-vis individuals within the larger, dominant cultural group. In other words, well-meaning legislation and policies that aim at liberating girls and women from patriarchal cultures and practices in effect negate the very agency and autonomy of girls and women within these groups that are fundamental to their experience of individual freedom and equality with other girls and women in the larger, dominant Western liberal democratic society.

Some key assumptions Okin makes that are problematic in relation to individual experiences are the following: First, that female circumcision is experienced negatively by all girls and women. This tendency to vicariously experience female circumcision as a harm and then to project this experience onto circumcised girls and women is poignantly highlighted in Hota's essay (this volume) in her description of one of her students who talked about feeling the pain of circumcision in her own body. Second, that individuals fit neatly into distinct dominant or minority cultural groups. The reality is that many so-called immigrants straddle multiple cultures and identities. When I joined my Kono female relatives on a plane to West Africa twenty-seven years ago, I was also a US-born and US-raised woman. And, finally, that agency can be expressed only through resistance to a cultural practice. Thus, the assumption goes, an individual who upholds or affirms a cultural tradition is not exercising agency.

This third point ignores the fact that individuals have multiple, often conflicting, cultural identities and that a practice such as female circumcision may not be experienced subjectively as harmful by women who identify (in some cases nonexclusively) with the cultural group that supports this tradition. As a woman born and raised in the United States, I opted out of the dominant US cultural tradition of not circumcising girls (and circumcising boys only) and embraced female (and male) circumcision, which is a part of my African ancestral tradition and supposedly inimical to the dominant gender and aesthetic norms of the Western society to which I also belong. A French feminist, Chantal Zabus, seemed to have the answer: In her 2007 book, Zabus suggested that it was in order to belong to my African culture (a culture she claims I could fathom only through "second hand knowledge of British Anthropology") that I chose initiation as an adult, thus my actions did not truly reflect agency (2007, 218). In her view, as a culturally lost in betwixt and between soul, I was not really rejecting anything; I was striving to belong to something, however unfamiliar.

> In Kono, [Ahmadu] seeks not only wholeness through excision but also an antidote to feelings of uprootment and displacement. Yet it is when she is experiencing the acute, punctual pain of excision that she acknowledges the United States as her home, that is, the country of her birth, of her being, and of her becoming whole despite her excision. (Zabus 2007, 220)

My response is to call for a broader, more fluid and less ethnocentric understanding of culture and agency that reflects multiple cultural identities and the wide range of choices that are available to people in today's world. Any effective concept of agency needs to acknowledge the prerogative of individuals to a wide range of choices, including the choice to uphold a cultural or ancestral tradition where there are other clear options available. My aunt was born in Sierra Leone and identified with her dominant Kono culture yet chose to opt out of female initiation as an immigrant to the United

States to fit in better with US gender norms. I was born in the United States and identified with dominant Western culture yet chose to opt in to female initiation to fit in better with the gender norms of my Kono mother, aunts, and grandmother. As I mentioned in the opening paragraph, we were both given the choice to "join" Bondo or not. In Okin and Zabus's view only my aunt exhibited agency because she rejected her African cultural tradition and embraced westernization. In my multicultural estimation, I believe that I also exhibited agency in rejecting a particular US cultural tradition (of circumcising boys only) and embracing a particular African cultural heritage that upholds a view of boys' and girls' circumcision as parallel and complementary. Choosing this or that cultural practice does not make me less or more American no more than rejecting this or that cultural practice makes my aunt more or less Kono. Likewise, I do not have less agency simply because the cultural tradition I chose is deemed un-American in the same way that my aunt does not have more agency simply because she chose to uphold the US tradition of not circumcising girls.

According to Okin (1999, 12), advocating for group rights is problematic for feminists (and all Western liberal-minded folk) because most cultures are suffused with ideologies and practices concerning gender. She posits a hypothetical situation (which then uncritically becomes real further along the essay) in which a culture endorses and facilitates the control of men over women, and that the more powerful male members are those in a position to determine and articulate the group's beliefs, practices, and interests. She states categorically that under such conditions the claims regarding group rights are actually antifeminist and limit the capacities of women and girls of that culture to live with human dignity equal to that of men and boys, and to live lives that are as freely chosen as they can. Okin's examples of extreme forms of subjugation of Western women include clitoridectomy and polygamy. She quotes a Western female journalist's interview with a female excisor in Africa as proof that clitoridectomy is meant to desexualize women and keep them faithful and subordinate in marriage (1999, 14) and she cites African women living in polygamous marriages in France as representative of the oppression and silencing of all women who live in polygamous societies (10).

Okin argues that advocates for group rights for minorities within liberal states ignore that cultural groups are not monolithic (there are important differences within groups) and that they are themselves gendered (with differences of power and advantages for men and women). She also criticizes the fact that advocates of group rights pay no attention to the private sphere or the realm of domestic or family life (1999, 12).

Okin argues that when liberal-minded Westerners do pay attention to these shortcomings, two important connections between gender and culture become quite apparent: First, the sphere of personal, sexual, and reproductive life that results in cultural practices affecting to a greater extent the lives of women and girls than lives of boys and men. Second, Okin posits that most cultures have as one of their principal aims the control of women by men and she cites examples of the founding myths of Judaism, Christianity, and Islam that are rife with attempts to control and justify the subordination of women. She states that these myths consist of a combination of denials of women's roles in reproduction; appropriations by men of the power to reproduce themselves; characterizations of women as overly emotional, untrustworthy, evil, or sexually dangerous; and refusal to acknowledge mother's rights over the disposition of children (1999, 13).

Further, Okin states boldly (despite her criticism of monotheistic Western religious traditions) that "while virtually all the world's cultures have distinctly patriarchal pasts, some—mostly, though by no means exclusively, Western liberal cultures—have departed far further from them than others" (1999, 16). Okin goes on to cite many examples of gender subordination in Western societies but still manages to conclude that "women in more liberal cultures are, at the same time, legally guaranteed many of the same freedoms and opportunities as men." And states further that "most families in such cultures, with the exception of some religious fundamentalists, do not communicate to their daughters that they are of far less value than boys, that their lives are to be confined to domesticity and service to men and children, and that their sexuality is of value only in marriage, in the service of men, and for reproductive ends" (1999, 17).

In the next section I present a detailed ethnographic description of the relevant aspects of Kono culture, history, and general way of life for many women in relation to female (and male) circumcision as a critique of Okin's caricaturization of women's supposedly dismal position in non-Western cultures. More specifically, I provide the ethnographic background for my own argument against anti–female genital mutilation legislation and zero-tolerance policies: That banning practices among minority groups that are legally permitted and accessible to members of the dominant cultural group is an infringement on the rights of individuals within the minority group to equality, nondiscrimination, and (parental) autonomy. My contention does not concern group rights versus minority rights per se but the rights of all individuals within a liberal democratic society to equality, autonomy, and nondiscrimination. How is it that the same operation I underwent in Sierra Leone during a traditional ceremony that honored my female ancestors is called female genital mutilation and is banned in many countries—even for adult women—but would be called female genital cosmetic surgery and would be my legal prerogative and no one's business if I had opted for the surgery in a high-end plastic surgery office in Bethesda?

An American Journey into Kono Womanhood

Okin's first and most basic assumption is that all the world is now and has always been patriarchal and has as its conspiratorial aim the control of women by men. In this section, I examine my own ethnic group, the Kono of eastern Sierra Leone, and how it is that as a liberated US college student I could possibly choose to identify with the supposedly oppressed women of this society who are subjected to female genital mutilation and polygamous marriages. Using several theoretical insights from my doctoral dissertation on the Mandinka in The Gambia (Ahmadu 2005) as well as my master's thesis on Bondo Society among the Kono in Sierra Leone (1996), I have tried to assess the symbolic meanings of female and male circumcision within Bondo (and Poro) initiation for the Kono. The claims I make in this section are derived from unpublished papers I have presented at my public lectures and scientific or professional conferences in the United States and abroad during the past ten years (Ahmadu 2013, 2014, 2015a, 2015b).

The Kono are a Mande-speaking ethnic group who are closely related to the Mandinka (Ahmadu 2005, 40). Like all Mande groups, the Kono came from a region that now includes Mali and Guinea. And, like all Mande speakers, the Kono practice male and female initiation and circumcision as complementary and parallel cultural and symbolic processes (Hardin 2003) that are performances of Mande creation (Ahmadu 2005, 219). The stereotypical view of male and female initiation within anthropology is that these rituals mark and celebrate the transition from boyhood to manhood and girlhood to womanhood respectively. I have used this Van Gennepian concept in much of my own writings, but it is far more appropriate to view these rituals as complex performances of a society's cosmology (Ahmadu 2005, 219–44). Like all good performances, initiation tells us (through the use of metaphor, rhetoric, drama, and so on) a story: In this case, the story is about the creation (or rather separation) of nature and culture, of natural human beings and enculturated social beings, of the elementary structures of kinship, of sex, gender, gendered social structures, of reproductive and ecological spheres of power, in short, of the world in which the cultural group lives and imagines itself as a distinct entity (Ahmadu 2005, 219).

In Sierra Leone, women's initiation, like men's, is a highly organized and hierarchical affair: The institution itself is synonymous with women's traditional power, their political, economic, reproductive, and ritual domains of dominance (Ahmadu 2013, 2014, 2015b; Bledsoe 1984; Boone 1979; Mac-Cormack 1975, 1979 and 1980; Hardin 1993). If Genesis is the written creation story of the Jews of Israel, initiation is the enacted creation story of the Mande people of West Africa.

In the following sections I demonstrate that contrary to Okin's thesis: (1) Female circumcision is not gender-based violence among the Kono but a practice that most view as complementary and parallel with male circumcision. (2) The symbolic meanings of female and male circumcision can be understood in reference to Mande creation myths that have as a key figure a matriarchal creator and, as some writers have observed about other parts of the world, a central theme of the natural androgeneity of humans (Broch-Due, Rudie, and Bleie 1993). (3) As I will go on to describe, female and male circumcision are about the creation of sex and gender and the separation of nature and culture (MacCormack and Strathern 1980; Strathern 1980). (4) Female sex and sexuality are celebrated in female initiation rituals and reified in the masquerades that women dance and parade in villages and towns (Ahmadu 2013, 2014, 2015b; Boone 1979). (5) Female sexual autonomy among the Kono coexists with a dual-sex social structure (baindenmoe and fadenmoe) in which senior women and senior men exercise political power (Hardin 1993). (6) Okin's Western feminist construction of female genital mutilation draws on assumptions about the body, female sexuality, and universalized patriarchy that are projected onto practitioners of traditional female circumcision practices.

Androgyny School of Thought

The most forceful theoretical models that explain female circumcision are associated with what I will refer to as the "androgyny school" on initiation (Broch-Due et al. 1993; Jonckers 1987; Zahan 1979). In her article "Making Incomplete," Strathern (1993) provides the following insight: "far from completing a person, it is as though initiation practices gender the person as an incomplete being" (42). That is to say, that initiation transforms a child who is considered somehow androgynous or "complete," having both male and female elements, into a single-sex, "incomplete" person. Strathern goes on to suggest that this "incomplete" person will then be directed in search of a cross-sex partner, also an "incomplete" single- (opposite) sex person. In marriage, these "incomplete" beings become "complete," male and female, and capable of procreation. Zahan (1979 makes a similar observation in his study of Bambara male initiation: "[W]hen children leave the n'domo brotherhood . . . they are circumcised, which means that they are now relieved of their androgynous nature, by the removal of their female element (represented by the foreskin) and directed towards the search of their social partner" (Zahan 1979, 17).

Jonckers, who like Zahan is a French-speaking anthropologist, also writes on a related Mande group that "La pensée Minyanka donne une portée symbolique à ces mutilations: il s'agit de supprimer le symbole femelle (le prépuce) chez l'homme et le symbole masculin (le clitoris) chez la femme" (Jonckers 1987, 90).

Bleie (1993) also provides applicable cross-cultural examples of themes of androgyny that provide a convincing framework for understanding women's voices among the Kono and the symbolic analysis I describe in what follows. In her study, Bleie discusses "a recurring theme in mythologies of androgeneity: That the androgyne is unable to procreate and must split into two pure halves to be made procreative, or to fake procreativity" (261). Bleie goes on to describe several ethnographic examples of this dialectic in local cosmologies, two of which are of particular importance to our purpose. Among the Gimi, Bleie explains, a woman and a man are joined as a pair, but must remain split and not merge in order to (re)produce offspring that are seen as androgynous, with dual origins (275). Bleie explains further that splitting is enhanced by deconstructing and detaching parts of the initiates' composite identities, thereby rendering them single-gendered and ready for marriage. The merging of female and male elements generates the basis for exclusively female or male claims to autonomous reproduction.

Androgyny and Mande Creation of Sex and Gender

According to Mande cosmology, there is a supreme, unseen, almighty God who is distant and has little to do with the human world (Zahan 1979); among the Kono the ultimate creator is Ya-tah, the one you met (Hardin 1993; Parsons 1964). In most oral traditions this unseen maker created, metamorphosed, or manifested as nature, the seen world, the earth, or—as Mande symbolism depicts—a matriarchal creator. This primordial, divine nature is wild and untamed and, according to Zahan (1979), goes about populating the world with forests, oceans, mountains, wild animals, and so on. The matriarchal creator possesses both feminine and masculine aspects, and so is sexually undifferentiated or ambiguous. Among the Bambara this matriarchal creator is referred to as Moussou Koroni Koundye (Zahan 1979). During my analysis of the meaning of Mandinka initiation rites and circumcision, I realized that the literal translation of Moussou Koroni Koundye is "an old woman spirit with a sweet/white head" (Ahmadu 2005, 225). In my view, as a Kono woman who is familiar with the Bondo/ Sande masks used in female initiation (more on this follows), this is a clear sexual reference to an uncircumcised penis/clitoris or the excess flesh that surrounds the glans (Ahmadu 2013, 2014, 2015a).

To make a long creation myth short, natural-born humans or children are viewed as replicas or reproductions of the androgynous matriarchal creator (Ahmadu 2013, 2014, 2015b). As part of nature, they too are un- defined and possess both male and female elements; like the matriarchal creator, they are whole. Boys possess the penis shaft, foreskin around the head, and a "vagina" (urethral opening) externally and girls also possess "foreskin" around the clitoral head and a vagina externally but the "penis" or clitoral shaft is internal. In male initiation rituals, the prepuce or fore- skin of the penis head is associated with femininity—arguably the excess skin or labia of Moussou Koroni (old woman spirit; Ahmadu 2005, 226– 30). Thus, removal of the foreskin represents the masculinization of the boy as well as the "opening of his eye" (because the urethral opening or "vagina" or "birth canal" is exposed). He now belongs to the community of single-sex Poro men that reproduces other single-sex men (in Poro ini- tiation rituals). He is not a whole man in the Western sense of the word, but an incomplete being, a husband called chee among the Kono or kee among the Mandinka (Ahmadu 2013, 2014, 2015a).

In parallel and complementary form the external clitoral or "penis" glans represents Moussou Koroni's masculinity, Koundye (sweet head). Thus, excision of the clitoral glans symbolizes the girl's feminization, her transformation into a single sex. Her separation from the masculine aspect of the maternal marks her new sexual status and entry into the community of single-sex women (Bondo) that reproduces other single-sex women (in Bondo initiation). Her labia minora is excised, just like the male foreskin, to reveal her vagina or symbolically to "open the eye" of the inner phallus (the internal clitoral shaft). The name of large initiation ceremonies among the Mandinka is *nyakabaa* literally meaning "open the eye of the mother/ spirit/creator" (Ahmadu 2005, 2013, 2014, 2015b). The initiated Bondo woman is now single-sex, not a whole woman in the Western sense of the word, but an incomplete being, or a wife called *musu* among the kono or *musoo* among the Mandinka (Ahmadu 2013, 2014, and 2015b). In short, initiated Poro men and initiated Bondo women possess both a phallus and vagina as a procreative tool (men externally and women internally). They are complementary and interdependent as *chee* and *musu* halves who will join together in marriage or heterosexual intercourse as one whole flesh. In men's ceremonies, men identify with and celebrate their differences from women; similarly women's ceremonies elaborate, exaggerate, and celebrate their differences from men, often ridiculing and belittling male sexuality and supposed social and sexual superiority (personal observation of initiation ceremonies in The Gambia and in Sierra Leone).

In men's ceremonies among other Mande groups, the secret masks such as the Komo are representations of the awesomeness of the vagina, female supernatural power, blood, and death (Brett-Smith 1984). In complementary form, women's ceremonies celebrate their own masks, which are representations of the "the sweet head," the uncircumcised clitoral glans. The rings around the neck of the Bondo mask are said to resemble the excess flesh around the head of the penis/clitoris and are a sign of beauty (Boone 1986). Women who have lines of extra flesh around their neck are said to be especially beautiful (Boone 1986 and personal observation). Most important, the head of the Bondo mask is invariably topped off with braids or hair ornaments of various sorts. This represents female ownership of the phallus, women's domination of the male sexual tool for their own pleasure and men's semen for procreation (Ahmadu 2005, 147–52). Ironically, while the women dance around the Bondo masquerade, it is an external representation of their sexual powers that is celebrated and enjoyed by all women communally during initiation. But for the Konomusu, as with the Gambian women I interviewed, Alice Walker's (1992) *Possessing the Secret of Joy* would not be a reference to the intimate pleasures of an external clitoral head (however sweet it is) but to a woman's phallus within, her internal clitoris that remains intact, very sexually functional and the site of both orgasm and conception (Ahmadu 2005, 136–51).

Thus, I have argued that through excision girls symbolically eschew childhood masculinity or androgyny and maternal attachment. Female initiation teaches that sexual and reproductive power resides with women and is represented internally—by the clitoral shaft that remains intact and very sensitive under the vaginal surface. Physiologically, this inner phallus constitutes the great bulk of the clitoral tissue and organ that initiated women say is responsible for powerful orgasms during sexual intercourse. Women I interviewed said that female contractions during orgasm trigger or facilitate male ejaculation and insemination, which ultimately leads to conception (Ahmadu 2005, 136–51). In my focus groups during fieldwork, many women of all ages stated clearly that there is no separation between orgasm and reproduction, that sexual pleasure facilitates conception and hence, procreation (Ahmadu 2005, 148). These beliefs were reinforced by what I observed in seclusion—the very sexually explicit songs and body movements girls learned as part of their training and instruction in dancing and, by extension, lovemaking.

Therefore, contrary to much of the rhetoric of the anti–female genital mutilation campaigns, the female sex and female sexuality are not oppressed in, through, or by these ritual practices. On the contrary, female sexual prowess, pleasure, and reproductive powers are embodied by the Bondo masks, which also represents the invisible clitoris or the hidden phallus beneath the vulva. The subcutaneous clitoris is celebrated and reified in the masquerades as the origins of creation, of nature, and of culture (Ahmadu 2013, 2014, and 2015b). In male rituals, the vagina and menstrual blood are feared as potent weapons of death and destruction. This cultural and symbolic context of female initiation and excision explains how it could be that Kono girls and women speak in almost reverential terms about the practice, their bodies, and the experience of womanhood (see Sunju Ahmadu film 2005). In short, excision, removal of the external clitoral glans and labia minora, what much of the world has been taught to think of as female genital mutilation is, for most Kono women and the women of Bondo, a powerful symbol of matriarchal power (Ahmadu 2013, 2014, and 2015b).

Mande Dual-Sex Societies, Female Circumcision, and Sexual Openness

According to some traditional rulers, the Kono, like most if not all Mande-speaking ethnic groups, were most likely at one time in history a predominantly matrilineal society, that is, inheritance and kinship or blood relations were traced solely through women (personal communication with chiefs in Kono, Sierra Leone, and Brikama, The Gambia). According to traditional elders, biological paternity was not culturally acknowledged (recall that female initiation rituals deny and appropriate male sexual and reproductive powers) and men could never make claims based on their supposed biological connection to a child or as genitor (Ahmadu 1996). The man responsible for caring for and protecting a woman's children was her own maternal uncle, her mother's brother who even today is referred to as a "small mother" or a sort of male mother among both the Kono (mbain) and the Mandinka (mbaring). A woman's eldest son would succeed his uncle as head of the family. The uncle's primary job was the protection of his sister and sister's children (Ahmadu 1996).

Women were not sexually controlled by their brothers or uncles because it did not matter who the biological father of her children were; all the children came under the legal protection of her brother or uncle (personal communication with Kono informants). A man who wanted to be sexually involved with a woman had to come and work under the latter's maternal uncle and provide services for the family for many, many years. They would live in the family compound or come and visit (personal communication with Kono informants). Royal women, or women whose sons were in line to rule, had to remain in the family compound, whereas younger sisters were permitted more freedom to reside elsewhere with their lovers. At no time could these male lovers lay claim to their biological children with the women—they were responsible for their own sister's children (Ahmadu 1996).

I came to gather all this information on women's sexual behavior in Kono after reflecting on some of my experiences in my father's village (Ahmadu 2000). My father had introduced me to several women who in turn introduced me to their male companions or "friends." My father once sensed that I was a bit confused and then he explained to me that these "friends" were the lovers of the women I met. The young males were there to assist the women with their "farms" and "gardens." A chief with many wives could not possibly take care of all of their needs, so it made sense that other, younger and stronger, unmarried men were available to lend a hand, my father would say mockingly. Since that time, I have heard young women in the villages (and even as far as the United States where I normally reside) shout at their husbands for one thing or another and insist that their husbands do not own their vaginas, that they are free to do with their vaginas whatever they wanted and to take their vaginas to whomever they choose. I have heard and continue to hear these sorts of protests and assertions by women so often that I am inclined to believe (and many informants have confirmed) that women are in fact the owners of their sexuality, whether married or not.

In a dual-sex society, women corule with men (Ahmadu 2005, 260). Typically, the queen sister (or queen mother) is responsible for what Okin would refer to as the "private" sphere—sexuality, reproduction, rice farming, and so on (Ahmadu 2005, 197). Except, in these circumstances, the line between public and private is blurred. Reproduction is hardly considered a private affair but involves the entire community—it is daughters, after all, who reproduce the ruling patrilineage or matrilineage. In large-scale female initiation or fertility ceremonies as described in the previous section, women demonstrate their power and control over male sexuality and reproduction. Among the Mande-speaking groups—traditional female initiation is a time and place of what even today's liberated Western feminists would refer to as female sexual license (Ahmadu 2005, 125). In initiation ceremonies, there are no "husbands" (Gamble 1998, 44); "wives" own their vaginas both ideologically and in practice:

> The ceremony was a woman's one, and no man should disturb them. Every woman was at liberty to do whatever she liked. No man was allowed to guard his wife during this period and if he heard that any man had beaten his wife during this period or fought with another man because he was joking or chatting with his wife, that man would be tied with a rope and kept in the chief's cell until the ceremony was over. Let no man ask a stranger where he was going if he found him in his women's quarters. All unmarried men should give up their houses to strangers. (Gamble 1998, 44)

Okin also would be surprised to learn that Mande male initiation is not about biological reproduction and fertility or controlling anyone's sexuality, let alone women's. These male rituals are about the transformation of androgynous boys into single-sex "husbands" or chee, who are defined as hunters, warriors, and chiefs, but not as biological fathers or progenitors (Ahmadu 2005, 59). The bloodletting that occurs in Mande male initiation rituals concerns the appropriation and harnessing of female substance (blood), which is associated with secret knowledge and supernatural power, which is further transformed into medicinal substances that men use for protection in hunting and warfare. As stated in the previous section, the symbol of power in men's rituals is the vagina, which is considered to be an awesome abyss and repository of supernatural knowledge. Harnessing these female sources of power continues to be the main preoccupations of men's initiation rituals today in Mande secret societies and the installation of chiefs.

Abrahamic Religion, Male Circumcision, and Control of Female Sexuality

Okin is certainly right about one thing: The idea of father as progenitor was given birth to by Judaism and the creation of the patriarchal God of Abraham (Okin 1999, 13–14). The symbolic appropriation of women's sexual and biological contributions to reproduction, as Okin rightly pointed out, is associated with Western origins of religion and specific cultural and historical expressions of patriarchy (Okin 1999, 13–14).

As I have demonstrated above for the Kono and other Mande groups, female circumcision is associated with a matriarchal creator, specifically with the creation or separation of male and female from an androgynous maternal being. However, Jewish male circumcision came to signify the creation of a male God and through Abraham a special male lineage that would rule the world and give birth to a male messiah or son who would save the world. This symbolism, as Okin observed, has involved imagery of male appropriation of female sexual power and reproductive capacities as well as the denial of biological motherhood—the exact reversal of the symbolism of Mande female circumcision, matrilineal social structure, and a matriarchal creator (Ahmadu 2005, 180).

Although there is no space to discuss it in detail here (Ahmadu, in preparation), I argue that from the west coast of Africa across to the eastern horn of the subcontinent, the deep symbolic meaning of female circumcision—whether Type I, II, or III—has a common ideological or religious origin: the belief in an androgynous matriarchal creator either as a consort or metamorphosis of the original unseen creator. I suggest that it is the expansion and imposition of Abrahamic religious traditions, the creation and worship of a unitary male, patriarchal God, as well as colonialism, modernity, and now Western second-wave feminism that has reshaped the meaning of female circumcision from its matriarchal origins to what much of the world recognizes today as a patriarchal practice. It is Abrahamic conceptualization of God as paternal creator, the passing on of His seed to male descendants to create an unblemished patrilineal line of descent via the recognition of father as progenitor, that necessitates the sexual control of women in marriage in order to keep the patriline pure and unadulterated. It is Western traditional and modern nuclear, monogamous ideals of marriage that are founded upon these patriarchal traditions and ideologies that require the sexual fidelity and virginity of women to ensure biological paternity of children (Ahmadu 2005, 182–84). It is Western societies that grant legal rights and authority to biological fathers that makes it compelling for men to advance cultural rules and norms about female honor and purity that shame many women into sexual monogamy to ensure that they know and society knows the identity of the biological father of their children.

Many traditional Kono women who lack formal Western education and serious attachment to any of the Abrahamic religions would laugh at the thought that they are the sexual possessions of their husbands or that they must give birth to the biological children of their husbands in order to maintain their respect and honor in society. As previously mentioned, to this day women in traditional Kono villages (especially those married in polygamous households) have male lovers and have children with these male lovers and these children are considered to be the legal responsibility of their husbands and continue to have legal rights within their husbands' lineages. As I demonstrated for the Mandinka, another Mande ethnic group, history has introduced radical changes in social structures and ideologies, matrilineages became paralleled with patrilineages, the mother's brother's responsibility for his sister and his sister's children were transferred via modern marriages and so-called religious marriages to a woman's husband, the man who has paid bridewealth to her mother's brother in order to have reproductive and legal rights over her children (Ahmadu 1996).

As with the Mandinka, among the Kono it is now the husband who gets to decide about his children's future and it is now his own son who will inherit his wealth. His wife now lives with him and away from her family (especially her brothers), which makes her vulnerable to abuse and exploitation (Ahmadu 1996). Even though according to Kono customary law, a man cannot make claims of biological paternity (he can only make claims to rights over children if he has married or produced bridewealth for his wife), Kono men who convert to Islam or Christianity can make those claims under the religious moral codes of those traditions. Further, they can demand girls' virginity and chastity, as well as marital fidelity from wives under the banner of religion which today has also come to stand for traditional culture.

More poignantly, the obsession with female sexual shaming, which was never a part of Kono traditional society, has become an everyday lived reality for many contemporary Kono women. Those who are educated or who see themselves as good Muslims or good Christian women have bought into the sexual ideologies of women in these religions and see themselves as a step above their illiterate and "promiscuous" counterparts. For educated Christian women of my mother's and even my generation, female circumcision took on new meaning—sexual restraint and dampening of sexual desire in women to guard their virginity and keep them faithful in marriage. Educated men who are Muslim or Christian also seek to defend female circumcision for its supposed dampening effect on female sexuality (personal communication in exchanges on social media sites). Among many Muslim men or male heads of household, traditional female initiation ceremonies—because of their association with "promiscuity" and un-Islamic gods and goddesses—are eschewed over purely medical operations and recitations of Koranic verses (personal communication with informants).

This is the contemporary context of female circumcision that has caused Western women from outside these cultures to view this practice as patriarchal vestiges of an ancient era that subjugates women and treats them as the sexual slaves of men so that they are "good wives" and "good mothers" who care nothing of their own pleasure but live to reproduce for men, serve men, and ensure the reproduction of patriarchy in their part of the world (Sanderson 1981). This is the context in which a female excisor in Mali could proudly tell a white female journalist (a representative of Western, patriarchal society) what the excisor felt the journalist most likely wanted to and was expecting to hear—that the practice of excision makes a woman a good wife by quelling her sexual desire and taking the edge off her sexual response. Had I interviewed this same excisor, and she knew I was an initiated Kono woman, I can guarantee her response would have been different. One could argue that the excisor would feel equally compelled to tell me what I wanted to hear—and this would probably be true—but I would walk away from this engagement with far more complex cultural knowledge and awareness of how women think and talk about sexual empowerment than I would if I were to presume a simple, universal, and timeless patriarchy theory.

Western women (and non-Western women who uphold this perspective) can have a view of female circumcision as the patriarchal sexual subjugation of women for and in the service of men and marriage only if they only see the starting point of history from the Greeks and Romans and of religion from the beginning of Judaism, as Okin clearly does (Okin 1999, 13–14). Ironically, many feminists, like Okin, argue that proponents of female circumcision cannot make a claim to history and culture because what they call female genital mutilation is about the sexual oppression of women globally but these same feminists, as Okin does, are quick to refer to cultural or historical instances to prove their point about global patriarchy. So, it is not that history and culture are irrelevant but it is that only a specific version of history and culture is permitted when talking about or dismissing the cultural and historical claims that make female circumcision a meaningful practice for many African and other non-Western women practitioners.

Discussion: Equal Rights and Multiculturalism

If Okin's main thesis is right, one is to conclude that if not for the ingenuity and political astuteness of Western women who have fought to liberate their own cultures from the worst forms of patriarchy and guaranteed certain legal rights for women over the years, the rest of the non-Western world pretty much lives under pre-Western feminist darkness and sub-ordination. What is antifeminist (and has disturbing racial overtones) is permitting women from a dominant society to impose their views of re-ality and their experiences on women within minority groups or immi-grant women who reside in the same Western liberal democracy. Dissent-ers within the cultural groups have been propped up as spokespersons for all women in the group—those who identify as female genital mutilation victims or now survivors are given the media attention and platform (even if not the bulk of funding to combat this supposed scourge within their communities)—while those who question the dominant Western feminist discourse are either ignored or dismissed as "stupid" and "brainwashed."

As a US woman and a Kono woman, my own work has been to coun-ter this dominant and oppressive female genital mutilation narrative, to give space and scope to women and girls within our minority immigrant groups to express their different experiences and, in many cases, their sup-port for this aspect of our traditions. (Other writers and anthropologists who have also been critical of the female genital mutilation metanarrative include Shweder 2013; Hernlund and Shell-Duncan 2007; Shell-Duncan and Hernlund 2000; Kratz 1994; Boddy 1991, PPAN 2012, Earp 2016, Johnsdotter and Essen 2004.) In my view, it is very important that women in my community do not allow ourselves to be labeled antifeminists sim-ply because we refuse to allow ourselves to be defined in a negative and ethnocentric way by others who consider themselves to be the true custodi-ans of the dominant culture or of the Western societies we all call home. A truly multicultural society like the United States is the cultural monopoly of no one single group and therefore cannot promulgate a single standard of womanhood or support restrictive interpretations of freedom, auton-omy, and equality. As a woman born to Kono immigrants to the United States, I choose to see female initiation through the eyes of those women who raised me—as my right and a privilege of my cultural heritage that no one has the unmitigated right or power to deny me, regardless of what she or he thinks of this practice. At the same time, my adult Kono aunt who declined "vacation cutting" (as most if not all US-born Sierra Leonean girls would today) had a right to reject what she did not deem to be a privilege and her reasons were respected.

We did not then nor do we now need oppressive laws that judge and label our cultural traditions in order to recognize this fundamental level of freedom of adults to choose what or what not to do with our own bod-ies. Although my aunt and I were adults, my sister and younger cousin did not have a choice, just like my brothers and most boys in the United States and various parts of the world. My sister turned out to be well in favor of our mother's decision; my cousin was more skeptical—why wasn't she informed? Why was she not given a choice? When it comes to minors and nonmedical genital operations, considerations about whether this is allowed to continue have to be taken together and include both genders, all ethnic groups whether dominant or minority, without special privileges being accorded to one sex over another or one cultural group over another because of assumptions made by members of dominant groups about the inherent superiority of their own sex, religion, cultural heritage, and so on (Earp 2016).

Susan Okin may well believe that Western liberal democracies afford more freedom, autonomy, and sexual rights and privileges to women than the rest of the world. As a born US citizen and daughter of Kono immigrants who has experienced both worlds (and others), I beg to differ that this is always the case when it comes to the status of women. As I have shown in this essay, Kono culture affords far more sexual freedom and license to women than my Euro American sisters can boast about in our Western liberal societies. Much of the sexual prerogatives of Kono women have been increasingly encroached upon through patriarchal cultural, religious, and legal impositions under colonialism, Christianization, Islamization, and now a modern state and global "human rights" agenda dominated by a Western women's movement that seeks to universalize and standardize the experience and interests of white, European, middle-class women. Kono women walking around in rural villages carrying buckets on their heads and babies strapped to their backs or squatting in open markets selling vegetables and fruits or laboring on rice farms under the hot sun may not seem that empowered to many of my well-heeled, university-educated, latte-drinking feminist friends. But Kono women, like other women the world over, do have their own definitions of empowerment and what it is to be woman. Most of all, many of these women value their ancestral heritage and female-only traditions.

As the same US woman who freely choose Kono initiation twenty-five years ago, I say "thanks but no thanks" to my present day feminist anti–female genital mutilation saviors: Instead of special protection for me against my cultural group, grant me equal rights with yourselves and men from the dominant Western culture to which I also belong; and allow me to determine for myself as an American and a Kono woman what is and what is not a patriarchal practice and what I can or cannot do with my own body. Grant me the same privilege of family privacy that is accorded to men and women from the dominant society to which I belong to decide which cultural, religious, or purely cosmetic practices from any number that exist among the diverse groups in society that I will or will not transmit to my own children—male and female. If there is to be an age of consent for nonmedical genital procedures, then this needs to be applied across all categories of groups and individuals. If we allow that, among some groups or for some individual cases, exceptions can be made, we also must allow similar exceptions in parallel cases within other groups or among other individuals under similar circumstances.

My freedom to choose is true feminism, as Okin (1999,10) herself defined the term, "the belief that women should not be disadvantaged by their sex, and they should be recognized as having human dignity equal to that of men, and that they should have the opportunity to live as fulfilling and as freely chosen lives as men can." Male and female circumcision are important to the human dignity of those who support these bodily practices and, for most Kono people, male and female circumcision are a reflection of the equality of the sexes. If men can choose to uphold their cultural traditions, women also must enjoy the freedom to uphold their parallel cultural traditions within Kono society. Concern for the rights of the child in this instance should not be gender- or sex-specific. Either there is a ban on all genital modifications on minors or certain operations ought to be permitted on children, irrespective of sex.

Even though for Okin multiculturalism is "harder to pin down," for me it is the same as my feminism—the belief that I should not be disadvantaged or discriminated against because of my ethnic, cultural, religious, or any other difference, that I have the same human dignity as any other person in the United States, and that I should have the opportunity to live as fulfilling and as freely chosen a life as any other US citizen. Multiculturalism as expressed through the extension of individual freedom and equality to all and across all groups in a pluralistic society (no special protection and no special privileges) is the best thing for group preservation, for feminism, and for all liberal societies. Multiculturalism is good for women!

Note

1. Terminology is a very contentious issue with respect to female genital surgeries among non-Western women (PPAN 2012). I use the term female (and male) circumcision or excision to refer specifically to those genital operations or procedures that are performed as customary procedures and are linked with a society's religious beliefs—whether or not these beliefs are stated as explicit reasons for the practice. I use the term male circumcision to include this definition but also to refer to the

secular and widespread practice of male genital surgeries in the United States that are customary but not necessarily for religious reasons. I use the term female genital mutilation when referring specifically to the perspective of opponents of the practice and the term female genital cosmetic surgery in reference to anatomically similar practices that are more prevalent among white, educated Western women residing mainly in Western countries.

References

Abdalla, R. 1982. *Sisters in Affliction: Circumcision and Infibulation of Women in Africa*. London: Zed Press

Ahmadu, Fuambai. 1996. *Fertility, Femininity and a "Matriarchal" Ideal: Bondo "Secret Society" and Female Circumcision among Kono Women*. Unpublished master's thesis. Department of Anthropology, London School of Economics.

———. 2000. "Rites and Wrongs: Excision and Power among Kono Women of Sierra Leone." In *Female "Circumcision": Interdisciplinary Perspectives*, edited by Bettina Shell-Duncan and Ylva Hernlund, 283–312. Boulder, CO: Lynne Rienner.

———. 2005. *Cutting the Anthill: The Symbolic Foundations of Female and Male Initiation among the Mandinka of The Gambia*. Unpublished PhD diss., London School of Economics, University of London.

———. 2009a. "Empowering Girls in Sierra Leone: Initiation into Bondo Society." In *The Child: An Encyclopaedic Companion*, edited by Richard Shweder, 168–69. Chicago: University of Chicago Press.

———. 2009b. "Disputing the Myth of Sexual Dysfunction of Circumcised Women." *Anthropology Today* 4 (6): 14–17.

———. 2013. "Sexual and Symbolic Meanings of Female Circumcision among Mande groups in West Africa, Part I." Paper presented at Law and Public Policy Fellows Program Seminar, Georgetown University Law Center, Washington, DC, May 30.

———. 2014. "Sexual and Symbolic Meanings of Female Circumcision among Mande groups in West Africa, Part II." Paper presented at the Law and Public Policy Fellows Program Seminar, Georgetown University Law Center, Washington, DC, July 3.

———. 2015a. "Is Mutilated to Circumcised as Female Is to Male? Challenging the Last Vestige of Inequality in Sub-Sahara Africa." Guest lecture sponsored by the Lecture Fund, Departments of Anthropology and African Studies, Georgetown University, Washington, DC, December 2.

———. 2015b. "Sexual and Symbolic Meanings of Female Circumcision among Mande groups in West Africa, Part III." Paper presented at the Law and Public Policy Fellows Program Seminar, Georgetown University Law Center, Washington, DC, May 20.

———. 2016. In preparation. The Hidden Female Phallus: Matriarchy, Circumcision and the Cosmology of the Clitoris in Gender Rituals among the Mandinka of The Gambia.

Ahmadu, Sunju. 2005. *Bondo: A Journey into Kono Womanhood*. Documentary film.

Bledsoe, Caroline. 1984. "The Political Use of Sande Ideology and Symbolism." *American Ethnologist* 11: 455–72.

Bleie, Tone. 1993. "Aspects of Androgyny." In *Carved Flesh/Cast Selves: Gendered Symbols and Social Practices*, edited by Vigdis Broch-Due, Ingrid Rudie, and Tone Bleie, 257–77. Providence, RI: Berg.

Boddy, Janice. 1982. "Womb as Oasis: The Symbolic Context of Pharaonic Circumcision in Rural Northern Sudan." *American Ethnologist* 9: 682–98.

———. 1991. "Body Politics: Continuing the Anti-Circumcision Crusade." *Medical Anthropology Quarterly* 5: 15–17.

Boone, Sylvia. 1979. *Sowo Art in Sierra Leone: The Mind and Power of Women on the Plane of the Aesthetic Disciplines.* PhD diss., Yale University.

———. 1986. *Radiance from the Waters: Ideals of Feminine Beauty in Mende Art.* New Haven, CT: Yale University Press.

Braun, Virginia. 2005. "In Search of (Better) Sexual Pleasure: Female Genital Cosmetic Surgeries." *Sexualities* 8 (4): 407–24.

Brett-Smith, Sara. 1984. "The Mouth of the Komo." *Journal of Anthropology and Aesthetics* 31: 71–96.

Broch-Due, Vigdis, Ingrid Rudie, and Tone Bleie, eds. 1993. *Carved Flesh/Cast Selves: Gendered Symbols and Social Practices.* Providence, RI: Berg.

Earp, Brian. 2016. "Between Moral Relativism and Moral Hypocrisy: Reframing the Debate on 'FGM.'" *Kennedy Institute of Ethics* 26 (2): 105–44.

El Guindi, Fadwa. 2006. "Had This Been Your Face, Would You Leave It as Is?" *In Female Circumcision: Multicultural Perspectives.* Philadelphia: University of Pennsylvania Press.

Gamble, David, and A. K. Rahman. 1998. "Mandinka Ceremonies." *Gambia Studies, No. 34.* David Gamble Papers, UCLA, Los Angeles.

Gollaher, David. 2000. *Circumcision: A History of the World's Most Controversial Surgery.* New York: Basic Books.

Goodman, Michael. 2011. "Female Genital Cosmetic and Plastic Surgery: A Review." *The Journal of Sexual Medicine* 8 (6): 1813–25.

Hardin, Kris. 1993. *The Aesthetics of Action: Continuity and Change in a West African town.* Washington, DC: Smithsonian Institution Press.

Hernlund, Ylva, and Bettina Shell-Duncan, eds. 2007. *Transcultural Bodies: Female Genital Cutting in Global Context.* New Brunswick, NJ: Rutgers University Press.

Jonckers, D. 1987. *La Société Minyanka du Mali: Traditions Communautaires et Développement Cotonnier.* Paris: L'Harmattan.

Johnsdotter, Sara, and Birgitta Essen. 2010. "Genitals and Aesthetics: The Politics of Genital Modifications." *Reproductive Health Matters* 18 (35): 29–37.

Kratz, Corinne. 1994. *Affecting Performance: Meaning, Movement and Experience in Okiek Women's Initiation.* Washington, DC: Smithsonian Institution Press.

Lightfoot-Klein, Hanny. 1989. *Prisoners of Ritual: An Odyssey into Female Genital Mutilation in Africa.* London: Harrington Park Press.

MacCormack, Carol. 1975. "Sande Women and Political Power in Sierra Leone." *West African Journal of Sociology and Political Science* 1, 42–50.

———. 1979. "Sande: The Public Face of a Secret Society." In *The New Religions of Africa,* edited by B. Jules-Rosette, 27–37. New Jersey: Ablex.

———. 1980. "Proto-Social to Adult: A Sherbro Transformation." In *Nature, Culture and Gender,* edited by Marilyn Strathern and Carol MacCormack, 95–118. Cambridge: Cambridge University Press.

———. 1982. "Control of Land, Labour and Capitol in Rural Southern Sierra Leone." In *Women and Work in Africa.* Boulder, CO: Westview.

MacCormack, Carol and Marilyn Strathern, eds. 1980. *Nature, Culture and Gender.* Cambridge, UK: Cambridge University Press.

Okin, Susan. 1999. "Is Multiculturalism Bad for Women?" In *Is Multiculturalism Bad for*

Women?, edited by Joshua Cohen, Matthew Howard, and Martha C. Nussbaum, 9–24. Princeton, NJ: Princeton University Press.

Parsons, Robert Thomas. 1964. *Religion in an African Society: A Study of the Religion of the Kono People of Sierra Leone in Its Social Environment with Special Reference to the Function of Religion in That Society*. Leiden, Neth.: Brill.

Public Policy Advisory Network on Female Genital Surgeries in Africa (PPAN). 2012. "Seven Things to Know about Female Genital Surgeries in Africa." *Hastings Center Report* 42: 19–27. doi: 10.1002/hast.81

Shell-Duncan, Bettina, and Ylva Hernlund, eds. 2000. *Female "Circumcision": Interdisciplinary Perspectives*. Boulder: Lynne Rienner.

Sanderson, Lillian Passmore. 1981. *Against the Mutilation of Women*. London: Ithica.

Shweder, Richard. 2013. "The Goose and the Gander: The Genital Wars." *Global Discourse* 3 (2): 348–66. doi: http://dx.doi.org/10.1080/23269995.2013.811923.

Strathern, Marilyn. 1993. "Making Incomplete." In *Carved Flesh/Cast Selves: Gendered Symbols and Social Practices*, edited by Vigdis Broch-Due, Ingrid Rudie, and Tone Bleie, 41–51. Providence, RI: Berg.

UNICEF. 2013. *Female Genital Mutilation/Cutting: A Statistical Overview and Exploration of the Dynamics of Change*. New York: UNICEF.

Walker, Alice. 1992. *Possessing the Secret of Joy*. San Diego, CA: Harcourt.

Zabus, Chantal. 2007. *Between Rites and Rights: Excision in Women's Experiential Texts and Human Contexts*. Stanford, CA: Stanford University Press.

Zahan, Dominique. 1979. *The Religion, Spirituality, and Thought of Traditional Africa*. Chicago: University of Chicago Press.

Section 2
Mental Health: Variations in Healthy Minds across Cultures

THIRTEEN

Cultural Psychology and the Globalization of Western Psychiatric Practices

RANDALL HORTON

Seattle University
Department of Psychology

The last two decades have seen models for diagnosing and treating mental illness developed in North America and Europe introduced into communities across the developing world in historically unprecedented ways. A host of forces, humanitarian, economic, and institutional, have been driving this expansion, and although these efforts appear to hold tremendous potential for benefiting diverse communities, certain problems within the US system of psychiatric research stand at risk of being recreated in the emerging international system and undercutting the promised benefits of expanded mental health care to communities across the globe. This chapter looks specifically at a pair of problems that cultural psychologists and anthropologists identified in the 1990s in the US psychiatric system. It examines problems of ethnocentric bias that have arisen in the process of establishing and validating the basic constructs of psychiatric medicine and the problem of untoward economic influences (on the part of pharmaceutical companies and other professional interest groups) shaping current practices of the field.

It approaches these issues by documenting some of the forces driving the current press for internationalization of psychiatric medicine. It looks at the ways that sociocultural dimensions of human experience (and the related problems of ethnocentrism and untoward influence) have been reflected in successive editions of the *Diagnostic and Statistical Manual of Mental Disorders* [DSM] and the *International Classification of Diseases* [ICD], the two most prominent systems of psychiatric classification being used internationally. It argues that the changing treatment of sociocultural issues in successive revisions to these manuals reflects the growing impact of research within cultural psychology and medical anthropology. Both disciplines have offered strong critiques of the epistemological assumptions that underpin uniformitarian discourses in psychiatry, and both have contributed exemplary studies that document similarities and meaningful variations in the psychological experience of illness across cultures. We begin with an examination of a particularly illuminating moment in the history of the cultural and multicultural psychology movements in the United States.

Ethnocentrism, Epistemological Conservatism, and the US Case

On the cusp of the millennium in the pages of the *American Psychologist*, Stanley Sue (1999), a leader of the multicultural psychology movement in the United States, offered a critique of what he saw as barriers to the publication of research on the psychological experiences of ethnic minorities in the United States. Although directed at the field of psychology as a whole, his critique applied with especial force to the domain of clinical psychological, and by extension, psychiatric research. He argued that in articulating its methodological commitments, the field of psychology in the United States had long emphasized the pursuit of internal validity. It had focused on refining experimental designs and statistical analyses, on improving procedures for isolating and controlling variables, on insisting on the random assignment of subjects, on the use of manipulation checks and rigorously validated measures. These were laudable and important methodological refinements, but the field, Sue argued, had simultaneously ignored certain basic issues with the external validity of its theories.

Specifically, he argued, a host of psychological theories, measures, and interventions—many of which were now serving as foundational theory for various subfields of the discipline—had been validated almost exclusively in studies of white Americans of European descent. Their validity for other ethno-cultural groups had been presumed but never rigorously tested. Sue argued that the existence of this established body of "validated theory" grounded in Anglo-European communities, bolstered by this selective application of methodological canons for internal validity, was producing a bias against the emergence, reception, and influence of theories and constructs grounded in studies of other ethno-cultural groups.

Sue (1999) observed that studies conducted with white US middle-class samples had long been seen as an acceptable basis for the assumption of general, universal validity of a theory. When studies using ethnic minority samples showed effects, however, their findings would often be deemed insufficient as a basis from which to generalize to other groups. The internal validity of such research would be strongly scrutinized, and its findings might be dismissed in the face of a more rigorously internally validated body of knowledge anchored in homogeneous majority samples. These problems were compounded by the facts that even basic descriptive research on psychological life in ethnic minority communities was lacking, that the process of developing and internally validating measures for use in such communities was expensive and time consuming, and that funding for work in these areas was scant.

Sue's contention was that, at least in the United States, white European American researchers had not just enjoyed a kind of home court advantage in the putatively impartial contest of psychological ideas, but that—because of the historic underrepresentation of ethnic minorities in the discipline—they could be said to have written the rules, served as the league officials, and appointed the referees who would adjudicate the contest. Sue noted, however, that the situation was beginning to change. He was writing in 1999, and for two decades the multicultural and the cultural psychological movements in the United States had been growing in strength and prominence. The multicultural movement was a coalition of professionals from diverse backgrounds—including African Americans, Hispanic and Asian immigrants, women and sexual minorities—who organized to address issues of discrimination, exclusion, and prejudice in the field of psychology. Responding to the concerns the movement had raised, in 1993 the National Institutes of Health had taken the important step of requiring that, barring exceptional circumstances, all supported clinical research needed to include women and ethnic minorities and the design of such studies needed to allow for tests of whether variables measured and interventions tested affected members of these groups differently.

Observing the existence of persisting barriers to research focused on ethnic minorities, however, Sue (1999) proposed at least four additional remedies. First, he argued, researchers in the field of psychology should explicitly state the populations upon whom theories have been tested and validated. Second, theories should be viewed as local in scope until they have been tested and cross-validated in other populations and settings. Third, psychological researchers should adopt a wider range of methods "including qualitative and ethnographic approaches" (1076) to broaden the knowledge base of the discipline. Finally, cross-cultural research in psychology should work harder to discern which aspects of culture or ethnicity are responsible for differences, and the way to do this would be to focus on the "meaning of ethnicity."

Readers of this volume will recognize in these recommendations core tenets of the discipline of cultural psychology as mapped out in the preceding decade by theorists like Bruner (1990) and Shweder (1991). Indeed, Sue's millennial remarks pointed toward the appreciable common ground between the cultural psychological and multicultural movements, a relationship that has, at times, been tested on the grounds of differences in the two movements' relative depth of commitment to value pluralism (see Hota, this volume; Shweder 2003) and by the cultural psychology's more complete break with the positivist epistemological stance of the broader discipline of psychology. The publication of Sue's remarks in the millennial issue of the *American Psychologist* suggests that the force of the critiques of both of these movements was beginning to be felt in the mainstream of the discipline.

Sue's millennial remarks raised serious concerns, though, for some of his readers. The ensuing exchange in the journal tracked strikingly with debates that cultural psychologists had been involved in throughout the 1990s. Guyll and Madon (2000), for instance, strongly objected to Sue's characterization of bias in the field. Although they allowed that a focus on issues of internal validity, or "theoretical conservatism" as they termed it, could indeed be producing the kind of effects Sue described (i.e., suppressing the emergence of evidence for cultural psychological differences, prioritizing constructs reflecting a white, middle-class, Eurocentric bias), a conservative epistemological stance, they argued, was essential for the progress of scientific knowledge. Further, they offered, there was no evidence of intent on the part of researchers in the field of psychology to discourage research into ethnic differences. Going on to address the pragmatics of Sue's recommendations, they characterized his call for psychologists to stop making default generalizations of research findings across ethnicities as "unworkable." They felt it would require researchers to accept as "a fundamental premise that individuals from different ethnic groups differ from each other with respect to all psychological processes" and lead to a "balkanization" of the discipline. They concluded (Guyll and Madon 2000, 1510) by articulating a specific ideal for the discipline: "The ultimate challenge of psychological science is the development of universal theory that can explain individual differences both within and across cultures."

This exchange was important because within it these authors voiced explicitly the disciplinary aspirations and fears—the moral goods, to use Shweder's (1991) terms—along with a set of supporting epistemological commitments—that cultural psychologists (see the introduction to this volume) have argued have implicitly governed psychological research in the United States for several decades. Psychology as a field has valorized the discovery of universal, pan-cultural theory as a Holy Grail of empirical research. By contrast, research seeking to describe and characterize—or even acknowledge the existence of—significant, locally bounded psychological processes has been seen, at best, as impractical or unworthy of attention from serious scholars, or at worst, as inviting chaos (or "balkanization") into the field and undermining the integrity of the discipline as a whole.

Sue (2000) rejoined that bias needed to be judged by the outcomes of a process, and it could accrue without intent or awareness on the part of actors involved. He clarified that his proposals would not require accepting as a premise the existence of psychological differences across human groups. Ethno-cultural differences should neither be presumed to be present nor absent: they should be investigated. Data should be collected, and conclusions should be drawn from the evidence that emerges.

Western Psychiatry in a Wider World: The US Case Writ Large

How does this exchange help to illuminate the current situation of globalizing psychiatry? Fifteen years later, looking at the accelerating diffusion of Western psychiatric research and practices internationally, one can see within this process a set of problems analogous to those that Sue (1999) described in domestic US research. Here too, scientific priority has been awarded to a body of research that arose and received its initial validation and conceptual elaboration in a limited human community in Western Europe and North America. As practitioners and institutions seek to extend the reach of this system, expand it to embrace a much wider swath of humanity, the forces that lead to ethnocentrism and bias in the US system seem to be duplicated, if not aggravated, in international settings. In tracing the extent of the problems of ethnocentric bias and the prioritization of existing psychiatric theory and practice, we will focus on the way these issues have been reflected through successive revisions in the authorized diagnostic systems for psychiatric disorders, the *International Classification of Diseases* (*ICD*) and *Diagnostic and Statistical Manual of Mental Disorders* (*DSM*).

In adopting the term "Western psychiatric practices," I will be referring to the body of knowledge, institutions, and practices whose central elements include the development and use of large-scale diagnostic classification systems, the *ICD* and the *DSM*, as well as diagnostic instruments like the Structured Clinical Interview for the *DSM* [SCID], interventions like cognitive behavioral or psychoanalytic therapy, and the use of psychotropic medications such as antidepressants and antipsychotic agents. Although well established in the high-income nations of Europe and North America, and certain urban centers of Asia and Latin America, the general elements of this system had, by the turn of the millennium, obtained at most a fragile foothold in many parts of the world (Jacob 2001). The last fifteen years, however, have witnessed a push to extend the reach of this system to low- and middle-income countries. Although much of this push has come from health- and development-focused institutions like the World Health Organization (WHO), and, in some cases, initiatives are developed in response to particular public health crises such as natural disasters (see Good and Good this volume), in many parts of the world, such as China and India, the resources and incentives for this expansion of psychiatric care are coming from private pharmaceutical corporations.

Publication in 2010 of journalist Ethan Watters's *Crazy like Us: The Globalization of the American Psyche* brought what had been a largely academic and policy debate about the merits of this expansion to a broader public audience. Drawing on published research and interviews with academic researchers, clinicians, and laypersons, Watters painted an image of globalizing psychiatry as development gone awry, one in which the presumption of expert, universally applicable knowledge of mental illness and its proper treatments by Western-trained clinicians and policymakers was leading to iatrogenic illnesses (as a new variety of anorexia took root and became endemic in the late 1990s in Hong Kong), to wasted resources (as evinced in post-tsunami mental health relief efforts in Sri Lanka), and the disruption of adaptive local systems of meaning and support (in responding to psychosis in Zanzibar and posttraumatic stress disorder in Sri Lanka).

Grounds for skepticism about the invariably benign effects of whole-scale adoption of Western psychiatric practices go back considerably further, however, to the WHO's own Collaborative Study on Determinants of Outcome of Severe Mental Disorders (Sartorius et al. 1986), which documented better outcomes for schizophrenia for individuals living in several less industrialized nations where modern psychiatric infrastructure and care were lacking. The factors leading to these outcomes are still being debated (Littlewood, Jadhav, and Ryder 2007). At the very least, however, research suggests that we cannot take for granted that introducing biomedical explanations and treatments for illnesses and mental disorders will engender more humane, less stigmatizing responses in a particular community than explanations cast in terms of processes such as spirit attack, possession states, humoral imbalances, or the effects of karma or moral sickness.

Institutional Pressures for Adoption of a Uniform Globalized Psychiatry

The impetus for organizations like the WHO to address what has become known as the Mental Health Gap across the developing world emerged in the 1990s, when investigators working with data from the WHO and World Bank's International Morbidity and Mortality Study introduced the construct of disability-adjusted life years (DALYs). With the creation and adoption of this new construct, researchers sought to quantify with a single metric the combined losses to society that accrued from both the premature death and disability associated with a wide range of diseases and injuries. Neurological, mental health, and behavioral conditions were included among them. Working with these data, Desjarlais, Evans, Goode, and Kleinman (1995) argued that previous analyses based solely on mortality figures had grossly underestimated the negative impact of untreated mental health and behavioral problems in communities around the world. This was because, beyond their simple contribution to premature mortality, conditions such as depression, psychotic disorders, and substance abuse tend to disable and incapacitate people in the most productive years of their lives. An analysis of data collected in 2010 (Murray et al. 2012), for instance, suggested that a cluster of behavioral and psychiatric conditions, specifically, depression, substance abuse, and anxiety and psychotic disorders, were together responsible for as much as 23 percent of years lost to disability, an enormous burden in terms of lost economic productivity and general human welfare. The term *mental health gap* was introduced to highlight the acuity of these problems relative to the scarcity of mental health providers and resources to address them in the developing world.

To address these concerns, the WHO adopted a Mental Health Global Action Program (mhGAP) in 2002, which it began to implement in 2008. With the critical shortage of psychiatrists, psychologists, primary-care doctors, and nurses in most low-income countries, this initiative has focused on task sharing and providing resources for training nonspecialized health workers to diagnose and treat a core subset of mental and behavioral disorders. Several models have been put forward (Lund et al. 2012; Rahman, Malik, Sikander, Roberts, and Creed 2008) for how to implement such efforts. Researchers acknowledge that the obstacles can be significant to building programs that are locally relevant, effective, and sustainable. The initiative represents a direct and concerted commitment to bring core elements of psychiatric diagnosis and treatment to communities in which they have had little or no presence to date.

In terms of its overall role in globally diffusing the system of psychiatric diagnosis and treatment, the WHO's impact is deeper and more pervasive even than its promotion of projects like mhGAP would suggest. Each of the WHO's 193 member states commits to surveying and reporting standardized morbidity and mortality data in terms of the categories of illness and disorder set forth in the *ICD* system. The data collected in this way is used by the WHO and national governments for tasks such as developing health-care priorities, confronting epidemiological concerns, and monitoring the health impact of policy changes and events. These are profoundly important tasks. As the emergent lingua franca of health and morbidity, governments and nongovernmental organizations around the world must use the *ICD*'s psychiatric nomenclature to access support and resources. In this respect, the role of the *ICD* parallels that of the *DSM* in the United States, where use of the latter is required to access not only government-funded mental health care, but reimbursement from third-party payers, and in determinations of long-term disability. Thus, the *ICD*—and to a lesser degree the *DSM*, which sees extensive use outside the United States across many parts of the English-speaking world—acts internationally as a force for uniform adoption of psychiatric nomenclature, and with this nomenclature comes an array of pressures for standardization of psychiatric education, training, and practice.

The Economic Impetus for a Global Psychiatry

Although care and deliberation can be said to characterize the best of these efforts from the WHO and development agencies in disseminating psychiatric knowledge and practices, the actions of international pharmaceutical companies toward these same ends appear rather less circumspect. Pharmaceutical companies based in the United States and Europe have invested millions of dollars in promoting the use of psychotropic medications in middle- and low-income countries. In many places these companies have been able to align their interests with those of physicians, researchers, public and private universities, scientific journals, and policymakers. Evidence suggests these companies have been able to influence these actors and to co-opt or corrupt the process of establishing the safety, efficacy, and appropriateness of diagnosing and treating psychiatric conditions with their products.

To look at just one example, in 2012 the British pharmaceutical firm, GlaxoSmithKline (GSK), paid out $3 billion to settle a lawsuit in the United States after engaging in an organized campaign to encourage doctors to prescribe its antidepressant Paxil to children, a use for which it was not approved (Foley 2012). The company was shown to have suppressed and distorted critical research findings and to have offered inducements to doctors to promote its medications that included paying out lavish consulting and speakers' fees to medical professionals and researchers and providing travel junkets with luxury hotel stays to popular destinations. Evidence suggests the company's corruption of the clinical research process in the United States is mirrored internationally.

In 2014 GSK was slapped with a half-billion-dollar fine by the government of the People's Republic of China. Investigators there alleged that since 2007 GSK spent the equivalent of $489 million in bribing Chinese doctors and hospital administrators to purchase and prescribe its medications, including its first-line psychotropic agents, Paxil and Wellbutrin (Neate 2013; Xinhua 2013). Company sales representatives were said to have engaged in practices similar to those documented in the US case. Owing perhaps to a more lax regulatory environment, the abuses in China extended further (Xinhua 2013), with the company authoring scientific presentations for doctors, paying speaker fees for conferences not even attended, and providing sexual favors for physicians and hospital administrators. Bloomberg News (2013) reported that GSK enjoyed massive returns on these investments, with its China-based sales increasing 20 percent over a single year during the period of these alleged abuses, generating the company $1.5 billion in revenue. A vital task for pharmaceutical companies in securing such windfalls from new markets is the increase in public acceptance of the legitimacy of psychiatric practices and in the diagnosis of specific psychiatric disorders.

Far from being immune to such influence, social scientists, anthropologists, and scholars of Japanese culture found themselves similarly co-opted, as Watters (2010) documented, in GSK's successful campaign to reshape traditional Japanese understandings of sadness/loss/depression. With the help of these experts, who were recruited though a lavish all-expense-paid conference junket to Indonesia, GSK's creative team crafted a new, less frightening understanding of depression to introduce into the Japanese cultural sphere. In magazine articles, films, and advertisements, consumers were asked to ponder the question: "Does your soul have a cold?" Reframed to be as benign and effective as an antihistamine for a runny nose, sales of the company's antidepressant medications exploded.

The flood of money and resources that these companies are mobilizing in their efforts to advance the use of psychiatric diagnostic categories is concerning. As in the United States, the example of GSK's activities in

China suggest the ability of powerful economic agents to coopt and corrupt the clinical research process. The adoption of a particular *DSM* or *ICD* diagnosis supports a particular understanding of the experience of distress and it anchors claims for a particular set of public health responses, in this case, pharmacological responses. In the process, important sociocultural, political, and historical dimensions of suffering are at risk of being ignored. As a result, public health priorities may be distorted, scarce social resources may poorly allocated, and the uniformitarian system of psychiatric diagnosis and care is further empowered, and the profits and stakes for parties with vested economic interests in the system increase.

The Changing Treatment of Culture in the *DSM* and *ICD*

Whether in the hands of pharmaceutical companies or development organizations, the *ICD* and *DSM* classifications systems serve as the narrow end of a wedge for opening societies to the influence of Western psychiatric practices. Ostensibly, these manuals are concerned only with the diagnosis of mental illness, but in practice, they anchor a host of other activities. They not only shape clinical-therapeutic research agendas and treatments, they guide legal and forensic evaluations and educational assessments and are integral to a variety of tasks related to health policy and development. The remainder of this chapter examines how the most recent editions of these manuals, *DSM-IV* and *V* and *ICD-10*, have approached issues of cross-cultural validity in the constructs they set out, and how research and theory generated in cultural psychology and related fields is beginning to affect and be reflected in these works.

Although quasi-independent in their editorial leadership, in their content, and in epistemological orientation, recent editions of the *DSM* and the *ICD* have been entwined root and branch. Since the 1970s, revisions to both manuals have been closely coordinated, and diagnostic codes for disorders from *DSM* are designed to be readily convertible into codes for the *ICD*. Historically, the publication in 1980 of *DSM-III* is held to have marked the inception of a new era in psychiatric diagnosis. This edition was the first to use clusters of descriptive phenomenological symptoms as the criteria for determining a diagnosis of a particular disorder (Alarcón 2009). This approach deliberately excised almost all references to the causes of a disorder from the criteria proposed to diagnose it. It also removed almost all references to sociocultural context from the defining characteristics of disorders (Raven and Parry 2012). Several years after the publication of *DSM-III*, the *ICD-10* followed suit, instituting similar procedures.

DSM-IV was published in 1994, and in a widely discussed critique of its handling of cultural issues, Kirmayer and Minas (2000, 439) offered that the main text of the manual treated cultural considerations as "minor qualifications to what are presumed to be culture-free diagnostic categories," and that the "absence of attention to meaningful social and cultural variables and parallel ethnographic research . . . leaves us with data that poorly reflect the local reality." Structurally, the manual presented information on the cultural dimensions of each particular diagnosis in a section that followed presentation of its primary diagnostic criteria. For many disorders no information was presented at all. On questions such as in which populations a disorder had been studied and on what grounds was its validity asserted for individuals from non-white, middle class US populations, readers were left largely in the dark. A brief Guide to Cultural Formulation was included in an appendix, along with a list of twenty-five culture-bound syndromes. The former set forth some useful guidelines for assessing individuals from cultural backgrounds that might differ from those of the clinician, but the catalog of culture-bound syndromes proved less useful. Derided as a "museum of exotica at the back of the book," the entries for conditions such as dhat, koro, or latah presented these disorders in what we will recognize as prototypical *DSM* style, through terse descriptions of deviant symptomatology, denuded of sociocultural context and without reference to the local beliefs and understandings in which the disorders make sense.

The main text of *ICD-10* (WHO 1992), the edition currently in use in much of the world, excluded entirely a discussion of social and cultural factors contributing to the shaping of psychiatric and behavioral disorders. A companion volume *ICD-10-CR* (WHO 1993), published a year later and designed for use by researchers, adopted an approach similar to that of the *DSM-IV*. In its annex, following the lead of the *DSM*, it offered a description of twelve "frequently described" culture-specific disorders with a caveat that these conditions might simply be variations of the core disorders presented in the main text. The contributions of both manuals to clinicians or policymakers seeking guidance for how to approach issues of cultural difference in providing mental health care in non-Western communities were underwhelming. The assumption of the universality of psychiatric theory, at least within the pages of these manuals, went largely unaddressed and unproblematized. Fortunately, outside their pages, significant work on these questions was taking place, and in the fifth edition of the *DSM*, the findings of cultural and transcultural psychologists and medical anthropologists found more of a place.

DSM-V: A New Beginning and Much of the Same

Indeed, against the backdrop of previous editions, *DSM-V*, published in 2013, represents a considerable improvement in its treatment of culture, though fundamental problems persist. This appears to directly reflect the work of cultural psychological scholars and anthropologist such as those represented in this volume. One sees improvement (and persisting problems), for instance, when, in explaining their rationale for discarding the term *culture-bound syndromes* used in *DSM-IV*, the editors of *DSM-V* make the following observations:

> The [former] term culture-bound overemphasizes the local particularity and limited distribution of cultural concepts of distress. The current formulation acknowledges that *all* forms of distress are locally shaped, including the DSM disorders. From this perspective, many DSM diagnoses can be understood as operationalized prototypes that started out as cultural syndromes, and became widely accepted as a result of their clinical and research utility. (APA 2013, 758)

Here for the first time, the *DSM*'s authors have acknowledged the contingent and constructed status of the primary diagnostic categories offered in the manual. The passage has the further virtue of emphasizing that the criterion most appropriate in explaining the elevated status of *DSM* categories is probably utility, rather than a correspondence to the natural contours of an underlying biological process. The passage is less helpful, however, in uncritically advancing what could be called a *myth of meritocratic promotion*. Cultural syndromes, the authors assert, may be promoted and registered as fully qualified *DSM* disorders when they have proven useful enough to clinicians and researchers. Like a popular cartoon for children in the United States that explained how a bill becomes a law, this account of the promotion of cultural syndromes to full-fledged *DSM* disorders elides the role that forces of historical privilege, vested economic interests, and access to social and institutional power often play in the process of promotion. If one is to accept the claim that the "utility" of a diagnostic category is the criterion that engenders promotion and retention in *DSM*—and there grounds in some cases to do so—then one ought at least to pose the question, *utility for whom?* The constituencies that our modern diagnostic systems serve are plural, and in addition to *mental health consumers* (to use that most American of terms), they minimally include pharmaceutical shareholders, government bureaucrats, academic researchers, and a variety of health and human services professionals. Several of these constituencies are disproportionately aggregated in the developed world. The influence of the *DSM* (and *ICD*) is, however, increasingly international in scope, and it seems important to ask whether these diagnostic categories are the most useful ones for members of communities that are linguistically, socially, and economically distant from seats of commerce, power, and international development, say in western Tibet or rural Guinea.

For each particular mental disorder, after setting forth diagnostic criteria and features, *DSM-V* offers an entry on *culture-related diagnostic issues*. These entries are quite brief for many disorders, but one finds in them, far more often than in *DSM-IV*, an admission of the limits of what is known, for example, about anxiety disorder, about which we read "little is known about the phenomenology of the disorder across cultures." For generalized anxiety disorder, we find "there is no information as to whether the propensity for excessive worrying is related to culture, although the topic being worried about can be culture specific" (APA 2013, 224). Such declarations in themselves constitute an improvement over the default approach most often adopted in *DSM-IV*, where, when entries on culture were included, they often simply stated the "expression" of symptoms of the disorder might vary in different settings.

In the case of several disorders, the *DSM-V* entry on culture-related diagnostic issues provides considerably more, in the form of a terse but useful summary of knowledge that has emerged from cultural psychological and anthropological work on related conditions and syndromes as they appear in other settings. These are typically disorders upon which considerable qualitative and ethnographic research has been undertaken, which has served as a foundation for complementary quantitative studies. The culture-related issues entries for panic disorder and social anxiety disorder epitomize this. The former, for instance, describes a range of well-researched panic-related syndromes, including attaques de nervios and khyall attacks, each with distinctive cultural provenance, a coherent phenomenology, and discrete explanatory models (e.g., Guarnaccia, Lewis-Fernandez, Marano 2003; Hinton, Park, Hsia, Hofmann, and Pollack 2009). The text still awards priority to the existing conceptualization of "panic disorder," referring to these regional syndromes as variations of this canonical disorder, but the account of them is far richer than any offered in corresponding commentary to the main disorders in *DSM-IV*.

These are significant improvements, and they reflect at least a cursory recognition of the growing body of high-quality research and scholarship into cultural psychiatry. This is encouraging, although shortcomings still

are apparent in even *DSM-V*'s basic editorial approach to sociocultural issues. Sections on "culture-related diagnostic issues," "development and
course," and "gender-related diagnostic issues," for instance, are presented
serially in discrete sections that follow the main diagnostic criteria for a
disorder. Like chastened participants in a twelve-step recovery group, cross-
talk between these sections appears almost entirely prohibited. Culture,
gender, and developmental processes are, of course, inextricably entwined.
They are mutually conditioned processes deeply shaped by historical and
social relationships of power. To treat these constructs as isolated demographic variables denudes them of meaning and effaces rather than illu-
minates important contours of the social experience of illness and distress.

The entry for bulimia nervosa may serve as an example. Under *development and course*, we read "Bulimia Nervosa most commonly occurs in adolescence or young adulthood. Onset before puberty or after age 40 is un-
common." The section on *culture-related diagnostic issues* states that "Bulimia
Nervosa has been reported to occur with roughly similar frequency in most
industrialized countries including the United States, Canada, many European countries, Australia, Japan, New Zealand, and South Africa." And the
entry under *gender-related diagnostic issues* reports that "Bulimia Nervosa
is far more common in females than males. Males are especially under-
represented in treatment-seeking samples, for reasons that have not been
systematically examined," (APA 2013, 349). A coherent account of the disorder would engage the unique appearance and meaning of symptoms and
behaviors in the light of gender expectations and the social-developmental
norms and experiences of particular historical communities. This humpty
dumpty approach adopted in *DSM-V*, breaking these out as isolated variables, seems to protect the core descriptive-phenomenological features of
the disorder from fracturing—one category will serve the world—but it is
otherwise mystifying.

The alternative, describing bulimia or similar forms of disordered eating (should one chose not to privilege the *DSM* construct) as they occur
in different sociohistorical contexts, examining the various conflicts that
they express and the meanings they carry, would highlight variations in
the characteristics of the disorder over time and space, rather than its unity
and coherence. Indeed, the practice of characterizing psychiatric disorders
while blanching of meaning all reference to the sociocultural contexts in
which they arise could be seen as performing a kind of control-rod function for the diagnostic system. It may prevent a critical mass of contextual
information from accumulating that would reveal the significant variability at the core of certain disorders. Resistance on the part of the manual's

editorship to engaging with meanings and contexts of disorder, acknowledging the sociohistorical contingency of categories in the system, or permitting challenges to the priority of existing categories of illness, echoes the resistance of psychological researchers in response to Sue's (1999) proposals to address bias in the US system. To do so would almost certainly decenter and fragment our diagnostic categories, a development that to some observers might constitute a "balkanization" of aspirations for a pan-cultural universally valid set of clinical practices. It might also lead, as Sue and proponents of cultural psychology have argued, to the emergence of more ecologically valid and locally relevant models for care.

In terms of one final issue of validity raised by Sue (1999), a section on "prevalence" follows each main entry for a disorder in *DSM-V*. The new manual usually, but not always, anchors the prevalence figures it reports for disorders with an indication of the geographic reference group(s) or population(s) from which they are derived. Although quite often this turns out to be from samples in the United States, there are more disorders in *DSM-V* for which international estimates are provided than in *DSM-IV*. In the still-too-frequent instances where no reference group is specified, the default appears to be the United States samples. Progress is evident here over *DSM-IV*, in which, for the majority of entries, a prevalence rate was offered with no explanation of where it was derived (beyond a note that it reflected, for instance, a "community-based sample") or where it might be appropriately applied.

The ambitions of the *DSM* and *ICD* manuals—to serve as a comprehensive guide for diagnosis of all significant forms of mental disorder in diverse multiethnic human communities—might lead a broadminded observer familiar with the diversity of illness experiences around the world to regard them simply as projects destined to fail. Clearly it would be impossible to provide a coherent description of even just the range of cultural syndromes, explanatory models, and idioms of distress that have been described in the cultural anthropological literature to date. *DSM-V* has followed tradition in offering its own modest *museum of exotica*, a brief Glossary of Cultural Concepts of Distress, with only nine entries this time, in its appendix. Despite some clarifications in terminology, the results in this regard remain unsatisfactory. The list is shorter and the clinical usefulness of entries as limited as before. In light of the enormous range and diverse expressions of human emotional and mental suffering—which the manual only hints at—was there not more that could be done?

Thankfully, in this regard, the editors of *DSM-V* have done more. Drawing on the work of cultural psychologists, psychiatrists, and anthropologists, the editors have provided a set of tools that appear to address the most pressing, practical needs of clinicians and researchers working in diverse communities. This takes the form of guidelines for the semistructured Cultural Formulation Interview (CFI) included in section III of the manual. The CFI draws on the work of Kleinman (1980 and 1988) and others, some of them contributors to the present volume (Good) on explanatory models of illness, and in several places it tracks closely to existing research and assessment instruments, such as the "Explanatory Model Interview Catalogue" (Weiss 1997). The main CFI interview, the one provided in text, helps clinicians explore patients' understandings of their problem, its causes and impact in their lives, and the wide range of possible coping responses and treatments they may have sought for it. Most important, it does so without tethering these understandings to Western psychiatric models.

The authors note that the CFI can be used when diagnostic assessment proves difficult as a result of differences between the backgrounds of clinician and client, when culturally distinctive syndromes or symptoms may be in play, when there is disagreement over the course of care, or when threats emerge to the client's engagement in treatment. Each of these are situations clinicians will routinely encounter in modern, multiethnic care settings in the West. More generally, they are situations that clinicians trying to bring psychiatric understandings to bear in communities far outside the urban Western care setting will confront at each and every step in their work.

The main CFI protocol alone is likely to prove useful to clinicians and researchers, but it is actually the set of twelve supplementary modules, accessible and freely downloadable from the APA's website, that offer the greatest promise for redressing the limits and deficits in the *DSM*'s primary diagnostic procedures. The supplementary modules enhance the richness of the CFI by providing guidelines for semistructured interviews to explore clients' experiences and concerns about illness-related stigma, prejudice and discrimination, gender and sexual orientation, acculturative experiences, care-giving expectations, and culturally grounded ideals for life-course development and potential sources of intergenerational conflict. The interviews invite clinicians and clients to engage in a much-needed restoration of social, political, and cultural context in the process of psychiatric assessment. They structure an encounter in which exploration of the role of intersecting social and cultural identities, meanings, and concerns in shaping a client's experience of illness are more than tolerated, they are valued and expected. The combined interview protocols should prove immensely valuable in helping clinicians and researchers enter into the assumptive worlds of their clients. It is to be hoped that they will see abundant use.

Prospects for the New Edition of the *ICD*

There is little to indicate that *ICD-11*, due out in 2017, will undertake more than a modest revision of its current system of psychiatric diagnosis. Indeed, we are at the stage where the *ICD's* structure and system of categorization appears to be functionally interleaved with so many other vital national and international projects that its core will need to remain serviceable and intact even as it is amended. In terms of its approach to cultural issues, the most important incremental change that has been proposed for the new edition appears to be a call to simplify diagnostic criteria for most psychiatric disorders, allowing clinicians a greater flexibility in applying the system across cultural settings where disorders may manifest differently. This may be, in part, a response to a pair of surveys (Evans et al. 2013; Reed, Correia, Esparza, Saxena, and Maj 2011) that the WHO commissioned of the largest international professional associations for psychiatrists and psychologists. Within that survey two-thirds of clinicians from both professions favored such a change. This might be a valuable change and may address central issues affecting the validity of the system in diverse settings.

Concluding Remarks

For all the encouraging developments in *DSM-V* and the potential for *ICD-11*, the authors of both manuals seem unable to diffuse a troubling, fundamental issue that the systems confront with their broader international use. For many communities around the world, *DSM* and *ICD* reflect a set of understandings that have not arisen organically within a society. Kleinman (2008, 14) established the concept of category fallacy, which he defined as "the reification of one culture's diagnostic categories and their projection onto patients in another culture, where those categories lack coherence and their validity has not been established" and this is ultimately what is at stake.

The problem maps in many respects back onto Sue's (1999) characterization of the privileged status of existing theory in US psychology. Although increasing numbers of investigators and care providers coming out of the fields of medical anthropology and cultural psychology are attentive to these issues (see Good and Good, this volume), it still is altogether rare that advocates for the internationalization of the Western psychiatric system candidly acknowledge the power that has accrued to it through simple historical priority, the power of getting there first. It is the power to establish the range of somatic, emotional, social, and political experiences that will be queried in a community and how these elements might be putatively linked. It is the power to establish the institutional and epistemological framework in which debates about the importance of diverging observations will be adjudicated. These forms of power carry within them the power to prescribe what types of interventions or responses are legitimate. This influence is reflected today in the simple fact that the majority of international publications and conference proceedings for psychiatry and psychology continue to be conducted in English, or to a lesser extent in French, Spanish, or the languages of other former European colonial powers.

Failure to address the groundedness of many of the practices of Western psychiatric medicine in the values and assumptions of European and US cultures, paired with a continued insistence on its portability, seems to carry at least two possible risks. On the one hand, these efforts may yield simple irrelevance. The system may just fail to take root and thrive in the new social environment. Where this occurs, we would expect to see low rates of service utilization, high dropout rates from treatment, and a generally lower efficacy of interventions among those who remain in treatment.

On the other hand, the new practices could take root and reproduce altogether too well. They might drive a global homogenization of human experiences of illness. This process carries with it the dangers attendant upon supplanting the indigenous forms of life in any complex ecosystem with mono-cultured strains. Under this scenario, the risks to communities would include undermining of locally adaptive systems of coping, reduced resiliency in the face of emerging psychiatric challenges, heightened vulnerability to manipulation, abuse, and waste by powerful commercial interests, and more intangibly, the loss to the world of unique forms of psychological life. For certain groups the effects might be worse. Among historically marginalized communities, the imposition of a culturally exogenous system of psychiatric care by political authorities might echo the destructive legacies of colonialism, abetting the devaluation of language, beliefs, and traditions.

But such accounts of the risks of top-down imposition of regimes of care, including scenarios of subversion through economic influence on policymakers and physicians, ignore an alternative possibility. More optimistic outcomes could result from the widespread emergence of culturally hybrid or creolized forms of healing and mental health care (Kirmayer 2006). Such forms might draw upon the expanding repertoire of psychiatric knowledge and practice, but they could also be local, distinctive, and grounded in the needs, values, and beliefs of the communities from which they emerge. The possibility for such developments seems not unlikely if we remember that cultural systems are open and fluid, subject to creative recombination by groups and individuals (Kirmayer 2006).

Indeed, one can find evidence of the hybridization of mental health practices in both the West and throughout much of the developing world. To cite just two examples, the practice of mindfulness, appropriated in the 1990s and 2000s by Western clinicians from a variety of Buddhist sources and traditions, has now become a central element of many psychotherapeutic regimes in the United States and Europe, an empirically validated treatment. Correspondingly, other practices of Mahayana Buddhism are in the process of being transformed through an extended dialogue between exiled Tibetan religious scholars and leaders like the Fourteenth Dalai Lama and cognitive and clinical scientists in the West. The bidirectional character of such flows and the many forces now in play encourage a cautious optimism about the emergence of a transformed and pluralistic "global psychiatry," or at least of a host of vital, locally inflected alternatives to such a psychiatry.

References

Alarcón, Renato D. 2009. "Culture, Cultural Factors and Psychiatric Diagnosis: Review and Projections." *World Psychiatry: Official Journal of the World Psychiatric Association* 8 (3): 131–39.

American Psychiatric Association. 1994. *Diagnostic and Statistical Manual of Mental Disorders: DSM-IV*. 4th ed. Washington, DC: American Psychiatric Association.

———. 2000. *Diagnostic and Statistical Manual of Mental Disorders: DSM-IV-TR*. 4th ed., text revision. Washington, DC: American Psychiatric Association.

———. 2013. *Diagnostic and Statistical Manual of Mental Disorders: DSM-5*. 5th ed. Washington, DC: American Psychiatric Association.

Bloomberg News. 2013. "Police Say Sexual Favors Spur $1.5 Billion Glaxo China Sales." Last modified July 16, 2013. http://www.bloomberg.com/news/2013–07–16/sexual -favors-spur-glaxo-s-1–5-billion-china-sales-police-say.html.

Bruner, Jerome S. 1990. *Acts of Meaning*. Cambridge, MA: Harvard University Press.

Desjarlais, Robert, Leon Eisenberg, Byron Good, and Arthur Kleinman. 1995. *World Mental Health: Problems, and Priorities in Low-Income Countries*. New York: Oxford University Press.

Evans, Spencer C., Geoffrey M. Reed, Michael C. Roberts, Patricia Esparza, Ann D. Watts, João Mendonça Correia, Pierre Ritchie, Mario Maj, and Shekhar Saxena. 2013. "Psychologists' Perspectives on the Diagnostic Classification of Mental Disorders: Results from the WHO-IUPsyS Global Survey." *International Journal of Psychology: Journal International De Psychologie* 48 (3): 177–93.

Foley, Stephen. 2012. "GlaxoSmithKline Pays $3bn for Illegally Marketing Depression Drug." *Guardian*, http://www.independent.co.uk/news/business/news/glaxosmithkline-pays-3bn-for-illegally-marketing-depression-drug-7904555.html.

Guarnaccia, Peter, Roberto Lewis-Fernández, and Melissa Rivera Marano. 2003. "Toward a Puerto Rican Popular Nosology: Nervios and Ataque de Nervios." *Culture, Medicine and Psychiatry* 27 (3): 339–66.

Guyll, Max, and Stephanie Madon. 2000. "Ethnicity Research and Theoretical Conservatism." *American Psychologist* 55 (12): 1509.

Hinton, Devon E., Lawrence Park, Curtis Hsia, Stefan Hofmann, and Mark H. Pollack. 2009. "Anxiety Disorder Presentations in Asian Populations: A Review." *CNS Neuroscience and Therapeutics* 15 (3): 295–303.

International Advisory Group for the Revision of ICD-10 Mental and Behavioural Disorders. 2011. "A Conceptual Framework for the Revision of the *ICD-10* Classification of Mental and Behavioural Disorders." *World Psychiatry* 10 (2): 86–92.

Jacob, K. 2001. "Community Care for Persons with Mental Disorders in Developing Countries: Problems and Possible Solutions." *British Journal of Psychiatry* 178: 296–98.

Kirmayer, Laurence J. 2006. "Culture and Psychotherapy in a Creolizing World." *Transcultural Psychiatry* 43 (2): 163–68.

Kirmayer, Laurence, and Harry Minas. 2000. "The Future of Cultural Psychiatry: An International Perspective." *Canadian Journal of Psychiatry* 45 (5): 438–46.

Kleinman, Arthur. 1980. *Patients and Healers in the Context of Culture: An Exploration of the Borderland between Anthropology, Medicine, and Psychiatry*. Comparative Studies of Health Systems and Medical Care; No. 3. Berkeley: University of California Press.

———. 1988. *Rethinking Psychiatry: From Cultural Category to Personal Experience*. New York: London: Free Press, Collier Macmillan.

Littlewood, Roland, Sushrut Jadhav, and Andrew G Ryder. 2007. "A Cross-National Study of the Stigmatization of Severe Psychiatric Illness: Historical Review, Methodological Considerations and Development of the Questionnaire." *Transcultural Psychiatry* 44 (2): 171–202.

Lund, Crick, Mark Tomlinson, Mary De Silva, Abebaw Fekadu, Rahul Shidhaye, Mark Jordans, Inge Petersen, Arvin Bhana, Fred Kigozi, Martin Prince, Graham Thornicroft, Charlotte Hanlon, Ritsuko Kakuma, David McDaid, Shekhar Saxena, Dan Chisholm, Shoba Raja, Sarah Kippen-Wood, Simone Honikman, Lara Fairall, Vikram Patel. 2012. "PRIME: A Programme to Reduce the Treatment Gap for Mental Disorders in Five Low- and Middle-Income Countries." *PLoS Medicine* 9 (12): E1001359.

Murray, Christopher, Theo Vos, Rafael Lozano, Mohsen Naghavi, Abraham D. Flaxman, Catherine Michaud. 2012. "Disability-Adjusted Life Years (DALYs) for 291 Diseases and Injuries in 21 Regions, 1990–2010: A Systematic Analysis for the Global Burden of Disease Study 2010." *Lancet* 380 (9859): 2197–2223.

Neate, Rupert. 2013. "GlaxoSmithKline 'The Big Boss' in £300m Bribery Scandal, China Says." *Guardian*. http://www.theguardian.com/business/2013/jul/15/glaxosmithkline-china-bribery-allegations.

Rahman, Atif, Abid Malik, Siham Sikander, Christopher Roberts, and Francis Creed. 2008. "Cognitive Behaviour Therapy–based Intervention by Community Health

Workers for Mothers with Depression and Their Infants in Rural Pakistan: A Cluster-Randomised Controlled Trial." *Lancet* 372 (9642): 902–9.

Raven, Melissa, and Peter Parry. 2012. "Psychotropic Marketing Practices and Problems: Implications for *DSM-5*." *Journal of Nervous and Mental Disease* 200 (6): 512–16.

Reed, Geoffrey M., João Mendonça Correia, Patricia Esparza, Shekhar Saxena, and Mario Maj. 2011. "The WPA-WHO Global Survey of Psychiatrists' Attitudes towards Mental Disorders Classification." *World Psychiatry* 10 (2): 118–31.

Sartorius, Norman, Assen Jablensky, Ailsa Korten, G. Ernberg, M. Anker, J. E. Cooper, and Robert Day. 1986. "Early Manifestations and First-Contact Incidence of Schizophrenia in Different Cultures. A Preliminary Report on the Initial Evaluation Phase of the WHO Collaborative Study on Determinants of Outcome of Severe Mental Disorders." *Psychological Medicine* 16 (4): 909–1028.

Shweder, Richard A. 1991. *Thinking through Cultures: Expeditions in Cultural Psychology.* Cambridge, MA: Harvard University Press.

———. 2003. *Why Do Men Barbecue? Recipes for Cultural Psychology.* Cambridge, MA: Harvard University Press.

Sue, Stanley. 1999. "Science, Ethnicity, and Bias: Where Have We Gone Wrong?" *American Psychologist* 54 (12): 1070–77.

———. 2000. "The Practice of Psychological Science." *American Psychologist* 54 (12): 1510–11.

Watters, Ethan. 2010. *Crazy like Us: The Globalization of the American Psyche.* New York: Free Press.

Weiss, Mitchell. 1997. "The Explanatory Model Interview Catalogue (EMIC): Framework for Comparative Study of Illness." *Transcultural Psychiatry* 34 (2): 235–64.

World Health Organization. 1992. *The ICD-10 Classification of Mental and Behavioural Disorders: Clinical Descriptions and Diagnostic Guidelines.* Geneva: World Health Organization.

———. 1993. *The ICD-10 Classification of Mental and Behavioural Disorders: Diagnostic Criteria for Research.* Geneva: World Health Organization.

Xinhua News Agency. 2013. "Pharma Giant in Bribery Scandal." *Xinhua News.* Last modified July 16, 2013. http://news.xinhuanet.com/english/health/2013–07/16/c_132543978.htm.

FOURTEEN

Toward a Cultural Psychology of Trauma and Trauma-Related Disorders

BYRON GOOD AND MARY-JO DELVECCHIO GOOD

Harvard University
Department of Anthropology and the Department of Global Health
and Social Medicine, Harvard Medical School

Introduction

The goal of this chapter is to reflect on the cultural psychology of trauma-related disorders, based on our work in postconflict Aceh, Indonesia. Psychiatric categories such as posttraumatic stress disorder, or PTSD, have long been "good to think with" for those interested in the interface of anthropology, psychology, and medicine (Good 1992). Too often, however, such discussions devolve into debates about whether psychiatric disorders are "real" and universal, though with cultural modification, or whether mental disorders are culturally constituted, distinctive of particular societies. The value of a cultural psychology perspective on such conditions is that it challenges us, in Shweder's (1991, 102) terms, to examine the relationships between "culturally constituted realities (intentional worlds) and reality constituting psyches (intentional persons)," reframing the debate between universalist and culturally relativist arguments about the nature of psychiatric categories and focusing attention on psychocultural processes. It suggests specific forms of coconstitution of "psyches" and cultural "worlds" that have been productive for scholars working in a number of disciplines. Shweder argues that taking multiple perspectives on such coconstitution rather than seeking a single solution is the most productive way to understand psychological processes as well as cultural worlds (Shweder 1991, 1999; Shweder and Sullivan 1993).

This chapter grows out of a decade of studying the traumatic effects of the conflict between the Free Aceh Movement (*Gerakan Aceh Merdeka* or

GAM) and the military forces of the government of Indonesia (*Tentara Nasional Indonesia* or TNI) on communities and individuals in the Indonesian province of Aceh, and of our efforts to support the development of mental health responses to the "remainders of violence" in posttsunami, postconflict Aceh, beginning in 2005.[1] In the aftermath of the Great Indian Ocean Tsunami (December 26, 2004) and after the peace agreement of August 15, 2005, the term *trauma* was ubiquitous among international nongovernmental organizations and intergovernmental agencies, and seeking support for forms of psychosocial and mental health activities needed little justification (B. Good, M. Good, Grayman, and Lakoma 2006, 38). The term *trauma*, however, had a longer history in Indonesia.[2] Just as the term *crisis* entered everyday Indonesian vocabulary in 1998 (the economic crisis was popularly dubbed *krisis moneter*, or *krismon*), so the term *trauma* entered into Indonesian popular discourse—borrowed directly as *trauma*—as part of the response to the May 1998 riots and attacks on the Indonesian Chinese community after the fall of Suharto and to several shocking terrorist bombings, particularly that in Bali in October 2002. The term *trauma* and support for trauma treatment, including PTSD programs, were part of the international aid programs that followed the Bali bombings (Dwyer and Santikarma 2007). *Trauma* was domesticated in Indonesian language and culture—particularly used as a verb, *saya trauma*, "I am experiencing trauma," or "I am traumatized'—and was present in everyday discourse in Aceh in the period after the tsunami.

The entry of the word *trauma* and the therapeutic apparatus of trauma treatment was clearly a globalizing process, supported by international agencies, training programs, and humanitarian support. In some cases, the effort to attract clients was crude. Dwyer and Santikarma (1997, 416) describe how PTSD programs in postbomb Bali represented traumatic memory as a challenge to social functioning: "one organization sponsored the placement of large public-service advertisements in Bali's major newspapers with the headline *"Ingin Melupakan?"* or "Do You Want to Forget?" Dwyer and Santikarma argue strongly, however, that "the use of the Indonesianized word *trauma* and the diagnostic category PTSD emerged not out of a unidirectional export trajectory in which Western knowledge of human biology and behavior is disseminated to a scientifically underdeveloped world, but out of the social and political relations that coalesced at a particular juncture in Indonesian history" (1997, 406).

We argue here that a cultural psychology needs to examine not only the interdependence of cultural and psychological processes, but the embedding of them into local political and historical processes. We suggest, however, that efforts to understand and criticize the linkages of terms like *trauma* and PTSD to global and local political processes do not necessarily imply that phenomena similar to what has come to be diagnosed as PTSD are not present or even ubiquitous in settings of mass violence or that the treatment of such disorders in clinical practice or mental health services is not valuable. A commitment to cultural psychology does not imply that each society—or individual—has unique forms of psychopathology, or that disorders with closely related psychological processes and phenomenologies do not exist across very diverse cultural settings (see Horton, this volume). In what follows, we briefly review recent critiques of the "export" of PTSD and trauma treatment as part of humanitarian work and then examine the use of the category PTSD and its treatment in clinical practice in postconflict Aceh. This clinical perspective, and the use of PTSD as a diagnostic and treatment category, will be juxtaposed to a perspective focused on the psychocultural and political processes through which trauma and its treatment are deployed and constituted. In the end we reflect on relationships among the clinical mandate and psychocultural and political analyses in the development of a cultural psychology of trauma-related disorders.

Critiques of the PTSD Category: Is PTSD a Pseudocondition?

The category PTSD and its deployment as part of humanitarian interventions has been subject to critique ever since the entry of PTSD into the American Psychiatric Association's *Diagnostic and Statistical Manual of Mental Disorder-III*, or *DSM-III*, in 1980 (American Psychiatric Association 1980). Trauma, memory, and PTSD have been the site of extended anthropological critique and exploration (see Good and Hinton 2009, 2015; B. Good, M. Good, and Grayman 2015; Hinton and Hinton 2015; Hinton and Lewis-Fernández 2010). Examples include Ian Hacking's (1995) fine work on memory, dissociation, and multiple personality disorder; Allan Young's (1995) groundbreaking work on the emergence of PTSD in the context of the rehabilitation of veterans of the Vietnam War; Paul Antze and Michael Lambek's (1996) drawing together of the growing ethnographic writing on trauma and memory, as well as a strand of writing—represented by that of Arthur Kleinman and his colleagues—that criticizes PTSD as the medicalization and professionalization of social suffering (Das, Kleinman, Ramphele, and Reynolds 2000; Kleinman and Kleinman 1991), in which anthropologists have levied sustained critical analysis of the psychiatric category PTSD as represented by the US diagnostic and statistical manuals. Anthropological analyses of trauma and PTSD have often been linked to broader critiques of humanitarian interventions in postconflict settings, particularly of the emergence of analyses of whole societies as "traumatized" and requiring repair, and the use of PTSD as a clinical and administrative category, used to determine rights to compensation and legal status of refugees, as well as treatment (e.g., Breslau 2004; Fassin and Pandolfi 2010; Fassin and Rechtman 2009; James 2004; Gross 2004; Pandolfi 2003, 2008).

Critical analyses such as these are embedded in broader debates about humanitarian governance, as well as the cross-cultural validity of PTSD. "Psycho-social interventions" focused on addressing "trauma" often support a "new form of international therapeutic governance," Pupavac has argued (2001, 358; see also Pupavac 2002, 2004, 2012). This claim is linked in turn to broader critical analyses of theories of economic development that understand violence as emerging in settings of poverty, weak states, and underdevelopment and as requiring liberal development aid and the reconstruction of societies as its remedy (Duffield 2001, 2002, 2012). These discussions incorporate many of the anthropological criticisms of the medicalization and professionalization of suffering in settings of violence and the pathologization of whole populations (Pupavac 2001; Summerfield 2004). Summerfield, principal psychiatrist for the Medical Foundation for Care of Victims of Torture in London and consultant to Oxfam on projects in war-affected settings, draws on anthropological writings for his critiques of the global deployment of psychiatric nosologies, arguing that

> for the vast majority of survivors posttraumatic stress is a pseudocondition, a reframing of the understandable suffering of war as a technical problem to which short-term technical solutions like counseling are applicable. These concepts aggrandize the Western agencies and their "experts" who from afar define the condition and bring the cure. There is no evidence that war-affected populations are seeking these imported approaches, which appear to ignore their own traditions, meaning systems, and active priorities. (Summerfield 1999, 1449)[3]

Summerfield's argument raises classic questions from cultural psychology about what could be meant by "real" as opposed to "pseudo" conditions. Summerfield's (2001) provocative claims about the "invention" of PTSD in the *British Medical Journal* seem on their face a parallel to Allan Young's (1995) classic statement in the introduction to his book, *The Harmony of Illusions: Inventing Post-Traumatic Stress Disorder*: "The disorder is not timeless, nor does it possess an intrinsic unity. Rather, it is glued together by the practices, technologies, and narratives with which it is diagnosed, studied, treated, and represented and by the various interests, institutions, and moral arguments that mobilized the efforts and resources" (Young 1995: 5).

Young goes on, however, to reject the suggestion that his saying PTSD is a "historical product" means that it is "not real." "On the contrary," Young writes,

> the reality of PTSD is confirmed empirically by its place in people's lives, by their experiences and convictions. . . . My job as an ethnographer of PTSD is not to deny its reality but to explain how it and its traumatic memory have been *made* real, to describe the mechanisms through which these phenomena penetrate people's life worlds, acquire facticity, and shape the self-knowledge of patients, clinicians, and researchers. (5–6)

The program set forth by Young, of exploring the ways that traumatic memory is "made real," penetrating people's life worlds and shaping self-knowledge, is more challenging—and productive—than engaging in debates over the status of PTSD. It is consistent with the development of a cultural psychology of trauma and trauma-related disorders.

PTSD as a Clinical Phenomenon in Postconflict Aceh

The data for our reflections on these issues grow out of five years (2005–2010) of collaboration with the International Organization for Migration (hereafter IOM) in addressing postconflict mental health problems in Aceh, the northernmost province of the island of Sumatra, in Indonesia.[4] On December 26, 2004, an intense earthquake off Aceh's west coast produced a massive tsunami, with three waves of nearly thirty meters devastating the coast, leaving mass destruction and approximately one hundred eighty thousand people missing and dead. The scope of the ensuing humanitarian response was unprecedented. By the end of February 2005, just two months after the tsunami, the UN's Humanitarian Information Center in Banda Aceh listed 320 organizations working in Aceh (Hedman 2008). The influx of international organizations brought to awareness a military conflict that had been largely hidden from view. Acehnese had been living under martial law since May 2003, and Indonesian security forces carried out a massive counterinsurgency campaign against Aceh's separatist rebels in the Free Aceh Movement (GAM, *Gerakan Aceh Merdeka*)—a protracted conflict that was launched in 1976 and intensified in the late

1980s. The massive humanitarian presence placed pressure on the government of Indonesia and GAM to reach a peace accord. With the signing of a peace agreement between representatives of the two parties in Helsinki on August 15, 2005, less than eight months after the tsunami, the role of national and international agencies and humanitarian groups dramatically increased in scope. Whereas the tsunami relief focused on the coastal communities, the peace process focused on communities up in the hills of Aceh, where the violence had been most intense.[5]

Because of our near-decade of work on mental health in Indonesia, particularly studies of early psychosis in Yogyakarta (which began in 1996), IOM asked the two of us to consult with them about providing psychosocial or mental health services as part of their response to tsunami-affected communities. After the signing of the Memorandum of Understanding between GAM and the Indonesian government, our attention shifted to focus primarily on communities most intensely affected by the conflict. In November 2005, we were invited by IOM to collaborate in conducting a psychosocial needs assessment in three districts of the northeast coast of Aceh that had suffered among the highest levels of violence from the initial stages of the conflict. In January 2006 we, along with a team of researchers from IOM and Syiah Kuala University in Banda Aceh, developed and piloted instruments for a quantitative survey and qualitative interviews, trained interviewers, and undertook a random sampling procedure for high-conflict subdistricts in the three districts.[6] During February, six months after the signing of the peace accords, the teams carried out research in thirty villages, interviewed 596 adults for the quantitative survey, seventy-five key informants, and seventeen GAM members in a kind of focus group. By late March we had initial findings of the survey, and by May we had completed a draft report on key findings.[7]

The survey and the interviews were not designed to determine whether PTSD as a clinical syndrome was present and at what rates in this population. The quantitative data showed the presence of extraordinarily high levels of experiences of violence, high rates of psychological symptoms (using classic symptom scales for depression, anxiety, and PTSD, adapted into terms commonly used in Indonesian), and a strong correlation between levels of violence an individual experienced and levels of distress. It also documented typical coping patterns and a broad desire for medical services to treat these problems (B. Good et al. 2006).

Perhaps equally important for us and for members of the research team were simply our experiences of hearing stories of what these villagers had lived through during the years prior to the signing of the Memorandum of Understanding.[8] As the Indonesian military became frustrated at its inability to find and defeat the shadowy military forces of GAM, soldiers increasingly turned their violence onto civilian communities believed to be the bases for GAM—the source of soldiers, food, and money. All men in a village would be rounded up and tortured in an effort to gather information about GAM. Whole villages would be forced to flee their homes, returning to find their houses empty, schools burned, and all food and animals confiscated. Women learned to survive, defending their homes, and when possible their men, and protecting each other from sexual violence (M. Good 2015). But men, women, and young people, even children, were threatened, beaten, and terrified, and many were forced to watch family and friends tortured and killed. Families were increasingly prevented from maintaining their fields, rice paddies, and gardens.

Working in collaboration with IOM, we produced a formal Psychosocial Needs Assessment (PNA1; B. Good et al. 2006), which, though politically sensitive, was published by IOM and used to build awareness of the level of violence and traumatic experiences of villagers in the high-conflict areas among government agencies and other humanitarian organizations. We also agreed to extend the survey to seventy-five more villages in the remaining eleven districts of Aceh, interviewed an additional 1,376 adults, and completed an analysis of violence and traumatic experience throughout the province (PNA2; M. Good et al. 2007).

Second, we actively advocated for IOM to develop a pilot program of mental health outreach teams, using Acehnese general practitioners and nurses, trained and supervised by an Acehnese psychiatrist, to provide general mental health services for villages in areas our research had shown to have suffered the highest levels of violence. We advocated and provided technical support for IOM to build mental health outreach teams that provided regular visits and mental health services in twenty-five villages in one northeast coast district. When this program proved feasible and effective, we helped IOM develop funding from the World Bank to extend the project to fifty more villages. In this second phase, the outreach teams identified and treated more than twelve hundred patients with mental health problems. We supported a formal evaluation program that interviewed 1,063 patients and family caregivers before, during, and after being treated by the program, carried out case studies of individuals who had been treated by the program, and interviewed families, community leaders, and health workers. These data were used to argue for increasing prioritization of mental health care in the public health system and for the development of programs of mental health services that by necessity rely on nonpsychiatrists (see B. Good, Grayman, and M. Good 2015; M. Good, B. Good, and Grayman 2010).

It is from within this position—working as advocates for mental health services for persons affected by violence as part of a nearly twenty-year conflict, working closely with clinicians providing services—that we address questions about PTSD and the cultural psychology of trauma-related conditions. Several initial points are important. First, collaborating with clinicians gives anthropologists access to data that are unavailable in any other manner. There is clear evidence that "debriefing," asking people to tell their stories after traumatic violence, is often harmful. Working closely with clinicians who are providing care, and talking with clinicians and those in care about their experiences, are ways anthropologists can ethically gather information about trauma-related conditions. Second, from within a clinical perspective, addressing questions about how local psychological processes and intentional worlds interact, or questions about whether PTSD is a form of "medicalization" or is a "pseudocondition," devolves into phenomenological questions about the nature of conditions these clinicians were responding to, how these conditions were perceived and interpreted culturally, whether they were genuine "disorders" rather than normal responses to difficult situations, and whether the medical interventions were useful. In a sense, all medical diagnoses, including psychiatric diagnoses, are "pseudoconditions," translations of embodied experience into a medical "project" through the "formative practices" of medicine (B. Good 1994, ch. 3). The question is how these are deployed, or "made real," in Young's terms, in distinctive cultural settings.[9]

From this perspective, we examine three critical questions: What is the local phenomenology of trauma-related disorders in this setting? Should medical treatment of these be viewed as "medicalization" of normal responses to violence? And were treatments effective? After a review of our findings, we can return to the initial questions about a cultural psychology of trauma-related conditions in Aceh.

The Phenomenological Question

The local phenomenology of trauma-related disorders in these communities emerged in the context of providing care (see B. Good, M. Good, and Grayman 2015). An extremely common initial presentation of distress, reflected in our interviews, in clinical interactions, and in the medical records, would begin with a simple statement, *jantung berdebar debar*, my heart pounds.[10] Those diagnosed as suffering a trauma-related disorder or

PTSD would often go on: *Saya sering takut,* I am often afraid. *Teringat,* I have memories that come unbidden to me. *Tidak bisa tidur dengan enak,* I cannot sleep well at night; *ada mimpi buruk,* I have nightmares or bad dreams, wake up feeling frightened, and cannot sleep again. *Gelisah,* I often feel restless, anxious, worried. My body feels weak, *lemah;* I lack spirit or energy, *semangat,* so that I am unable to go off to work in the rice paddies or the gardens. In some cases, these symptoms were presented as such—as symptoms—to the physicians or a member of the medical team, with narrative content emerging after several meetings with the clinicians, when a close enough relationship was established to recount horrifying memories, such as those described in the beginning of this chapter. In other cases, the narratives came first, with symptoms essentially describing the embodied response to the events that had occurred. Physicians would then inquire further to determine more specific diagnoses.

Two characteristics of those whose condition most represented that described clinically as PTSD are especially noteworthy. First, the symptoms of intense, intrusive memories were clearly marked by the Indonesian verb *teringat,* "to remember" in the sense of intrusive memories, coming unbidden, in contrast with the verb *mengingat,* to remember in the sense of an active remembering process. In some cases, individuals described intrusive memories as producing acute episodes of extreme fear or anxiety, with symptoms meeting criteria for panic attacks, as well as nightmares in which these events were vividly reexperienced. The boundary between acute remembering, often with intense anxiety, and reexperiencing of the kind popularly described as "flashbacks" is often unclear in Aceh. Patients being treated would describe acute, intrusive remembering of terrible events they had witnessed directly, things that had been done to them, or in some cases events they had only heard about when a family member was tortured or killed. Some would describe seeing such events being played out as though on a video—in some cases, even if they had not seen the events directly. Many would describe becoming anxious in specific places in their villages or their homes where terrible events had happened, or in some cases having extremely acute memories be triggered when they were in such settings. And many described avoiding going out in crowds or trying to avoid the specific places where these events had occurred.

Second, equally striking was the fact that many of those persons the clinicians labeled as suffering PTSD would, at some point early in their care, tell stories of what they had witnessed or experienced as though they had occurred very recently. We recall cases in which stories were told to us, or to clinicians (who retold the stories to us), with great vividness and a sense that they had occurred in the past days or in recent months, even though the war had ended at least two and a half years earlier. We or the clinicians would later learn that the events had happened years before, in some especially memorable cases up to sixteen years earlier. Although Indonesian language does not neatly distinguish present and past tense, these stories were told as though in the vivid present, as recent occurrences that were cause for current, ongoing anxiety. As we will note below, after treatment, the same patients would tell or refer to these stories as clearly being a part of their past.

Disorder versus Medicalization of Normal Responses to Violence

Some argue that PTSD represents a medicalization of normal responses to violence. It is our view that it is normal to experience anxiety—terror— during times of violence, and it is inappropriate to consider intrusive memories, anxiety, and withdrawal as a disorder such as PTSD during a period of violence or of great insecurity and realistic fear that the violence may recur. The medical project we are describing began thirty months after the peace agreement, which had led to a complete cessation of the fighting and, after some months, withdrawal of the Indonesian special forces from the region. Mental health workers in the IOM project diagnosed and treated approximately 11 percent of the total adult population of the villages in these high-conflict areas—in areas in which over 80 percent of adults reported having experienced combat (B. Good, M. Good, and Grayman 2015). Of all patients treated for mental health problems, 33 percent (40 percent of males, 29 percent of females) were given a diagnosis of PTSD by the clinicians—less than 4 percent of the total adult population. Analysis of data from the total clinical sample indicated individuals described themselves as having been able to work on average twenty-eight hours per week prior to their suffering "this emotional problem," but only ten hours per week after they suffered the problem. The clinicians were thus using the label PTSD for a very small part of the population who continued to suffer severe symptoms thirty months or longer after the end of the conflict, and who suffered significant disability caused by the problem.

Did Treatment Lead to Recovery?

A critical question from a clinical perspective is whether treatments lead to recovery. The primary modes of treatment in this project were medical, with regular follow-up to the villages and supportive counseling.

(Data indicated that 47 percent of the patients were given an antidepressant medication, 44 percent an antianxiety medication, and 3 percent an antipsychotic medication. 74 percent of the sample reported having used a medication for six months or less, with antianxiety drugs usually being provided for quite short periods.) The quantitative data provide strong evidence that this patient group had high levels of symptoms when they entered treatment, that symptoms declined markedly, social functioning improved, and those treated reported subjectively that their symptoms had gotten better (B. Good, M. Good, and Grayman 2013, 2015). At the end of the intervention program, 1 percent of patients indicated their symptoms were worse than when they entered treatment; 16 percent the same; and 83 percent better (37 percent), much better (38 percent), or extremely improved (9 percent). Whereas the patients estimated that at the time they were ill their ability to work had declined to a mean of ten hours per week, at the end of the program that mean increased to forty-one hours per week.

Our case studies documented examples of recovery. One of the most dramatic experiences was to observe individuals, who early in treatment would discuss the violence they had experienced in the vivid present tense, go on to talk about these same events near the end of treatment as part of their past. There was no sense of having "forgotten" the violence or the losses associated with it, but many described the episodes of intense, intrusive memories as having declined in frequency and intensity or largely stopped. Many were clear that they remembered our earlier interviews but indicated that they were now better, now able to work, and that they did not want to think back on or retell the stories of what had happened to them.

PTSD and Its Treatment in Aceh: Reflections from Clinical Observations

Our research was not designed to investigate the validity of the PTSD construct or its diagnostic criteria in Aceh, or even to provide deep analyses of the cultural or religious dimensions of postconflict traumatic experience. Our work was oriented toward determining public levels of mental health problems, advocating for an increase in the investment in mental health services, developing and evaluating particular service approaches for a setting with extremely low mental health resources, and assessing effectiveness in order to improve clinical services and advocate for support for such services.

From this perspective, several things were clear. Phenomena similar to clinical descriptions of PTSD were found in a significant—but limited—number of persons who entered into treatment when it was made available in these villages. These individuals suffered a "disorder," in the sense of continued distress and disability, when the majority of adults in these communities had been able to move forward with their lives. Treatment helped people get better. For the vast majority, somatic symptoms, depression, anxiety, panic attacks, sleep disorders, and intrusive traumatic memories were all present to some extent, co-occurring rather than neatly discrete conditions, and all were expressed in a variety of local idioms of distress. Descriptions of "complex trauma" were more relevant for what clinicians observed than classic *DSM* or *ICD* diagnostic descriptions. These individuals suffered long periods of traumatic violence, rather than a single event, and could be diagnosed with multiple, comorbid disorders rather than a single discrete condition. The term *trauma* was ubiquitous in these communities and lessened any stigma associated with mental health care. But people did not commonly use named illness categories—either local categories or terms such PTSD—but described symptoms and feelings in common, embodied, and processual rather than categorical terms.

Exploring recovery, and how much was due to broader social recovery rather than the effects of treatment, would require an extended discussion. Clearly the most important public mental health intervention was stopping the war, negotiating a settlement, and removing the Indonesian special forces. But this project began thirty months after the Memorandum of Understanding, and the treatment was directed at those persons who had not recovered. From a clinical perspective, patients were largely happy to be given medical treatment and medications, and there were limited reports of people being nonadherent to medications. The most common antidepressant available was amitriptyline, which is quite sedating. For persons who had not slept well for months or years, however, this was sometimes welcome, enabling individuals to sleep, which in turn allowed local psychocultural or religious processes of healing to take effect. The antidepressants used may have also had antipanic qualities, reducing the acute episodes of intrusive memories and accompanying terror. On the other hand, having medical personnel come to their village, in vehicles from international organizations, listening to them and acknowledging what they had been through, returning regularly and being available, may have played a critical role in the clinical recovery of many of the patients treated.

From the perspective of clinicians engaged in good-quality mental health programs, many of the anthropological and political critiques of the use of the term PTSD and the development of treatment programs seem quite wide of the mark. Indeed, the imperative to provide care in postconflict settings, the importance of developing systems of care of high quality in such settings, and the importance of attending to issues such as training and supervision, making medications continuously available, using monitoring and evaluation to ensure quality of care, and building mental health into local public health systems seem far more pressing than many of the issues raised by those who critique the global expansion of the trauma concept and psychosocial services.

Psychocultural and Political Perspectives on Trauma-Related Disorders

Having reflected on postconflict trauma-related disorders in Aceh from the perspective of those committed to providing care, it is important to acknowledge the partiality of this view. A cultural psychology of trauma and PTSD requires equal attention to psychocultural processes and to their deep relation to what Dwyer and Santikarma (2007) call "posttraumatic politics." Discussions of trauma always cast light on some forms of violence and hide or reproduce others. *Trauma* entered the Indonesian vocabulary during the period of the fall of Suharto (1998), when speaking about the repression associated with the regime was just beginning to be possible.[11] It was dangerous to speak openly about the role of the military in instigating the violence that erupted against the Chinese-Indonesian communities in Jakarta, Solo, and other Indonesian cities, and the raping of Chinese women in Jakarta, which accompanied the resignation of Suharto. Activists who sought to help these women reported being followed and harassed by the security forces. *Trauma* was a coded way of speaking about the violence associated with the regime, and professional associations, such as the Indonesian Psychiatric Association, were extremely hesitant to speak openly about trauma and trauma treatment.

For the international community, the Bali bombing in 2002 was a prototypical act of terrorism, and trauma treatment was seen as a means of responding to individuals as well as the entire Balinese population, presumed to have been traumatized by the event. But hidden by this focus on terrorism and communal "recovery" was a smaller movement of human-rights activists attempting to place on the agenda the mass killings of 1965 and 1966 that brought Suharto to power. This Balinese activist community, Dwyer and Santikarma (2007, 407) report, found that by framing the terrorist bombings as an event of extraordinary, unprece-dented horror—as an exemplary site of trauma—PTSD programs not only tended to negate the experiences of tens of thousands of Balinese survivors of one of the worst mass crimes of the 20th century, . . . but also risked ignoring the continuing suffering of Balinese living with structures of so-cial and economic inequality that became even more pronounced after the bombings.

When we met with a group of GAM members as part of our initial psycho-social needs assessment in Aceh, the leaders of the group were very clear: "Trauma is not our language. Human rights is our language" (M. Good, B. Good, and Grayman 2010, 247–48). For mental health activists, on the other hand, the language of trauma, particularly to describe the effects of the tsunami on survivors, was useful in emphasizing the magnitude of mental health problems facing Aceh and the importance of seeking in-ternational support for building a comprehensive mental health system. Although mental health specialists participated in training workshops for teachers, health care workers, and other government workers focused on how to recognize and respond to the effects of trauma, there was a broad consensus about the importance of building comprehensive mental health services, rather than focused trauma treatment. Syiah Kuala University, for example, resisted suggestions to develop a trauma center but invested in building a new program in clinical psychology.

Trauma and trauma treatment are thus linked intimately to local "post-traumatic politics." These are in turn mediated through psychocultural pro-cesses. Although the words *trauma* and *stres* are used commonly in Aceh —though with quite different meanings than in English—the term *recov-ery* is seldom used to describe coming to terms with a profound loss or trauma. Instead, Acehnese regularly use the religious terms *pasrah* (surren-der, acceptance) and *ikhlas* (sincere—in one's moral commitment to ac-cepting what God has given), as well as *sabar* (patience; see Samuels 2012, chapter 3, for a full discussion) to describe the process of working through trauma or loss. One experiences the immediate shock of *trauma*, but must come to accept this by sincerely surrendering to God. The alternative is to risk becoming *stres*, permanently crazy, as a result of these events. Acehnese never talk of "forgetting"—who could forget the effects of the tsunami or the conflict—but of accepting, surrendering oneself to what was given by God, and thus working through the experience. It was widely agreed by Acehnese that despite the terrible magnitude of the tsunami—a nurse told us of losing twenty-seven members of her family, and one of the physicians who became a psychiatrist told of losing three hundred members of her extended kin when the city of Calang was wiped out—it was easier to accept the tsunami than the trauma associated with the conflict. Many we interviewed continued to express anger at the Indonesian military for what they had done—and many Acehnese feel that only a genuine acknowledgment of the human-rights violations would allow them to come fully to terms with the violence. "If you know someone has done something to you, and they come into your house and say, 'I did such and such, I'm sorry,'" a former GAM leader told us, "the matter would be easily finished. But if that person comes into your house and sits with you, but does not acknowledge what he has done, how can the matter be finished?" Such acknowledgment from the government of Indonesia has never come. Trauma and trauma treatment, or "trauma healing," as our friends from government ministries would say wistfully of our work, focuses attention on individual suffering, often allowing the historical events and the structures that produce and reproduce violence to remain unchallenged.

One central argument throughout this essay has been that trauma, traumatic disorders, and trauma treatment are best seen both as psychocultural processes and at the same time as fundamentally political and societal. These are more intimately linked than has often been acknowledged within cultural psychology, and they deserve further theorization and investigation (see B. Good, M. Good, Hyde, and Pinto 2008).

Concluding Thoughts

This chapter is a sketch of some elements of what would constitute a cultural psychology of trauma, trauma-related disorders, and PTSD. Too often the clinical, the cultural, and the political are set off against one another. There are good reasons for this. Trauma and trauma treatment have become areas of scientific specialization, focused particularly on the biological and psychological, with too little attention to the social, political, and moral. Humanitarian agencies have used trauma and trauma treatment as means of gaining donor support, and political violence and collective historical trauma often are made invisible by the focus on the individual and the clinical. Political critique often fails to recognize the moral challenge of responding to the mental health consequences of mass violence. And a huge enterprise of funded research on trauma treatment almost never focuses on how to build public mental health programs in postconflict settings with enormous burdens of trauma-related suffering in settings with extremely low mental health resources. It is in this contested domain that a genuine cultural psychology of trauma and trauma-related disorders can be developed, and no single position will constitute such a discipline.

Notes

1. We first used this term in a conference we organized, *The Future of Aceh: The Remainders of Violence and the Peace Process in Nanggroe Aceh Darussalam*, which brought together representatives of both sides of the conflict and peace process, as well as key humanitarian and mental health actors, at the Harvard Asia Center, October 24–27, 2007.
2. Dwyer and Santikarma (2007) have the fullest discussion of this issue, and detailed analysis of the conflicts over the use of the term in Bali after the 2002 bombing. See also M. Good, B. Good, and Grayman (2010) and B. Good et al. (2006).
3. See also Summerfield (2000, 2001, 2004, 2008); see B. Good, M. Good and Grayman (2015) for a critical evaluation of this position.
4. Our primary publications on this work are found in M. Good, B. Good and Grayman (2010); M. Good (2010, 2015); B. Good (2012); B. Good, Grayman, and M. Good (2015); B. Good, M. Good, and Grayman (2015); Grayman, M. Good, and B. Good (2009).
5. Important works on the conflict and peace process include Reid (2006), Aspinall (2005, 2009), and Drexler (2008). See M. Good and B. Good (2013) for a comparison of the peace processes in posttsunami and Aceh and Sri Lanka.
6. Jesse Grayman, our PhD student and collaborator at the time of this work, led the project on the ground and was coordinator in all stages of instrument development, sampling, and implementation of the research.
7. See B. Good et al. 2006, M. Good et al. (2007), and B. Good, M. Good, and Grayman (2015) for a full discussion of the two psychosocial needs assessment surveys, methods, instruments, and findings.
8. Discussion of such stories is found in M. Good, B. Good and Grayman (2010), B Good (2012, 2015), M Good (2010, 2015).
9. See Good and Hinton (2015), the introduction to our edited book *Culture and PTSD: Trauma in Global and Historical Perspective*, for a development of this argument of comparative studies of how PTSD is "made real" in diverse settings and programs. For elaboration of this issue in relation to our Aceh data, see B. Good, M. Good and Grayman (2015).
10. This analysis reports symptoms in Bahasa Indonesia, or Indonesian language. Local villages in our region spoke primarily Acehnese. The Indonesian terms, here, are translations of Acehnese and the terms used when Acehnese spoke Indonesian.
11. We have not done a full search of the use of the term *trauma* in Indonesia prior to this time. During the second half of the 1990s, both before and after the fall of Suharto, there was widespread violence in Indonesia—violence surrounding the late elections under Suharto, religious and communal violence, militarized violence in Aceh, East Timor, and Papua. Some of this was discussed locally as Indonesian communities "running amok" (B. Good and M. Good 2001, 2010; B. Good, Subandi,

and M. Good 2007). In Aceh, Danish groups collaborated with Acehnese torture survivors to launch a local Acehnese relief organization, RATA, in the late 1990s, to support those tortured by the military in Aceh.

References

American Psychiatric Association. 1980. *Diagnostic and Statistical Manual of Mental Disorder* (3rd ed.). Text revision. Washington, DC: American Psychiatric Association.

Antze, Paul, and Michael Lambek, eds. 1996. *Tense Past: Cultural Essays in Trauma and Memory*. London: Routledge.

Aspinall, Edward. 2005. "The Helsinki Agreement: A More Promising Basis for Peace in Aceh?" *Policy Studies* 20. Washington, DC: East-West Center.

———. 2009. *Islam and Nation: Separatist Rebellion in Aceh, Indonesia*. Stanford, CA: Stanford University Press.

Breslau, Joshua. 2004. "Cultures of Trauma: Anthropological Views of Posttraumatic Stress Disorder in International Health." *Culture, Medicine and Psychiatry* 28 (2): 113–26.

Das, Veena, Arthur Kleinman, Mamphela Ramphele, and Pamela Reynolds, eds. 2000. *Violence and Subjectivity*. Berkeley, CA: University of California Press.

Drexler, Elizabeth. 2008. *Aceh, Indonesia: Securing the Insecure State*. Philadelphia: University of Pennsylvania Press.

Duffield, Mark. 2001. "Governing the Borderlands: Decoding the Power of Aid." *Disasters* 25 (4): 308–20.

———. 2002. "Social Reconstruction and the Radicalization of Development: Aid as a Relation of Global Liberal Governance." *Development and Change* 33 (5): 1049–71.

———. 2012. "Risk Management and the Bunkering of the Aid Industry." In *The End of the Development-Security Nexus? The Rise of Global Disaster Management, edited by* Fredrik Soderbaum and Jens Stilhoff Sorensen. Special issue, *Development Dialogue* 58: 21–36.

Dwyer, Leslie, and Degung Santikarma. 2007. "Posttraumatic Politics: Violence, Memory, and Biomedical Discourse in Bali." In *Understanding Trauma*, edited by Laurence Kirmayer, Robert Lemelson, and Mark Barad, 403–32. Cambridge: Cambridge University Press.

Fassin, Didier, and Mariella Pandolfi, eds. 2010. *Contemporary States of Emergency: The Politics of Military and Humanitarian Interventions*. New York: Zone.

Fassin, Didier, and Richard Rechtman. 2009. *Empire of Trauma: An Inquiry into the Condition of Victimhood*. Princeton, NJ: Princeton University Press.

Good, Byron J. 1992. "Culture and Psychopathology: Directions for Psychiatric Anthropology." In *New Directions in Psychological Anthropology*, edited by Theodore Schwartz, Geoffrey M. White, and Catherine A. Lutz, 181–205. Cambridge: Cambridge University Press.

———. 1994. *Medicine, Rationality, and Experience: An Anthropological Perspective*. Cambridge: Cambridge University Press.

———. 2012. "Theorizing the 'Subject' of Medical and Psychiatric Anthropology." R. R. Marett Memorial Lecture. *Journal of the Royal Anthropological Institute* 18 (3): 515–35.

Good, Byron J., and Mary-Jo DelVecchio Good. 2001. "Why Do the Masses so Easily Run Amuk? Madness and Violence in Indonesian Politics." *Latitudes* 5: 10–19.

———. 2010. "*Amuk* in Java: Madness and Violence in Indonesian Politics." In *A Reader in Medical Anthropology: Theoretical Trajectories, Emergent Realities, edited by* Byron Good,

Michael Fischer, Sarah Willen, and Mary-Jo DelVecchio Good, 473–80. Malden, MA: Wiley-Blackwell.

Good, Byron J., Mary-Jo DelVecchio Good, and Jesse Grayman. 2013. "A New Model for Mental Health Care?" *Inside Indonesia* (online journal), December 2, 2013. http://www.insideindonesia.org/current-edition/a-new-model-for-mental-health-care.

Good, Byron J., Mary-Jo DelVecchio Good, and Jesse Grayman. 2015. "Is PTSD a 'Good Enough' Concept for Postconflict Mental Health Care? Reflections on Work in Aceh, Indonesia." In Hinton and Good, *Culture and PTSD*, 387–416.

Good, Byron J., Mary-Jo DelVecchio Good, Jesse Grayman, and Matthew Lakoma. 2006. *Psychosocial Needs Assessment of Communities Affected by the Conflict in the Districts of Pidie, Bireuen, and Aceh Utara*. Jakarta: International Organization for Migration. http://ghsm.hms.harvard.edu/uploads/pdf/good_m_pna1_iom.pdf.

Good, Byron J., Mary-Jo DelVecchio Good, Sandra Teresa Hyde, and Sarah Pinto. 2008. "Postcolonial Disorders: Reflections on Subjectivity in the Contemporary World." In *Postcolonial Disorders*, edited by Mary-Jo DelVecchio Good, Sandra Hyde, Sarah Pinto and Byron Good, 1–39. Berkeley, CA: University of California Press.

Good, Byron J., Jesse Grayman, and Mary-Jo DelVecchio Good. 2015. "Humanitarianism and 'Mobile Sovereignty' in Strong State Settings: Reflection on Medical Humanitarianism in Aceh, Indonesia." In *Medical Humanitarianism: Ethnographies of Practice*, edited by Sharon Abramowitz and Catherine Panter-Brick, Philadelphia: University of Pennsylvania Press.

Good, Byron J., and Devon E. Hinton. 2009. "Introduction: Panic Disorder in Cross-Cultural and Historical Perspective." In *Culture and Panic Disorder*, edited by Devon Hinton and Byron Good, 1–28. Stanford, CA: Stanford University Press.

———. 2015. "Introduction: Culture, Trauma, and PTSD." In Hinton and Good, *Culture and PTSD*, 3–49.

Good, Byron J., M. A. Subandi, and Mary-Jo DelVecchio Good. 2007. "The Subject of Mental Illness: Psychosis, Mad Violence and Subjectivity in Indonesia." In *Subjectivity: Ethnographic Investigations*, edited by João Biehl, Byron Good, and Arthur Kleinman, 243–72. Berkeley: University of California Press.

Good, Mary-Jo DelVecchio. 2010. "Trauma in Post-Conflict Aceh and Psychopharmaceuticals as a Medium of Exchange." In *Pharmaceutical Self: The Global Shaping of Experience in an Age of Psychopharmacology*, edited by Janis H. Jenkins, 41–66. Santa Fe, NM: SAR Press.

———. 2015. "Acehenese Women's Narratives of Traumatic Experience, Resilience and Recovery." In Hinton and Hinton, *Genocide and Mass Violence*, 280–300.

Good, Mary-Jo DelVecchio, and Byron J. Good. 2013. "Perspectives on the Politics of Peace in Aceh, Indonesia." In *Radical Egalitarianism: Local Realities, Global Relations*, edited by Felicity Aulino, Miriam Goheen, and Stanley J. Tambiah, 191–208. New York: Fordham University Press.

Good, Mary-Jo DelVecchio, Byron J. Good, and Jesse Grayman. 2010. "Complex Engagements: Responding to Violence in Postconflict Aceh." In *Contemporary States of Emergency: The Politics of Military and Humanitarian Interventions*, edited by Didier Fassin and Mariella Pandolfi, 241–66. New York: Zone.

Good, Mary-Jo Delvecchio, Byron J. Good, Jesse Grayman, and Matthew Lakoma. 2007. "A Psychosocial Needs Assessment of Communities in 14 Conflict-Affected Districts in Aceh." Jakarta: International Organization for Migration. http://ghsm.hms.harvard.edu/uploads/pdf/good_m_pna2_iom.pdf.

Grayman, Jesse, Mary-Jo Delvecchio Good, and Byron J. Good. 2009. "Conflict Night-mares and Trauma in Aceh." *Culture, Medicine and Psychiatry* 33 (2): 290–312.

Gross, Corina Salis. 2004. "Struggling with Imaginaries of Trauma and Trust: The Refugee Experience in Switzerland." *Culture, Medicine and Psychiatry* 28 (2): 151–67.

Hacking, Ian. 1995. *Rewriting the Soul: Multiple Personality and the Sciences of Memory.* Princeton, NJ: Princeton University Press.

Hedman, Eva-Lotta E. 2008. "Back to the Barracks: Relokasi Pengungsi in Post-Tsunami Aceh." In *Conflict, Violence, and Displacement in Indonesia*, edited by Eva-Lotta Hed-man. Ithaca, NY: Cornell Southeast Asia Program Publications.

Hinton, Devon E., and Alexander L. Hinton, eds. 2015. *Genocide and Mass Violence: Mem-ory, Symptom, and Recovery.* Cambridge: Cambridge University Press.

Hinton, Devon E., and Roberto Lewis-Fernández. 2010. "The Cross-Cultural Validity of Posttraumatic Stress Disorder: Implications for *DSM-5*." *Depression and Anxiety* 28 (9): 783–801.

Hinton, Devon E., and Byron J. Good, eds. 2015. *Culture and PTSD: Trauma in Global and Historical Perspective.* Philadelphia: University of Pennsylvania Press.

James, Erica Caple. 2004. "The Political Economy of 'Trauma' in Haiti in the Democratic Era of Insecurity." *Culture, Medicine and Psychiatry* 28 (2): 127–49.

Kleinman, Arthur, and Joan Kleinman. 1991. "Suffering and Its Professional Transfor-mation: Toward an Ethnography of Interpersonal Experience." *Culture, Medicine and Psychiatry* 15 (3): 275–301.

Pandolfi, Mariella. 2003. "Contract of Mutual (In)Difference: Governance and Humani-tarian Apparatus in Contemporary Albania and Kosovo." *Indiana Journal of Global Le-gal Studies* 10: 369–81.

———. 2008. "Laboratories of Intervention: The Humanitarian Governance of the Post-communist Balkan Territories." In *Postcolonial Disorders*, edited by Mary-Jo DelVec-chio Good, Sandra Teresa Hyde, Sarah Pinto, and Byron J. Good, 157–86. Berkeley: University of California Press.

Pupavac, Vanessa. 2001. "Therapeutic Governance: Psycho-Social Intervention and Trauma Risk Management." *Disasters* 25: 358–72.

———. 2002. "Pathologizing Populations and Colonizing Minds: International Psycho-social Programs in Kosovo." *Alternatives: Global, Local, Political* 27: 489–511.

———. 2004. "Psychosocial Interventions and the Demoralization of Humanitarianism." *Journal of Biosocial Science* 36: 491–504.

———. 2012. "Global Disaster Management and Therapeutic Governance of Communi-ties." In *The End of the Development-Security Nexus? The Rise of Global Disaster Manage-ment*, edited by Frederik Soderbaum and Jens Stilhoff Sorensen. Special issue, *Devel-opment Dialogue* 58: 81–98.

Reid, Anthony, ed. 2006. *Verandah of Violence: The Background to the Aceh Problem.* Singa-pore: Singapore University Press.

Samuels, Annemarie. 2012. *After the Tsunami: The Remaking of Everyday Life in Banda Aceh, Indonesia.* Unpublished PhD diss., Leiden University, the Netherlands.

Shweder, Richard A. 1991. *Thinking through Cultures: Expeditions in Cultural Psychology.* Cambridge, MA: Harvard University Press.

———. 1999. "Why Cultural Psychology?" *Ethos* 27 (1): 62–73.

Shweder, Richard A. and Maria A. Sullivan. 1993. "Cultural Psychology: Who Needs It?" *Annual Review of Psychology* 44: 497–523.

Summerfield, Derek. 1999. "A Critique of Seven Assumptions behind Psychological

Trauma Programmes in War-Affected Areas." *Social Science and Medicine* 48 (10): 1449–62.

———. 2001. "The Invention of Post-Traumatic Stress Disorder and the Social Usefulness of a Psychiatric Category." *British Medical Journal* 322: 95–98.

———. 2004. "Cross-Cultural Perspectives on the Medicalization of Human Suffering." In *Posttraumatic Stress Disorder: Issues and Controversies,* edited by Gerald M. Rosen, 233–45. Chichester, UK: Wiley.

Young, Allan. 1995. *The Harmony of Illusions: Investing Post-Traumatic Stress Disorder.* Princeton, NJ: Princeton University Press.

FIFTEEN

The Risky Cartography of Drawing Moral Maps: With Special Reference to Economic Inequality and Sex-Selective Abortion[1]

RICHARD A. SHWEDER

University of Chicago
Harold Higgins Swift Distinguished Service Professor in the
Department of Comparative Human Development

During much of the twentieth century, the ranking of cultures, civilizations, and religions from better to worse was out of fashion in US cultural anthropology. "Mirror, mirror on the wall, which is the best way of life of them all?" was a question US cultural anthropologists stopped asking. In the first decades of that century Franz Boas (the founder of the US version of the discipline) and his so-called relativistic thinking had displaced the so-called cultural evolutionary "white man's burden" universal civilization reasoning of an even earlier era. By the time I entered graduate school in anthropology at Harvard University in 1966 it was more or less unacceptably invidious to use expressions such as "primitive," "savage," "barbaric," "heathen," or even "underdeveloped" to characterize cultural groups. As it turns out that displacement was only temporary.

In recent decades global moral mapping has become popular again, even in cultural anthropology. Moral mapping has been on the ascendency ever since the rise of global feminism and of various other universalizing human rights and humanitarian projects in which global means universal and universal implies uniformity. It has been on the rise ever since the fall of the Berlin Wall and the emergence of a "Washington Consensus" premised on the view that "the West is best and its ways are likely to take over the world." In light of this striking pendulum swing in attitudes toward the normative comparative analysis of cultural groups, this essay explores ways

to do so while avoiding ethnocentrism and the associated hazards of parochial arrogance and the dark art of invidious comparison.

Two examples of normative comparative analysis will be the main foci
of the essay. The first concerns economic inequality in the United States.
Among liberal egalitarians in the United States these days there is a progressive's sense of national crisis and a perception of decline associated
with the belief that economic inequalities have been growing for the past
fifty years and are greater today than in the decades prior to 1965. A dys-
topian picture of the country has gone viral, depicting a caste-like society
increasingly divided between those who have and those who have not, or,
alternatively, between those who own the country and those who do not.
(See for example figure 15.1, taken from Saez and Piketty 2003, but which
includes data updated by the authors in March 2012; also Piketty 2014; for
a critique, see Furchtgott-Roth 2014.) The topic has been a hot one for presidential candidates in the United States. Bernie Sanders talked about it all
the time during his campaign. The second example concerns sex-selective
abortion in India and the associated portrait of the Indian subcontinent
as a patriarchal society where violence against women runs so deep that
even the womb of Indian mothers is a dangerous place for a female fetus.
I hope to illustrate the value of approaching normative comparisons from
a cultural psychology of morality perspective. The exercise raises questions
about the reality and ecological validity of that picture of income inequality and fundamentally reframes that portrait of sex discrimination.

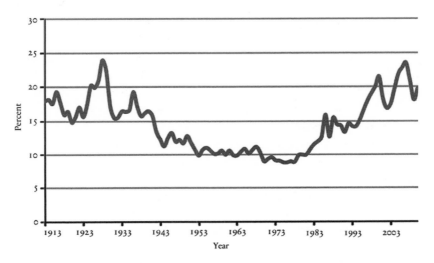

15.1. Percentage of national income (pre-tax income plus capital
gains) held by the top 1% of earners, 1913–2010

The Cultural Psychology of Morality: Are You
Now or Have You Ever Been a Relativist?

There is an inviting aphorism formulated by the anthropologist Clifford
Geertz that states: Relativism disables judgment; absolutism removes judgment from history. Geertz tried to find some kind of middle path between
relativism and absolutism. He believed in normative judgment but only
when it did not pretend to be context-free. Nevertheless, his adage, while
true and important, is incomplete. It omits the fact that even a context-rich
comparative normative judgment about the value (or shortcoming) of a
local way of life must be framed and ultimately justified by reference to
moral absolutes. No genuine knowledge of particulars is possible without
that type of implicit or explicit framing.

Despite Geertz's efforts to find a middle way between relativism and
absolutism, I suspect it will not surprise many readers to be told that "Are
you now or have you ever been a relativist?" is an accusation often directed
at contemporary cultural anthropologists, and the discipline is sometimes
portrayed as soft on superstition. Perhaps the label was reinforced by the
decision of the members of the 1949 Executive Board of the American Anthropological Association (AAA) to decline to endorse the United Nations
Declaration on the Rights of Man, which was a document designed to help
save the world by identifying universal standards for making normative
judgments about other societies.

The AAA board members of 1949 gave several reasons for their skepticism, including the following: (1) That "the aims that guide the life of
every people are self-evident in their significance *to that people*" [my emphasis; their implication being that the UN Charter was a guide whose stated
aims for an ideal way of life was largely ethnocentric and had an illusory
air of self-evidence largely because its ideals were culturally familiar to its
authors]; (2) that "respect for differences between cultures is validated by
the scientific fact that no technique of qualitatively evaluating cultures has
been discovered" [I interpret this terse and not entirely transparent comment about respect for diversity to be an endorsement of the emotive principle that when it comes to matters of taste about the valued ends of life
they are subjective and beyond the scope of logic and science and hence
there can be no way to rationally argue about them]; and (3) that "there
can be no full development of the individual personality as long as the
individual is told, by men who have the power to enforce their commands,
that the way of life of his group is inferior to that of those who wield the
power" [the implication being that the presumptively absolute and decep-

tively self-evident rights explicated in the UN declaration are really part
of a global project of Western cultural domination, and might actually be
harmful to the development of autonomous individuals who should be
left free to embrace alternative cultural traditions. [Of course that invoca-
tion of the principles of harm and autonomy might suggest the existence of
at least two moral absolutes posited or presupposed by the AAA Executive
Board members].

It is noteworthy that despite the skeptical views of AAA Executive Board
members in 1949, there can be little doubt that qualitative (and quantitative) evaluative comparisons (including accusations of universal human
rights violations), are quite prevalent today, not only in the media but all
over the social science disciplines (including cultural anthropology). This
is especially so when the topic turns to gender relations; economic inequality; undemocratic political structures; the raising, educating, and disciplining of children; and various so called illiberal cultural customs or so-called
harmful traditional practices (from arranged marriages to the reshaping of
the genitals of both boys and girls).

To avoid misunderstanding, let me acknowledge the following point
from the outset: Whenever and wherever there really does exist a blueprint
or objective moral charter for the design of the most exemplary human society (and we can be reasonably confident we actually know what it is) then
a refusal to use it as a global standard for morally mapping the world and
promoting moral progress would be irrational. But that is a very big "if,"
with respect to which doubts sometimes do legitimately arise in the minds
of thoughtful people, such as the members of the American Anthropological Executive Board in 1949. Those who have such doubts fear that moral
maps once drawn will get used to justify righteously motivated but debatable save-the-world crusades. They harbor such anxieties because they suspect that the enterprise is often (not always but often) a high-minded form
of cultural imperialism engaged in by those who are powerful or wealthy
enough to mandate that everyone should see and value the world in only
one way, namely according to the dominant group's preferred (and quite
possibly parochial) set of terms.

There are universal objective truths about the physical world—for example, that force equals mass times acceleration everywhere you go on the
globe. And I myself have no difficulty accepting that there exist some absolute and genuinely self-evident universal or undeniably valid rules of moral
reason. Such truths or rules command and deserve uncritical respect of the
sort some nineteenth-century and early-twentieth-century philosophers associated with what they called "moral intuitions." For example, that one

ought to give every person their due, treat like cases alike and impartially apply rules of general applicability (justice); protect those who are vulnerable and in one's charge (beneficence); and respond to the urgent needs of others if the sacrifice or cost to oneself is slight.

Nevertheless it is quite another thing to assert that the existing contemporary social norms and moral judgments of one's own group should be viewed as the best and most accurate representations and manifestation of those universal moral truths. One hopes (or at least I hope) that it still remains a basic methodological principle in cultural anthropology to be wary when those in possession of power and wealth assert that whatever they desire is the kind of thing that all morally sensitive and fully rational human beings ought to desire. So let me turn to some current cases, where you may find it hard to rise above history and local context and bracket your own initial powerfully evaluative culturally shaped attachments and impulses. I can only hope you will be willing for the moment and for the sake of the argument to suspend your initial sense of disbelief about some of the things I am about to say.

Brief Summary of the Two Examples of Comparative Normative Analysis

With regard to the first example, I am going to raise some doubts about the way comparisons have been made in the economic inequality debates and discuss a conflict or tradeoff I refer to as the equality-difference paradox. These doubts initially arose in my own mind when I first learned that (when viewed from the comparative perspective of household income distributions) the poorest community in the United States is a vibrant culturally distinctive and expanding Jewish village in Upstate New York.

Those doubts were reinforced when I began to read the literature on economic inequality. I realized that economics is a much softer social science than I had supposed, and that the problem of method variance in accounting categories, measurement procedures, and designs for comparative research is a major problem. For example, I discovered that assessments of current income, assessments of current net worth, and assessments of current spending or consumption patterns yield rather different portraits of the degree of economic inequality in the United States. To cite one example, utilizing an intragenerational comparative design, Auerbach, Kotlifoff and Koehler (2016) recently discovered that "the top 1 percent of 40–49-year-olds ranked by resources account for 18.9 percent of total cohort net wealth and 13.4 percent of total cohort current income, but only 9.2 percent of total cohort remaining lifetime spending."[2]

In other words, a projected lifetime spending measure revealed far greater economic equality in the United States than comparisons based on static cross-generational measures of net worth or current income. Here is one take-home message from their study: Any picture of economic inequality based on either contemporary income distributions prior to taxation (the decision whether to measure income prior to or after taxation is itself a potential source of method-variance) or based on cross-cohort distributions of wealth at single points in time is probably going to be an inaccurate depiction of a person's standard of living and is probably not a good predictor of his or her life-course economic status as poor, middle class, or rich. The soft side of quantitative economic inequality information becomes obvious once it is realized that the "hard data" may tell you more about the way things are measured and counted (measuring instruments used, comparative design properties, decisions about what to count and what not to count, etc.) than about economic realities per se.

When trying to picture economic realities, even simple demographic facts can be eye-opening and complicate the scene: A substantial portion of US citizens in the bottom 20 percent of the annual earned-income distribution today are college students (whose future economic prospects are favorable) and retirees (most of whom have financial assets and a spending capacity and may be long lived). Thus, comparisons of yearly income distributions comparing generations at two points in time, 1925 versus 2005 for example, can be very misleading, especially if the demographics of a population have shifted—for example, with more young people in college now than in 1925 or with more unemployed retired people in the population with assets but no current income (due to increases in longevity) now than in 1925. The income data may tell you less than you imagine about a worrisome historical increase in economic inequalities. It is possible it is a shadow indicator of a more benign demographic story about changes in the prevalence of certain social statuses (student, retiree) in the general population.

With regard to the second example examined in this essay—the practice of sex-selective abortion in India—I critique a type of invidious comparison stunningly expressed by a senior Indian government official, who looked me in the eye and said to me when I was last in New Delhi: "If it were not for the British, India would still be a land of barbarians." This is a view shared by many members of the English-speaking cosmopolitan elite in India. It is a view shared by many of my US friends. At issue will be a depiction of India as a place where parents do not like girls and want to get rid of them by means of prenatal gender detection devices and subsequent selective abortion. The practice often gets interpreted as a measure of the backwardness of that ancient civilization in comparison with modern Western civilization. I am going to deconstruct and then reconstruct that comparison. Mother India, it turns out, does a better job than Uncle Sam at keeping the womb safe for girls; and sex-selective abortion in India is not part of a cultural war against women.

My overall aim, however, is to highlight some of the challenges that arise when one tries to morally map different ways of life. I hope to do this without totally rejecting the aims and possibilities of developmental analysis. Addressing that point toward the end of the essay I will suggest that robust cultural pluralism of the type defended by at least some cultural anthropologists (I am one of them) is not only compatible with a normative comparative analysis but actually must be grounded in some base set of moral absolutes that make comparison possible. But my main concern will be to caution against invidious comparisons, especially those that are so artfully done they seem obviously true and induce in us a spontaneous sense of moral superiority.

The Poorest Community in the United States Is Jewish

Jews are known to be the richest ethnic group in the country, and so when I discovered that the poorest community in the United States is Jewish, that hamlet drew my attention. It is a community where 60 percent of the residents qualify for food stamps and live below the poverty line as defined by the official standards used in debates about income inequality. It might not be surprising that there are Talmudic lessons being learned by the devout in that poorest of all US communities, where the men of the community spend much of their time in bible study. After a brief visit to the community, I engaged in my own Talmudic exercise: spending day and night trying to answer some doubt-ridden take-home questions about what is real and what is unreal in our current inequality debates.

Questions such as these: If the current official way of counting designates this Jewish village as the poorest, could there be something wrong with the way we currently measure and portray the realities of income inequality in the United States? And by extension: What is the most sensible way to think about the shape of US income distributions in a complex multicultural society such as the United States, where promoting equality and embracing life-style diversity may not be harmonious goals; and where many individuals and groups are not terribly eager to turn themselves into upwardly mobile highly paid marketable assets in a global economy or to have an equal opportunity to sacrifice their distinctive way of life at the altar of Mammon? Could it be that income inequality comes with the territory and might even be a vital measure of the freedom of peoples in a multicultural society to live by different lights? What if income equality could be achieved by flattening out cultural variety, bleaching the country of its life-style differences, and cleansing it of its group diversity? That has happened historically in some countries in Europe at various points in their history and appears to be a process in full force today, for example in France, where even the modest clothing styles of Muslim women is increasingly viewed as a threat to national security and the social order. During the recent 2016 presidential election season in the United States there was (and even now in the United States there still is) an ongoing contentious debate over multiculturalism and immigration. It remains to be seen whether European style ethno-nationalism is going to become an American way too. As you can see, even a brief visit to the poorest community in the land can be an assumption-questioning (and potentially frame-shattering) experience for anyone caught up in the inequality debates.

Conversations about economic inequality and diversity in the United States do seem to be almost everywhere these days. Public policy forums are ablaze in partisan disputes about whether to raise the minimum wage and culture war quarrels about whether it is shameful to be in the top 1 percent, or whether there should even be a top 1 percent. In academic circles there is much discussion about the obscenely rich leaving behind everyone else in the upper half of the yearly income distribution, largely provoked by statistical analyses showing a gradual increase in the high-end concentration of monetary earnings beginning in the 1960s and accelerating over the past twenty-five years (Bryan and Martinez 2008; Saez and Piketty 2003; Piketty 2014; see figure 15.1 above).

Many other voices have entered the conversation. For a while the well-known public television program "News Hour" conducted weekly interviews with members of Congress about their legislative proposals for closing the gap between the rich and the poor. Inside the Washington beltway, the vision of middle-class consumers disappearing from malls in the land of the free and the home of the brave to be replaced by oligarchs having fun at the expense of an impoverished underclass has gained political currency. Several prominent private foundations—the William T. Grant Foundation, the Russell Sage Foundation—have redirected their research funding priorities so as to better understand the distribution of economic resources in the United States and to trace the consequences of income inequality for the overall well-being of US children, families, and communities.

But what exactly is really real and what is unreal (or unrealistic) in this national conversation? A closer look at the way of life of the residents of the poorest community in the United States is unexpectedly eye-opening. We are not talking about a Lakota Indian reservation in North Dakota or Mexican-US border settlements in Presidio County, Texas, which are locations very near the bottom of our country's monetary earnings hierarchy. We are talking about Kiryas Joel, an ultra-orthodox Yiddish-speaking Hasidic village of 21,357 souls who carry forward their distinctive Jewish lifestyle in a one-square-mile incorporated region of New York State; who spend much of their time studying biblical texts (if you are a man) or raising a family (if you are a woman); who do not really care if their sexual division of labor in the family does not maximize household income; and who (whether you are a man or a woman) expend a great deal of effort maintaining a holy community and sanctified family life according to their understandings of divine law (including instructions for food preparation, ritual purity, modesty, dress, and perhaps almost everything else).

That lifestyle does not place a high value on going to college in the service of mainstream upper-middle-class conceptions of career success. Very few of the adult members of the community (almost all of whom are native-born Americans) have or have ever wanted a college degree. It is also a very youthful village where more than 60 percent of the residents are under eighteen years of age. This is understandable from the fertility rate in the community and the average number of persons living in a household (5.7), which are among the highest in the country.

The median household income in Kiryas Joel is record-breaking too, on the low side ($23,336 based on 2012 census records). The average per capita monetary income amounts to only $6,948 per year. Yet the population of the village is expanding. Hasidic Jews keep moving into this suburban enclave, admiring its communal purity, and the average value of owner-occupied housing units in the community ($365,600) is above the median for New York State.

In 2011 the UCLA historian of Jewish life David Myers and the USC legal scholar Nomi Stolzenberg wrote about the origins of this residential community in the 1970s and the legal status of the now incorporated village. Kiryas Joel (the Village of Joel) was named after Rabbi Joel Teitelbaum, a holocaust survivor and charismatic anti-Zionist leader[3] who aimed to create a site of insular purity for Satmar Hasidim outside New York City. If you visit Kiryas Joel, as I did a few years ago, you will encounter a distinctive village (although one no more exotic to the sensibilities of most New Yorkers than an Amish community) where language, dress, gender relations, dietary restrictions, family life customs, and religious practices are reminiscent of Jewish life as one might imagine it in a nineteenth-century Hungarian shtetl. Myers and Stolzenberg invite us to recognize that the creation of this Hasidic enclave is consistent with "a long-standing American tradition—a potent strain of communitarianism—which permits difference and segregation, not least religious difference and segregation." (See for example, Fischer 1989.) There are, of course, many long-standing US traditions, including potent strains of liberal individualism, but that is not what this particular community is about.

How Poor Are They?

Do the astonishingly and distressingly low official household and per capita incomes of the residents of Kiryas Joel actually index a way of life that is poor, wretched, desperate, or devoid of self-affirming purpose? Clearly not, and that is a problem for anyone who thinks the official numbers that get analyzed and debated in discussions of rising inequality in the United States are true reflections of the actual standard of living of a person or a people, whether in Sioux County, North Dakota; Presidio County, Texas; or Orange County, New York. Speaking as an anthropologist interested in the way of life of actual peoples and communities I am tempted to say that in and of themselves the official quantified numbers on household income lack "ecological validity."

Around the time Myers and Stolzenberg described the potent communitarian origins of the village, Sam Roberts, a correspondent for the *New York Times*, began wondering what the poverty numbers really meant in Kiryas Joel. How hard or soft were those numbers? Did they reveal very much about the actual well-being of members of the community?

Figuring that out and interpreting the numbers is a Talmudic exercise in and of itself. For it matters what you count, and how you count it. And the counting process is less straightforward and more inviting of interpretation than you might think. Roberts noticed several factors contributing to the overall welfare of this close-knit Jewish village, which extended far beyond the official measures. Income-based statistical distributions may seem literal and up-close-and-personal to macroeconomists calculating and recalculating cutoffs for the top 1 percent and the poverty line on a computer screen. But the numbers are not really real in and of themselves. They are quite distanced from lived realities. They are so narrowly focused they overlook many relevant features of the local scene. Kiryas Joel turns out to be an existence proof of the hazards of using such data to draw strong inferences about the general welfare of a real community.

There are many hazards. Some are associated with the discretionary nature of accounting categories and procedures. Some are associated with decisions about what and how to compare. Some are associated with our limited capacity to measure the realities of "social capital." For example, unattended to and thus unaccounted for in standard income-based poverty numbers are the monetary earnings flowing into Kiryas Joel's communally owned nonprofit butchery that sells lots of kosher chickens. Not counted is the income flowing into a successful matzah bakery owned by a local synagogue. Not counted are the public transfers (for example, food stamps, tax credits) that are available to many of residents of Kiryas Joel precisely because (on the basis of earned income data prior to transfers) they are officially classified as living below the poverty line. Not counted are the welfare benefits that flow from publicly financed institutions in the village, such as a maternal care facility and a secular public school for disabled local children. Such factors are indicators of a community's well-being (and of the individual benefits that accrue from this type of communitarian living) but they are not part of the official calculation of yearly per capita or household income that are at the heart of the national conversation about increasing inequalities in the United States.

There are other types of welfare-enhancing benefits to life in communitarian villages. One begins to notice these benefits once the unit of assessment is broadened, moving from personally earned monetary income to other less readily quantifiable factors. The Jewish people who live in Kiryas Joel spend much of their time engaged in spiritually meaningful, value-congruent activities expressive of their distinctive lifestyle, cultural inheritance, and theological calling. Some of those activities (the kosher butchery, for example) may produce economic benefits for the community as a whole. But not all welfare involves material resources. The devout in the community have the benefit of what our economists (with their primary focus on material wealth, economically productive activities, monetary income, and things one can buy, sell, and consume) might classify as noneconomic welfare-enhancing "leisure time," which enables the men to spend much of the day intensively engaged in the highly valued project of Torah study, while many of the women in the community undertake the equally valued "leisure-time" project of raising Jewish families. In Kiryas Joel raising a family is not a "second shift." It is not a "first shift" either; because it is experienced as a meaningful calling rather than a wealth-producing job.

For the devout, those who are prepared to embrace this particular strain of communitarianism and its worldview, there may even be a welfare-enhancing value assigned to unpaid voluntary service or low-paid work at private religious schools. And the most vulnerable members of the community seem assured of some local safety-net-like protections, whether from local acts of charity, bartered exchanges, or subsidized housing. In other words, the so-called social capital of this Hasidic village makes it possible to provision the basic needs of in-group members while they go about their religiously motivated business of being reproductively successful in both the biological and cultural sense. It may take a village to pull this off; perhaps even a culturally homogeneous village where the residents feel bound to each other by religion, ethnicity, and common historical fate, and not just by happenstance or convenience.

Some readers may be inclined to harshly judge this entire lifestyle. That response is predictable from the reality of ideological factions, lifestyle diversity, and variations in metaphysical beliefs and visceral attachments in a multicultural society such as the United States, but that is definitely not my intended message. Speaking as a cultural anthropologist (and with due respect for those economists who might argue otherwise) lifestyles differ in part because not everyone has the same hopes and aspirations or conceptions of the good life. The lessons I draw from Kiryas Joel are not moral judgments about the ideal way of life for all of humanity but rather some assumption-questioning thoughts (and some additional questions) about the character and future of US national values, especially equality and diversity.

Do the Numbers Match Reality?

The first thought is that current income inequality measures are not a mirror of inequalities in household standard of living or of general community welfare. They do not serve us well in current debates about the distribution of well-being in the United States, or about how best to identify and assist those who need it and really do lead desperate and impoverished lives, or about the most effective social policies for protecting the vulnerable. That thought—that the numbers do not match reality—was fully anticipated by Kenneth Prewitt (2013), former director of the United States Census Bureau, when he wrote: "It will take decades of gradual re-engineering to match census statistics to demographic realities." Prewitt had in mind problems with the way the government tries to map group diversity in the United States (counting, classifying, and keeping genealogical records on our citizens using outdated, inadequate, or misleading ethnic and racial classifications), but his point holds for the way we count, measure, and portray economic inequality as well. He believed that rational social policymaking in the United States depends on the intelligent use of quantitative data, but he was aware that the current numbers are misleading.

Numbers can be deceiving. Everyone knows this. Economists and survey researchers are well aware of the enormous methodological difficulties of accurately measuring, evaluating, and representing the overall poverty or welfare of a community. They have to make decisions all the time about what to count and what not to count, even in simply estimating household income. Should the value of those food stamps be counted as income? How about the tax credits or other transfers of wealth you receive? Are we talking about pretax or posttax income? Should the value of your monetary earnings be adjusted to take account of regional differences in cost of living?

Economists also know that measures of household income, measures of household wealth (total net worth), and measures of overall welfare of persons and peoples do not always tell the same story about rising (or declining) inequality in the United States. As Kevin Bryan and Leonardo Martinez (2008) observe in their *Economic Quarterly* essay "On the Evolution of Income Inequality in the United States," "the increase in income inequality observed in recent decades has not been reflected in an increase in wealth inequality" (114). They go on to point out that "the only major change in the wealth distribution in the 20th century is a massive reduction in the wealth share of the top of the distribution between 1929 and 1945" (114). Unlike the rising inequalities in the income distribution, the inequalities in the household wealth distribution did not accelerate in the 1990s, and the national distribution of total wealth has remained relatively unchanged for nearly seven decades. To make matters even more complicated, the economist Diana Furchtgott-Roth (2014) has shown that, if one looks at spending and consumption patterns, one discovers that current "Differences in per-person spending, from the lowest income fifth [the bottom 20 percent] to the highest [the top 20 percent] are not different from 25 years ago" (13). As a way of explaining the apparent increase in income inequality in recent decades, she draws our attention to the demographic composition of households in the top and bottom 20 percent of the income distribution. She suggests that the representation of growing income inequalities as an economic problem is partly a mirage that keeps us from noticing demographic differences between those at the top of the income distribution and those at the bottom. She writes: "The lowest-income group contains at least three significant groups of individuals. Some have low incomes because of lack of employment and are searching for jobs or better paying jobs. A second group comprises elderly people who may have small amounts of retirement income, but substantial assets such as stocks and a house. A third group consists of students or recent graduates whose education level ensures that they will have a prosperous future. Clearly, the first group is a social problem in need of a solution, but not the other two" (12).

Indeed, when economists turn their attention to estimating an individual's lifetime spending capacity, adjusted for the realities of a progressive tax system and redistributive wealth transfers of various kinds, the picture of economic inequality changes yet again. Auerbach, Kotlikoff, and Koehler (2016) adopt this approach. They conceptualize and estimate economic well-being in terms of what households are likely to spend over their remaining lifetime. As they note: "One can estimate remaining lifetime spending based on a) estimated lifetime resources—the household's current net wealth and its current and projected future labor earnings; b) the taxes it will pay and transfer payments it will receive, in present expected value; and c) assumed life-cycle consumption smoothing behavior subject to borrowing constraints" (2). Their striking finding is that "The distribution of remaining lifetime spending, while still highly unequal, is considerably more equal than either net wealth or current income" (7).

Nevertheless, it is the income distribution that has been at center stage in the national conversation about inequality. The gap or dispersion in the upper quintiles of the distribution with its rising concentration of yearly income at the very high end of the distribution has become grist for the fertile imaginations of politicians, storytellers, and left- and right-wing commentators, who value simple conclusion-demanding master narratives that carry a preferred moral or emotional punch.

Some Varieties of Spin: The Appeal of a Simple Master Narrative

There are many imaginative stories one can spin to interpret the representation in figure 15.1 of changes in the percentage of national income (pretax plus capital gains) held by the top 1 percent of earners between 1913 and 2010. This is especially so because the rising income inequalities pointed to today have occurred before in US history, for example, in the decades just prior to 1913 and World War I. Those earlier decades are not shown in figure 15.1 but analogies abound. The period from 1870 to 1914 was an era when diverse peoples migrated to the United States and some of our citizens thought of the United States as a "world federation of nations." But the melting pot was abruptly turned off shortly after the First World War I. In 1924 we sealed our borders. For the next several decades the United States became more culturally homogeneous and, lo and behold, incomes in the United States became more equal. In 1965 immigration policy was liberalized. Once again we welcomed the diverse peoples of the world to our shores. Is it just a coincidence that income inequalities began increasing just about the same time? Yet that 1870 to 1914 era also resembled the 1970 to 2016 era in other ways. It too was a period of rapid technological and industrial change, with all that implies for those who are entrepreneurial and have the social capital, the cultural capital, and the financial capital plus the individual talent, luck, and desire to cash in. And so, in looking at the income numbers and the history of those numbers, there are many types of stories to be told with different types of political spin.

In a sense, all the current anxious attention to income inequalities per se is ironic because the annual incomes of the citizens of the United States are far more equally distributed than the distribution of their net worth or household wealth (which includes all holdings and assets). Of course, as noted earlier, all estimates of income or wealth are the products of many debatable calculation decisions and they vary somewhat from study to study (and author to author). Perhaps it goes without saying that dispassionate analysis is at a premium these days and has not been the strong suit of partisan commentators. Nevertheless, it appears that for the past several decades the share of annual income taken home by the top 1 percent has been somewhere between 10 and 20 percent while the share of US wealth owned by the top 1 percent is about twice that amount. (Auerbach, Kotlikoff, and Koehler [2016] suggest that the top 1 percent own 24.1 percent of all net worth, while there are others who might say that 35 percent is not a bad guess—there is fair amount of guesswork in all these numbers.)

Speaking as an anthropologist curious about the ways we assess and represent the well-being of local communities I would like to suggest that Kiryas Joel is a warning sign that something is seriously wrong with the way we currently measure, compare, portray, and debate the lived reality of economic inequality in the United States. Income-based definitions of impoverishment classify the village of Kiryas Joel as the poorest in the land, yet a broader assessment approach leads to a very different conclusion about the status of their welfare, standard of living, and overall well-being. It is not a squalid village, the basic needs of its residents are taken care of, and their way of life is thick with meaning and purpose. The sooner we move to a broader assessment approach the better, while taking into account the social capital advantages of a potent communitarian life.

The Equality-Difference Paradox

I would also like to suggest that Kiryas Joel is not an outlier or a radically atypical case. Quite the contrary, it is an ideal case for understanding a more general social process that some social scientists refer to as "the equality-difference paradox." The equality-difference paradox refers to the tradeoff between the amount of economic equality and the amount of cultural (or lifestyle) diversity achievable within any particular society (see Shweder 2008). The basic idea is that promoting economic equality and expanding the legal and ethical scope for cultural diversity (of the sort seen in Kiryas Joel) are not harmonious goals. Witness the fact that those countries in the world with the most egalitarian distributions of income, such as Croatia, Slovenia, Denmark, and even Rwanda, are also among the most culturally homogeneous. The tradeoff goes both ways—complex, multi-ethnic, culturally heterogeneous countries such as the United States, Brazil, India, and Israel tend to be relatively unequal in income distributions. Perhaps this is because egalitarian redistributive norms are more likely to gain popular support in culturally uniform populations where the members of the group have a visceral sense of kinship, trust, and fellow feeling for one another (see Alesina, Glaeser, and Sacerdote 2001; also Putnam 2007).

Michael Jindra (2014), the University of Notre Dame anthropologist, examines the paradox in a groundbreaking essay titled "The Dilemma of Equality and Diversity." Reviewing the literature on lifestyle diversity in family life, the raising of children, time management, work, and consumption, he makes the point that for many individuals and groups in a diverse society such as the United States, maintaining one's way of life is more important than the pursuit of economic gain. He writes that the high achievement pattern comes at a cost "so for many the sacrifices required for upward mobility are simply not thought to be worth it." One should not be too surprised if the parents living in Kiryas Joel and in other potently communitarian minority group communities around the country do not always aim to liberate their children from family, community, and group history or insist that their children acquire those marketable skills or become the kind of "capitalist tools" that will make them upwardly and outwardly mobile and cosmopolitan in a global economy.

The picture of the United States as a liberal pluralistic society where individuals and groups can be both different and equal is a moral ideal for many US academics (see Shweder, Minow, and Markus 2002, 2002; Shweder 2008). It is thus understandable that the equality-difference paradox has long been a taboo topic in the social sciences. Both multiculturalists and egalitarians have preferred to keep it out of sight.

Multiculturalists do not like to acknowledge that income equality is most easily achieved in a society by flattening out its cultural variety (for example, by getting rid of Hasidic enclaves or Native American Indian reservations or Mexican-US border settlements). They fear that, if the news gets out that the value of diversity is in tension with the value of economic equality, diversity will lose out and egalitarian values will be put to nefarious political use by Anglo-American ethno-nationalists for whom "united we stand" or "make America great again" implies cultural uniformity. Multiculturalists worry that the goal of achieving economic equality might then be used to justify an aggressive defense of the country against immigration and an aggressive assault on ethnic and religious diversity. The 2016 US presidential election has intensified that fear.

Egalitarians too do not like to acknowledge that the greater the legal and ethical scope for lifestyle diversity in a society, the more likely the resources of that society will be unequally distributed. They find it hard to believe (and nearly impossible to accept) that in the United States there are individuals and groups who actually reject East and Left Coast upper-middle-class bourgeois notions of achievement and success, and do so by choice, spending most of their time doing something that is not wealth-producing like studying the Torah or having babies and taking care of their children.

It may be painful to acknowledge contradictions in one's way of life, but the national moral conversation we in the United States ought to be having is about the irreconcilability of diverse core values. It is about whether one would rather be economically equal but culturally uniform or culturally diverse but economically stratified. It is about how best to strike a balance of values in a real world where economic equality and cultural diversity do not go hand in hand. The equality-difference paradox suggests that the more we lean toward tolerance and making space for robust cultural diversity, the more we will need to accept that there will be economic inequalities between cultural groups by virtue of the differences in their lifestyles, the way they raise their children, and what they think is of value;[4] and the more we try to make all factions or cultural groups equally skilled and financially well off in the Davos-world-economic-forum sense, the more we will erode those institutions (such as the freedom of parents to control the education of their children) that keep us diverse. Unfortunately, that is not the conversation we are having. In our ideologically divided society it seems to be much easier (probably more profitable, and possibly more fun, although less and less so these days) to just continue the culture wars and engage in an oracular national debate about the true meaning of numeric changes in the dispersion characteristics of a highly aggregated income distribution on the computer screen (as in figure 15.1). But that is a long way from the realities of the poorest community in the United States or the lessons we might learn about what is real and what is unreal in current debates about income inequality and the implication of economic inequality for social cohesion in a multicultural society such as the United States.

"If It Were Not for the British, India Would Still Be a Land of Barbarians"

My second example is not a fraught and provocative morally loaded normative comparison across periods of time in the history of an income distribution. Instead, it concerns the invidious moral mapping of ways of life. As noted earlier, this type of normative comparative view goes in and out of fashion in the academic world and mainstream media: In during the heyday of British and French colonial expansion one hundred years ago, when many Europeans acted as if they were the Chosen People bringing the light onto others; and out during the waning years of European colonialism and the waxing of national independence movements in Asia and Africa; but back again with a vengeance since the fall of the Wall in 1989 and the rise of the "end of history" thinking among the Anglicized and Francophile cosmopolitan elites of the world. This type of "West is best" (and its ways will eventually spread throughout the world) thinking is especially manifest when, as I mentioned, the conversation turns to the topics of gender and global feminism, as for example in discussions of sex-selective abortion in India, which is a specific example of normative comparative analysis upon which I shall focus.

According to that particular moral mapping, the Indian subcontinent is a place where violence against women runs so deep in the local culture that even the womb of Indian mothers is a dangerous place for a female fetus. As noted earlier, the practice thus gets interpreted as a measure of the backwardness of that ancient civilization in comparison with modern Western civilization. How well does that normative comparison stand up to analysis? Is it true and just, or is it invidious?

I believe dispassionate comparative analysis actually suggests that Mother India does a better job than Uncle Sam at keeping the womb safe for girls. How can this be so, in light of the widely publicized depiction of abortion decisions in India as a tactic in a cultural war against women?

"Missing Girls"

First some background. Ever since the initial reports of a monstrous gang rape of a young woman in New Delhi in 2012, the global media has been relentless in its disparagement of gender relations on the subcontinent. Much of the coverage interprets the brutal criminal act as a symbol of South Asian cultural misogyny. Journalists, bloggers, and letter writers have not only felt free to defame Mother India for everything from her social norms on female comportment in public spaces, to her customary family and status-related constraints on a woman's choice in the selection of a marriage partner, to reports of sexual abuse in the extended joint family, to bride burnings and kitchen deaths attributed to insufficient dowry gifting. One of the barbarisms one hears much about is sex-selective abortion. According to this depiction, South Asian parents do not like girls and seek to get rid of them by means of prenatal gender detection devices and subsequent elective abortion, which is a source of "missing girls" in the Indian population and a measure of the backwardness of that ancient civilization when it comes to the protection of women.

There is one pretty fundamental problem with this particular horror-inducing picture of the hazards of the womb for girls in India. It does not stand up well to critical comparative analysis. Question: In which country is a female fetus at greater risk for her life from an elective abortion—India or the United States? Answer: At least with respect to the risk of becoming a missing person from an elective abortion, the womb is a safer place for female fetuses in India than in most countries of the world, including the United States. How can this be so?

The obvious (but often overlooked) answer is that elective abortions in India are relatively rare in comparison with the United States, even if strongly sex selective under the rather special circumstances associated with their occurrence. I will have more to say about those special circumstances in a moment. But first let's compare the risk of an elective abortion for female fetuses in India and the United States. The elective abortion rate in India is approximately 3 percent. This is low in comparison with most countries. By way of contrast, the elective abortion rate in the United States is approximately 22 percent. (The average global rate is 26 percent, and there are countries in the world where more than 50 percent of pregnancies are voluntarily terminated.) Consequently, despite differential fertility rates (higher in India) and a massive difference in population size (India's is four times as great) there are twice as many abortions annually in the United States (approximately 1.2 million per year) than in India (approximately six hundred thousand per year).

Demographers who study population dynamics talk about "missing girls" in the Indian population as a result of elective abortions. Whether intended or not, this type of morally suggestive language invites us to think about the Indian fetus as a person in jeopardy of a particular type of harm, namely the denial of its rights to representation in the general population as defined and surveyed by demographers. A study published in *The Lancet* (Jha et al. 2011) suggests that 4.5 million is a cautious estimate of the total number of Indian females who are missing from the general population because of elective abortion in the first decade of the twenty-first century (2001–2011).

What would the results be if we tried to estimate the number of "missing girls" in the United States over that same period of time, relying on readily available demographic facts about elective abortions? Here one starts with the assumption that for the most part elective terminations of a pregnancy in the United States are sex-blind and equal opportunity occasions governed by norms of gender indifference. Consequently, it seems reasonable to assume that in nearly 50 percent of the cases it is a female fetus whose life will be terminated. Six million is a cautious estimate of the total number of female fetuses who were aborted between 2001 and 2011 in the United States.

Those numbers invite two conclusions. First, if you allow yourself to adopt the perspective of a female fetus (a potential "missing girl"), the overall risk of having your life terminated by an elective abortion is far greater in the United States than in India. Second, if you really believe that aborting a female fetus is a form of violence against women, then there is far more of that type of violence in the United States than in India. In that regard, the customs of Mother India provide better protection to girls than do the customs of Uncle Sam.

Such conclusions are provocative. I imagine most readers will grant that a decision by a mother to abort a fetus is more likely in the United States than India. And, upon a moment's reflection, it becomes evident that as a consequence of the discrepancy between a 22 percent abortion rate (of which almost 50 percent of aborted fetuses are female) and a 3 percent abortion rate (of which most are female) females fetuses are at greater risk of having their life voluntarily ended in the United States than in India. (I hope it goes without saying that male fetuses too are at greater risk in the United States than in India, and the male abortion risk differential between the United States and India is greater than the female abortion risk differential; US male fetuses are much more likely to go missing than their Indian counterparts.) Nevertheless, the global moral mapping of gender relations publicized by the media ever since the dreadful crime in New Delhi has not featured Mother India as a patron Goddess protecting female fetuses from harm. Moreover, given the popularity of the received image of Indian women as victims of cultural misogyny it would not be surprising if the reader of this essay reacted with some skepticism to this current challenge to that media picture.

One can imagine the following objection. Although it is instructive to learn that abortions are relatively rare events in India, the principle of non-discrimination and gender indifference is a self-evidently valid moral rule that ought to be universally binding when deciding whether to terminate a pregnancy. Even if only 3 percent of pregnant Indian females engage in sex-selective abortion, those who do so are engaging in vicious gender discrimination expressive of a pervasive cultural hatred of women, which Indian women themselves have been culturally conditioned to perpetuate. The crime is their culture.

Montaigne's Wisdom: Be Slow to Judge Little-Known Others

In proposing a response to this retort, I am going to follow the advice offered to posterity by the great sixteenth-century ironist Michel de Montaigne (1580) in his famous essay "On Cannibals." Montaigne, who wrote during an earlier age of Western interventions into the lives of alien peoples, was reluctant to let the cosmopolitan elites of his own era make the world safe for European condescension. He designed his essay as a mirror in the face of which his Renaissance readers might notice, and reflect on, the uncivilized qualities in their own way of life and be more circumspect in their judgments about "barbarians."

Montaigne's take-home messages later became standard recommendations for researchers in cultural anthropology. When judging other cultures, beware of the illusory air of moral superiority that so naturally arises as you invest the familiar popular acceptances of your own society with strong sentiment and experience them as self-evident truths. Rushing to judgment can be hazardous. Be slow to demonize the way of life of little-known others. Distinguish facts from factoids. Try to see the world from the native point of view. Bracket your own impulsive emotional reactions. Have a closer look before arriving at strong moral conclusions.

Taking a closer look, what are the special circumstances associated with sex-selective abortions in India? Who are the 3 percent? What are they thinking? Why do they do it? Unlike India, the vast majority of elective abortions in the United States result from choices made by unmarried women. They chose to abort their pregnancy because they do not want to disrupt the pattern of their personal lives (including their commitments to work and school), or because they feel they cannot afford to have a child, or simply because they want to delay family formation or never form a family at all.

The circumstances are quite different in India and special in their own way. Local context matters. The 3 percent of pregnant women who elect to terminate their pregnancy are typically married mothers who are deeply embedded in family life and who already have one or two daughters. It is a highly significant fact that abortions in India, relatively infrequent as they are, are *not* sex selective for first-born children. And if that first-born child is a male, there is no sex selection for the second-born child or for the third-born child either. Indian abortions are not motivated by a general hatred of women. Getting rid of girls is not a cultural custom, any more than getting rid of children is a cultural custom in the United States with its 22 percent gender-indifferent abortion rate. Indeed, females are worshiped, honored, and empowered in many contexts in Indian society.

It is true that in general Indian women would prefer to have at least one son. In that respect, they are just like many men and women in Europe and the United States. Unlike most women in Europe and the United States, those few women in India who do abort a fetus are trying to have some control over that outcome for the sake of the well-being of the entire family (its females and males). In that respect, they are corporate or communal in their aspirations and primarily concerned about the welfare of the patrimony of which they are a part and in which they play a crucial part.

For a married Indian woman who is embedded in a thick family life and has already given birth to one or two daughters, the aggregate welfare effects of having at least one son can be substantial. There are dowry-related effects on one's financial ability to arrange a suitable and status-preserving marriage for the girls in the family. There are effects on one's ability to be an ancestral guardian and perpetuator of the kinship group and family line. There are potential effects on the mother herself, who—in consideration of the nature of residence patterns, kinship affiliation, and group formation in India—is more likely to be dependent on her sons than her daughters for care, protection, and shelter in her old age.

And who are the 3 percent? Unlike the United States, where there is a tendency for abortions to be more common among those who are poor, in India women who terminate a pregnancy tend to be relatively well-educated, financially well-off urbanites who have embraced the cosmopolitan values of family planning and population control and have accepted the message of the ubiquitous Indian family planning posters that idealize a four-person nuclear family consisting of a mother, a father, a daughter, and a son. In other words, the 3 percent who elect to terminate a pregnancy in India are members of the emerging urban middle class who feel empowered by pro-choice and family-privacy values (and are able) to make use of modern technologies to exercise parental control over their reproductive life.

There may be wisdom in Montaigne's advice for feminist organizations. Drawing moral maps of the cultures of the world and seeking to be a light unto all others is a risky business. If the mirror on the wall tells you "you are the best of them all," insist on a waiting period before arriving at strong and emotion-laden moral judgments about the gender relations of others. Many feminists in the United States insist that the fetus is not a person, whether female or male; and ever since the 1973 *Roe v Wade* Supreme Court decision, a fetus in the United States, whether female or male, does not have either an individual right or a gender-based group right to representation in the general population. Most feminist organizations are advocates of family privacy, doctor-client confidentiality, and freedom of choice with regard to terminating a pregnancy, as am I, and would reject the idea that an abortion is a form of violence against the fetus, whether female or male. Presumably, they would reject as well any sweeping disparagement of US culture that interpreted the 22 percent abortion rate with its norm of gender indifference as expressive of an US cultural hatred of children.

All that changes when the feminist gaze turns its attention to the Indian womb. All of a sudden, the fetus (or at least the female fetus) becomes a person and feminist organizations embrace a pro-life policy agenda demonizing and criminalizing the activities of doctors who are prepared to assist pregnant Indian women who wish to exercise freedom of choice in the service of the welfare of their families. In the eyes of some Indian women and their doctors, that appearance of hypocrisy seems quite real. Normative comparisons and the moral mapping of cultures can be hazardous. There continues to be great wisdom in Montaigne's advice that one should be slow to judge little known others.

Notes

1. I am grateful for the confidence reflected in the selection of the title for this book and for the conviction of the editors that the refrain "universalism without uniformity" gives expression to a significant idea. I myself view that idea as supportive of a definition of the discipline of cultural psychology as the study of the fate and diverse manifestations of universals in history, and also expressive of the notion that human beings cannot live by ecumenism alone. That motto was also used to name two roundtable sessions at the 2014 American Anthropological Association Meetings in Washington, DC, where Julia Cassaniti and Usha Menon conspired to gather together some of my dearest academic friends, colleagues, and former students—representing several generations of a lively academic moiety specializing in the comparative study of cultural mentalities—and invited them to react to a few of my favorite mantras: universalism without the uniformity; one mind, many mentalities; culture and psyche make each other up; seeing is not believing; reality testing is a metaphysical act; original multiplicity (that last phrase expressing the view that at birth we do not come into the world as blank slates and each of us is diverse and complex from the start, bearing traces of our history and prepared to selectively realize and add substance to potential capabilities developed over "deep time"). I was honored and humbled by the celebration. And pleased as well to have had that opportunity to expound a bit on one of my favorite maxims for researchers in cultural psychology: namely, that the knowable world is incomplete if seen from any one point of view, incoherent if seen from all points of view at once, and empty if seen from nowhere in particular. Given that choice between incompleteness, incoherence, and emptiness, the study of cultural psychology more or less requires that you opt for incompleteness and then stay on the move between alternative points of view, which is one of the things I try to do in this essay on the equality-difference paradox and the morally provocative topic of sex-selective abortion in India. I am also touched by the affections of my friends, colleagues, and former students (including their roasts and toasts, and even some of their boasts) communicated in entertaining and serious ways during our gatherings in the nation's capital and for their scholarly contributions to the comparative study of cultural mentalities made manifest in the various essays in this book. If one were to draw a tree of academic ancestry in US cultural psychology, I believe one would discover that almost all the contributors to this volume (Paul Rozin is fictive kin) were either students of the famous psychological anthropologist John Whiting (as was I) or students of students of John Whiting. Already out there pursuing careers in the profession are students of students of students of John Whiting, many, perhaps most, of whom are probably unaware of their descent line from his eponymous spirit (and beyond Whiting to some of his teachers—anthropologists and psychologists—back in the 1930s who had joined together in a great experiment in interdisciplinary social science at the Yale University Institute of Human Relations). My own contribution to this volume is an attempted demonstration of what I take to be some of the implications of the idea of universalism without uniformity for cultural critique.

2. Their estimate of remaining lifetime spending or consumption included estimates of remaining lifetime benefits from redistributive government transfers of wealth (including progressive taxation).

3. Rabbi Teitelbaum and Satmar Hasidim more generally view the aspirations of the Zionist movement as an arrogant abrogation of biblical prophesies about the timing of the creation of a Jewish homeland and State of Israel, which is scripted biblically to occur after the return of the Messiah. Hence Zionism is judged by the Satmar to be a transgression against divine will.

4. One implication of the equality-difference paradox is that not all economic inequality is the product of oppression, exploitation, or vicious discrimination. A second implication is that even in a pure merit-based system of economic distribution economic differences between cultural groups may emerge, for some of the reasons described in this essay.

References

Alesina, Alberto, Edward Glaeser, and Bruce Sacerdote. 2001. "Why Doesn't the US Have a European-Style Welfare State?" Harvard Institute of Economic Research Discussion Paper 1933. https://dash.harvard.edu/bitstream/handle/1/12502088/1209137.pdf ?sequence=2.

Auerbach, Alan J., Lawrence J. Kotlikoff, and Darryl Koehler. 2016. "U.S. Inequality, Fiscal Progressivity, and Work Disincentives: An Intragenerational Accounting." NBER Working Paper No. w22032. Washington, DC: National Bureau of Economic Research. http://www.nber.org/papers/w22032.

Bryan, Kevin A. and Leonardo Martinez. 2008. "On the Evolution of Income Inequality in the United States" *Economic Quarterly* 94 (2): 97–120. https://www.richmondfed .org/publications/research/economic_quarterly/2008/spring/bryanmartinez.cfm.

Executive Board of the American Anthropological Association. 1947. "Statement on Human Rights." *American Anthropologist* 49 (4): 539–43.

Fischer, David H. 1989. *Albion's Seed: Four British Folkways in America.* New York: Oxford University Press.

Furchtgott-Roth, Diana, ed. 2014. *Income Inequality in America: Fact and Fiction.* E21 Issue Brief, Economic Policies for the 21st Century at the Manhattan Institute. http://www .economics21.org/files/e21ib_1.pdf.

Jha, Prabhat, Maya A. Kesler, Rajesh Kumar, Faujdar Ram, Usha Ram, Lukasz Aleksandrowicz, Diego G. Bassani, Shailaja Chandra, and Jayant K. Banthia. 2011. "Trends in Selective Abortions of Girls in India: Analysis of Nationally Representative Birth Histories from 1990 to 2005 and Census Data from 1991 to 2011." *Lancet* 377 (9781): 1921–28. http://www.thelancet.com/pdfs/journals/lancet/PIIS0140-6736(11)60649 -1.pdf.

Jindra, Michael. 2014. "The Dilemma of Equality and Diversity." *Current Anthropology* 55: 316–34.

Minow, Martha, Richard A. Shweder, and Hazel Markus, eds. 2008. *Just Schools: Pursuing Equality in Societies of Difference.* New York: Russell Sage Foundation.

Montaigne, Michel de. 1580. "On Cannibals." http://public.wsu.edu/~brians/world_civ/ worldcivreader/world_civ_reader_2/montaigne.html.

Myers, David N., and Nomi M. Stolzenberg. 2011. "Kiryas Joel: Theocracy in America?"

Huffington Post, December 4. http://www.huffingtonpost.com/david-n-myers/kiryas -yoel-theocracy-in-america_b_1124505.html.

Piketty, Thomas. 2014. *Capital in the Twenty-First Century*. Cambridge, MA: Harvard University Press.

Prewitt, Kenneth. 2013. "Fix the Census' Archaic Racial Categories." *New York Times*, August 21. http://www.nytimes.com/2013/08/22/opinion/fix-the-census-archaic-racial -categories.html?emc=eta1&_r=0.

Putnam, Robert. 2007. "E Pluribus Unum: Diversity and Community in the Twenty-First Century." The Johan Skytte Lecture. *Scandinavian Political Studies* 30: 137–74.

Roberts, Sam. 2011. "A Village with the Numbers, Not the Image, of the Poorest Place." *New York Times*, April 20. http://www.nytimes.com/2011/04/21/nyregion/kiryas-joel-a -village-with-the-numbers-not-the-image-of-the-poorest-place.html?_r=0.

Saez, Emmanuel, and Thomas Piketty. 2003. "Income Inequality in the United States." *Quarterly Journal of Economic* 118: 1–39.

Shweder, Richard A. 2008. "After Just Schools: The Equality-Difference Paradox and Conflicting Varieties of Liberal Hope." In *Just Schools: Pursuing Equality in Societies of Difference*, edited by Martha Minow, Richard A. Shweder, and Hazel Markus, 254–90. New York: Russell Foundation Press.

Shweder, Richard A., Martha Minow, and Hazel Markus, eds. 2000. *The End of Tolerance: Engaging Cultural Differences*. Special issue, *Daedalus: Journal of the American Academy of Arts and Sciences* 129 (4).

———. 2002. *Engaging Cultural Differences: The Multicultural Challenge in Liberal Democracies*. New York: Russell Sage Foundation.

INDEX